# VMware vSphere 6.5 Cookbook
## *Third Edition*

Over 140 task-oriented recipes to install, configure, manage, and orchestrate various VMware vSphere 6.5 components

**Abhilash G B**
**Cedric Rajendran**

BIRMINGHAM - MUMBAI

# VMware vSphere 6.5 Cookbook
## *Third Edition*

Copyright © 2018 Packt Publishing

**Commissioning Editor:** Vijin Boricha
**Acquisition Editor:** Heramb Bhavsar
**Content Development Editor:** Sharon Raj
**Technical Editor:** Vishal K. Mewada
**Copy Editor:** Safis Editing
**Project Coordinator:** Virginia Dias
**Proofreader:** Safis Editing
**Indexer:** Francy Puthiry
**Graphics:** Kirk D'Penha
**Production Coordinator:** Melwyn Dsa

First published: October 2016
Second edition: October 2017
Third edition: January 2018

Production reference: 1190118

Published by Packt Publishing Ltd.
Livery Place
35 Livery Street
Birmingham
B3 2PB, UK.

ISBN 978-1-78712-741-8

www.packtpub.com

mapt.io

Mapt is an online digital library that gives you full access to over 5,000 books and videos, as well as industry leading tools to help you plan your personal development and advance your career. For more information, please visit our website.

# Why subscribe?

- Spend less time learning and more time coding with practical eBooks and Videos from over 4,000 industry professionals

- Improve your learning with Skill Plans built especially for you

- Get a free eBook or video every month

- Mapt is fully searchable

- Copy and paste, print, and bookmark content

# PacktPub.com

Did you know that Packt offers eBook versions of every book published, with PDF and ePub files available? You can upgrade to the eBook version at www.PacktPub.com and as a print book customer, you are entitled to a discount on the eBook copy. Get in touch with us at service@packtpub.com for more details.

At www.PacktPub.com, you can also read a collection of free technical articles, sign up for a range of free newsletters, and receive exclusive discounts and offers on Packt books and eBooks.

# Contributors

## About the authors

**Abhilash G B** (@abhilashgb) is a virtualization specialist, author, designer, and a VMware vExpert 2014-2017 who specializes in the areas of data center virtualization and cloud computing.

He has been in the IT industry for more than a decade and working on VMware products and technologies since the start of 2007. He sold several VMware certifications including VCIX6-DCV, VCAP4/5 -DCA, VCP3/4/5/6-DCV, VCP-Cloud, and VCP6-NV. He is also the author of the five other books.

*I dedicate this book to my family. Without their patience and support, this book would not have been possible. Thanks to the Technical Reviewer Mathias Meyenburg for his valuable input. Special thanks to the entire Packt team for their support during the course of writing this book.*

**Cedric Rajendran** is a senior staff engineer in technical support with VMware. He has around 13 years of experience covering a wide spectrum of technologies.

He holds a master's degree specializing in International Business. He has served in the fields of Network Ops, Technical Support, and Consulting. His core strengths are on the server and storage virtualization.

He has authored a book on VMware Virtual SAN, holds advanced certifications with VMware, and is also a TOGAF certified Enterprise Architect.

*I dedicate this book to my family, Samantha, Ankita, Dom, Annie, mum, and dad for their encouragement and support.*

*Special thanks to my dear daughter, Samantha. Her intriguing questions about pony were a welcome interruption when work gets tiring.*

*As with my first project, proceeds from this book would be donated to the children at Gerizim.*

# About the reviewer

**Mathias Meyenburg** is an accomplished business unit manager, solution architect, and senior consultant with more than 15 years of experience in the IT industry.

From a system administrator to large-scale data center operations and administration, his career has evolved through constantly updating and expanding his know-how as well as acquiring advancing certifications, CCNA, MCP, and VCP to name a few.

In 2016, he was recruited by vleet GmbH as a solution architect and senior consultant for server and desktop virtualization specializing in vSphere, vROPS, NSX, and vSAN.

> *I would like to express my gratitude to my wife Andrea who had to carry the burden while I was occupied with this book and my career and who lovingly looked after our kids while studying herself.*

# Packt is searching for authors like you

If you're interested in becoming an author for Packt, please visit `authors.packtpub.com` and apply today. We have worked with thousands of developers and tech professionals, just like you, to help them share their insight with the global tech community. You can make a general application, apply for a specific hot topic that we are recruiting an author for, or submit your own idea.

# Table of Contents

# Preface

With more and more data centers being virtualized using its technologies, VMware is still the undisputed leader in providing virtualization solutions ranging from server virtualization to storage and network virtualization. Despite the efforts from Citrix and Microsoft, VMware's vSphere product line is still the most feature-rich and futuristic in the virtualization industry. Knowing how to install and configure the latest vSphere components is important to give yourself a head start toward virtualization using VMware. This book covers the installation and upgrade of the vSphere environment and also the administration tasks that one would commonly need to handle when managing a VMware infrastructure.

VMware vSphere 6.5 Cookbook is a task-oriented, fast-paced, practical guide to installing and configuring vSphere 6.5 components. It will take you through all of the steps required to accomplish various configuration tasks with less reading. Most of the tasks are accompanied by relevant screenshots and flowcharts with the intention to provide visual guidance as well. The book concentrates more on the actual task rather than the theory around it, making it easier to understand what is really needed to achieve the task. However, most of the concepts have been well-described to help you understand the background and working.

## Who this book is for

This book is for anyone who wants to learn how to install and configure VMware vSphere components. It is an excellent handbook for administrators or for anyone looking for a head start in learning how to upgrade, install, and configure vSphere 6.5 components. It is also a good task-oriented reference guide for consultants who design and deploy vSphere.

## What this book covers

Chapter 1, *Upgrading to vSphere 6.5*, will teach you how to upgrade your existing environment to the vSphere 6.5, and you will also learn how to migrate vCenter running on Windows to appliance.

Chapter 2, *Greenfield Deployment of vSphere 6.5*, will show you how to perform a fresh deployment of VCSA 6.5 and installation of ESXi 6.5. You will also learn how to deploy External Platform Services Controller.

Chapter 3, *Using vSphere Host Profiles*, will show you how to use Host Profiles to push a configuration change, performing host customizations, remediating noncompliant hosts. You will also learn how to copy settings between host profiles.

Chapter 4, *Using ESXi Image Builder*, you will learn how to use ESXi Image Builder using both the new vSphere Web Client GUI and CLI. You will learn how to create image profiles from either an existing image profile and fresh profile from scratch.

Chapter 5, *Using vSphere Auto Deploy*, you will learn how to deploy stateless and stateful ESXi host without the need to have to run the ISO installation on the server hardware.

Chapter 6, *Using vSphere Standard Switches*, you will learn how to set up vSphere Networking using the standard Switches.

Chapter 7, *Using vSphere Distributed Switches*, will teach you how to set up vSphere Networking using vSphere Distributed Switches. You will also learn how to migrate networking from standard vSwitches to the Distributed Switches. You will also learn configuring advanced features, such as NetFlow, Port Mirroring, and Private VLANs.

Chapter 8, *Creating and Managing VMFS Datastore*, will show how to create VMFS Datastores.

Chapter 9, *Managing Access to the iSCSI and NFS Storage*, will show how to configure and manage access to the iSCSI and NFS storage.

Chapter 10, *Storage IO Control, Storage DRS, and Profile-Driven Storage*, will show methods to consume storage resource effectively, by controlling queue depths, reacting space and latency thresholds, and automating the usage of tiered storage.

Chapter 11, *Creating and Managing Virtual Machines*, will teach how to create virtual machines, configure its settings, create and manage templates, and also export them to OVFs. You will also learn how to create content libraries.

Chapter 12, *Configuring vSphere 6.5 High Availability*, will discuss how to configure High Availability on a cluster on ESXi hosts. You will also learn how to configure native high availability for vCenter Servers.

Chapter 13, *Configuring vSphere DRS, DPM, and VMware EVC*, will discuss how to pool compute resources from a cluster of ESXi hosts to enable efficient virtual machine placement and automate mitigation of resource imbalance in a cluster. You will also learn how to reduce power consumption of a cluster by changing the power state of underutilized hosts.

Chapter 14, *Upgrading and Patching using vSphere Update Manager*, will teach how to manage the life cycle of ESXi Hosts by patching and updating the environment.

Chapter 15, *Using vSphere Certificate Manager Utility*, will show how to generate certificate signing requests and replace certificates for a vSphere Environment.

Chapter 16, *Using vSphere Management Assistant*, will show how to deploy and configure vMA to run commands/scripts remotely on ESXi.

Chapter 17, *Performance Monitoring in a vSphere Environment*, will describe how to use esxtop and vCenter Performance Graphs to monitor the performance of a vSphere environment.

# To get the most out of this book

You will learn about the software requirements for every vSphere component covered in this book in their respective chapters, but to start with a basic lab setup, you will need at least two ESXi hosts, a vCenter Server, a Domain Controller, a DHCP server, a DNS server, and a TFTP Server. For learning purposes, you don't really need to run ESXi on physical machines. You can use VMware Workstation to set up a hosted lab on your desktop PC or laptop, provided the machine has adequate compute and storage resources. For shared storage, you can use any of the free virtual storage appliances listed as follows:

- OpenFiler can be downloaded at https://www.openfiler.com.
- HP StoreVirtual Storage can be downloaded at http://www8.hp.com/in/en/products/data-storage/storevirtual.html.

# Download the color images

We also provide a PDF file that has color images of the screenshots/diagrams used in this book. You can download it from http://www.packtpub.com/sites/default/files/downloads/VMwarevSphere65CookbookThirdEdition_ColorImages.pdf.

# Conventions used

There are a number of text conventions used throughout this book.

`CodeInText`: Indicates code words in text, database table names, folder names, filenames, file extensions, pathnames, dummy URLs, user input, and Twitter handles. Here is an example: "Browse the ISO ROM contents and navigate to the `migration-assistant` folder."

Any command-line input or output is written as follows:

```
Set-ExecutionPolicy RemoteSigned
```

**Bold**: Indicates a new term, an important word, or words that you see onscreen. For example, words in menus or dialog boxes appear in the text like this. Here is an example: "On the **Configure Ports** screen—you are not allowed to make any changes. Click on the **Next** button to continue."

Warnings or important notes appear like this.

Tips and tricks appear like this.

# Sections

In this book, you will find several headings that appear frequently (*Getting ready*, *How to do it...*, *How it works...*, *There's more...*, and *See also*).

To give clear instructions on how to complete a recipe, use these sections as follows:

# Getting ready

This section tells you what to expect in the recipe and describes how to set up any software or any preliminary settings required for the recipe.

# How to do it...

This section contains the steps required to follow the recipe.

# How it works...

This section usually consists of a detailed explanation of what happened in the previous section.

# There's more...

This section consists of additional information about the recipe in order to make you more knowledgeable about the recipe.

# See also

This section provides helpful links to other useful information for the recipe.

# Get in touch

Feedback from our readers is always welcome.

**General feedback**: Email `feedback@packtpub.com` and mention the book title in the subject of your message. If you have questions about any aspect of this book, please email us at `questions@packtpub.com`.

**Errata**: Although we have taken every care to ensure the accuracy of our content, mistakes do happen. If you have found a mistake in this book, we would be grateful if you would report this to us. Please visit `www.packtpub.com/submit-errata`, selecting your book, clicking on the Errata Submission Form link, and entering the details.

**Piracy**: If you come across any illegal copies of our works in any form on the internet, we would be grateful if you would provide us with the location address or website name. Please contact us at `copyright@packtpub.com` with a link to the material.

**If you are interested in becoming an author**: If there is a topic that you have expertise in and you are interested in either writing or contributing to a book, please visit `authors.packtpub.com`.

# Reviews

Please leave a review. Once you have read and used this book, why not leave a review on the site that you purchased it from? Potential readers can then see and use your unbiased opinion to make purchase decisions, we at Packt can understand what you think about our products, and our authors can see your feedback on their book. Thank you!

For more information about Packt, please visit packtpub.com.

# 1
# Upgrading to vSphere 6.5

In this chapter, we will cover the following topics:

- vSphere 6.5 core components
- Planning vSphere upgrade
- Upgrading from vSphere 5.5 or 6.0 to vSphere 6.5
- Upgrading vCenter Server on Microsoft Windows
- Using the vCenter 6.5 Migration Assistant
- Upgrading vCenter Server - Migrating from Microsoft Windows to VCSA
- Upgrading the vCenter Server Appliance
- Upgrading ESXi Hypervisor

## Introduction

The goal of this chapter is to help you understand and execute the process of upgrading your core vSphere infrastructure to VMware vSphere 6.5. The core includes your ESXi Hypervisor, vCenter Server, and vCenter Server's components. The upgrade of the third layer products that leverage the core vSphere infrastructure, such as vCloud Director and VMware Horizon View, are not covered in this chapter as they are beyond the scope and purpose of this book.

Before we begin, let me introduce you to the core infrastructure components that will be upgraded:

- **VMware vCenter Server**: The viability of an upgrade or the need for a new build will depend on the current version of vCenter and the supported upgrade path.
- **vCenter Single Sign-On**: These are authentication components. They will come into the picture if you are upgrading from vSphere 5.5 to 6.5.
- **vCenter Inventory Service**: This is no longer a separate service in vCenter 6.5.
- **vSphere Web Client**: This can be upgraded if the current version is 5.5; if not, it will be a new installation of this component.
- **vSphere Platform Service Controller (PSC)**: If you are upgrading from vSphere 6.0 to 6.5, you will need to review the current deployment model and apply an apt strategy to upgrade PSC.
- **vSphere Update Manager**: VUM should be updated to the latest version before it can be used to upgrade ESXi hosts managed by the vCenter VUM is integrated with. VUM components are now built-in to the vCenter Appliance.
- **vSphere Auto Deploy**: This is a requirement to upgrade vSphere Auto Deploy to the same version of vCenter Server.
- **VMware ESXi**: This can be upgraded by booting the server using the ISO image, using vSphere Update Manager, or updating the image profile if the existing servers are auto-deployed.

# vSphere 6.5 core components

The following components form the foundation of vSphere 6.5 environment and its management:

- **Hypervisor**: VMware ESXi 6.5
- **Core management layer**: VMware vCenter Server 6.5
- **Authentication and core services layer**: VMware Platform Services Controller
- **Upgrade and patch management layer**: VMware Update Manager 6.5

# Hypervisor – VMware ESXi 6.5

ESXi Hypervisor is the abstraction layer that enables running of different virtual machines sharing the same physical hardware resources. VMware ESXi 6.5 has significant scalability enhancements. Let's compare and contrast the scalability improvements since ESXi 5.5:

| Feature | vSphere 5.5 | vSphere 6.0 | vSphere 6.5 |
|---|---|---|---|
| Logical processors (CPUs) | 320 | 480 | 576 |
| Physical memory | 4 TB | 6 TB – 12 TB | 12 TB |
| NUMA nodes | 16 | 16 | 16 |
| vCPUs | 4,096 | 4,096 | 4,096 |
| Storage LUNs per host | 256 | 256 | 512 |
| VMFS datastore per host | 256 | 256 | 512 |
| Virtual machines per host | 512 | 1,024 | 1,024 |

Refer to the VMware vSphere 6.5 *Configuration Maximums* guide for more information regarding the scalability maximums at `https://www.vmware.com/pdf/vsphere6/r65/vsphere-65-configuration-maximums.pdf`.

A brief insight into all the new features made available with vSphere 6.5 has been put together in the VMware's technical whitepaper *What's New in VMware vSphere® 6.5* at `http://bit.ly/vSphere65WhatsNew`. Although I have shortened the URL for your benefit, you can always Google for the title text to find this whitepaper.

As the whitepaper introduces the components pretty neatly, we will not be doing the same in this book. This book will introduce you to the new changes in the respective chapters.

# Core management layer – VMware vCenter 6.5

Unlike the previous releases wherein although the appliance was a neater solution, it still lacked something in terms of features and functionalities. Not every aspect of the vSphere management element layer was integrated into the appliance, but that is about to change with vSphere 6.5. VMware vCenter 6.5 Appliance (**vCenter Server Virtual Appliance (vCSA)**) is the new king. It has features that are not available with the Windows version of vCenter. Features such as **Native High Availability (NHA)** and **Native Backup and Restore (NBR)** are only available with the appliance version of vCenter Server. We will cover NHA and NBR in `Chapter 2`, *Greenfield Deployment of vSphere 6.5*.

One component that always stayed out of the box was **vCenter Update Manager** (**VUM**). It was always required to have it installed on a Windows machine. VUM is now available as a component integrated into vCSA.

The vCSA Management has also been greatly improved, especially providing more insight into the built-in PostgreSQL database and its usage. VMware is slowly moving away from its dependence on Microsoft SQL and Oracle database instances.

# Authentication and core services layer – vSphere Platform Services Controller

VMware has bundled the essential services, such as the **Single Sign-On** (**SSO**), Inventory Service, and certificate management, into a single manageable solution named the **Platform Services Controller** (**PSC**). The PSC can be installed on the same machine as the vCenter, installed on a separate supported Windows machine, or run as an integrated component of the vCSA. Refer VMware KB Article 2147672 for supported topologies(https://kb.vmware.com/s/article/2147672).

SSO is an authentication gateway, which takes the authentication requests from various registered components and validates the credential pair against the identity sources added to the SSO server. The components are registered to the SSO server during their installation. We will delve deeper into PSC, and its components in Chapter 2, *Greenfield Deployment of vSphere 6.5*.

# Upgrade and patch management layer – vCenter Update Manager 6.5

**vCenter Update Manager** (**VUM**) is a solution that is used to upgrade or patch your vSphere environment. Keep in mind though that it can only be used to patch/upgrade ESXi hosts and perform some additional tasks, such as VMware tools and virtual machine hardware upgrade. Starting with vSphere 6.5, VUM is no longer required to be installed on Windows machines. It is now fully integrated into the vCenter Appliance and is enabled by default. Also, its reliance on the vSphere C#-based client has been removed. It can now be fully operated using the vSphere Web Client. You will learn more about VUM in Chapter 14, *Upgrading and Patching Using vSphere Update Manager*.

# Planning vSphere upgrade

A vSphere upgrade will require careful assessment of the existing infrastructure. You will need to ensure that the server hardware is compatible with ESXi 6.5. If the existing infrastructure has vCenter components on Microsoft Windows, then you will need to verify whether the current Windows Servers versions are supported for the installation of vCenter 6.5 and its components. If the existing environment has other third layer components, such as the VMware NSX, vRealize Automation, vRealize Operations Manager, vCenter Site Recovery Manager, then it becomes essential to verify whether upgrading the core vSphere components will leave the third layer components unsupported/incompatible. In this section of the chapter, you will learn how to check the hardware compatibility of the existing server hardware, check Windows Server operating system compatibility with the vSphere 6.5 components, and verify third layer product interoperability with the core vSphere 6.5 management components. We will also review various upgrade paths available based on the existing vSphere environment's version and deployment models.

# How to do it...

The following procedure walks you through the steps involved in planning a vSphere upgrade:

1. **Hardware capacity and software requirements check**: As with any new vSphere version, vSphere 6.5 does come with revised hardware capacity and software requirements. It is important to understand these requirements during the planning phase. VMware provides access to more than one form of reference material that would help you understand the hardware and software requirements to deploy a vSphere environment. One of the primary reference sources is the *product documentation* and in this case, the *vSphere 6.5 Installation and Configuration* guide (`https://docs.vmware.com/en/VMware-vSphere/6.5/vsphere-esxi-vcenter-server-65-installation-setup-guide.pdf`). Another source that is always kept up to date is **VMware Knowledge Base** (`https://kb.vmware.com/s/`).

2. **Hardware compatibility check**: The existing server hardware should be verified for its compatibility with ESXi 6.5. It is done by looking up the current server hardware's make and model in the **VMware Compatibility Guide**, which can be accessed at `https://www.vmware.com/resources/compatibility`.

3. **vCenter component compatibility checks**: The existing Microsoft Windows Servers hosting the vCenter components should be verified for its supportability with vCenter 6.5 and its components.

4. **Product interoperability check**: vCenter being the core management layer, there are other solutions that connect with vCenter through APIs to provide its services. Therefore, it becomes critical to verify whether the solution vendors, be it VMware or third party, has a vCenter 6.5 compatible solution yet. Also, consider upgrading the solutions and its plugins before you upgrade to vCenter 6.5. For instance, the first release of vSphere 6.5 did not add support for NSX. It was vSphere 6.5.0a that added support for NSX 6.3.

5. **Upgrade paths**: Depending on the current vSphere version and its deployment model, the process of upgrading to vSphere 6.5 could differ. Hence, it is important to understand the upgrade paths available. The oldest possible version that supports a direct upgrade is vSphere 5.5.

6. **Download vSphere 6.5 components** https://my.vmware.com/web/vmware/downloads: Download the vCenter Appliance or vCenter for Windows based on the platform decision that you have arrived at. Here is what you will need to download:

   - VMware vSphere Hypervisor (ESXi ISO) with VMware Tools
   - VMware vCenter and modules for Windows (ISO) or VMware vCenter Server Appliance (ISO)

# How it works...

The chances of successfully upgrading your vSphere environment without affecting the supportability and compatibility of your existing components will completely depend on how you plan and execute the upgrade. Once you have taken care of the hardware and software dependencies discussed in this section, you can safely execute the upgrade scripts to perform the upgrade. We will cover vSphere 5.5 to 6.5 and vSphere 6.0 to 6.5 upgrades in separate sections.

# Upgrading from vSphere 5.5 or 6.0 to vSphere 6.5

vSphere 5.5 is the oldest supported version of an upgrade to vSphere 6.5. Before we begin, let's review vSphere 5.5 component architecture so that we have a clear understanding of what needs to be upgraded. vSphere 5.5 had separate components.

If you have environments running versions older than vSphere 5.5, you will either need to update the components to vSphere 5.5 first or perform a fresh installation of vSphere 6.5 and then move the workloads to the new environment. In such cases, it is quite possible that the older hardware is no longer supported to host vSphere 6.5 or its components. Use the steps provided in the *Planning vSphere upgrade* section to review your current environment.

## How to do it...

In this section, we will cover the steps involved in upgrading a vSphere 5.5 environment to vSphere 6.5:

1. **Backup the current configuration**: Take snapshots of SSO, vCenter, and database VM before you start the upgrade. Also, take backups of the database if vCenter is running on a physical machine and using an external database.
2. **Upgrade SSO servers to vSphere 6.5 PSC**: Regardless of the platform (Windows or vCSA), the Single Sign-On component servers should be upgraded from 5.5/6.0 to vSphere 6.5 before the vCenter upgrade.
3. **Upgrade vCenter to VCSA 6.5**: For instructions on how to migrate from Windows to VCSA 6.5, read the section *Upgrading vCenter Server - Migrating from Microsoft Windows to VCSA* of this chapter. Single Sign-On and other services will be migrated. vCenter 6.5 can also be installed on a Windows Server, so upgrading vCenter can also be performed without having to rebuild a new machine. Read the section *Upgrading vCenter Server on Microsoft Windows* for instructions. In either case, a database upgrade will be performed.

 VCSA 6.5 no longer supports the use of an external database. Hence, the current database will be migrated to a PostgreSQL database.

4. **Upgrade vSphere Update Manager**: VUM will be upgraded and made part of the vCenter Server if the current vCenter system being upgraded also has VUM installed on it. If VUM is installed on a separate machine, which is mostly the case in enterprise infrastructures, then you will need to run the vCenter Migration Assistant on the VUM machine as well.

5. **Use vSphere Update Manager to upgrade the hosts to ESXi 6.5**: Read the `Chapter 14`, *Upgrading and Patching using vSphere Update Manager* for instructions on how to use VUM to upgrade ESXi hosts by scheduling upgrades/updates.

6. **Use vSphere Update Manager to upgrade the virtual machine hardware and VMware tools**: Read `Chapter 14`, *Upgrading and Patching using vSphere Update Manager*, for instructions.

# How it works...

When you upgrade from vSphere 5.5 to vSphere 6.5, you start with upgrading all the SSO instances. When the SSO instances are upgraded, the existing vSphere 5.5 environment will remain unaffected and will also be accessible via the already existing instance of the vSphere Web Client. If the existing SSO is not embedded, then the upgrade will result in a separate vSphere 6.5 PSC instance. The result remains the same regardless of the platform vCenter is deployed on. If you have more than one vCenter server connecting to the same SSO domain, then post the upgrade of one of the vCenter Servers, the newer vSphere Web Client 6.5 can be used to view/manage both vSphere 6.5 and 5.5 vCenter Servers. If you have more than one SSO/PSC servers, then upgrading one among them will not affect any of the services including vCenter Servers, except for the linked mode configuration, which will not be able to link two disparate vCenter versions.

Another important aspect to keep in mind is that the **Platform Services Controller** (PSC) and vCenter Server (Appliance or Windows) will manage two separate sets of services. The following table lists some of the services managed by both the components:

| Platform Service Controller | vCenter Server |
|---|---|
| VMware Appliance Management Service | vSphere Web Client |
| VMware License Service | vSphere Auto Deploy |
| VMware Component Manager | vSphere Syslog Collector |
| VMware Identity Management Service and **Secure Token Service** (STS) | vSphere ESXi Dump Collector |
| VMware Certificate Service | vCenter Update Manager |

# Upgrading vCenter Server running Microsoft Windows

vCenter 6.5 can be installed on a supported Microsoft Windows Server operating system. Therefore, it is possible to upgrade your existing Windows-based vCenter 5.5/6.0 to 6.5. Before we cover the steps involved in the upgrade, we will review the hardware and software requirements for vCenter 6.5:

- **Hardware requirements**: It is important to make sure that the current system (physical/virtual) hosting the vCenter Server meets the hardware requirements for vCenter 6.5 as laid out by VMware. You should also take into account the growth factor, regarding the number of ESXi hosts and VMs that you expect to manage shortly. To start with, if the upgrade requires you to form an external Platform Service Controller, you will need a machine with at least two CPUs/vCPUs and 4 GB of memory. And the vCenter Server regardless of it using an embedded/external PSC the hardware requirement remains the same; it starts at two CPUs/vCPUs and 10 GB of memory up to 24 CPUs/vCPUs and 48 GB of memory. Storage space requirements for vCenter regardless of using an embedded or external PSC is the same, 17 GB (`Program Files`, `ProgramData`, and `System` folder) and 4 GB (`Program Files`, `ProgramData`, and `System` folder) for an external PSC. The storage space requirement will sometimes have to be reviewed if you plan to host `ProgramData` and `Program Files` folders separately for VMware components on a different Windows drive ( sometimes, on a separate *VMDK*).

- **Software requirements**: Because you are upgrading from an older version of vCenter, it is possible that Windows Server version compatibility has changed for the newest version. Use the VMware Knowledge Base article (`https://kb.vmware.com/s/article/2091273`) to review the list of the supported operating systems. In this case, if you are upgrading from 5.5 or higher, you might already be running on a supported Windows Server operating system. Needless to say, it is important to verify before you proceed with the upgrade.

Although VCSA 6.5 has a fully scalable version of PostgreSQL database, the version embedded in Windows-based vCenter is limited for use in environments up to 20 ESXi hosts and 200 virtual machines. If you have an environment larger than that, you will need to and maybe are already using an external Microsoft SQL or Oracle Database. This is an*other valid reason to move to the vCenter Server Appliance model.*

# How to do it...

The following procedure will walk you through the steps required to perform an in-place upgrade of vCenter and its components using the vCenter installer:

1. At first, download the latest version of vCenter 6.5 Windows ISO and map it to the machine running the current version of vCenter 5.5/6.0.
2. Browse the contents of the ISO and run the `autorun.exe` file as a local system administrator or with a user that has local system administrator rights, to bring up the vCenter installer.
3. On the vCenter installer screen, click on the **Install** button to start the installation wizard.
4. On the **Welcome to VMware vCenter Server 6.5 Installer** screen, click on the **Next** button to continue.
5. Accept the EULA and click on the **Next** button to continue.
6. On the **vCenter Single Sign-On and vCenter Credentials** screen, supply the SSO administrator password and click on the **Next** button to let the installer run the pre upgrade checks.
7. On the **Configure Ports** screen—you are not allowed to make any changes. Click on the **Next** button to continue.
8. On the **Upgrade Options** screen, you can choose to migrate all or some of the historical data and the configuration or just the configuration. Choose an intended option and click on the **Next** button to continue:

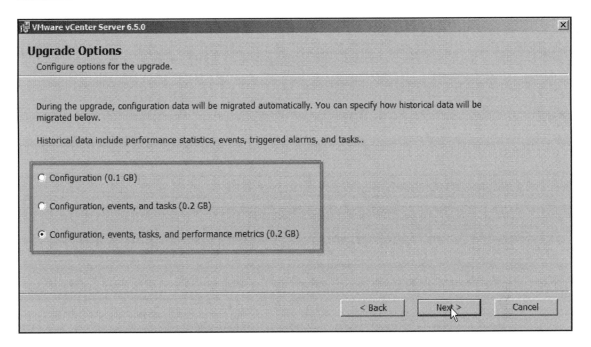

9. On the **Destination Directory** screen, you can choose to change the `Program Files` and `ProgramData` locations for this installation. You can also choose to modify the location of the `export` folder, which is used by the installer to export current configuration. Make intended changes and click on **Next** to continue.

10. On the next screen, you can choose either join or not join VMware's **Customer Experience Improvement Program**. Make an intended selection and click on **Next** to continue.

11. On the **Ready to Upgrade** screen, confirm that you have backed-up your vCenter Server by selecting the checkbox **I verify that I have backed up this vCenter Server machine** and click on the **Upgrade** button.

12. The installer will now perform the upgrade, and if successful, it will display a **Setup Completed** wizard screen, where you click on **Finish** to close the wizard:

13. Once done, you should be able to log in to the Web Client to view and manage the upgraded vCenter Server. If everything looks good, you can delete the `export` folder to free up some disk space.

# How it works...

The installer will remove the older components, import the data, and perform a new installation of vCenter 6.5 and its components. The amount of time the upgrade would take to finish successfully is very dependent on the amount of data that needs to be imported into the new installation and don't be surprised if the upgrade runs for more than 30-40 minutes. Once the installation is complete, you will be able to access vCenter 6.5 using vSphere Web Client. If there is more than one vCenter to upgrade, the procedure remains the same. However, the vSphere 6.5 Web Client would still let you view and manage the older version of vCenter.

# Using the vCenter 6.5 Migration Assistant

To upgrade and migrate vCenter 5.5/6.0 components running on Windows Servers, vCenter 6.5 comes with a new tool named the **vCenter Migration Assistant**. The procedure to run the migration-assistant is the same whether you are trying to upgrade an external SSO, PSC, or Update Manager or an embedded version of these. The migration-assistant should be run on the machines hosting these services separately, before initiating the vCenter Migration/Upgrade. The migration/upgrade process will migrate data from all the components server with an active migration-assistant session.

# How to do it...

The following procedure will walk you through the steps involved in running the vCenter Migration Assistant to enable the migration of configuration and performance data to the appliance:

1. Mapping the VCSA 6.5 ISO to the machine running the Windows-based version of vCenter 5.5/6.0.
2. Browse the ISO ROM contents and navigate to the `migration-assistant` folder. Copy the entire folder to a location on your Windows-based vCenter machine:

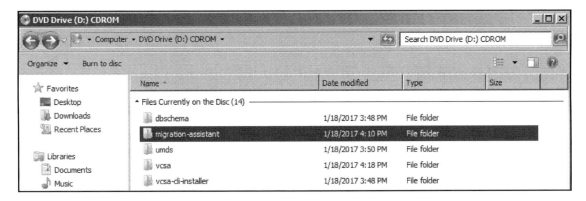

3. Browse the contents of the `migration-assistant` from the hard drive location and run the executable `VMware-Migration-Assistant.exe` as an administrator:

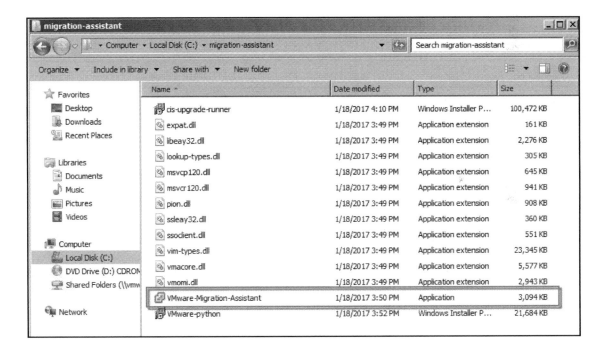

4. This will bring up a Windows CLI interface, and you will be prompted for the SSO administrator password. Type in the password and press *Enter*. *You will also be prompted for service account credentials if the vCenter Server Windows service is run with a service account's privileges.* Type in the password and press *Enter*:

5. You will now see the migration-assistant running prechecks and eventually warn you about extension/plugins that cannot be upgraded using this process. For instance, I have got an SRM plugin that cannot be upgraded. It will also display the source vCenter's configuration, and the expected resultant configuration post a successful upgrade:

6. There is nothing more to do with the migration-assistant tool at this point, but do not close it.
7. You are now all set to run the VCSA installer's Migrate or Upgrade wizards.

# Upgrading vCenter Server – Migrating from Microsoft Windows to VCSA

VMware with the release of vSphere 6.5 will now let you migrate an existing vCenter Server Windows installation, be it vCenter 5.5 or 6.0, to vCenter Server Appliance 6.5. This form of migration will let you move from any deployment model (embedded or external SSO/PSC) and any external database (Microsoft SQL, SQL Server Express, or Oracle). All the database contents will be migrated to an embedded PostgreSQL database within the appliance. Keep in mind that although it allows moving from any topology, it does not allow modifying the topology while migrating.

VCSA is now a fully featured vCenter component bundle and supports only an embedded PostgreSQL database. VMware might do away with the Microsoft Windows version for the next release.

Virtual machine requirements, there are no operating system level requirements because this is an appliance and VMware is using the **JeOS (Just Enough Operating System)** version of Linux named the Photon OS with all the required libraries bundled.

To learn more about Photon OS, visit the GitHub repository at https://vmware.github.io/photon/.

However, it is important to understand the sizing requirements. The compute requirements for VCSA are similar to that of a Windows installation. If the upgrade requires an external Platform Service Controller, you will need a machine with at least two CPUs/vCPUs and 4 GB of Memory. Starting with two CPUs/vCPUs and 10 GB of memory up to 24 CPUs/vCPUs and 48 GB of memory, the compute requirements for the vCenter Server remains the same regardless of the type of database configured - embedded or external. The virtual machine storage requirements are stated slightly differently, though. If deployed alone, PSC will require 60 GB of storage space. For more details on the requirements, refer to the VMware vSphere 6.5 Upgrade Guide.

# Getting ready

To perform this migration, you will need access to the vCenter Server Appliance 6.5 ISO downloaded from https://my.vmware.com/web/vmware/downloads. Also, because this will deploy a new appliance virtual machine, you will need to decide on the following factors:

- **Placement location**: This is is the vCenter inventory location where you would like to place the VCSA VM. The location could be a cluster, a resource pool or just a VM folder.
- **Datastore**: You will need to decide on an appropriate datastore to store the appliance.

 You will need access to a machine other than the one that is hosting vCenter 6.0/5.5 to complete the upgrade. It can even be a Linux or macOS machine.

# How to do it...

The following procedure will walk you through the steps involved in migrating and upgrading a vCenter 5.5/6.0 installation to a vCenter Server 6.5 Appliance with an embedded database:

1. Use the migration-assistant to perform the pre-checks and ready the source vCenter Server and its component servers for migration. Read the section *Using the vCenter 6.5 Migration Assistant* of this chapter for instructions.
2. Once you have readied the vCenter and its components using migration-assistant, map the VCSA ISO to a non-vCenter machine because the source will be *shut down* during the migration.

3. At the non-vCenter machine, browse the contents of the VCSA ISO ROM, navigate to `vcsa-ui-installer`, and choose a subdirectory corresponding to your operating system (`lin64`, `mac`, and `win32`). In this case, we will navigate to the `win32` directory and run the executable `installer.exe` as an administrator to bring up the **vCenter Server Appliance 6.5 Installer** window:

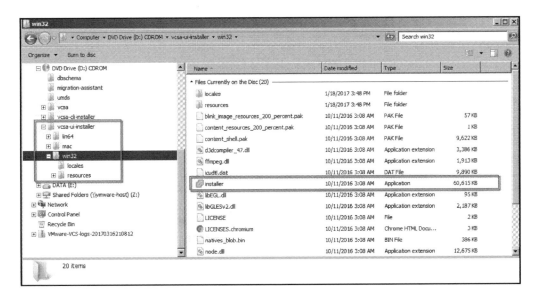

4. On the **vCenter Server Appliance 6.5 Installer** wizard window, click on **Migrate** to bring up the **Migrate - Stage 1: Deploy appliance** window. Click on **Next** to continue.

5. Click on the **Migrate - Stage 1: Deploy appliance** window and then click on **Next** to continue.

6. Accept the EULA and click on **Next** to continue.

7. Supply the source Windows vCenter's FQDN/IP and the SSO administrator's password to proceed further:

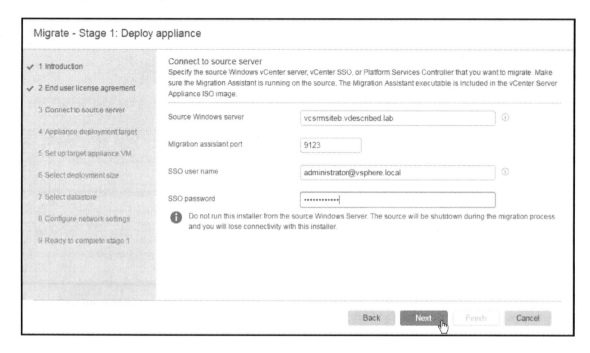

8. Click on **Yes** to accept the source vCenter Server's SSL certificate.

9. Supply the FQDN/IP and the credentials of the vCenter Server or ESXi host to deploy the VCSA VM:

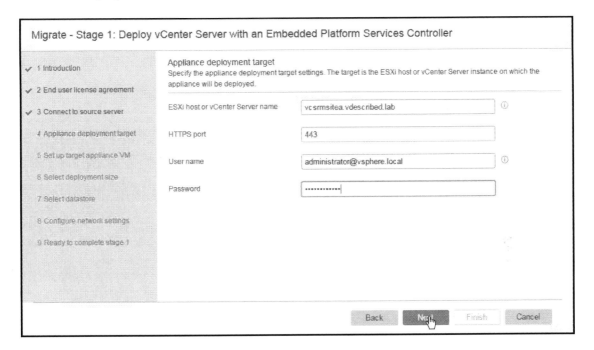

10. Click on **Yes** to accept the vCenter/ESXi SSL certificate.

11. Select a datacenter or VM folder from the destination vCenter inventory and then click on **Next**:

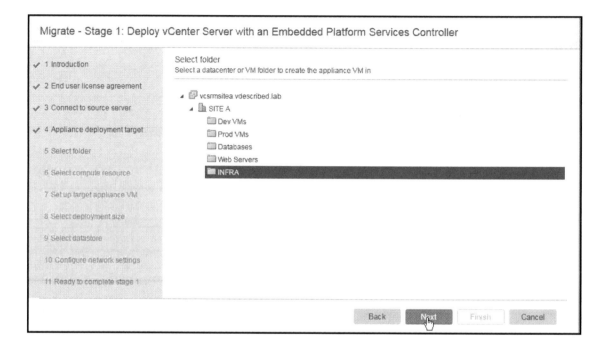

12. Select a cluster or a host from the vCenter inventory to deploy the VCSA VM and Click on **Next** to continue:

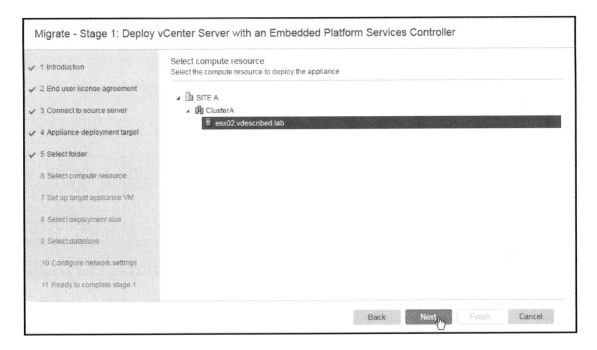

13. Supply **VM name** for the VCSA Appliance and set the **Root password**. Click on **Next** to continue.

14. Choose an intended VCSA **Deployment size** and **Storage size**. Click on **Next** to continue:

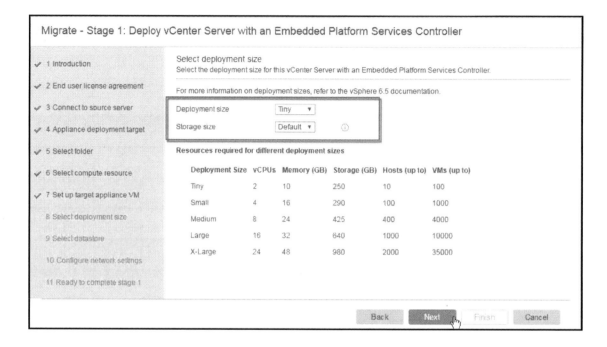

15. Select a datastore for the VCSA VM and click on **Next** to continue:

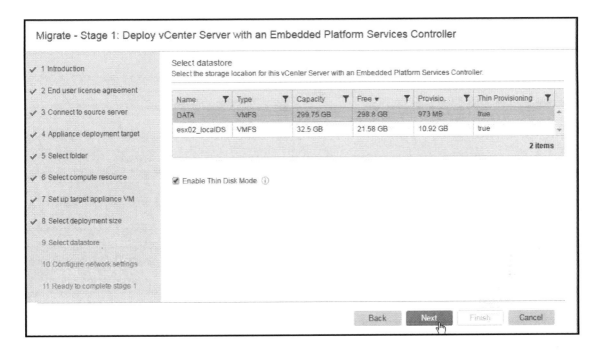

16. Choose a port group and a temporary static IP configuration, which will enable the appliance VM to communicate with the source vCenter and migrate configuration and other data:

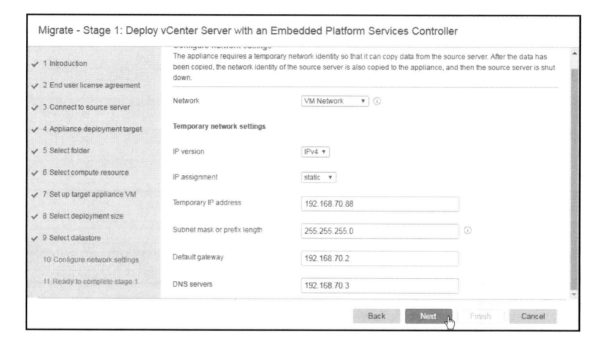

17. On the **Ready to complete stage 1** screen, review the settings and click on **Finish** to start the deployment:

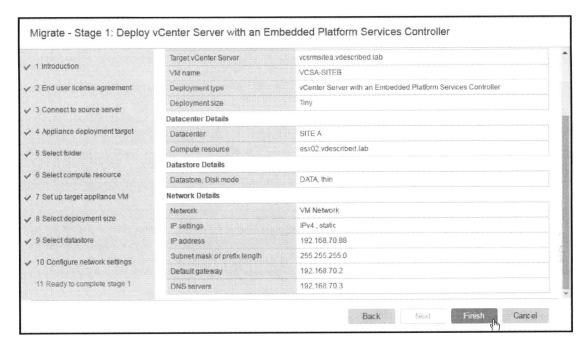

18. Once the deployment is complete, click on **Continue** to proceed to the stage-2 of the deployment process. Stage-2 is where you let VCSA VM connect to the source vCenter and initiate the data migration.
19. On the **Migrate - Stage 2** screen, click on **Next** to continue.

20. You will be prompted with the same set of warnings generated by the migration-assistant. Click on **Close** to continue.

21. The wizard will prompt you to join the same Active Directory domain as the source vCenter. Supply the credentials of an Active Directory user with the permissions to join a machine to the domain and click on **Next**:

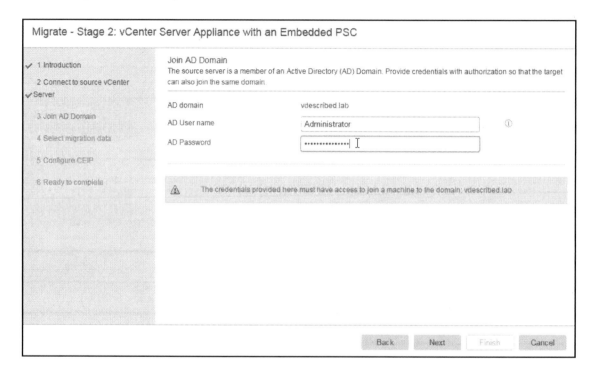

22. On the **Select migration data** screen, you can choose to migrate all or some of the historical data and the configuration or just the configuration. Select an intended option and click on **Next** to continue:

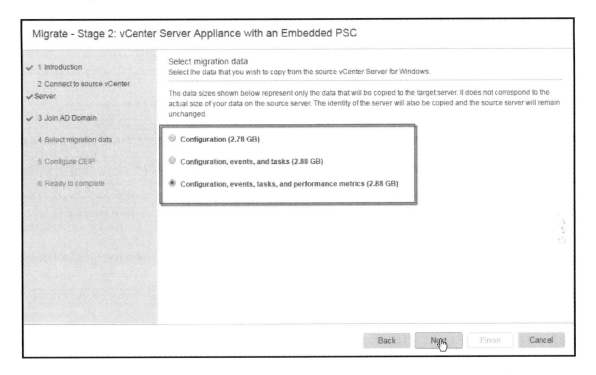

23. Choose to either join or not join the VMware CEIP and click on **Next** to continue.

24. On the **Ready to complete** screen, review the settings and confirm that you have backed-up your vCenter Server by selecting the checkbox **I have backed up the source vCenter Server and all the required data from the database** and click on **Finish** to start the migration and configuration of the VCSA:

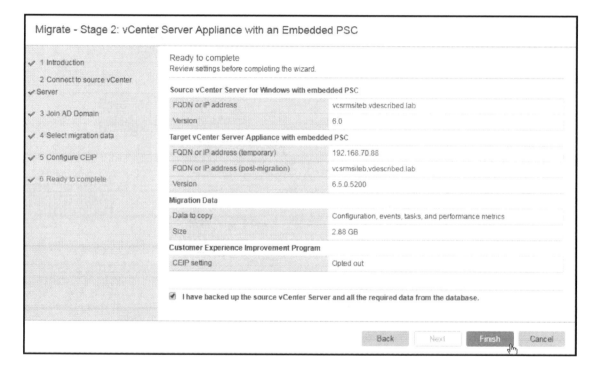

25. You will be warned about the fact that the source vCenter will be shut down during this process. Click on **OK** to acknowledge and continue.

26. The data migration will begin, and once done, it will shut down the source vCenter and configure the appliance VM.

27. Once the process completes successfully, click on **Close.**

28. You should now be able to login to the vSphere Web Client or the new HTML client to view and manage the new vCenter.

# How it works...

The migration process deploys a vCSA Appliance and imports the data from the vCenter windows installation. It retains vCenter Server's IP address, UUID, hostname, SSL certificates, and management object reference IDs; therefore once the installation is complete, the vCenter Server Windows machine is shutdown. If for any reason the upgrade fails and the vCenter Windows machine is shut down, all you need to do is to power-off the VCSA VM and power-on the vCenter Windows machine. The upgrade and migrate process will not make any changes to the source Windows machine.

# Upgrading the vCenter Server Appliance

An existing vCenter 5.5/6.0 Appliance can be upgraded to VCSA 6.5. This is done using the upgrade wizard of the vCenter Appliance installer. An upgrade does not change the current deployment model; if the vCSA is accompanied by external SSO/PSCs, then they will need to be upgraded first. The upgrade procedure is the same for both vCSA and PSC appliances.

# Getting ready

If the vSphere 5.5/6.0 environment has any of its component, running on Windows Server, then the migration-assistant should be run to ready those component servers. Read the instructions in the section *Using the vCenter 6.5 Migration Assistant*.

# How to do it...

The following procedure will guide you through the steps required to upgrade an existing vCSA 5.5/6.0 and its components to VCSA 6.5:

1. Once you have readied the Windows component servers using migration-assistant, map the VCSA ISO to a machine that can be used to reach the source VCSA over the network. The machine used for this purpose can be running Windows, Linux or macOS.

2. Browse the VCSA ISO ROM contents and navigate to `vcsa-ui-installer` and choose a subdirectory corresponding to your operating system (`lin64`, `mac`, `win32`). In this case, we will navigate to the `win32` directory and run the executable `installer.exe` as an *administrator* to bring up the **vCenter Server Appliance 6.5 Installer** window.

3. On the **vCenter Server Appliance 6.5 Installer** wizard window, click on **Upgrade** to bring up the **Upgrade - Stage 1: Deploy appliance** window. Click on **Next** to continue.

4. Accept the EULA and click on **Next** to continue.

5. Supply the source VCSA's FQDN/IP and the SSO administrator's password and also the FQDN/IP and the credentials of the vCenter Server or ESXi host managing the source VCSA.

6. Click on **Yes** to accept the source vCenter Server's SSL certificate.

7. On the **Appliance Deployment Target** screen, supply the FQDN/IP and the credentials of the vCenter Server or ESXi host to deploy the VCSA VM.

8. Click on **Yes** to accept the vCenter/ESXi SSL certificate.

9. Supply **VM name** for the vCSA Appliance and set the **Root password**.

10. Choose an intended VCSA **Deployment size** and **Storage size**. Click on **Next** to continue.

11. Select a datastore for the VCSA VM and click **Next**.

12. Choose a port group and a temporary static IP configuration, which will enable the appliance VM to communicate with the source vCenter and migrate configuration and other data.

13. On the **Ready to complete stage 1** screen, review the settings and click on **Finish** to start the VCSA 6.5 deployment.

14. Once the deployment is complete, click on **Continue** to proceed into the stage-2 of the deployment process. Stage-2 is where you let the VCSA VM connect to the source vCenter and initiate the data migration.

15. On the **Upgrade - Stage 2** screen click **Next** to continue.

16. You will be presented with the pre-upgrade check result. One of the important recommendations/warnings will be to configure your destination cluster's DRS automation level to manual. This is to make sure that the appliance VM is not being moved around by DRS during the upgrade process. Click on **Close** to continue.

17. On the **Select migration data** screen, you can choose to migrate all or some of the historical data and the configuration or just the configuration. Select an intended option and click on **Next** to continue.

18. Choose to either join or not join the VMware CEIP and click on **Next** to continue.

19. On the **Ready to complete** screen, review the settings and confirm that you have backed-up your vCenter Server by selecting the checkbox **I verify that I have backed up this vCenter Server machine** and click on **Finish** to start the migration and configuration of the VCSA.

20. You will be warned about the fact that the source vCenter will be shut down during this process. Click on **OK** to acknowledge and continue.

21. The data migration will begin, and once done, it will shut down the source vCenter and configure the appliance VM.

22. Once the process completes successfully, click on **Close**.

23. You should now be able to log in to the Web Client to view and manage the new vCenter.

# Upgrading ESXi Hypervisor

Once you have vCenter Server upgraded to version 6.5, the next step is to upgrade the ESXi hosts. The upgrade procedure will depend on the current deployment architecture. For instance, if all your ESXi hosts were deployed using the VMware Auto Deploy server, then you'll have to update the image profile sourcing the streamed image using a new offline bundle. As Auto Deploy is covered in Chapter 5, *Using vSphere Auto Deploy*, in this chapter, we will cover the upgrade of the ESXi host using the installation media. VMware ESXi can also be upgraded by running the ESXi installer on each of the servers or use vSphere Update Manager to perform the same activity. You will learn about patching/upgrading ESXi hosts using VUM in Chapter 14, *Upgrading and Patching using vSphere Update Manager*.

# Getting ready

Before you begin any upgrade, it is very important to plan for it. So what would you need to do to perform an upgrade of ESXi? You would, of course, need the ISO image downloaded from VMware's website, but you would also need a method to present the ISO to the physical machine so that it can boot from it. Most of the modern server equipment's have a methodology to avoid the need to burn ISO to a physical DVD medium and then insert it into the DVD drive of the physical machine. If you are an administrator, you might already be aware of terms such as ILO (HP), DRAC (Dell), and KVM Manager (Cisco). These are web-based tools that will connect to an RAC on the server and enable remote access to the server's console via the Web. Enough said on what is available out there; let's make a list of what you need to begin the upgrade:

- The ESXi 6.5 Hypervisor ISO image can be downloaded from VMware's downloads page https://my.vmware.com/web/vmware/downloads
- Access to the remote console of the server on which the upgrade will be performed

# How to do it...

The following procedure will walk you through the steps involved in upgrading ESXi 5.5/6.0 to ESXi 6.5 using the ESXi installer:

1. Boot the host with the ESXi 6.5 installer ISO mapped to it.
2. Choose ESXi 6.5 standard installer from the boot menu and press *Enter*:

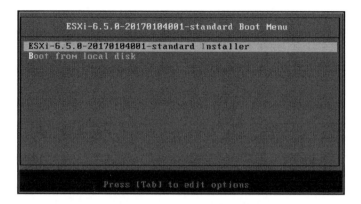

3. Once the installer is fully loaded into the memory, you will be prompted with a **Welcome to the VMware ESXi 6.5.0 Installation** screen. Now press *Enter* to continue.
4. To accept the EULA and continue, press the function key *F11*.
5. Select the storage device that has the previous installation of ESXi and press *F1* to view the disk details:

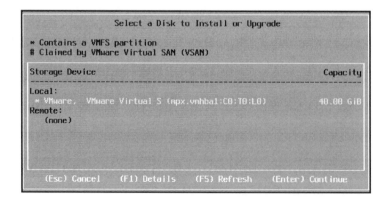

6. On pressing *F1*, it will show you the **Disk Details**. In this case, it has detected an ESXi 6.0 installation. Press *Enter* to go back to the **Select a Disk to Install or Upgrade** screen:

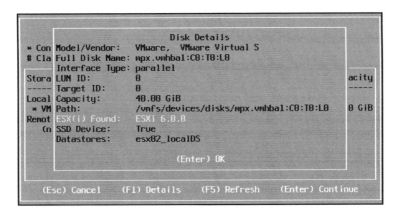

7. At the **Select a Disk to Install or Upgrade** window, press *Enter* to continue.
8. On the **ESXi and VMFS Found** window, select the option **Upgrade ESXi, preserve VMFS datastore** and press *Enter* to continue:

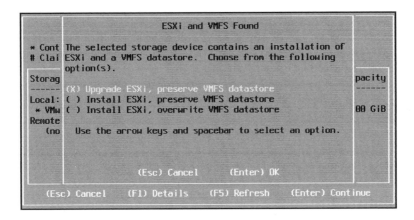

9. On the **Confirm Upgrade** window, select the **Upgrade** option by pressing the *F11* key:

10. If the upgrade completes successfully, you will be presented with an **Upgrade Complete** success window. Now press *Enter* to reboot the ESXi host.

11. After a reboot, you should be able to see the ESXi 6.5 DCUI welcome screen.

You should now be able to connect to this vCenter using the embedded host client as well. If the host was managed by a vCenter, then the inventory should now show this ESXi host connected.

# There is more...

Once you have vCenter and Update Manager upgraded and configured for use, the ESXi host upgrades can be performed using VUM in a much more effective manner. You will be able to run the upgrades simultaneously on more than one ESXi host using VUM remediation. You will learn more about this in Chapter 14, *Upgrading and Patching using vSphere Update Manager*.

It is important to note that although there are means to retain your Microsoft Windows servers to run the vCenter components, there is no longer a compelling reason to do so. The vCenter Server Appliance is the way ahead, and you need not be surprised to see VMware completely removing the dependency on Microsoft OS or external databases in its future releases.

# 2
# Greenfield Deployment of vSphere 6.5

In this chapter, we will cover the following recipes:

- Deploying VMware ESXi 6.5
- Configuring the ESXi Management Network
- Deploying vCenter Server Appliance 6.5
- Deploying External Platform Service controllers
- Deploying vCenter Servers in Enhanced Linked Mode
- Configuring SSO identity sources
- Assigning users and groups to vCenter Server

## Introduction

vSphere components ESXi and vCenter Server form the foundation of any modern day data center that is virtualized using VMware. Planning the deployment of these components and its execution is important as it forms the base for any other solution. We reviewed how scalable ESXi 6.5 is when compared to ESXi 5.5 or 6.0 in the previous chapter. Also, as mentioned in the previous chapter, there is no practical reason to use a Microsoft Windows Server to host vCenter and its components any longer. The vCenter appliance is the future, and with vSphere 6.5, VCSA is not a fully functional appliance with VUM integrated into it. For the same reason, we will not cover the installation of vCenter on a Windows server in this chapter.

# Deploying vSphere ESXi 6.5

The very first component that you will install in a fully virtualized VMware environment is the ESXi hypervisor. Although there are different methods of deploying ESXi 6.5, which include the use of auto deploy or an installation script, we will review how ESXi can be deployed using the interactive installer.

## Getting ready

The installation of ESXi 6.5 is pretty straightforward. It is recommended that you refer to the **VMware Compatibility Guide** web page to verify whether the server hardware is compatible with ESXi 6.5; this is available at `http://www.vmware.com/resources/compatibility/search.php`. Once you have made sure that the server hardware is compatible, the next step is to make sure that the server meets the hardware capacity requirements:

- The host should have at least two 64-bit x86 CPU cores
- AMD **No Execute** (**NX**) and Intel **Execute Disable** (**XD**) processor functions are to be enabled in the server BIOS
- To be able to run 64-bit operating systems on virtual machines, you will need to enable the use of hardware virtualization (Intel VT-x or AMD RVI) in the server BIOS
- A minimum of 4 GB of physical memory for hypervisor alone and an additional 4 GB to start hosting virtual machines

For more details on the hardware requirements, refer to the *ESXi Hardware Requirements* section of VMware vSphere 6.5 Installation and Configuration Guide (`https://docs.vmware.com/en/VMware-vSphere/6.5/vsphere-esxi-vcenter-server-65-installation-setup-guide.pdf`).

## Downloading ESXi 6.5 and mapping it to the server

You will need the ISO image downloaded from VMware's website, but you would also need a method to present the ISO to the physical machine so that it can boot from it. Most modern server equipment has a methodology to avoid the need to burn ISO to a physical DVD medium and then insert it into the DVD drive of the physical machine. If you are an administrator, you might already be aware of terms such as ILO (HP), DRAC (Dell), and KVM Manager (Cisco).

These are web-based tools that will connect to a **Remote Access Card (RAC)** on the server and enable remote access to the server's console through the web. Enough said on what is available out there; let's make a list of what you need to begin the upgrade:

- The ESXi 6.5 hypervisor ISO image downloaded from VMware's downloads page `https://my.vmware.com/web/vmware/downloads`
- Access to the remote console of the server on which the installation will be performed

# How to do it...

The following procedure will guide you through the steps involved in deploying ESXi 6.5 using the interactive installer:

1. Boot up the server with the ESXi 6.5 ISO mapped to it.
2. On the ESXi 6.5 standard boot menu, select the standard installer, as shown, and press the *Enter* key to continue:

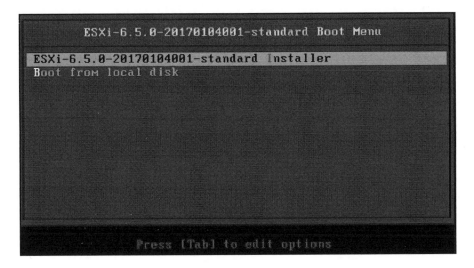

3. Once the installer is fully loaded into the memory, you will be prompted with a **Welcome to the VMware ESXi 6.5.0 Installation** screen. Now, press the *Enter* key to continue.

4. To accept the EULA and continue, press the *F11* function key.

5. On the **Select a Disk to Install or Upgrade** screen, select a storage device to install ESXi on it. Make a cautious effort to select the correct disk for the installation, as this will erase any data on the selected disk. The selection can be made using the *up/down arrow* keys. With the intended storage device selected, you can optionally hit the *F1* function key to view the details of the storage device selected. This is another way to make sure that you have selected the correct disk for the installation. In this case, the installer has only detected a device attached to the local controller. If necessary, you could hit *F1* to fetch more details about the device:

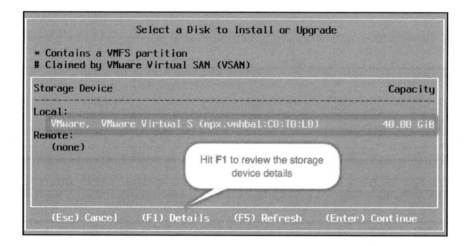

6. (Optional step) On hitting *F1*, you will be presented with the storage device details. Review the details and hit *Enter* to exit the details screen and return:

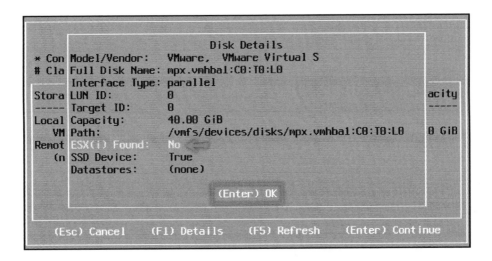

7. (Optional step) When you are back to the **Select a Disk to Install or Upgrade** screen, hit *Enter* to confirm the selection and continue.

8. Select the keyboard layout and hit *Enter* to continue. The default is **US Default**.

9. Supply a root password and hit *Enter* to continue.

 At this stage, the installer will scan the server hardware for additional information or prerequisites that it would need to proceed further. If any of the pre-checks fail, you will be warned accordingly. For instance, if you do not have Intel VT-x or AMD-V enabled in the BIOS, then it will warn you about that. It can also warn you about unsupported devices detected during the scan. Most warnings will not stop you from proceeding further, but will only indicate what will not be configured or supported. Hit *Enter* to continue.

10. At the **Confirm Install** screen, review the device that will be erased and partitioned. Hit *F11* to start the installation or hit *F9* to go back and make any changes needed.

11. You will now see the **Installing ESXi 6.5.0** screen showing the progress of the installation. This will take a few minutes to complete.

12. Once the installation is complete, you will be presented with an **Installation Complete** message screen. At this point, eject or unmount the CD/DVD drive or image, and hit *Enter* to reboot the machine.

13. A rebooting server message is displayed, indicating that the server is about to be rebooted. There is nothing that you have to do on this screen.

14. Once the reboot is complete, you will be at the main screen for ESXi 6.5.0:

```
VMware ESXi 6.5.0 (VMKernel Release Build 4887370)

VMware, Inc. VMware Virtual Platform

2 x Intel(R) Core(TM) i7 CPU 960 @ 3.20GHz
4 GiB Memory




Download tools to manage this host from:
http://192.168.70.129/ (DHCP)
http://[fe80::20c:29ff:fe7f:ec61]/ (STATIC)



<F2> Customize System/View Logs                          <F12> Shut Down/Restart
```

15. Once the installation is complete, you will need to supply the basic network configuration. The next recipe, *Configuring ESXi Management Network*, covers this.

# Configuring ESXi Management Network

After the ESXi installation is complete, it is essential to configure its management network before it can be accessed. The management network is what makes the ESXi become a part of a network. It is backed by a VMkernel network interface. We will learn more about these in the networking chapter. The ESXi hypervisor runs a DHCP client, so it does procure a DHCP address if there is a DHCP server on its network; but, in most cases, that is not enough. For instance, if your management network is on a VLAN, then you will need to configure the VLAN ID. Also, it is recommended that the ESXi hosts be assigned with a static IP address. Hence, it becomes important to configure the management network of an ESXi host after it is installed. In this recipe, we will use the **Direct Console User Interface (DCUI)** to achieve this.

# Getting ready

You will need access to the host's console via its IPMI interface DRAC/ILO/KVM, the root password, and the TCP/IP configuration that you would like to assign to the ESXi Management Network.

# How to do it...

The following procedure will walk you through the steps required in setting up the TCP/IP configuration for the ESXi's Management Network:

1. Connect to the console of the ESXi host. Hit the *F2* function key to log in to the DCUI by supplying the root password.
2. Select **Configure Management Network** and hit *Enter*:

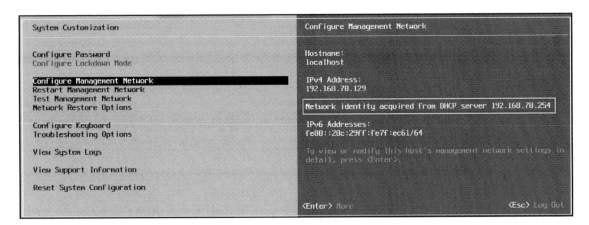

3. You will now be presented with options to select the **Network Adapters** for the management network, supply an optional VLAN, configure IPv4 and IPv6 settings, and DNS settings.

4. The **Network Adapters** option can be used to assign more adapters to the
**Management Network** port group. Once you have selected the NICs to use, hit
*Enter* to return to the **Configure Management Network** menu:

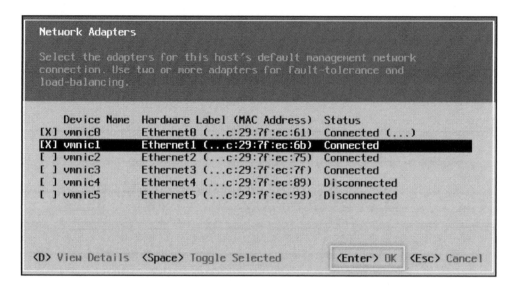

5. Select **IPv4 Configuration** and hit *Enter*. Use the keyboard arrow keys to select
the **Set static IPv4 address and network configuration** option and hit the
spacebar to confirm the selection. Supply the static **IPv4 Address**, **Subnet Mask**,
and **Default Gateway**, hit *Enter* to save the settings, and return to the **Configure
Management Network** menu:

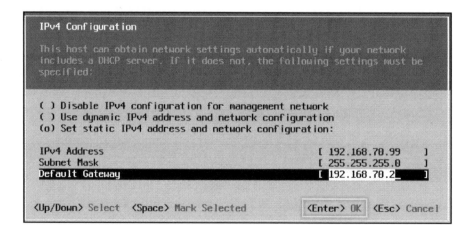

6. Select **DNS Configuration** and hit *Enter*. Supply the primary and alternate DNS servers and the hostname. Hit *Enter* to save the settings and return to the previous menu:

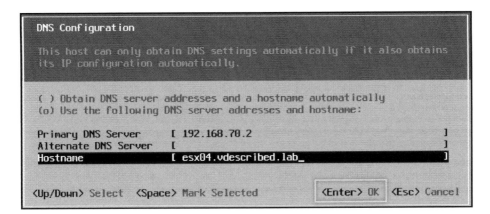

 If you do not supply an FQDN, then make sure you configure a custom DNS suffix. The option to do so is available on the **Configure Management Network** screen.

7. (Optional step) Use the **Custom DNS Suffixes** option to enter the **Suffixes**:

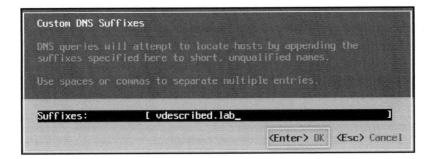

8. (Optional step) To assign a VLAN ID to the management network, select **VLAN (optional)**, hit *Enter*, supply the VLAN number, and hit *Enter* again to return to the **Configure Management Network** screen:

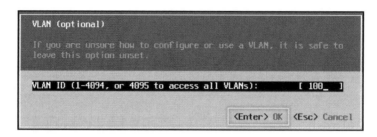

9. Once you are done with all the network configuration, while on the **Configure Management Network: Confirm** screen, hit *Esc* to be prompted to apply the changes by seeking consent for a restart of the management network. Hit *Y* to apply the settings.

10. If you go back to the DCUI of this ESXi host, it should now show the static IP configured:

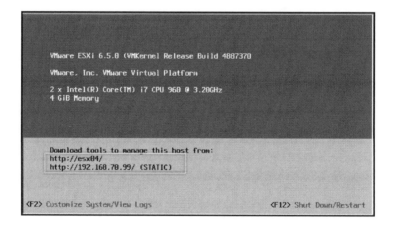

11. With the networking configured, you should now be able to connect to the ESXi host using the vSphere Client or add the host to a vCenter Server. Both can be achieved only if the ESXi management IP is reachable from the machine where the vSphere Client is installed or from the vCenter machine.

# There is more...

IPv6 is enabled by default. If you do not intend to use version 6, then it can be disabled from the **Configure Management Network** screen.

Select **IPv6 Configuration** and hit *Enter* to bring up the **IPv6 Configuration** window. Hit the spacebar to disable the selection, and then hit *Enter*:

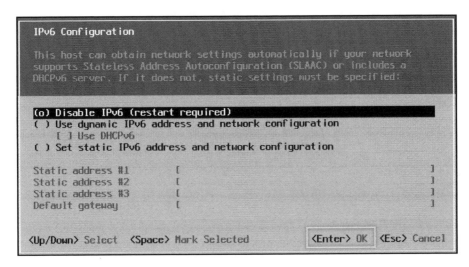

Disabling IPv6 will require a reboot of the ESXi host for the network changes to take effect.

# Deploying vCenter Server Appliance 6.5

vCenter Server Appliance 6.5 comes with a GUI installer that can run from different platforms (Windows, Linux, or macOS). The installer by itself has software and hardware requirements that need to be met for optimal performance during installation:

| Operating system | CPU | Memory | Storage |
|---|---|---|---|
| macOS Mavericks/Yosemite/El Capitan | 4 cores or vCPUs at 2.4 GHz | 8 GB | 150 GB |
| Windows 7, 8, 8.1, and 10 | 4 cores or vCPUs at 2.3 GHz | 4 GB | 32 GB |
| SUSE 12 (64-bit) or Ubuntu 14.04 (64-bit) | 2 cores or vCPUs at 2.3 GHz | 4 GB | 16 GB |

# How to do it...

The following procedure will guide you through the steps involved in deploying VCSA 6.5 with an embedded PSC:

1. Map and browse the contents of the VCSA ISO ROM, navigate to `vcsa-ui-installer`, and choose a subdirectory corresponding to your operating system (`lin64`, `mac`, `win32`). In this case, we will navigate to the `win32` directory and run the executable `installer.exe` as an administrator to bring up the **vCenter Server Appliance 6.5 Installer** window:

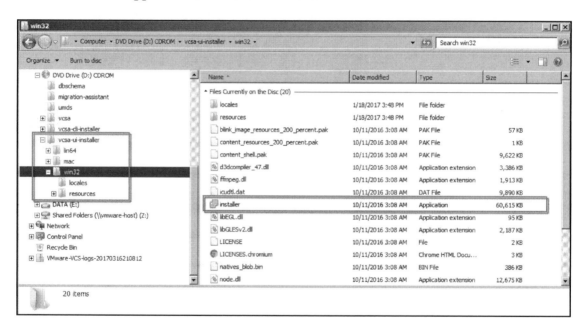

2. On the **vCenter Server Appliance 6.5 Installer** window, click **Install** to bring up the **Install - Stage 1: Deploy Appliance** window. Click **Next** to continue:
3. Accept the EULA and click **Next** to continue.

4. Choose a deployment type. In this case, we are deploying a **vCenter Server with an Embedded Platform Services Controller.**

5. The same installation wizard can be used to deploy external PSCs and vCenter Servers without PSCs as well. Click **Next** to continue.

6. On the **Appliance deployment target** screen, supply the IP address/FQDN and the credentials of the vCenter or the ESXi host the appliance VM will be deployed onto. In this case, the target is an ESXi host. Click **Next** to continue:

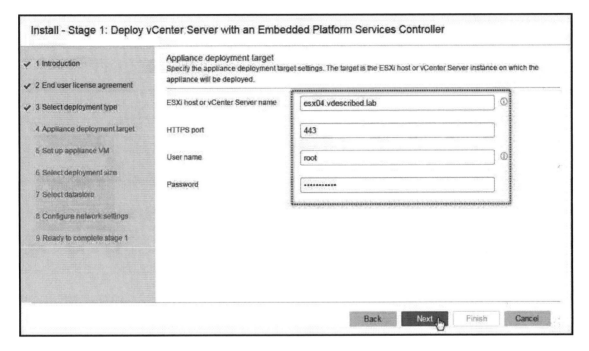

7. Click on **Yes** to accept the target host's SSL certificate.

8. On the **Setup appliance VM** screen, supply a name for the VM and set the password for its root user. Click **Next** to continue.

9.  Select an intended deployment size and click **Next** to continue:

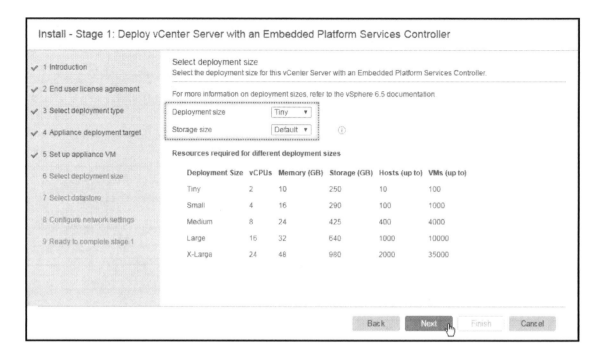

10. Select a datastore to place the appliance VM in. You can perform the **Thin provisioning (TP)** on the VMDKs if you choose to, by selecting **Enable Thin Disk Mode**. Click **Next** to continue:

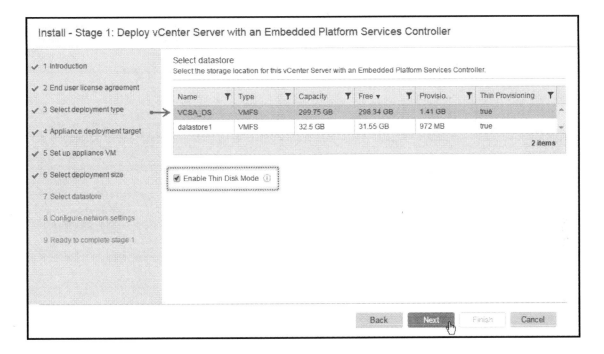

11. On the **Configure network settings** screen, supply a **System name** (which can either be the IP address or FQDN for the appliance) and the IP configuration. Click **Next** to continue:

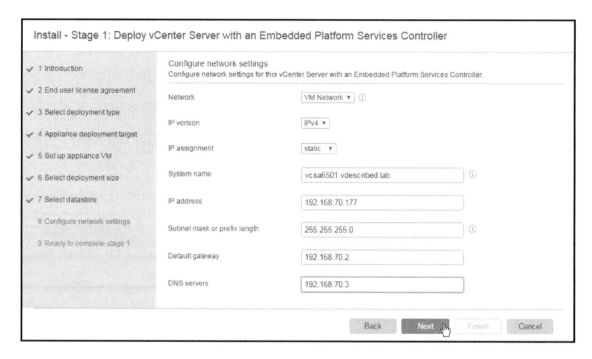

If you do not specify a **System name**, then the IP address will be used as the actual system name. The system name will be used in the SSL certificates of the appliance VM.

12. On the **Ready to complete stage 1** screen, review the settings and click **Finish** to deploy the appliance.

13. Once the deployment completes successfully, you will be presented with a screen indicating deployment is complete. Click **Continue** to start the stage 2 installer wizard.

If you accidentally close the wizard or choose to continue at a later time, then the stage 2 installer can be started by connecting to the appliance administration URL: `https://VCSA IP` or `FQDN:5480` and using the **Set up vCenter Server Appliance** option.

14. On the **Install - Stage 2: Set Up vCenter Server Appliance with an Embedded PSC** screen, click **Next** to continue.

15. On the **Appliance configuration** page, the IP configuration will be pre-populated. However, you will need to decide on the **Time synchronization mode**. You can either choose to synchronize time with the ESXi host or use **NTP servers**. It is recommended to time synchronize all your vSphere components with an NTP server. Supply the **NTP servers** IP address(s) and click **Next** to continue:

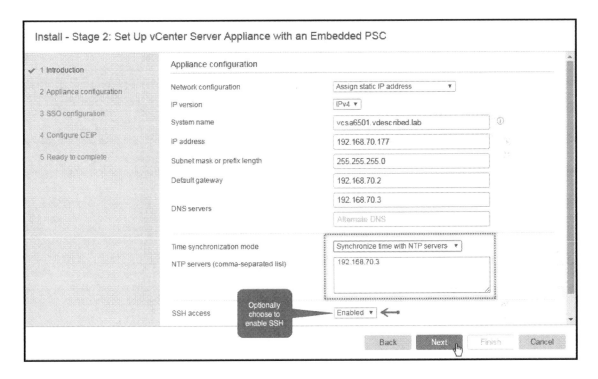

16. On the **SSO configuration** screen, supply an **SSO domain name** (the default is vsphere.local), set the password for the SSO administrator, and add a **Site name**:

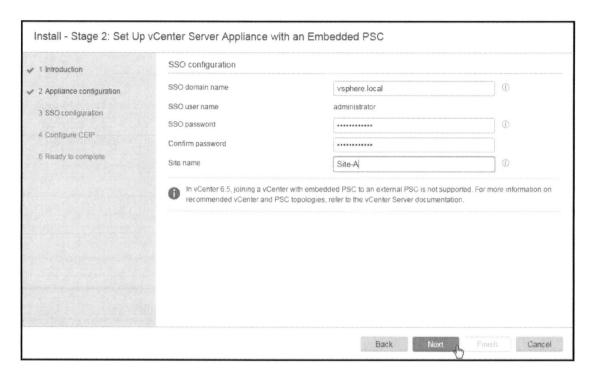

Using vsphere.local as the **SSO domain name** is perfectly fine, unless you want to change it. Changing the default SSO domain name is only possible with vSphere 6.0 and above.

17. On the **Configure CIEP** screen, choose whether or not to join the **Customer Experience Improvement Program (CEIP)** and click **Next** to continue.
18. On the **Ready to complete** screen, review the settings and click **Finish** to initiate the configuration of services in the appliance.
19. Once the appliance setup is complete, you will be presented with a screen indicating this. Click **Close** to exit the wizard.

You should now be able to connect to the vCenter Server using the **vSphere Web Client** URL provided in the previous screen. URL https://FQDN or IP of the appliance:443/vsphere-client/.

# Deploying External Platform Services controllers

Starting with vSphere 6.0, VMware have bundled essential services such as the SSO, inventory service, and certificate management into a single manageable solution called the **Platform Services Controller** (**PSC**). The PSC can be installed on the same machine as the vCenter, installed on a separate supported Windows machine, or a PSC running on the virtual appliance.

## Getting ready

Before we learn to deploy PSC, it is important to understand that there is more than one deployment model supported by VMware. Although PSC can be deployed as an embedded service along with VCSA, VMware does not support the pairing of an embedded PSC instance with an external PSC. Therefore, it is important to decide on the deployment model before we proceed:

- **Single PSC model**: A single PSC servicing more than one vCenter. The PSC in this case is a single point of failure.
- **Shared SSO domain PSC model**: More than one PSC servicing the same SSO domain. Although the PSC is not a single point of failure, there is no automated failover if one of the PSCs fail. The PSCs can be of different SSO sites.
- **PSCs behind a load balancer**: More than one PSC servicing the same SSO domain and same SSO site. No single point of failure at the PSC layer. If one of the PSCs fails, then the load balancer will redirect future requests to the surviving PSC node. However, this requires the use of an NSX Edge or a third-party load balancer.

VMware supports the pairing of PSC instances regardless of the platform (appliance or Windows) they are deployed on.

# How to do it...

The procedure to deploy an external SSO has two stages. The first stage is similar to deploying a VCSA and most of the critical configuration is done in stage 2. We will also cover the steps required to join a PSC to an existing SSO domain for high availability and multi-site configuration. The steps will be covered in two separate parts, part-1 will cover the deployment of a new PSC for a new SSO domain and part-2 will cover joining a PSC to an existing SSO domain.

## Part 1 – Deploying a PSC for a new SSO domain

The following procedure will help you deploy a new PSC appliance for a new SSO domain:

1. Map and browse the contents of the VCSA ISO ROM, navigate to `vcsa-ui-installer` and choose a subdirectory corresponding to your operating system (`lin64`, `mac`, `win32`). In this case, we will navigate to the `win32` directory and run the executable `installer.exe` as an administrator to bring up the **vCenter Server Appliance 6.5 Installer** window.

2. On the **vCenter Server Appliance 6.5 Installer** window, click **Install** to bring-up the **Install - Stage 1: Deploy appliance** window. Click **Next** to continue.

3. Accept the EULA and click **Next** to continue.

4. On the **Select deployment type** screen, select **Platform Services Controller** and click **Next** to continue.

5. On the **Appliance deployment target** screen, supply the IP address/FQDN and credentials of the vCenter or the ESXi host the appliance VM will be deployed onto. In this case, the target is an ESXi host. Click **Next** to continue.

6. Click **Yes** to accept the target host's SSL certificate.

7. On the **Setup appliance VM** screen, supply a name for the VM and set the password for its root user. Click **Next** to continue.

8. Select a datastore to place the appliance VM. You can perform the Thin provisioning on the VMDKs if you choose to, by selecting **Enable Thin Disk Mode**. Click **Next** to continue.

9. On the **Configure network settings** screen, supply a **System name** (which can either be the IP address or FQDN for the appliance) and the IP configuration for the PSC, and click **Next** to continue:

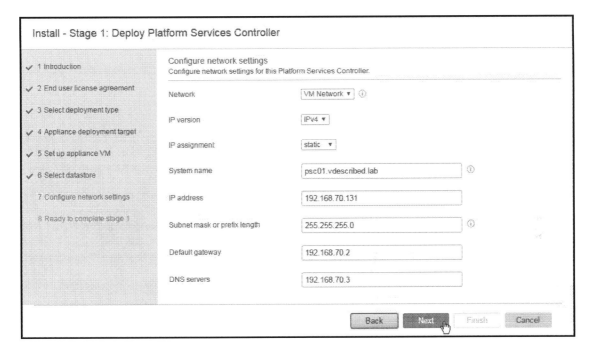

10. On the **Ready to complete** stage 1 screen, review the setting and click **Finish** to deploy the PSC appliance VM.
11. Once the deployment completes successfully, you will be presented with a screen indicating this. Click **Continue** to start the stage 2 installer wizard.
12. On the **Install - Stage 2: Set Up Platform Services Controller Appliance** screen, click **Next** to continue.
13. On the **Appliance configuration** screen, configure **Time synchronization** and click **Next** to continue.

14. On the **SSO configuration** screen, choose the option to **Create a new SSO domain** and supply the **SSO domain name**, **SSO password**, and SSO **Site name** values, and click **Next** to continue:

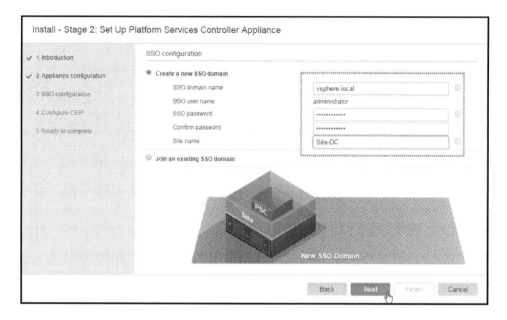

15. On the **Configure CEIP** screen, choose whether or not to join VMware CIEP and click **Next** to continue.
16. On the **Ready to complete** screen, review the setting and click **Finish**.
17. The installer will warn you about the fact that you will not be able to pause or stop the installation once started. Click **OK** to continue.
18. Once the installation completes successfully, you will be presented with a screen indicating this. Click **Close** to exit the wizard.

# Part 2 – Joining a PSC to an existing SSO domain

The following procedure will help you deploy a new PSC appliance and join it to an existing SSO domain for high availability or multi-site configurations:

1. Follow steps 1 through 11 from the section *Part 1 – Deploying a PSC for a new SSO domain* to deploy a new PSC.

Keep in mind that each PSC appliance will need a unique Appliance VM Name, FQDN, and IP configuration.

2. Once deployed, on the **Install - Stage 2: Set Up Platform Services Controller Appliance** screen, click **Next** to continue.
3. On the **Appliance configuration** screen, configure **Time synchronization** and click **Next** to continue.
4. On the **SSO configuration** screen, choose the option to **Join an existing SSO domain** and supply the FQDN or IP address of the existing PSC appliance, the **SSO domain name** you intend to join, and the **SSO password**. Click **Next** to continue:

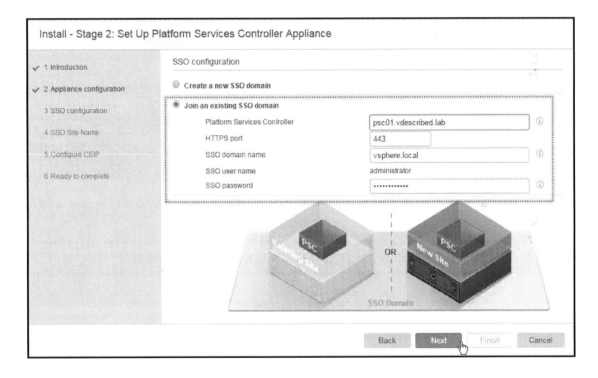

5. On the **SSO Site Name** screen, you can either choose to join an existing SSO site or create a new SSO site:

- If you intend to join an existing site, then select **Join an existing site** and select the **SSO site name** from the drop-down box:

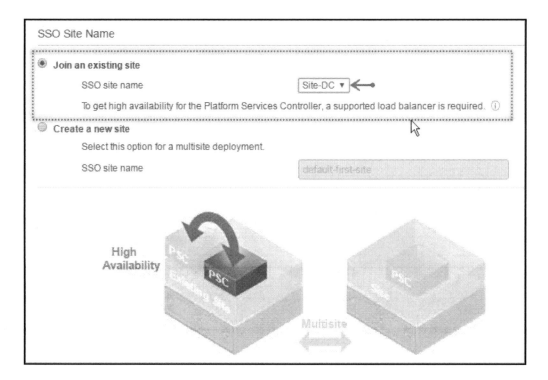

- If you intend to create a new site for a multi-site setup like SRM, then select **Create a new site** and supply an **SSO site name**:

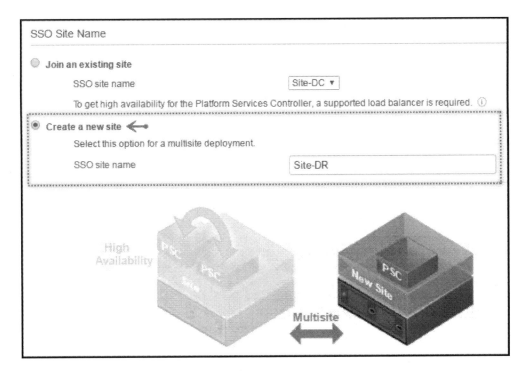

SSO Site Name

○ Join an existing site

    SSO site name                Site-DC ▾

    To get high availability for the Platform Services Controller, a supported load balancer is required. ⓘ

◉ Create a new site ⟵

    Select this option for a multisite deployment.

    SSO site name                Site-DR

6. With the desired option selected (in this case, I have chosen to create a new site Site-DR), click **Next** to continue.

7. Choose whether or not to join VMware CEIP and click **Next** to continue.

8. On the **Ready to complete** screen, review the setting and click **Finish**.

9. The installer will warn you about the fact that you will not be able to pause or stop the installation once started. Click **OK** to continue.

10. Once the installation completes successfully, you will be presented with a screen indicating this. Click **Close** to exit the wizard.

The previous procedure (part 1 and part 2) will result in an environment with the PSCs psc01 and psc02 joined to the same SSO domain, vsphere.local, in a multi-site mode.

> As mentioned before, VMware does not support the pairing of an embedded PSC with an external counterpart. The installer also does this pre-check and throws a warning.

# How it works...

The PSC can become a single point of failure if it is not protected. If a PSC becomes unavailable, then the vCenter or the components that were using the PSC will not be able to allow new connections or user sessions. Already active connections or sessions would continue to remain active. The same applies to the vCenter service as well. If, for any reason, the vCenter service is stopped, then you will not be able to restart it without the PSC being available.

You can have more than one PSC deployed for a set of vCenters; they sync data between them, but high availability is not built into them. This means that, if one of the PSCs fails for any reason, the existing ones would not take over the role of the failed PSC. To achieve high availability, you will need to put the PSC nodes behind a network load balancer.

The PSC VMs should be in an HA-enabled cluster for increased resiliency.

A PSC has the following components:

- VMware Certificate Authority
- VMware SSO
- VMware Licensing Service

# VMware Certificate Authority

**VMware Certificate Authority** (**VMCA**) is a service that helps manage the certificates used by vCenter, its components, and the ESXi hosts it manages. It offers a command-line interface. It is a requirement that the certificates and the private keys are stored in a VMCA key store, with the exception of the ESXi host certificates, which are stored locally on the hosts.

We will learn more about VMCA in Chapter 14, *Upgrading and Patching using vSphere Update Manager*.

# VMware Single Sign-On

VMware SSO is an authentication server released with vSphere 5.1. With version 5.5, it has been re-architected so that it is simple to plan and deploy and easier to manage. With vSphere 6.0 and 6.5, it is now embedded into the PSC.

 With vSphere 5.1, SSO had an option to use an external database. However, starting with vSphere 5.5, this was no longer possible; SSO now uses an embedded PostgreSQL database.

It is an authentication gateway, which takes the authentication requests from various registered components and validates the credential pair against the identity sources added to the SSO server. The components are registered to the SSO server during their installation.

Here are some of the components that can register with VMware SSO and leverage its ability, and these components, in SSO terms, are referred to as SSO clients:

- VMware vCenter Server
- VMware vCenter inventory service
- VMware vCenter Orchestrator
- VMware vShield manager
- VMware vCloud Director (partial integration)
- VMware vSphere Web Client
- VMware vSphere Data Protection
- VMware log browser

Once authenticated, the SSO clients are provided with a token for further exchanges. The advantage here is that the user or administrator of the client service is not prompted for a credential pair (username and password) every time it needs to authenticate.

SSO supports authenticating against the following identity sources:

- Active directory
- Active directory as an LDAP server
- Open LDAP
- Local OS

## VMware licensing service

The VMware licensing service is designed to act as a repository that will host the licensing information of all VMware products that are compatible with the PSC. Now that licensing is managed by a separate service, you will no longer have to perform license management on every vCenter Server in your environment. Since every vCenter 6.0 will have a PSC associated to it, license management is no longer dependent on the availability of vCenter. License information is replicated between only those PSCs which are in the same SSO domain.

# Deploying vCenter Servers in Enhanced Linked Mode

In large environments, there can be more than one vCenter Server deployed to manage resources; it is beneficial to view all the vCenter inventories from a single management plane. This can be achieved using Enhanced Linked Mode.

**Enhanced Linked Mode** (**ELM**) enables the linking of more than one vCenter Server, be it vCenter installed on a Windows machine or the VCSA. Although it is referred to as a method to link vCenter Servers together, the actual linking happens between the PSCs the vCenters are connected to. It is done by making the PSCs join a single SSO domain. This is a requirement. The PSCs in the same SSO domain will replicate roles and permissions, licenses, and other details, letting the administrator perform a single login into the vSphere Web Client to view and manage inventory objects of all the linked vCenter Servers.

 Enhanced Linked Mode doesn't work with the standard vSphere Client. It is only supported with the vSphere Web Client.

# How to do it...

To enable Enhanced Linked Mode, all you need to do is make the PSCs corresponding to the vCenter Servers participate in the same SSO domain. For instructions on how to perform this activity, refer to the *Deploying External Platform Services controllers* section of this chapter. Keep in mind, though, that you will only be able to join/pair PSCs during its installation or deployment.

You have CLI options to repoint a vCenter to a different PSC, but you cannot point an already deployed/installed PSC to a different SSO domain.

In scenarios where you intend to link already deployed vCenter Servers, deploy a new PSC in the same SSO domain and repoint one of the vCenter Servers to the newly deployed PSC. For instructions on how to repoint vCenter to PSC, read the VMware Knowledge Base article *How to repoint vCenter Server 6.x between External PSC within a site (2113917)* `https://kb.vmware.com/kb/2113917`.

# Configuring SSO identity sources

An identity source is nothing but a repository of users and groups. These can be the local operating system users, Active Directory, or OpenLDAP and VMDIR sources.

## How to do it...

The following procedure will guide you through the steps required to add identity sources to the SSO server:

1. Use vSphere Web Client to connect to vCenter Server. The URL will use the following syntax:

   ```
   https://<IP Address or FQDN>:9443/vsphere-client
   #Examples:
   https://localhost:9443/vsphere-client
   https://vcsa6501.vdescribed.lab:9443/vsphere-client
   ```

2. Log in using the default SSO administrator and its domain (the default is `vsphere.local`).

3. Use the vCenter inventory list to go to **Administration**:

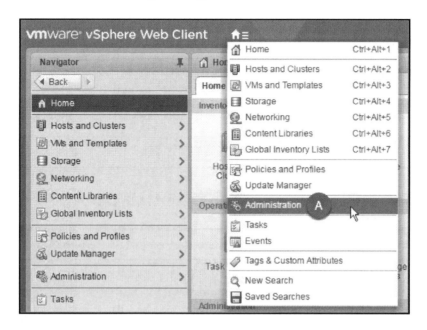

4. Click on **Configuration** from the **Single Sign-On** category on the left-pane, navigate the **Identity Sources** tab, and click on the green ✚ icon to bring up the **Add identity source** wizard:

5. On the **Add identity source** wizard screen, select an identity source type. In this case, we have selected **Active Directory as an LDAP server**. Click **Next** to continue:

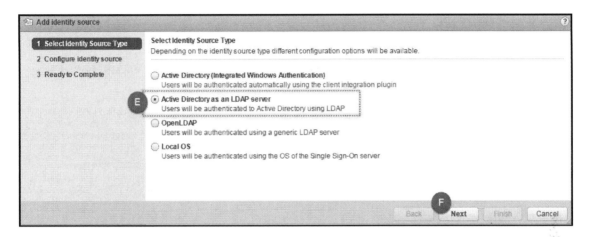

6. Supply the AD identity source details and click **Next** to continue:

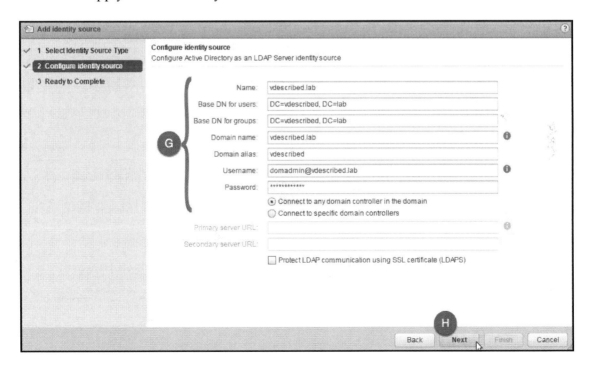

7. On the the **Ready to Complete** screen, review the settings and click **Finish.**

8. The **Identity Sources** tab should now list the newly added AD LDAP source:

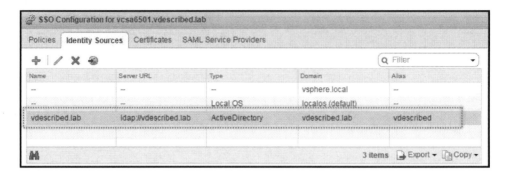

9. Verify whether the AD LDAP domain added can list its users/groups by navigating to **Users and Groups** under the **Single Sign-On** category on the left pane and switching the domain selection to the newly added AD LDAP source:

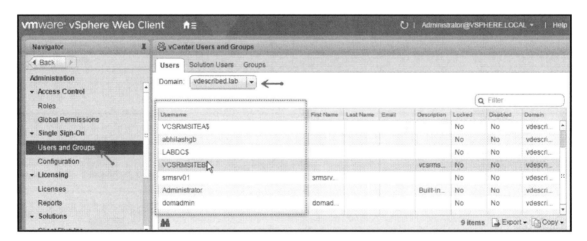

# Assigning users and groups to vCenter Server

Be it a simple installation or component installation, you will only be able to connect to vCenter Server using the SSO administrator (`administrator@vsphere.local`) after the installation. This is because, by default, the SSO administrator is assigned the vCenter administrator role. Most environments require other users to be able to connect to the vCenter Server. To make this possible, you will need to manually assign an access role to the user/group you would like to provide access to.

## Getting ready

Make sure that the domain from which you will be selecting a group/user is added as an identity source. For instructions, read the *Configuring SSO identity sources* section of this chapter.

## How to do it...

The following procedure will guide you through the steps required to assign access roles to a user/group:

1. Log in to the vSphere Web Client interface as the SSO administrator and select the vCenter Server from the inventory.
2. With the vCenter Server selected, navigate to the **Permissions** tab and click on the green ✚ icon to bring up the **Add Permission** window:

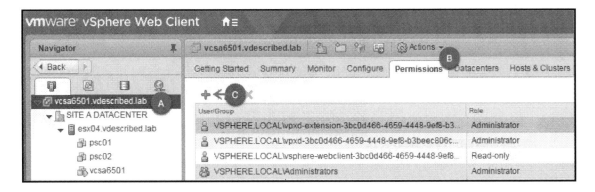

3. In the **Add Permission** window, click **Add...** to bring up the **Select Users/Groups** window:

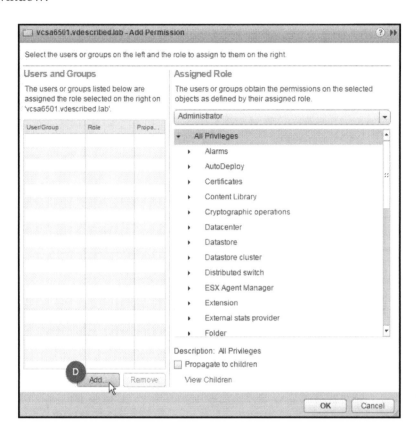

4. In the **Select Users/Groups** window, change the domain to the one you would like to add a group/user from; find and select the user/group, click on **Add,** and then **OK** to return to the **Add Permission** window:

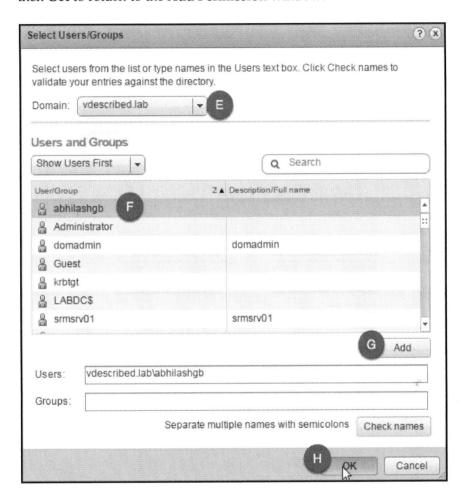

5. In the **Add Permission** window, select the user, assign a role, and click **OK**:

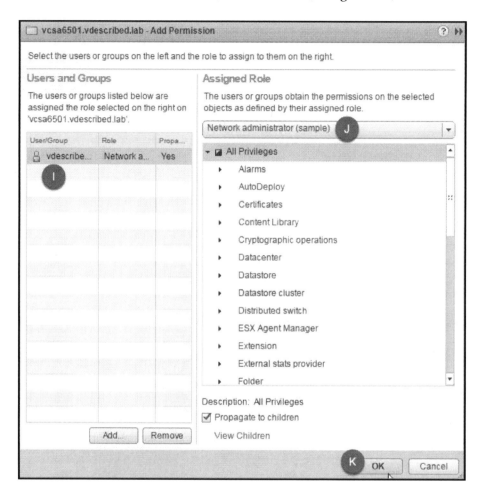

6. The **Permissions** tab will now show the newly added user/group and the role assigned in the **User/Group** tab:

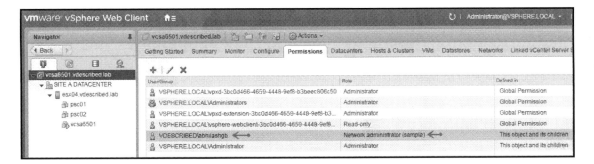

You should now be able to use vSphere Client, vSphere Web Client, or any other connection type (API) to connect to vCenter Server using the added user.

# 3
# Using vSphere Host Profiles

In this chapter, we will cover the following recipes:

- Preparing a reference host
- Creating Host Profiles
- Attaching/detaching ESXi hosts to/from a Host Profile
- Performing host customizations
- Checking Host Profile compliance of ESXi host(s)
- Scheduling Host Profile compliance checks
- Remediating non-compliant ESXi host(s)
- Using Host Profiles to push a new configuration change
- Copying settings between Host Profiles
- Exporting Host Profiles
- Importing Host Profiles
- Duplicating Host Profiles

## Introduction

It is of prime importance to make sure that every ESXi host in a cluster is configured identically to achieve operational efficiency at the cluster level. There is a lot of configuration that would go into an ESXi host after it is deployed. These include the general/advanced settings, storage, and networking configuration, licensing, and so on. With the number of ESXi hosts that can be part of a cluster or vCenter increasing with every release of vSphere, the amount of work to be done manually will also increase.

Starting with vSphere 4.1, VMware introduced a method to extract the configuration from an ESXi host and form a configuration template, often referred to as a blueprint or golden image. Such a configuration template is called a **vSphere Host Profile**. It is important to note that Host Profiles require Enterprise Plus Licenses applied.

It is important to note that Host Profiles require Enterprise Plus Licenses applied to the ESXi hosts.

Host Profiles help an administrator to maintain compliance with configuration standards on a set of ESXi hosts. They can also be used to make a configuration change to be pushed to all the hosts attached to the template, without the need to make the change on each of the hosts manually. For instance, if the NTP time source for the environment has changed, then there is a need to make this change on every host using the time source. Such a change can be pushed through a Host Profile. Another example would be a change in the VLAN ID for the virtual machine network on a cluster of ESXi hosts configured with standard vSwitches. Since the hosts are using standard vSwitches, the VLAN ID should be manually specified on the virtual machine port group on each of the hosts in the cluster. This manual work can be avoided by editing the Host Profile and then pushing the VLAN ID change to the entire cluster.

So, what does a Host Profile look like, and what does it contain? Host Profiles, once created, are presented to the user as GUI objects in the vCenter Server. Host Profiles contain configuration policies that are either fetched from the reference host or added to the Host Profile at a later stage.

A Host Profile can contain the following information:

- Advanced configuration settings
- General system settings
- Networking configuration
- Security and services
- Storage configuration

Not all advanced configuration settings can be configured using a Host Profile. VMware Knowledge Base article *2001994* has more details: https://kb.vmware.com/kb/2001994.

# Preparing a reference host

A reference host is prepared so that its configuration can be extracted and saved to a Host Profile, which becomes the golden image. It is important that you take extra care in configuring the reference host since this configuration will be applied to the rest of the hosts in the cluster/environment. The following flowchart provides an overview of the procedure:

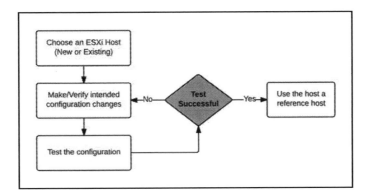

# How to do it...

The following procedure will help you prepare a reference host for generating a Host Profile:

1. You can deploy a new ESXi host or use an existing host for this purpose.
2. Configure the `basic/advanced/storage/network` settings on your chosen host, as you will need them on all the other ESXi hosts.
3. Deploy and run a few virtual machines on the reference ESXi hosts and make sure that everything is functioning as expected. For instance, verify whether the VMs are reachable over the network.
4. If everything works as you want it to, then you have the reference host ready.

# Creating Host Profiles

The Host Profile is created by extracting the host configuration information from a reference ESXi host. Once created, it will be listed as an object of the type Host Profile in the Host Profiles **Objects** tab.

Keep in mind that you will need access to a vCenter Server to create Host Profiles. This is because the object data corresponding to the Host Profiles created is saved in the vCenter Server database.

# Getting ready

Before you begin, make sure that you have identified a reference host to extract the configuration and form a template. For instructions on how to prepare a reference host, read the previous recipe, *Preparing a reference host*.

# How it works...

The following procedure will help you create a Host Profile from a reference host:

1. Log in to the vSphere web client and navigate to the reference ESXi host from the inventory.
2. Right-click on the ESXi host, navigate to **Host Profiles** | **Extract Host Profile**:

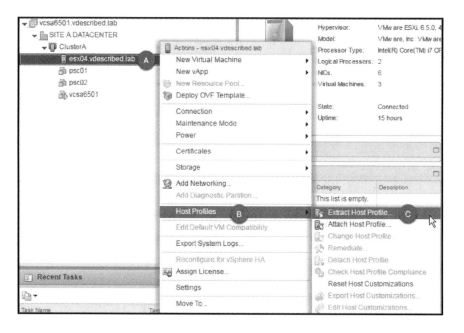

3. On the **Extract Host Profile** wizard screen, supply a **Name** for the profile and an optional **Description** and click **Next** to continue:

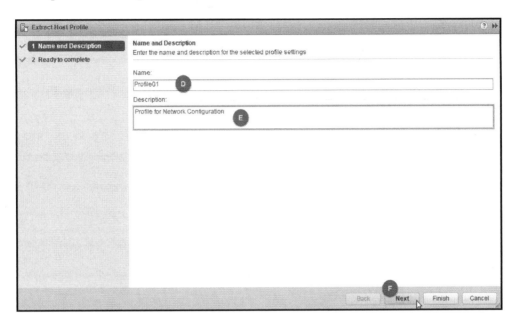

4. On the **Ready to complete** screen, there is nothing much to review; click **Finish** to create the profile.

# How it works...

 In vSphere 5.5, a Host Profile, once created, would still be related to the reference host. New configuration changes should be made to the reference host and pushed to the Host Profile. Starting with vSphere 6.0 this is no longer the case; the extracted profile is independent of the host it was extracted from. Due to this independence, you can now copy settings between Host Profiles. Read the recipe, *Copying settings between Host Profiles* for instructions on how to achieve this.

# Attaching/detaching ESXi hosts to/from a Host Profile

The whole purpose of creating a Host Profile is to automate the large-scale configuration of ESXi hosts. Before you can apply a Host Profile to any ESXi host, there should be a way to associate the host with the Host Profile. This is done in the vCenter by attaching the ESXi hosts to the Host Profile. Such an association is subsequently used for compliance checks and remediating new configuration changes.

If for any reason, you decide not to associate a host with a particular Host Profile, then you could choose to detach the host from the Host Profile. Both the attach/detach operations are performed using the same workflow wizard.

## How to do it...

The following procedure will walk you through the process of attaching or detaching ESXi host/hosts from a Host Profile.

1. Log on to the **vSphere Web Client** and use the key combination *Ctrl + Alt + 1* to navigate to the inventory home:

2. At the inventory home, click on **Host Profiles** to view all the profiles already created:

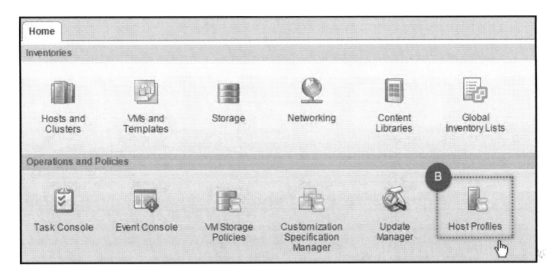

3. Right-click on the Host Profile (**Profile01**) and click on **Attach/Detach Hosts and Clusters...**:

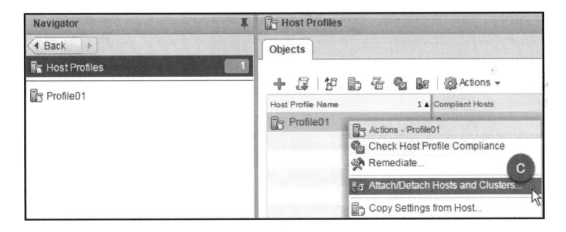

4. On the **Attach/Detach Host and Clusters** wizard screen, you can choose to attach an entire cluster of hosts or individual hosts. Detaching would require the items to be moved to the left pane using the **Detach** or **Detach All** button. If you are attaching many hosts, then choose the option to **Skip Host Customization**, which can be less laboriously accomplished by using a (.csv) file to import customization. Read the recipe, *Performing host customizations* for more details. Click **Finish** to complete the attach/detach operation:

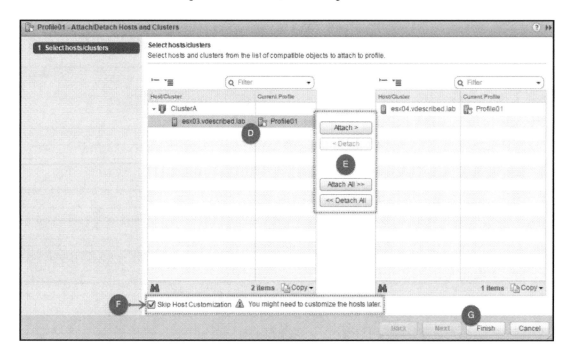

5. (Optional) If you do not choose to skip the host customization you will be presented with a **Customize host** screen, supply the host/s specific information such as the VMkernel interface configuration. Once done, click on **Finish** to attach the selected host/cluster to the Host Profile:

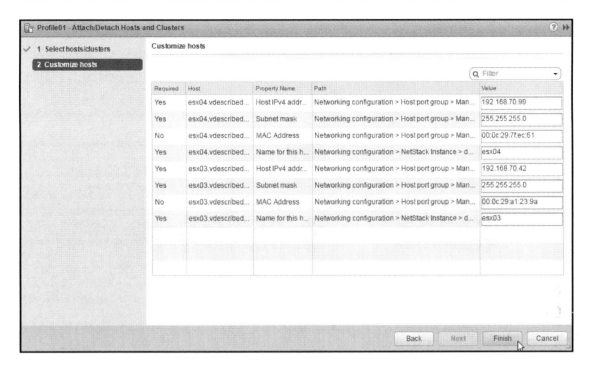

6. You should see an **Attach Host Profile** task completed successfully in the **Recent Tasks** pane.

# Performing host customizations

vSphere Host Profiles help you publish configuration standards across clusters of ESXi hosts. However, every host will have a set of unique settings which needs to be customized as well. When you attach ESXi hosts to a Host Profile, you will be allowed to customize the hosts that are being added. However, if you are dealing with a large set of hosts, supplying the values through the **Attach/Detach Host and Clusters** wizard will be a laborious task. An alternative and efficient method would be to prepare a customizations (.csv) file with the host-specific values and use it to perform the host customization.

The following flow chart provides a high-level overview of the procedure:

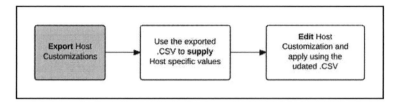

# Getting ready

You need to make sure that all the ESXi hosts that need to be customized are attached to the Host Profile you would be generating the customization file for. To learn how to attach hosts to a Host Profiles, read the recipe *Attaching/detaching ESXi hosts to/from Host Profile*.

# How to do it...

The following procedure will guide you through the steps involved in performing a host customization:

1. Log in to the vSphere Web Client and use the key combination *Ctrl + Alt + 1* to navigate to the inventory home.
2. At the inventory home, click on **Host Profiles** to view all the profiles already created.
3. Right-click on the Host Profile and click on **Export Host Customizations...**:

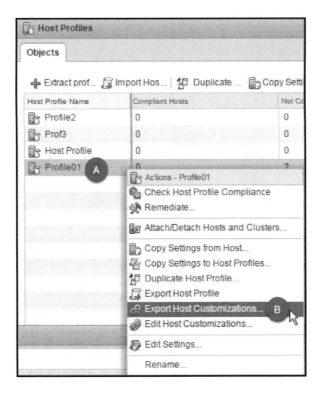

4. On the **Export Host Customizations** window, click **Save** to save the file as a .csv file:

5. Use a spreadsheet tool like Microsoft Excel to edit the contents of the file and supply the host-specific values.

6. Right-click on the Host Profile and click on **Edit Host Customizations...**:

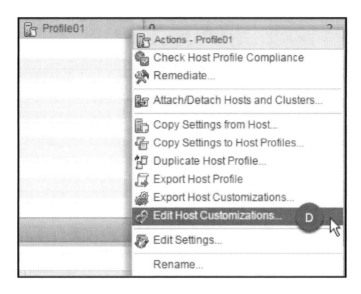

7. On the **Edit Host Customization** wizard, select all the applicable ESXi hosts and click **Next** to continue:

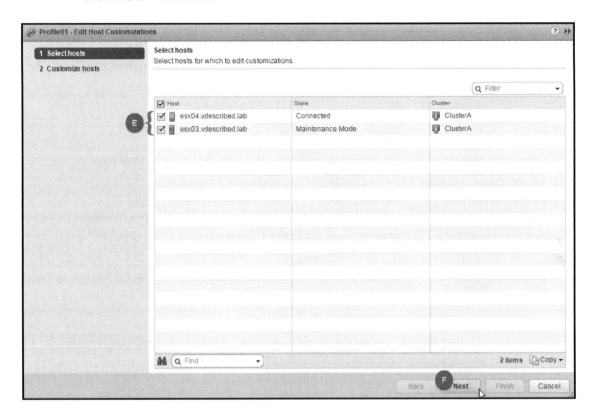

8. On the **Customize hosts** screen, click on **Browse** and select the host customization file. If the file selected is ready and is validated successfully, the same will be indicated. The wizard screen will show the values populated from the .csv file. Click on **Finish** to apply the customization:

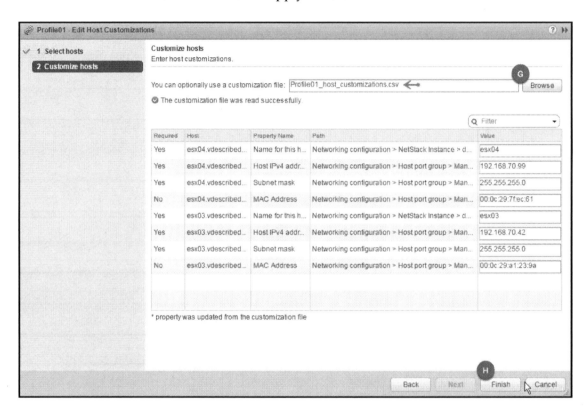

9. The **Recent Tasks** pane will show a task named **Update host customizations** complete successfully:

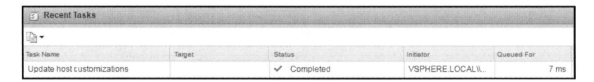

# Checking Host Profile compliance of ESXi host(s)

To ascertain that the ESXi hosts in a vSphere environment adhere to the organization's configuration standard, they can be examined for compliance against a Host Profile extracted from a reference host that was configured to meet the organization's standard.

## Getting ready

Before you could check the profile compliance of an ESXi host, it should be attached to the Host Profile. Read the instructions in the recipe, *Attaching/Detaching ESXi hosts to/from Host Profile* to achieve the same.

## How to do it...

The following procedure will walk you through the steps involved in checking the profile compliance of ESXi hosts:

1. Log in to the vSphere Web Client and use the key combination *Ctrl + Alt + 1* to navigate to the inventory home.
2. At the inventory home, click on **Host Profiles** to view all the profiles already created.

3. Right-click on the Host Profile and click on **Check Host Profile Compliance**:

4. You should see a compliance check task completed against each of the ESXi hosts attached to the Host Profile:

# How it works...

Checking a host for its compliance against an associated Host Profile will compare the host's configuration with the configuration settings in the Host Profile. If any of the configuration policy/settings in the Host Profile are not present on the host, the host is tagged as non-compliant. Non-compliant hosts can be remediated to meet the configuration requirements.

# Scheduling Host Profile compliance checks

You can also create a scheduled task to periodically run a Host Profile compliance check on the hosts or the cluster attached to a Host Profile.

# Getting ready

Before you could run or schedule profile compliance on an ESXi host, it should be attached to a Host Profile. Read the instructions in the recipe *Attaching/Detaching ESXi hosts to/from Host Profile* for achieving the same.

# How to do it...

The following procedure will guide you through the steps involved in scheduling profile compliance checks:

1. Log on to the vSphere Web Client and use the key combination *Ctrl + Alt + 1* to navigate to the inventory home:

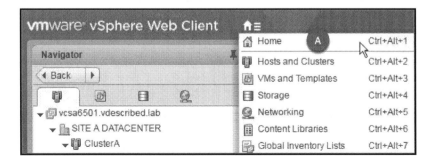

2. At the inventory home, click on **Host Profiles** to view all the profiles already created:

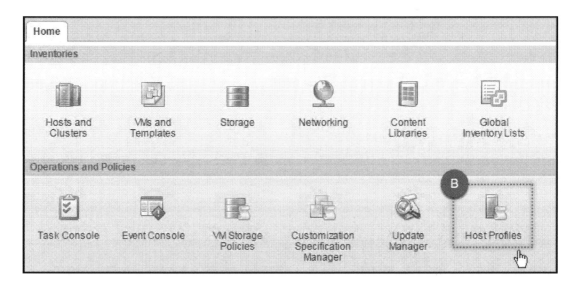

3. Double-click on the Host Profile you would like to create a scheduled task for:

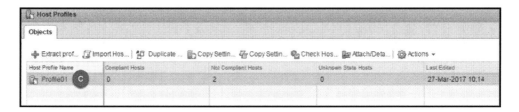

4. Navigate to the **Monitor | Scheduled Tasks** tab and click on **Schedule a New Task | Check Host Profile Compliance**:

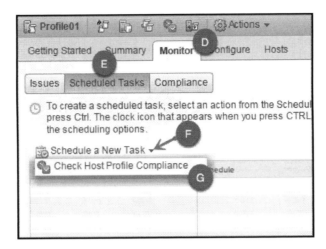

5. On the **Check Host Profile Compliance (scheduled)** window, click on **Scheduling options**.

6. On the **Scheduling options** screen, supply a **Task name**, optional **Task description** and click on **Change** to configure the scheduler:

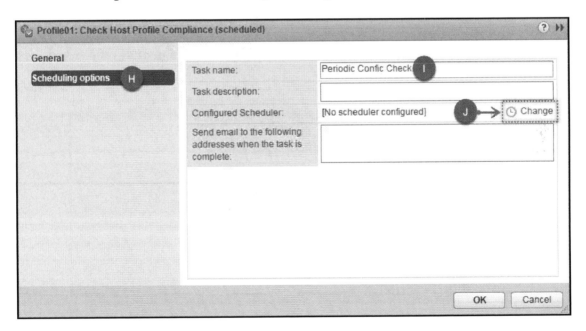

7. On the **Configure Scheduler** screen set an intended schedule and click **OK** to save the settings and return to the **Check Host Profile Compliance (scheduled)** window:

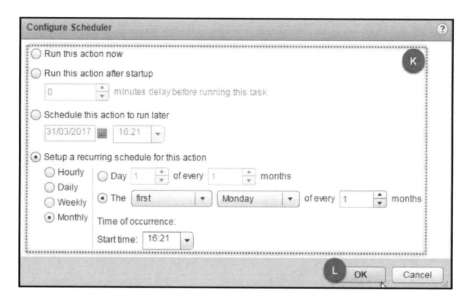

8. On the **Check Host Profile Compliance (scheduled)** window, supply an optional email address and click **OK**:

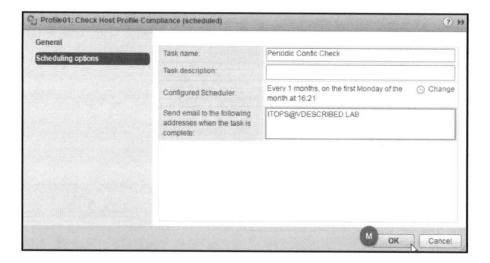

9. Once done, the **Scheduled Tasks** tab will list the newly created task:

# Remediating non-compliant ESXi hosts

An existing ESXi host or a newly added ESXi host that is found to be non-compliant with a Host Profile, to which it has been attached, needs a configuration change to make it compliant. Such changes are automated with the help of the remediate operation. The remediate operation will modify the configuration of the host to match the profile. The following flow chart shows a general overview of the remediation process:

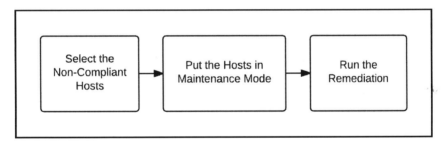

# Getting ready

Remediation can be issued directly on a Host Profile, which in turn will provide you with an option to remediate all the ESXi hosts attached to the profile, or you can issue remediation on a per host basis. Regardless of the method you choose, the hosts you intend to remediate should be put into maintenance mode.

# How to do it...

The following procedure will guide you through the steps involved in remediating non-compliant hosts:

1. Log in to the vSphere Web Client and use the key combination *Ctrl + Alt + 1* to navigate to the inventory home.
2. At the inventory home, click on **Host Profiles** to view all the profiles already created.
3. Right-click on the Host Profile and click **Remediate...** to bring up the **Remediate Hosts Based on Host Profile** wizard:

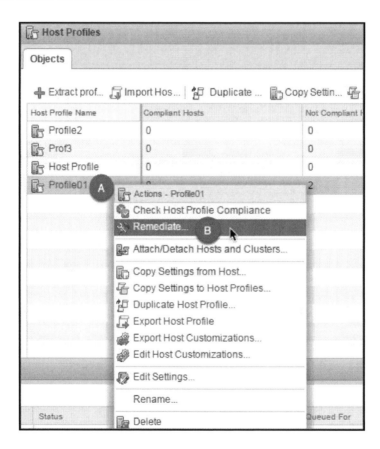

4. On the **Remediate Hosts Based on Host Profile** wizard screen, you will be presented with a list of hosts attached to the Host Profile. Select the hosts to remediate and click **Next** to continue:

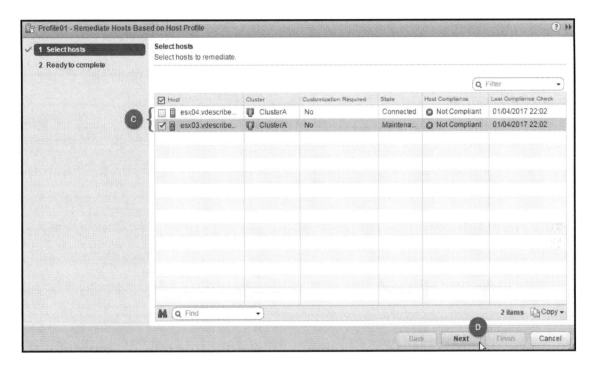

5. (Optional) You will be presented with the **Customize Hosts** screen if the host that you are trying to remediate has a compliance status of **Unknown**. You can either choose to use a customization file or enter the value on this screen. If you are dealing with a significant number of hosts, it only makes sense to use a customization file. Read the recipe, *Performing host customizations* to learn how to prepare the customization file.

6. On the **Ready to complete** screen, click on the **Pre-check Remediation** button to run a check to determine whether a successful remediation of the hosts selected is possible. If the checks return a **Ready to remediate** status, then click **Finish**:

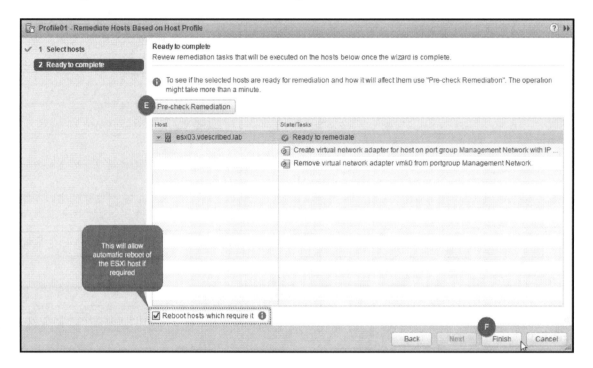

If the checks return an error, then you will need to fix the issue and re-run the pre-check again, before you can initiate the remediation.

After the remediation completes, relaunch the compliance check on the host to verify. Read the recipe, *Checking Host Profile compliance of ESXi host(s)* for instructions.

# Using Host Profiles to push a configuration change

The whole purpose of using Host Profiles is to effortlessly push the required configuration onto the ESXi hosts without the need for a manual configuration activity per ESXi host. This would not just come in handy when you deploy a new infrastructure but also when you want to push a new configuration to all the ESXi hosts.

The following flow chart shows a high-level overview of the whole procedure:

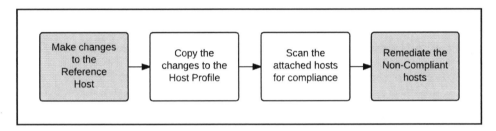

# How to do it...

The following procedure will walk you through the steps involved in pushing/publishing new configuration changes to the ESXi hosts attached to a Host Profile.

1. Make the necessary configuration change to a reference host.

2. Right-click on the Host Profile and select the option, **Copy Settings from Host...**:

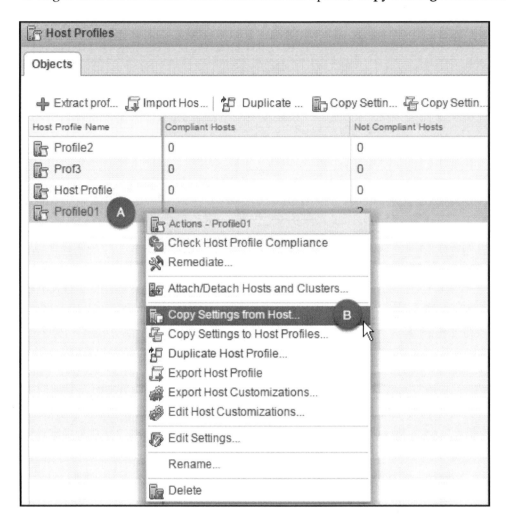

3. On the **Copy settings from host** window, choose the host the changes were made on in the first step and click **OK**:

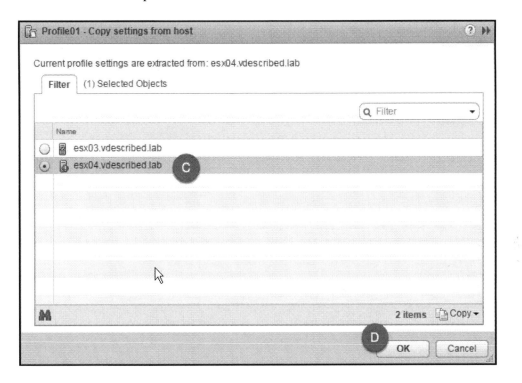

4. You should see an **Update host profile** task complete successfully in the **Recent Tasks** pane:

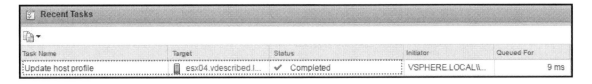

5. Run a Host Profile compliance check using the instructions in the recipe, *Checking Host Profile compliance of ESXi host(s)*.
6. Remediate the non-compliant ESXi host using the instructions in the recipe, *Remediating non-compliant ESXi hosts*, to push the new configuration change.

# Copying settings between Host Profiles

It is entirely possible in a large environment that you arrive at a configuration change that needs to be published across different sets of hosts or let's say, **host clusters**. Since a host or a cluster can only be attached to a single Host Profile at any point in time, there should be a way to publish configuration changes across clusters. And it wouldn't make any sense in duplicating Host Profiles whenever such a need arises. vSphere 6.5 Host Profiles will now let you copy settings from a Host Profile to one or more other Host Profiles.

The following flow chart shows a high—level overview of the whole procedure:

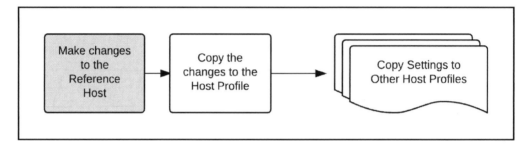

# How to do it...

The following procedure will guide you through the steps involved in copying settings between Host Profiles:

1. Log in to the vSphere Web Client and use the key combination *Ctrl + Alt + 1* to navigate to the inventory home.
2. At the inventory home, click on **Host Profiles** to view to all the profiles already created.

3. Right-click on the Host Profile you would like to copy settings from and click on **Copy Settings to Host Profiles...**:

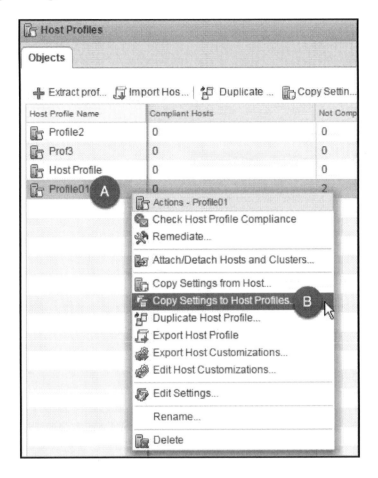

4. On the **Copy Setting to Host Profiles** wizard's **Select settings** screen, choose the configuration to be copied. In this example, I am choosing to export an **Advanced configuration option**. Make the selection and click **Next** to continue:

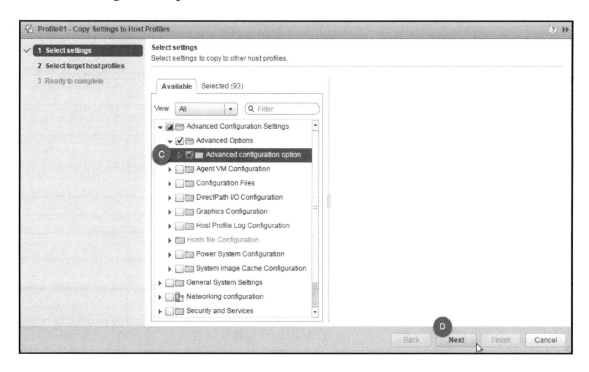

5. On the **Select target host profiles** screen, choose the Host Profiles to copy the settings to and click **Next** to continue:

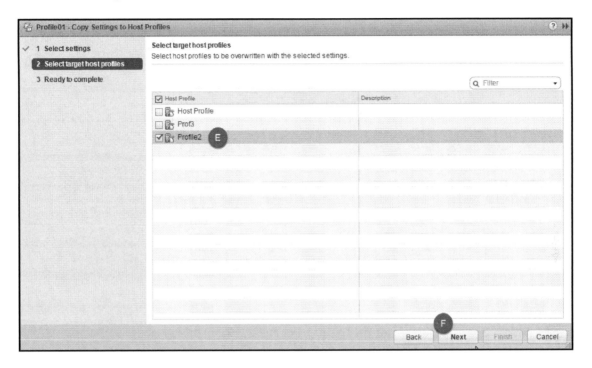

6. On the **Ready to complete** screen, review the settings and click **Finish** to start copying the settings:

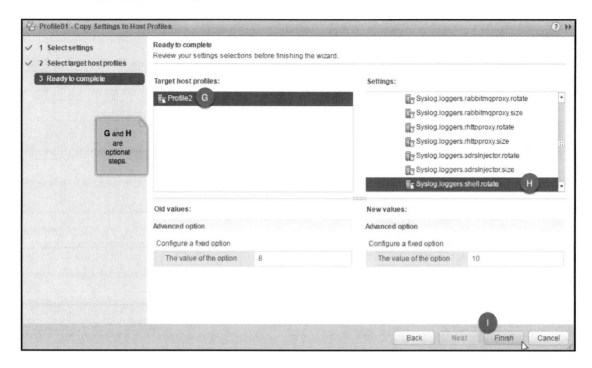

7. You should see a **Copy settings to host profiles** task complete successfully in the **Recent Tasks** pane:

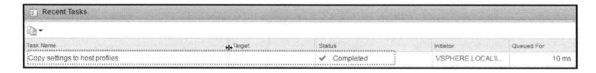

# Exporting Host Profiles

The vSphere Host Profiles can be exported to back up or transport the configuration. The exported data is stored in an XML data file with the extension (`.vpf`). Since this is an XML file, the contents of the file can be viewed using any text editor, so the passwords are not exported into this file. This file can then be imported into the vCenter Server as a Host Profile object.

# How to do it...

The following two procedures will guide you through the steps involved in exporting and importing Host Profiles:

1. Log in to the vSphere Web Client and use the key combination *Ctrl + Alt + 1* to navigate to the inventory home.
2. At the inventory home, click on **Host Profiles** to view all the profiles already created.
3. Right-click on the Host Profile and click on **Export Host Profile**:

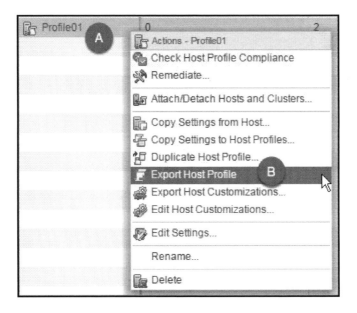

4. After the retrieval of the profile data, you will be prompted to acknowledge the information that the passwords will not be exported. Click **Save**:

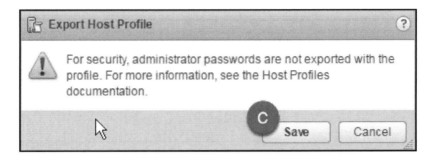

5. In the **Save As** windows, supply a name for the profile file and click **Save**.
6. You should see an **Export host profile** task complete successfully in the **Recent Tasks** pane:

# Importing Host Profiles

Exported .vpf files can be imported as Host Profile objects using the **Import Host Profile** wizard. For instance, if you were to build a new data center in your environment which will be managed by a new vCenter, and if the hosts in the new data center should be configured identically to an existing data center host, then a Host Profile from the existing data center can be exported and then imported into the new vCenter so that it can be applied to the new hosts.

# How to do it...

The following procedure will help you import .vfp files as Host Profiles:

1. Log in to the vSphere Web Client and use the key combination *Ctrl + Alt + 1* to navigate to the inventory home.

2. At the inventory home, click on **Host Profiles** and click on **Import Host Profile**:

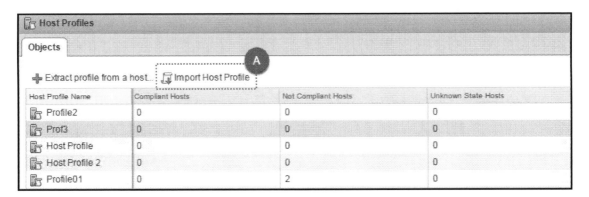

3. On the **Import Host Profile** windows, browse and add the .vpf file, supply a name for the new profile that will be created and click **OK**:

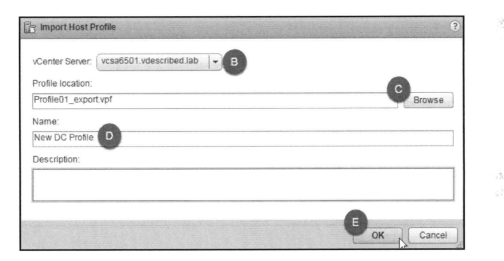

4. The **Recent Tasks** pane should show a **Create a host profile** task completed successfully option:

# Duplicating Host Profiles

An existing Host Profile can be cloned to create a duplicate of the same. This can be achieved by using the duplicate Host Profile operation. Duplicating a Host Profile will not retain the hosts that were attached to the source profile.

## How to do it...

The following procedure will guide you through the steps involved in duplicating a Host Profile.

1. Log in to the vSphere Web Client and use the key combination *Ctrl + Alt + 1* to navigate to the inventory home.
2. At the inventory home, click on **Host Profiles** and click on **Duplicate Host Profile...**:

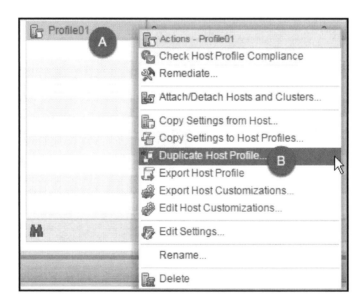

3. On the **Duplicate Host Profile** wizard, supply a **Name** and an optional **Description** and click **Next** to continue.
4. On the **Ready to complete** screen, click **Finish** to initiate the clone operation.
5. The **Recent Tasks** pane should show a **Create host profile** task complete successfully.

# 4

# Using ESXi Image Builder

In this chapter we will cover the following recipes:

- Enabling ESXi Image Builder service for vSphere Web Client GUI
- Preparing an ESXi Image Builder CLI environment
- Downloading an ESXi offline bundle
- Importing a software depot
- Creating an online software depot
- Creating a custom depot
- Creating image profiles using an existing image profile
- Creating image profiles from scratch
- Comparing image profiles
- Moving image profiles between software depots
- Exporting image profiles

# Introduction

ESXi Image Builder is used to custom-build ESXi bootable images. There are several use cases, but the most prominent one is the server hardware vendor using ESXi Image Builder to custom package their drivers along with the ESXi image. Image Builder is, in fact, used to create ESXi image profiles, which can then be exported as ISO images containing bootable ESXi images. We will learn more about image profiles later on in this chapter. With the previous vSphere versions, all the Image Builder actions were performed using its PowerCLI plugin. Starting with vSphere 6.5, VMware introduced a vSphere Web Client GUI making it much easier to use the Image Builder service. In this chapter, we will learn to use image profiles using both GUI and the CLI.

## vSphere ESXi Image Builder architecture

Before we find out how to use Image Builder, let's review the architecture and its components:

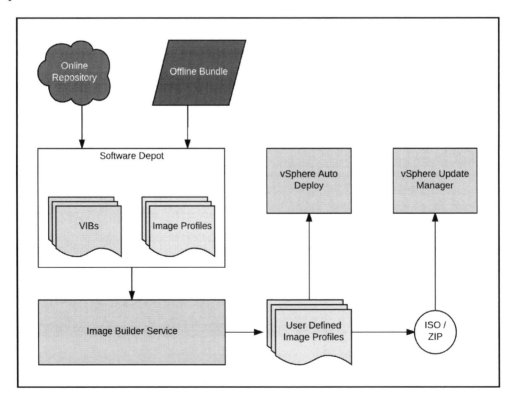

An offline bundle is an archive that can either be the entire ESXi image or a driver bundle. It is a collection of VIBs, their corresponding metadata, and the image profiles. All VMware ESXi offline bundles will have more than one VMware defined image profile. It is the first thing that the ESXi Image Builder will need to perform any of its tasks. It is presented as a software depot to the Image Builder service. Therefore a software depot is nothing but a collection of image profiles and VIBs.

An image profile is a predefined or custom-defined set of VIBs and ESXi boot image that can be addressed as a single package. Image profiles are primarily used to deploy, upgrade, and patch auto deploy ESXi hosts. To learn more about vSphere Auto Deploy read *Chapter 5, Using vSphere Auto Deploy*.

A **vSphere Installation Bundle** (**VIB**) is a packaged archive that contains a file archive, an XML configuration file, and a signature file. Most OEM hardware vendors bundle their drivers as VIBs.

# Enabling ESXi Image Builder service for vSphere Web Client GUI

As mentioned earlier in the chapter, starting with vSphere 6.5, ESXi Image Builder now has a graphical user interface for folks who do not want to deal with the CLI.

# How to do it...

The following procedure will walk you through the steps involved in enabling the Image Builder service for use with the vSphere Web Client:

1. Log in to the vSphere Web Client and navigate to **System Configuration** from the inventory home:

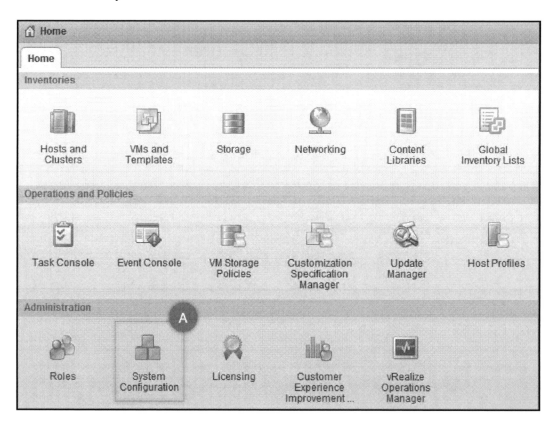

2. On the **System Configuration** screen, click on **Services** to list all the services available:

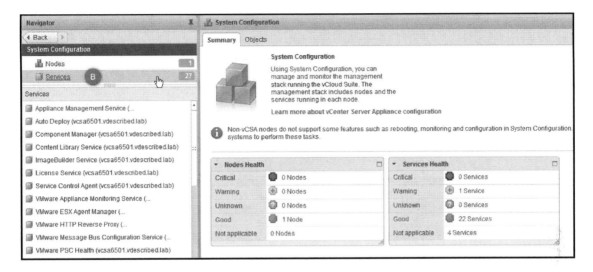

3. Right-click on the **ImageBuilder Service** and click on **Start**:

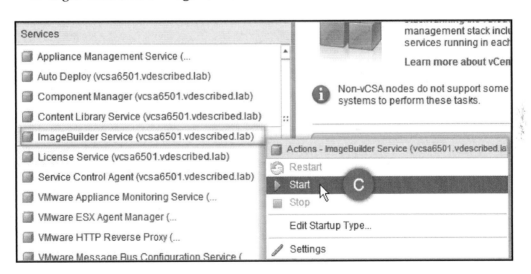

4. Since Image Builder GUI is a part of **Auto Deploy** GUI, you will need to start the auto deploy service as well. Right-click on the **Auto Deploy** service and click **Start**:

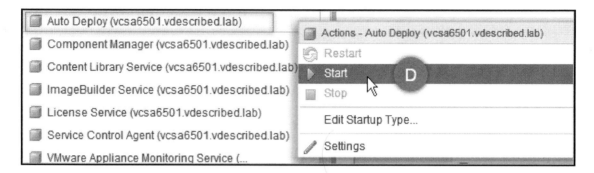

5. The **Recent Tasks** pane should show **Start Service** task complete successfully.
6. Exit the vSphere Web Client, re-login and navigate to **Auto Deploy** from the inventory home, to view the **Auto Deploy** interface:

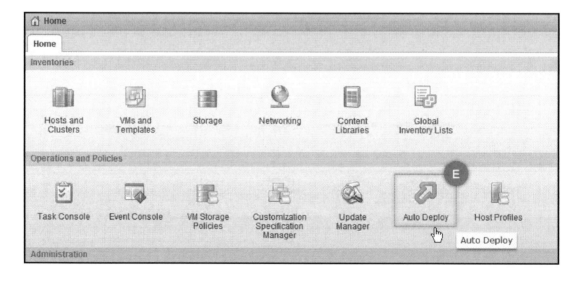

7. (Optional, but recommended). You can configure the service to automatically reboot on startup on the host by changing its startup type. Right-click on the service and click on **Edit Startup Type...**:

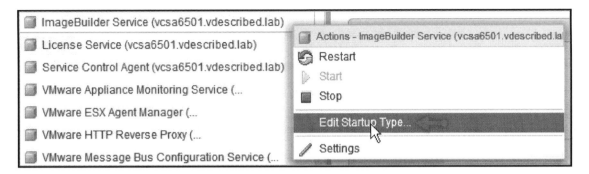

8. (Optional, but recommended) On the **Edit Startup Type** window, set the startup type to **Automatic** and click **OK**:

# Preparing an ESXi Image Builder CLI environment

To be able to use Image Builder CLI, you are required to install VMware PowerCLI 6.5 or later. The Image Builder snap-in is built into PowerCLI.

## Getting ready

The machine you choose to install VMware PowerCLI 6.5 on, requires Microsoft PowerShell 3.0 or later pre-installed. It is recommended that you install Windows Management Framework 3.0 or later, to meet this requirement.

# How to do it...

The following procedure will guide you through the process of installing PowerCLI and configuring it for first use:

1. Go to VMware's download portal at `https://my.vmware.com/web/vmware/downloads`.

2. At the downloads page, using the search field to look up `VMware PowerCLI` and download **VMware PowerCLI 6.5 Release 1** (at the time of reading, you might find a newer version. Install the most recent version to proceed).

3. Run the `VMware-PowerCLI-6.5.0` installer as an administrator and progress through the wizard screens with the default options and click **Finish**. The installation is straightforward and needs no special configuration.

4. Once done, double-click on the PowerCLI desktop icon to bring up the **VMware-PowerCLI** window.

5. Issue the following command to set the execution policy to remotely signed and select *Y* to execute the policy:

    `Set-ExecutionPolicy RemoteSigned`

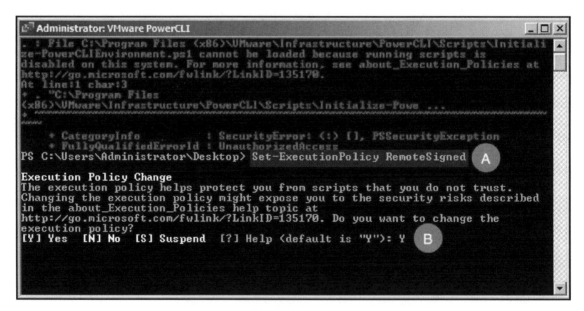

6. Close the PowerCLI session and re-launch it:

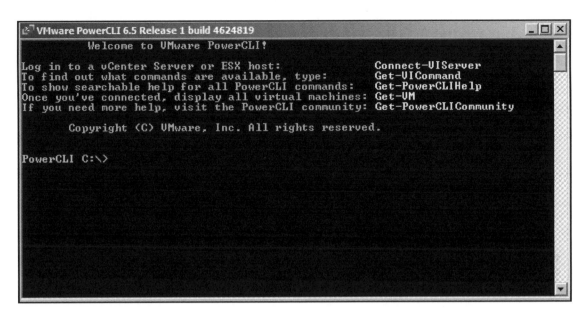

7. You are now all set to use the Image Builder cmdlets.

# Downloading an ESXi offline bundle

You cannot use the ESXi installer ISO as an offline bundle. The ESXi offline bundle has to be downloaded separately.

## How to do it...

The following procedure will guide you to download the ESXi offline bundle:

1. Navigate to the VMware's download portal at `https://my.vmware.com/web/vmware/downloads`.

2. At the downloads page, using the search field to look up `ESXi 6.5`; use the hyperlink from the search result to get to the ESXi 6.5 downloads page:

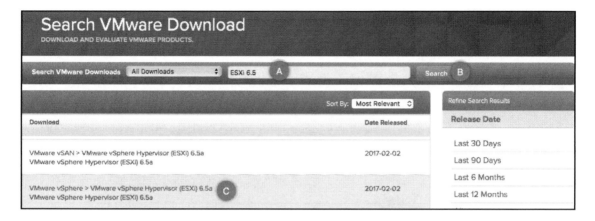

3. Download **VMware vSphere Hypervisor (ESXi) Offline Bundle**:

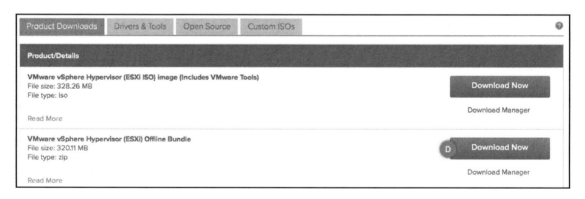

4. The file downloaded will be a ZIP archive.

# Importing a software depot

The very first step before you can create, clone, or manage image profiles, is to present the VMware ESXi Image Builder with a software depot. As introduced at the beginning of the chapter, a software depot is nothing but an ESXi offline bundle presented to the Image Builder.

# How to do it...

The following procedure will guide you through the steps involved in importing a software depot from an offline bundle:

1. Log in to the vSphere Web Client and navigate to the **Auto Deploy** plugin screen.
2. On the **Auto Deploy** screen, navigate to the **Software Depots** tab and click on the ⬆ icon to bring up the **Import Software Depot** window:

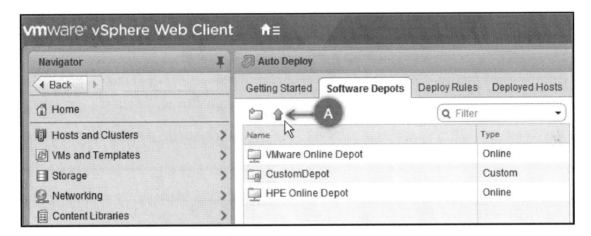

3. On the **Import Software Depot** window, supply a **Name** for the depot and click **Browse...** to locate and select the ESXi65_OfflineBundle. With the offline bundle selected, click **Upload** to begin uploading the package to the **Auto Deploy** server:

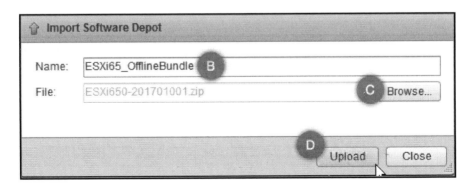

4. You will now see the bundle being uploaded to the Image Builder.

5. Once the upload completes, click **Close** to return to the **Software Depots** tab:

The uploaded files will be stored in the
`/storage/imagebuilder/depot` directory of the VCSA appliance:

6. The **Recent Tasks** pane should show a **Connect depot** task complete successfully:

| Task Name | Target | Status | Initiator |
|---|---|---|---|
| Connect depot | vcsa6501.vdescrib... | ✓ Completed | com.vmware.imagebuilder |

7. Refresh the vSphere Web Client, and you will see the **Software Depots** tab list the newly created software depot:

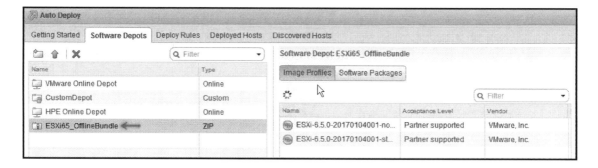

# There's more...

You can use the Image Builder CLI to achieve the same task. Before you begin, keep in mind that each vSphere PowerCLI session is like a  temporary work desk and exiting a session will clear your work desk. So, it is necessary for you to import what you need to work on into the PowerCLI session. An offline bundle is imported into a PowerCLI session as a software depot to allow for the cloning of image profiles, or the use of VIBs included in the bundle, to create a **custom depot**, for instance.

The following procedure will walk you through the steps involved in importing an offline bundle into a VMware PowerCLI session:

1.  Launch a VMware PowerCLI session.
2.  Use the `Add-SoftwareDepot` command to import the required offline bundles. The command requires you to provide the path of the offline bundle.
3.  Run the `GetEsxSoftwareDepot` command to list all software depots imported into the PowerCLI session.
4.  Additionally, you could issue the `$DefaultSoftwareDepots` command to verify which of the added software depots is the default:

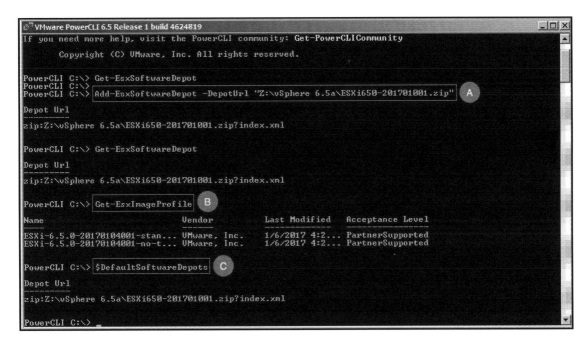

Unlike with the Image Builder GUI, the CLI method does not upload anything to the VCSA appliance storage. However, anything that you add to the PowerCLI session is temporary and is lost after you exit the session.

# Creating an online software depot

Software depots can be sourced from online repositories as well. The repository can be VMware hosted or vendor hosted. These depots may or may not contain image profiles. Some depot will only contain software packages.

## Getting ready

To be able to create an online software depot you will need to have the depot URLs handy. Here are some sample URLs:

- **VMware**: `https://hostupdate.vmware.com/software/VUM/PRODUCTION/main/vmw-depot-index.xml`
- **HPE**: `http://vibsdepot.hpe.com/index.xml`
- **Dell**: `http://vmwaredepot.dell.com/index.xml`

## How to do it...

The following procedure will guide you through the steps involved in importing a software depot from an offline bundle:

1. Log in to the vSphere Web Client and navigate to the **Auto Deploy** plugin screen.
2. On the **Auto Deploy** screen, navigate to the **Software Depots** tab and click on the icon to bring up the **Add Software Depot** window:

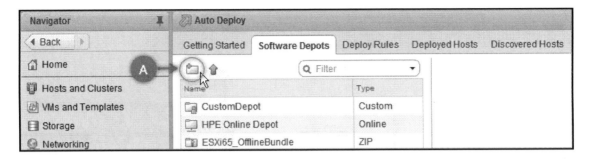

3. On the **Add Software Depot** window, select **Online Depot**, supply a **Name**, URL, and click **OK** to create the online depot:

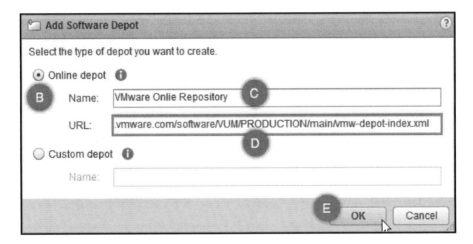

4. You should see a **Connect depot** task complete successfully in the **Recent Tasks** pane.

# There's more...

Online Software Depots can also be added using the Image Builder CLI. The process is identical to adding an offline bundle. The depot URL used will be an online `https` URL instead of a hard disk location:

1. Launch a VMware PowerCLI session.
2. Use the `Add-SoftwareDepot` command to import an offline bundle. The command requires you to provide the URL of the online repository.

3. Run the `GetEsxSoftwareDepot` command to list all software depots imported into the PowerCLI session.

4. Additionally, you could issue the `$DefaultSoftwareDepots` command to verify which of the added software depots is the default:

# Creating a custom depot

The Image Builder GUI will require you to create a custom depot to allow the cloning or creation of new image profiles. Pre-defined image profiles can only be cloned to a custom depot. You can think of custom depot as a work desk for customizing image profiles.

# How to do it...

The following procedure will help you create a custom depot:

1. Log in to the vSphere Web Client and navigate to the **Auto Deploy** plugin screen.

2. On the **Auto Deploy** screen, navigate to the **Software Depots** tab and click on the
   icon to bring up the **Add Software Depot** window:

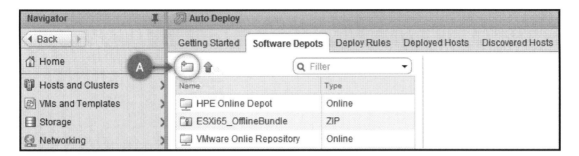

3. On the **Add Software Depot** window, choose to create a **Custom Depot** and
   supply a **Name** for the depot. Click **OK** to create the depot:

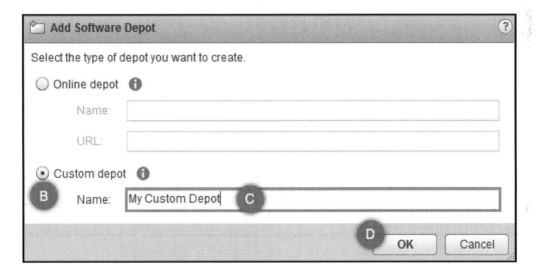

4. You should see a **Connect depot** task complete successfully in the **Recent Tasks**
   pane.

# Creating image profiles using an existing image profile

Image profiles can be created by cloning a predefined image profile. Predefined image profiles are read-only. Hence they cannot be modified. Cloning will let you create an exact copy of the image profile with the read-only property set to false, thereby letting you modify the profile.

## Getting ready

To be able to create the image profiles you would need a software depot/s with the required predefined image profiles and software packages already presented to the Image Builder service. Read the recipes, *Importing a software depot* and *Creating an online software depots* to learn how to present offline and online-depots to the Image Builder. Also, create a custom depot before you proceed. Read the recipe, *Creating a custom depot* for instructions.

## How to do it...

The following procedure will guide you through the steps involved in creating an image profile by cloning a predefined image profile:

1. Log in to the vSphere Web Client and navigate to the **Auto Deploy** plugin screen.
2. On the **Auto Deploy** screen, select the **Software Depots** you would like to clone the **Image Profiles** from. In this case, we have selected the depot created by importing an offline bundle.
3. With the intended software depot selected, navigate to the image profiles tab and select the image profile you would like to clone.

4. With the image profile selected, click on the Clone Image Profile icon to bring up the **Clone Image Profile** wizard:

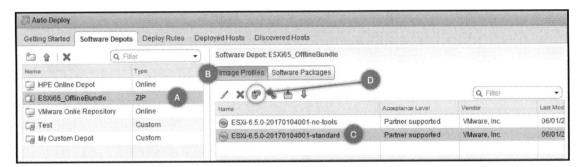

5. On the **Clone Image Profile** wizard screen, supply a **Name**, **Vendor**, **Description** (optional) and choose the destination **Software depot**. Click **Next** to continue:

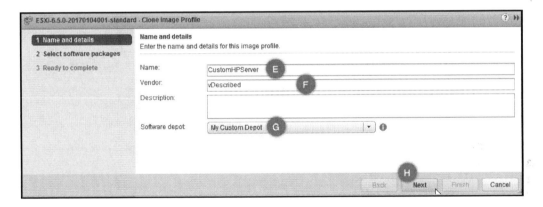

6. On the **Select software packages** screen, set a desired **Acceptance level** for the image profile, choose a software depot to fetch the packages from, select the packages and click **Next** to continue:

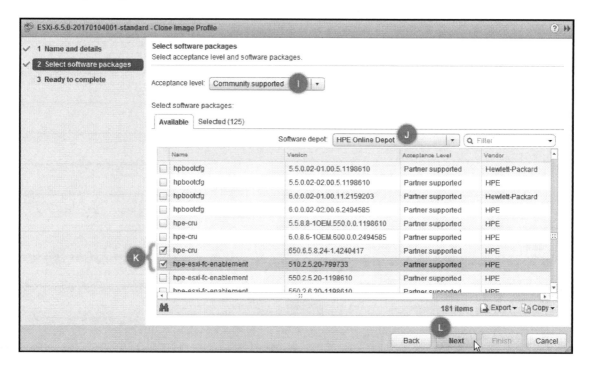

7. On the **Ready to complete** screen, review the setting and click **Finish** to start the clone operation.

8. You should see a **Connect depot** task complete successfully in the **Recent Tasks** pane.

9. Once done, the custom depot will list the newly cloned image profile. Verify whether it has the desired vendor **Name**, **Acceptance Level**, and the packages:

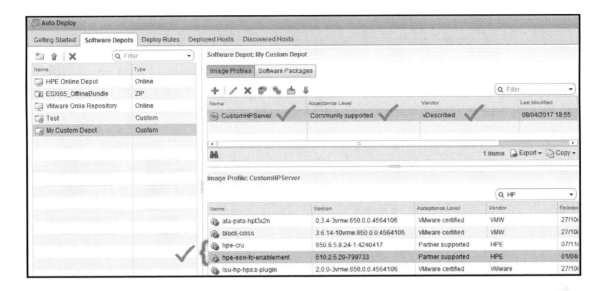

# There's more....

You can also use ESXi Image Builder CLI to clone an image profile. Unlike the GUI method, you are not required to create a custom depot for this activity. In this case, the VMware PowerCLI session becomes the work desk for this activity:

1. Launch a VMware PowerCLI session.
2. Use the `Add-SoftwareDepot` command to import an offline bundle. The command requires you to provide the path to an offline depot or the URL of the online repository.
3. Define an array variable to hold the output of the command `Get-EsxImageProfile`.
4. List the contents of the array variable to verify it has the desired content.
5. Use the `New-EsxImageProfile` command to create a new image profile by cloning the desired image profile. Use the `array[n]` representation to address the correct image profile.

6. Run the `Get-EsxImageProfile` command to list all the image profiles. You should see the newly created image profiles:

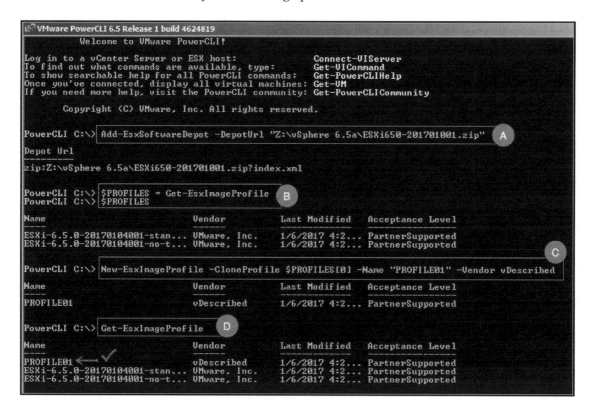

# Creating image profiles from scratch

Image profiles can be created from scratch. Meaning you need not depend on a predefined image profile to form a new image profile. However, it is important to make sure that you include at least one ESXi base image and a bootable kernel module.

# Getting ready

To be able to create image profiles from scratch, you will need offline or online software depot(s) with the required predefined image profiles and software packages already presented to the Image Builder Service. Read the recipes, *Importing a software depot* and *Creating an online software depot* to learn how to present offline and online-depots to the Image Builder. Also, create a custom depot before you proceed. Read the recipe, *Creating a custom depot* for instructions.

# How to do it...

The following procedure will guide you through the steps involved in creating an Image Profile from scratch:

1. Log in to the vSphere Web Client and navigate to the **Auto Deploy** plugin screen.
2. On the **Auto Deploy** screen, select the software depot you would like to create the image profile within, navigate to the **Image Profiles** tab and click on the **New Image Profile...** ✚ icon to bring up the **New Image Profile** wizard:

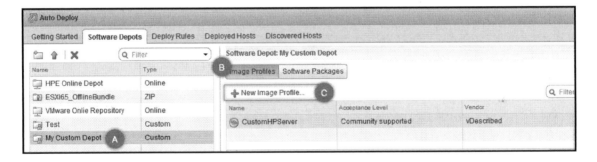

3. On the **New Image Profile** wizard screen, supply a **Name, Vendor, Description** (optional) and choose the destination **Software depot**. Click **Next** to continue:

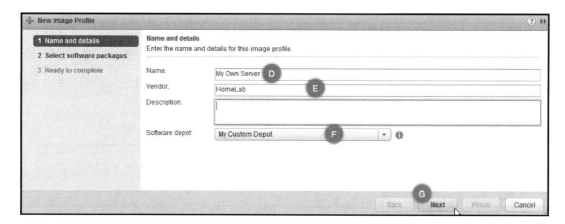

4. On the **Select software packages** screen, set a desired **Acceptance level** for the image profile, choose a software depot to fetch the packages from, add an ESXi base and boot image and its dependencies and select the other required packages and click **Next** to continue:

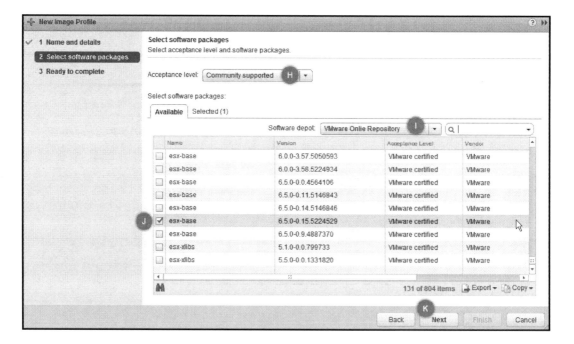

5. Since this is an example, I have included only the **esx-base** image, **esx-tboot** module and their dependencies. In the real world, you will need additional software packages to form a functional ESXi image.

6. On the **Ready to complete** screen, review the setting and click **Finish** to create the profile:

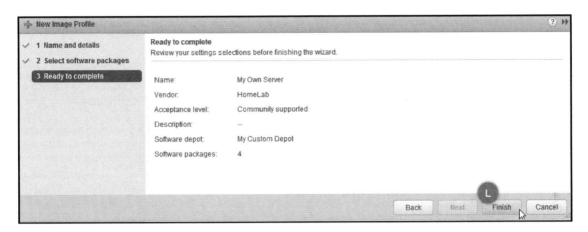

7. Once done, verify whether the image profile has the desired **Acceptance Level**, vendor **Name** and software packages:

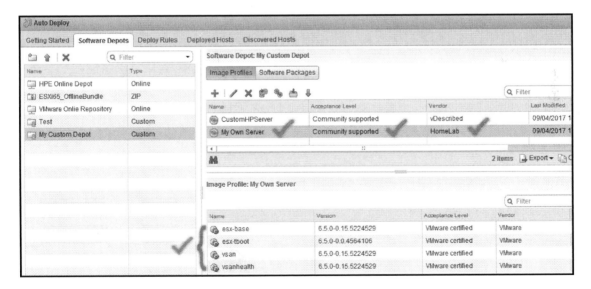

# There's more...

ESXi Image Builder CLI can be used to create an Image Profile from scratch. Unlike the GUI method, you are not required to create a custom depot for this activity, since the VMware PowerCLI session becomes the work desk in this case.

Here is how you do it:

1. Launch a VMware PowerCLI session.
2. Use the `Add-SoftwareDepot` cmdlet to import an offline bundle. The command requires you to provide the path to an offline depot or the URL of the online repository.
3. Use the `Add-EsxSoftwareDepot` cmdlet to add all the needed offline bundles to the vSphere PowerCLI session.
4. Assign the `Get-EsxSoftwareDepot` cmdlet output to an array variable.
5. Use the `Get-EsxSoftwarePackage` cmdlet to generate a list of required software packages.
6. Assign the output of the `Get-EsxSoftwarePackage` command to a variable.
7. Use the `New-EsxImageProfile` cmdlet to create a new image profile including the desired software package list stored in the variable.
8. Export the image profile to an ISO or offline bundle:

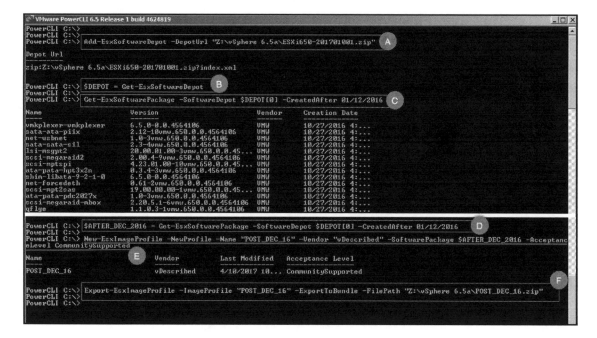

# Comparing image profiles

Sometimes, it becomes necessary to compare the difference between two image profiles. For instance, you can compare two different versions of ESXi to know what's upgraded or changed. The Image Builder GUI provides a very intuitive workflow to do this.

# How to do it...

The following procedure will walk you through steps involved in comparing two image profiles using the GUI. In this example, we will be reviewing an ESXi 6.0 image profile with ESXi 6.5:

1. Log in to the vSphere Web Client and navigate to the **Auto Deploy** plugin screen.
2. On the **Auto Deploy** screen, select **Software Depots**, navigate to **Image Profiles**, select the image profile to compare and click on **Compare To** to bring up the **Compare Image Profile** screen:

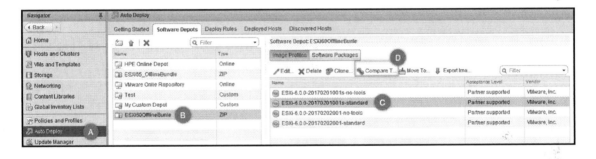

3. On the **Compare Image Profile** screen, click on **Select image profile...** to bring up the **Select Image Profile** window:

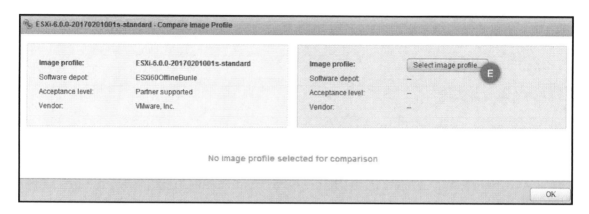

4. On the **Select Image Profile** window, choose the desired **Software depot**, select the image profile and click **OK** to make the selection and return to the **Compare Image Profile** screen:

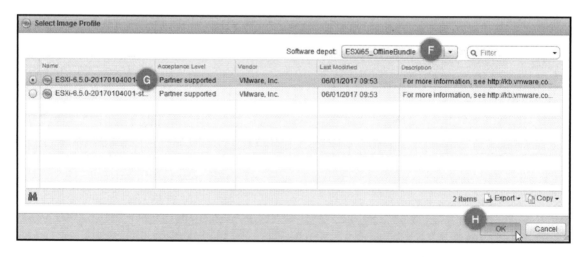

5. The **Compare Image Profile** screen will now present you with the comparison options—**Upgraded**, **Downgraded**, **Additional**, **Missing**, and **Same**. All the options are self-explanatory. Once you have finished with comparing the image profiles, you can click **OK** to close the window:

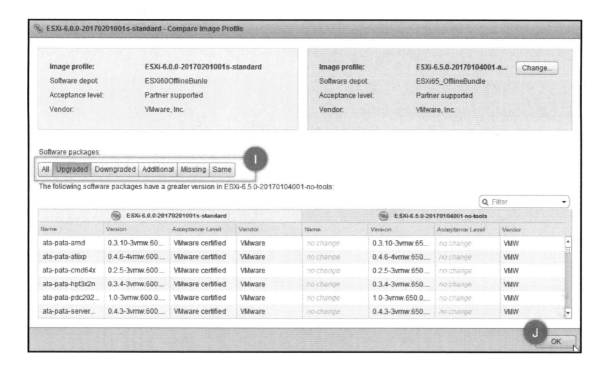

# Moving image profiles between software depots

You can move image profiles between two custom software depots. A common use case is to use a single software depot as a staging area to prepare an image profile and then move the desired ones to a separate software depot.

Image Builder GUI uses software depots as a work desk to manage and manipulate image profiles.

# How to do it...

The following procedure will help move image profiles between custom software depots:

1. Log in to the vSphere Web Client and navigate to the **Auto Deploy** plugin screen.
2. On the **Auto Deploy** screen, select a **My Custom Depot**, navigate to its **Image Profiles** tab, right-click on the image profile to move and click **Move To...**:

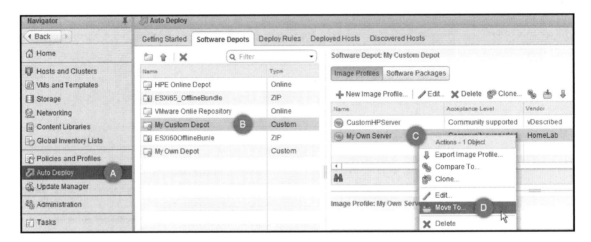

3. On the **Move Image Profile** window, use the dropdown to select the desired destination depot and click **OK**:

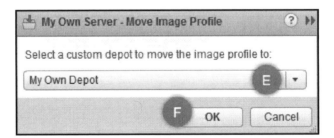

4. Verify whether the destination depot lists the moved image profile:

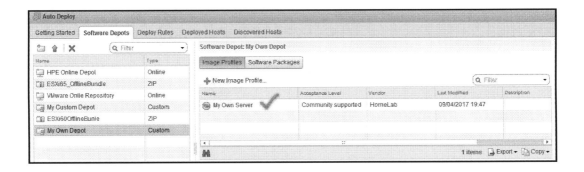

# Exporting image profiles

The whole purpose of using ESXi Image Builder is to create custom ESXi bootable images. Customization is achieved by manipulating ESXi image profiles. The procedure reaches fruition only when you can generate a bootable ISO or a usable offline bundle. The Image Builder GUI can be used to export image profiles as ISOs or offline bundles (`.zip`).

# How to do it...

The following procedure will help you export image profiles:

1. Log in to the vSphere Web Client and navigate to the **Auto Deploy** plugin screen.
2. On the **Auto Deploy** screen, select a **My Custom Depot**, navigate to its **Image Profiles** tab, right-click on the image profile to move and click **Export Image Profile...**:

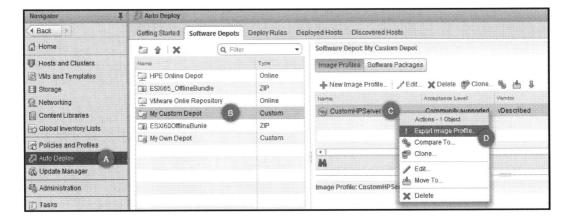

3. On the **Export Image Profile** window select the export type and click **Generate image** to begin the export. The export might take a few minutes to finish:

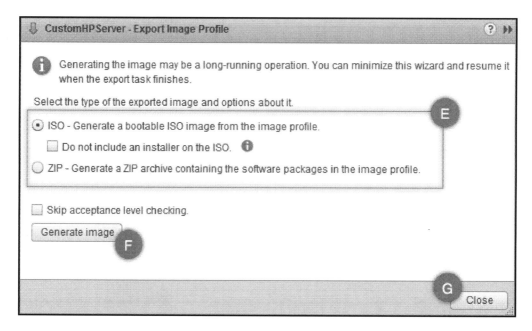

4. The export might take a few minutes to finish.
5. Once done, click **Close** to exit the **Export Image Profile** window.

# There's more...

Image profiles can be exported to ISO or offline bundles (.zip) using the Image Builder CLI. Although the GUI method is more intuitive, it is handy to know the CLI method. The commands syntaxes are:

```
Export-EsxImageProfile -ImageProfile "<Profile Name>" -ExportToIso -
FilePath "<Destination hard disk location for the ISO>"
Export-EsxImageProfile -ImageProfile "<Profile Name>" -ExportToBundle -
FilePath "<Destination hard disk location for the .zip file>"
```

Here is an example:

```
PowerCLI C:\> Export-EsxImageProfile -ImageProfile "PROFILE01" -ExportToIso -FilePath "Z:\vSphere 6.5a\PROFILE01.iso"
PowerCLI C:\>
PowerCLI C:\>
PowerCLI C:\> Export-EsxImageProfile -ImageProfile "PROFILE01" -ExportToBundle -FilePath "Z:\vSphere 6.5a\PROFILE_OfflineB.zip"
PowerCLI C:\>
```

# 5

# Using vSphere Auto Deploy

In this chapter, we will cover the following recipes:

- Enabling vSphere's auto deploy service
- Configuring a TFTP server with the files required to PXE boot servers
- Configuring a DHCP server to work with auto deploy
- Preparing the vSphere environment – create host profile, configure the deploy rules and activating them
- Enabling stateless caching
- Enabling stateful install

# Introduction

In a large environment, deploying, and upgrading ESXi hosts is an activity that requires a lot of planning and manual work. For instance, if you were to deploy a set of 50 ESXi hosts in an environment, then you might need more than one engineer assigned to perform this task. The same would be the case if you were to upgrade or patch ESXi hosts. The upgrade or the patching operation should be done on each host. Of course, you have vSphere update manager that can be configured to schedule, stage, and remediate hosts, but again the process of remediation would consume a considerable amount of time, depending on the type and size of the patch. VMware has found a way to reduce the amount of manual work and time required for deploying, patching, and upgrading ESXi hosts. They call it vSphere auto deploy. In this chapter, you will learn not only to design, activate, and configure vSphere auto deploy but also to provision the ESXi hosts using it.

# vSphere auto deploy architecture

vSphere auto deploy is a web server component that, once configured, can be used to quickly provision a large number of the ESXi hosts without the need to use the ESXi installation image to perform an installation on the physical machine. It can also be used to perform the upgrade or patching of the ESXi hosts without the need for vSphere update manager. Now, how is this achieved? vSphere auto deploy is a centralized web server component that lets you define rules that govern how the ESXi servers are provisioned. It, however, cannot work on its own. There are a few other components that play a supporting role for auto deploy to do its magic and here they are:

- The auto deploy service
- A DHCP server with scope options 66 and 67 configured
- A TFTP server hosting files for a PXE boot
- Servers with PXE (network boot) enabled in their BIOS
- Host profiles configured at the vCenter server

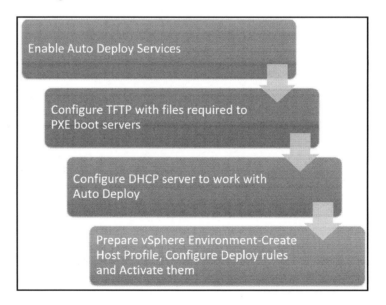

The **ESXi Host** first begins to network boot by requesting for an IP address from the **DHCP Server**. The **DHCP Server** responds with an IP address and the DHCP scope options providing the details of the **TFTP Server**. The **ESXi Host** then loads the **PXE** boot image from the **TFTP Server** to bootstrap the machine and subsequently sends an **HTTP Boot Request** to the **Auto Deploy Server**, to load an **ESXi Image** into the host's memory. The image is chosen based on the rules created at the **Auto Deploy Server.** The workflow is shown here:

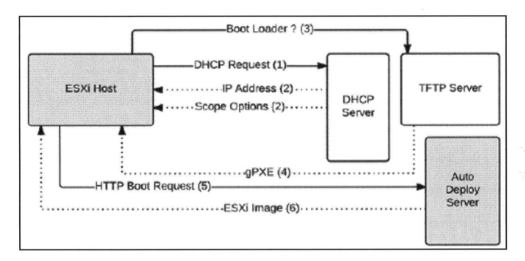

# Enabling vSphere auto deploy service

Auto deploy services, by default, are left disabled and need to be enabled explicitly. Understandably so, unless the environment warrants having specific features, they are left disabled to keep the resource consumption optimal. There are two specific services that need to be enabled to ensure that auto deploy functions as desired. In this recipe, we shall walk through the process of enabling the auto deploy service and image builder service on the vCenter Server Appliance.

# How to do it...

The following procedure walks us through enabling the appropriate services to activate Auto Deploy:

1. Log in to vCenter Server Appliance.
2. Navigate to **Home** | **Administration** | **System Configuration** as illustrated in the following screenshot:

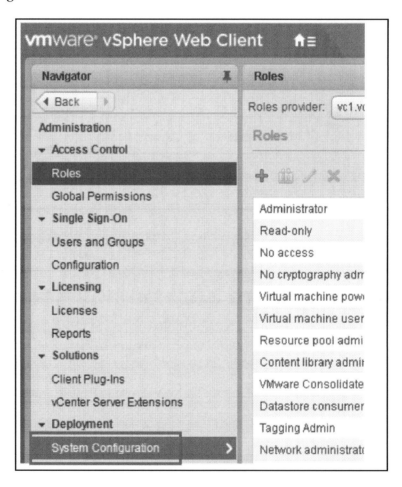

3. Click on **Nodes** and select the intended vCenter instance and **Related Objects** as shown here:

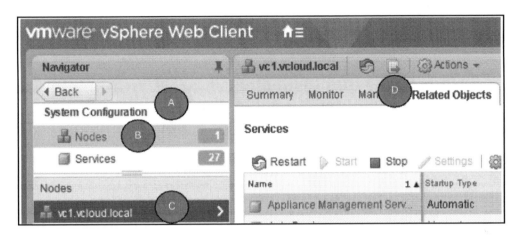

4. Highlight **Auto Deploy** service and click on **Start**.
5. Click on **Settings** and set **Automatic** to start automatically as shown here:

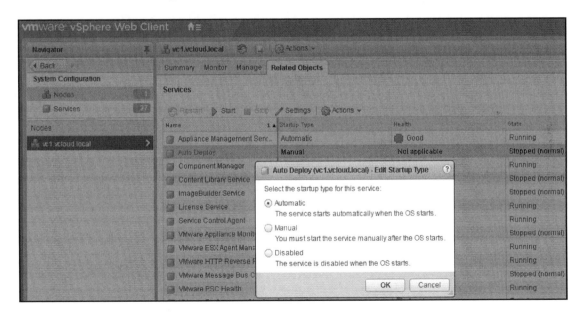

6. Highlight **ImageBuilder Service** and click on **Start**.
7. Click on **Settings** and set **Automatic** to start automatically.

8. Confirm that services are started from the **Recent Tasks** pane:

# How it works...

Auto deploy services are, by default, left to start manually although integrated with vCSA. Hence, if the environment warrants having the feature, the administrator has to enable the service and set it to start automatically with vCenter.

# Configuring TFTP server with the files required to PXE boot

**Trivial File Transfer Protocol** (**TFTP**) enables a client to retrieve a file and transmit to a remote host. This workflow concept is leveraged in the auto deploy process. Neither the protocol nor the workflow is proprietary to VMware. In this recipe, we shall use an open source utility to act as the TFTP server, there are other variants that can be used for similar purposes.

# Getting ready

Download SolarWind TFTP server at `https://www.solarwinds.com/free-tools/free-tftp-server`.

# How to do it...

The following procedure would step you through configuring the TFTP server to be PXE boot ready:

1. Log in to vCenter Server Appliance.
2. Navigate to **Home** | **vCenter** | **Configure** | **Auto Deploy**
3. Click on **Download TFTP Boot Zip** instance as depicted here:

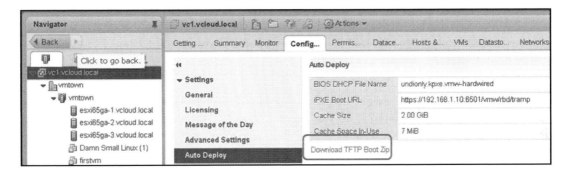

4. Extract the files to the TFTP server folder (`TFTP-Root`) as demonstrated in the following screenshot:

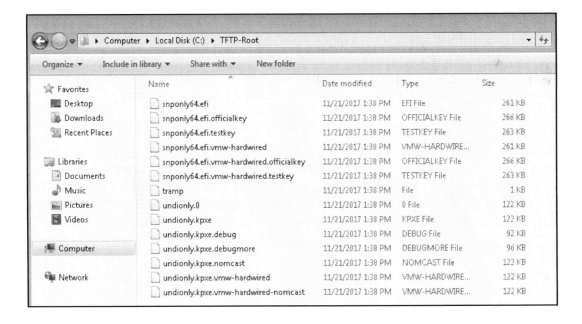

5. **Start** the TFTP service as shown here:

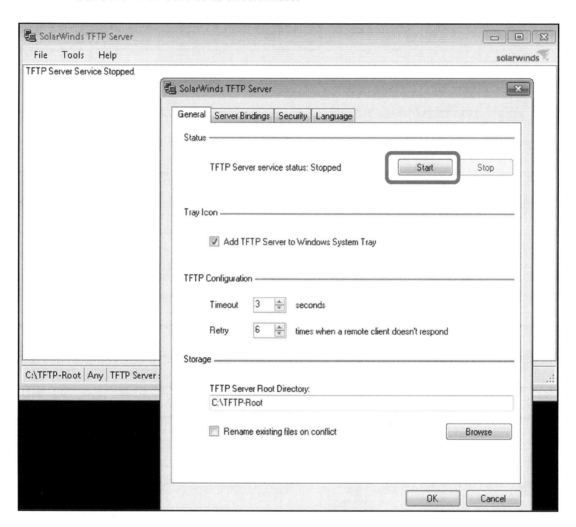

# How it works...

TFTP is primarily used to exchange configuration or boot files between machines in an environment. It is relatively simple and provides no authentication mechanism. The TFTP server component can be installed and configured on a Windows or Linux machine. In this recipe, we have leveraged a third-party TFTP server and configured it to provide the relevant PXE files on demand. The TFTP server, with the specific PXE file downloaded from vCenter, aids the host in providing a HTTP boot request to the auto deploy server.

# Configuring the DHCP server to work with auto deploy

Once the auto deploy services and TFTP servers are enabled, the next most important step in the process is to set up the DHCP server. The DHCP server responds to servers in scope with an IP address and specifically redirects the server to the intended TFTP server and boot filename. In this recipe, we shall look into configuring the DHCP server with TFTP server details alongwith the PXE file that needs to be streamed to the soon-to-be ESXi host. In this recipe, we shall walk through setting up a Windows-based DHCP server with the specific configuration that is prevalent. Similar steps can also be repeated in a Unix variant of DHCP as well.

## Getting ready

Ensure that the TFTP server has been set up as per the previous recipe. In addition, the steps in the following recipe would require access to the DHCP server that is leveraged in the environment with the appropriate privileges, to configure the DHCP scope options.

## How to do it...

The following procedure would step through the process of configuring DHCP to enable PXE boot:

1. Log in to the server with the DHCP service enabled.
2. Run `dhcpmgmt.msc`.

3. Traverse to the scope created for the ESXi IP range intended for PXE boot.

4. Right click on **Scope Options** and click on **Configure Options...** as shown in the following screenshot:

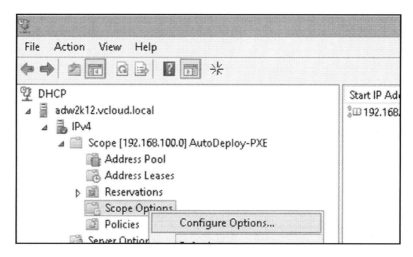

5. Set values for scope options **066 Boot Server Host Name** to that of the TFTP server.

6. Set values for scope options **067 Bootfile Name** to the PXE file `undionly.kpxe.vmw-hardwired` as demonstrated here:

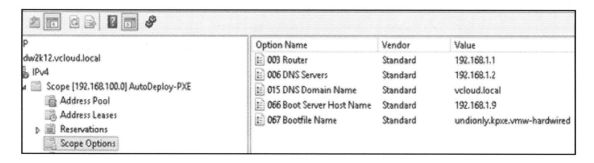

# How it works...

When a machine is chosen to be provisioned with ESXi and is powered on, it does a PXE boot by fetching an IP address from the DHCP server. The DHCP scope configuration option **66** and **67** will direct the server to contact the TFTP server and load the bootable PXE image and an accompanying configuration file.

There are three different ways in which you can configure the DHCP server for the auto deployed hosts:

1. Create a DHCP scope for the subnet to which the ESXi hosts will be connected to. Configure scope options 66 and 67.
2. If there is already an existing DHCP scope for the subnet, then edit the scope options 66 and 67 accordingly.
3. Create a reservation under an existing or a newly created DHCP scope using the MAC address of the ESXi host.

Large-scale deployments avoid creating reservations based on the MAC addresses, because that adds a lot of manual work, whereas the use of the DHCP scope without any reservations is much preferred.

# Preparing vSphere environment – create host profile, configure the deploy rules and activate them

Thus far, we have ensured that auto deploy services are enabled, and the environmental setup is complete in terms of DHCP configuration and TFTP configuration. Next, we will need to prepare the vSphere environment to associate the appropriate ESXi image to the servers that are booting in the network. In this recipe, we will walk through the final steps of configuring auto deploy by creating a software depot with the correct image, then we will create auto deploy rules and activate them.

# How to do it...

The following procedure prepares the vSphere environment to work with auto deploy:

1. Log in to vCenter Server.
2. Navigate to **Home** | **Host Profiles** as shown here:

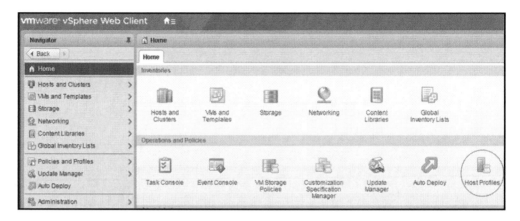

3. Click on **Extract Profile from host** as shown:

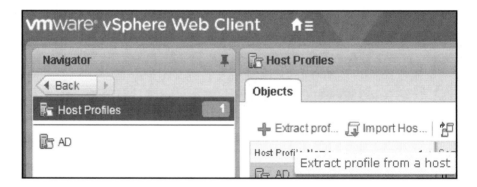

4. Choose a reference host based on which new hosts can be deployed and click on **Finish**:

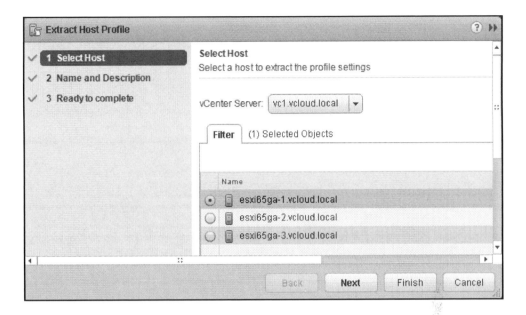

5. Navigate to **Home** | **Auto Deploy**.

6. Click on **Software Depots** | **Import Software Depot**, provide a suitable name and browse to the downloaded offline bundle as shown here:

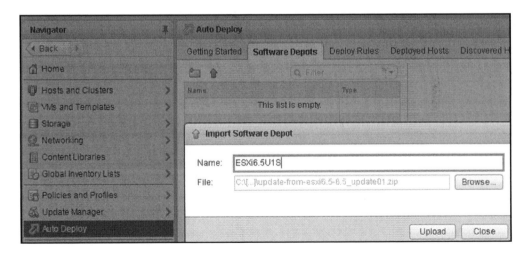

7. Click on the **Deploy Rules** tab and then click on **New Deploy Rule**.

8. Provide a name for the rule and choose the pattern that should be used to identify the target host; in this example we have chosen the IP range defined in the DHCP scope, also multiple patterns can be nested for further validation:

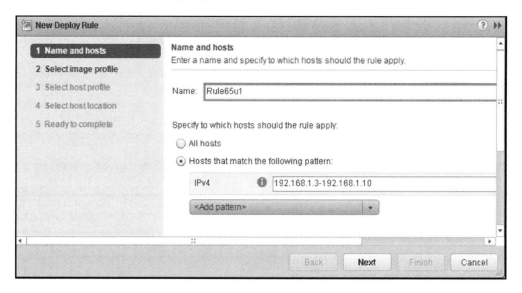

9. Choose an image profile from the list available in the software depot as shown here:

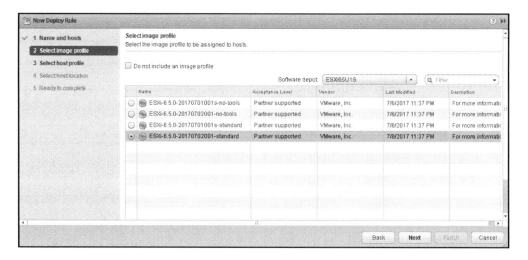

10. (Optional) Choose a host profile as shown here:

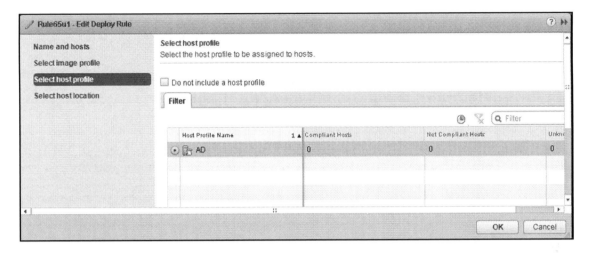

11. (Optional) In the **Select host location** screen, select the inventory and click on **OK** to complete:

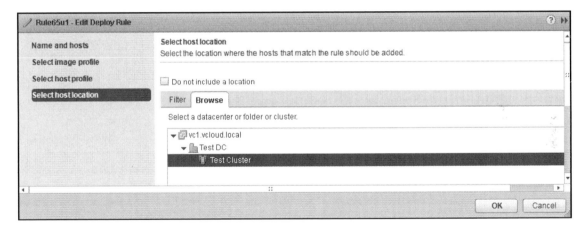

12. Click on **Activate/Deactivate rules**.

13. Choose the newly created rule and click on **Activate** as shown here:

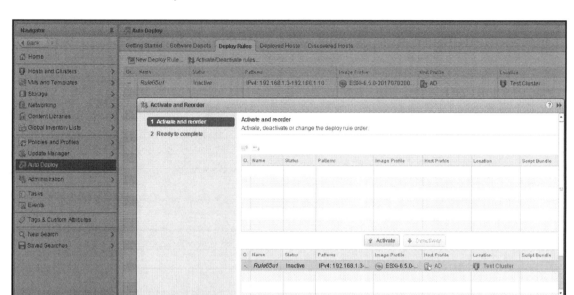

14. Confirm that the rule is **Active** as shown here:

# How it works...

To prepare the vSphere environment for auto deploy, we perform the following steps:

1. Create a host profile from a reference host, a host profile conserves the efforts in replicating much of the commonly used configuration parameters typically used in the environment. There is a natural cohesion of the feature with auto deploy.

2. Create a software depot to store image profiles, typically more than one depending on the environment needs.

3. Create deploy rules to match specific hosts to specific images.

In a complex and large infrastructure, there could be heterogeneous versions of products in terms of software, hardware, drivers, and so on. Hence, the auto deploy feature enables the creation of multiple image profiles and a set of rules through which targeted deployments could be performed. In addition, auto deploy use cases stretch beyond the typical deployments to managing the life cycle of the hosts, by accommodating updates/upgrades as well.

There are two primary modes of auto deploy:

- **Stateless caching**: On every reboot, the host continues to use vSphere auto deploy infrastructure to retrieve its image. However, if auto deploy server is inaccessible, it falls back to a cached image.
- **Stateful install**: In this mode, an installation is performed on the disk and subsequent reboots would boot off the disk. This setting is controlled through the host profile setting system cache configuration.

# Enabling stateless caching

In continuation of the previous recipe, an administrator can control if the ESXi hosts boots from the auto deploy on every instance of reboot, or perform an installation through auto deploy and have subsequent reboots to load image from disks. The option to toggle between stateless and stateful is performed by amending the host profile setting. In this recipe, we shall walk through the steps to enable stateless caching.

## How to do it...

1. Log in to vCenter Server.
2. Navigate to **Home** | **Host Profiles**.
3. Select the host profile and click on **Edit host profile**.

4. Expand **Advanced Configuration Settings** and navigate to **System Image Cache Configuration** as shown here:

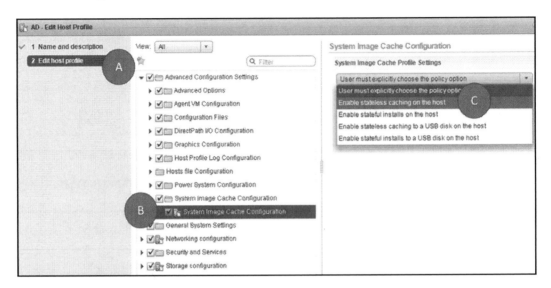

5. Select on **Enable stateless caching on the host** or **Enable stateless caching to a USB disk on the host**.

6. Provide inputs for **Arguments for first disk** or leave at default: this is the order of preference of disk on which the host would be used for caching. By default, it will detect and overwrite an existing ESXi installation, if the user indicates the specific disk make, model or driver used, the specific disk matching the preference is chosen for caching:

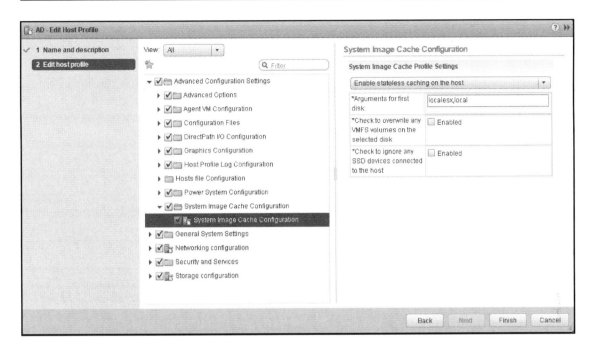

7. For the option **Check to overwrite any VMFS volumes on the selected disk,** leave it unchecked. This would ensure that if there were any VMs on the local VMFS volume, they are retained.

8. For the option **Check to ignore any SSD devices connected to the host,** leave it unchecked. You may need to enable this setting only if you have SSD for specific use cases for the local SSD, such as using **vFlash Read Cache** (vFRC).

# How it works...

The host profile directs the installation mode in an auto deploy-based deployment. In a data center where we see blade architectures prevalent, the local storage is rather limited and data is more often stored in external storage with the exception of hyperconverged infrastructures. The stateless caching feature specifically aids in such scenarios to limit dependency on local storage. In addition, users may also choose the option to enable stateless caching to USB disk.

# Enabling stateful install

While the stateless caching feature is predominantly built to tackle disk specific limitations on server hardware, the stateful install mode is more of a legacy installation through PXE mechanism. Apart from the installation procedure that is set to scale, it mimics the attributes of a standard manual installation. In this recipe, we shall walk through the steps to enable stateful install.

## How to do it...

1. Log in to vCenter Server.
2. Navigate to **Home** | **Host Profiles**.
3. Select the host profile and click on **Edit host profile**.
4. Expand ;**Advanced Configuration Settings** and navigate to **System Image Cache Configuration** as shown here.
5. Click on **Enable stateful install on the host** or **Enable stateful install to a USB disk on the host**:

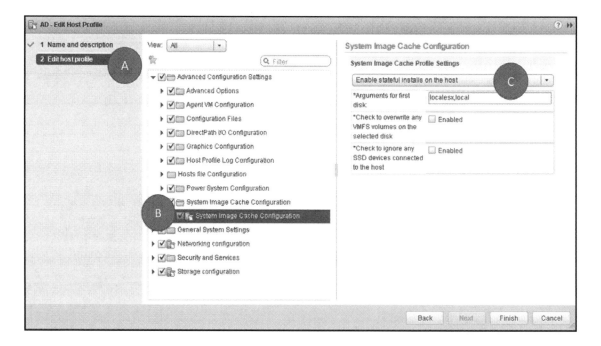

6. Provide inputs for **Arguments for first disk** or leave at default: this is the order of preference of disk on which the host would be used for installation. The administrator may also indicate the specific disk make, model or driver used, the specific disk matching the preference is chosen for installation.

7. For the option **Check to overwrite any VMFS volumes on the selected disk,** leave it unchecked. This would ensure that if there were any VMs on local VMFS volume, they are retained.

8. For the option **Check to ignore any SSD devices connected to the host,** leave it unchecked; you may need to enable this setting only if you have SSD for specific use cases for the local SSD such as using vFRC.

# How it works...

In the stateful install mode of deployment, the device on which the host needs to be installed is governed by the host profile. There is also granular control provided to the user to specifically locate the disks of specific make or model for target installation. As discussed earlier, this mimics more or less the manual installation methodology to persistently install the ESXi image onto the disk.

# 6
# Using vSphere Standard Switches

In this chapter, we will cover the following recipes:

- Creating a vSphere Standard Switch
- Creating VMkernel interfaces on a vSphere Standard Switch
- Creating custom VMkernel TCP/IP stacks
- Creating virtual machine port groups on a vSphere Standard Switch
- Managing physical uplinks on a vSwitch
- Configuring security, traffic shaping, teaming, and failover on a vSphere Standard Switch

## Introduction

Networking is the backbone of any infrastructure, be it virtual or physical. It enables connections between various infrastructure components. When it comes to traditional server-side networking components, we often talk about one or more physical adapters cabled to a physical switch. But things would slightly change when you install a hypervisor on a server and run a virtual machine atop. So why and what should change?

Firstly, now that we create virtual machines on the hypervisor, each of the virtual machines would need a network identity to enable it to become part of a network. Therefore, we create vNICs on the virtual machine that will appear as a network adapter to the guest operating system (Windows/Linux) that runs inside the virtual machine.

Now that we have taken care of the network connection for the virtual machine, the second hurdle is to let the virtual machines communicate over the network. On a server, since there would a limited number of physical NICs, it is a challenge to present these NICs to individual VMs. For instance, if you were to run 20 VMs on a host with 4 physical NICs, then there should be a way to effectively allow all the VMs to share the physical NIC resources. The sharing of physical network interface hardware is achieved by enabling a layer of abstraction called the vSphere Standard Switch (there is another kind though, called the vSphere Distributed Switch, which will be discussed in the next chapter).

vSphere Standard Switch (or simply vSwitch) is a software switching construct, local to each ESXi host, and it provides a network infrastructure for the virtual machines running on that host. It enables aggregating network connections from multiple vNICs, applies network configuration policies on them, and also pins them to the physical network adapters on the ESXi hosts for traffic flow. Unlike a physical switch, a vSphere Standard Switch is not a managed switch. It doesn't learn MAC addresses and build a **Content Addressable Memory** (CAM) table like a physical switch, but it has just enough intelligence built into it to become aware of the MAC addresses of the virtual machine vNICs connected to it. There are two other layers of abstraction called the virtual machine port groups and VMkernel port group. A port group, in general, is a method to group a set of virtual ports on a vSwitch under a common configuration umbrella. A virtual machine port group can only be used for connecting virtual machine network interfaces to it. And every VMkernel interface will require its own VMkernel port group.

Unlike the virtual machine port group that allows you to connect more than one virtual machines to it, a VMkernel port group can only house a single VMkernel interface. This is only the case with vSphere Standard Switch port groups, though.

# Creating a vSphere Standard Switch

A vSphere Standard Switch operates at the VMkernel layer. By default, a vSwitch vSwitch0 is created during ESXi installation. In this section, we will learn how to create a new vSwitch using the vSphere Web Client and also the ESXi command-line interface.

# Getting ready

Before you create a Standard Switch, you will need the following details handy:

- **Name of the vSwitch**: Most organizations follow a naming standard. It is essential to arrive at an accepted naming format.
- **Physical uplinks**: Not all uplinks are configured to pass all traffic. It is important to make sure you identify the correct uplinks. For example, it is possible that only a fixed number of VLANs are trunked to a port the uplink is cabled to.

# How to do it...

The following procedure will help you create a Standard vSwitch using the vSphere web client graphical user interface:

1. Log in to the vSphere Web Client, navigate the vCenter inventory and select the ESXi host to create the vSphere Standard Switch on.

2. With the ESXi host selected, navigate to **Configure** | **Networking** | **Virtual Switches** to view the existing vSphere Standard Switches on the host. Click on the ⬛ icon to bring up the **Add Networking** wizard:

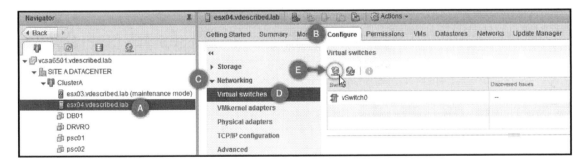

3. On the **Add Networking** wizard, set the connection type as **Physical Network Adapter** and click **Next** to continue:

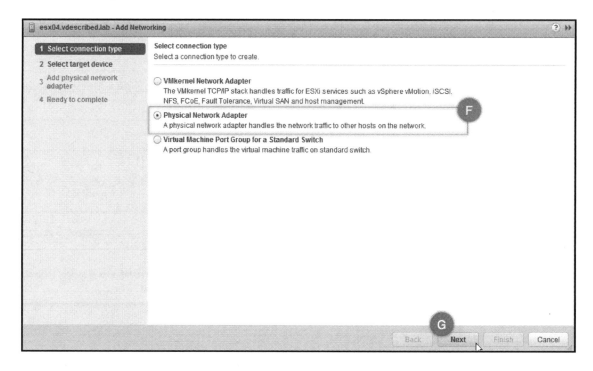

You can choose the other connection types depending on what you are trying to achieve. For instance, if you were creating a new VMkernel interface or a virtual machine port group on a new or an existing switch, you could choose the appropriate connection type. In this case, since we are only creating a new standard switch, we will be using the **Physical Network Adapter** as the connection type.

4. On the **Select target device** screen, choose to create a **New standard switch** and click **Next** to continue:

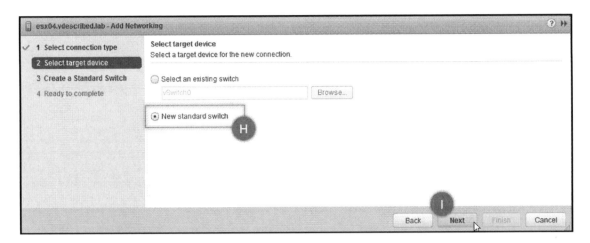

5. On the **Create a Standard Switch** screen, you can assign physical adapters for the switch. This is done by clicking on the ✚ icon to bring up the **Add Physical Adapters to the Switch** window:

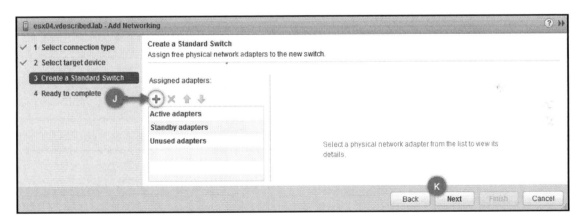

6. On the **Add Physical Adapters to the Switch** window, select (or multi-select) the required adapters, choose a failover group (active or standby or unused) and click **OK** in the wizard screen:

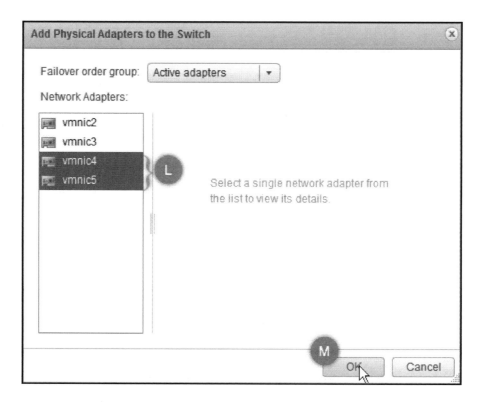

The default Failover order group is Active adapters. If you do not explicitly choose a group, all the added adapters will become active traffic carrying adapters for the vSphere Standard Switch.

7. On the **Ready to complete** screen, review the setting and click **Finish** to create the vSwitch.

8. The **Recent Tasks** pane should show an **Update network configuration** screen completed successfully:

9. The new vSwitch should now be displayed under **Configure** | **Networking** | **Virtual** switches:

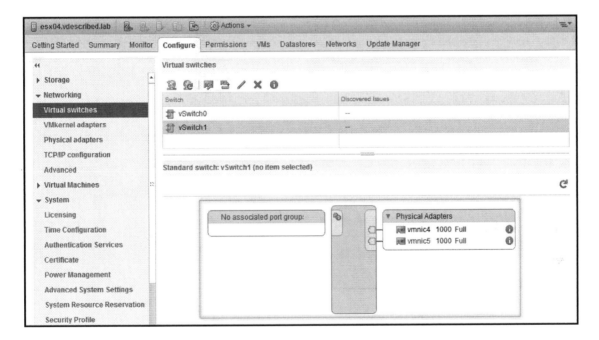

# There is more...

vSphere Standard Switches can also be created using the ESXi CLI. The following procedure will help you achieve the same:

1. SSH into the ESXi host as `root` use a direct console access method such as HP ILO or DRAC and login as `root`.

2. List all available vmnic adapters using the command `esxcfg-nics -l`.

3. Use the following command syntax to create a new standard vSwitch:

```
# esxcli network vswitch standard add -v <Name of the vSwitch>
```

4. Add an uplink to the newly created standard vSphere switch using the following command syntax:

```
# esxcli network vswitch standard uplink add -u <Name of the vmnic>
-v <Name of the vSwitch>
```

5. Issue the following command to view the details on the newly created vSwitch:

```
# esxcli network vswitch standard list -v <Name of the vSwitch>
```

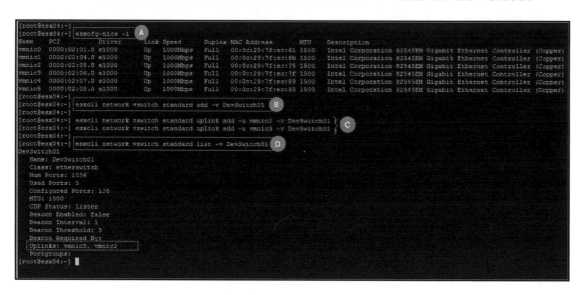

6. We could enable vMotion and FT functionalities on a selected VMkernel interface by using the following commands:

```
vim-cmd hostsvc/vmotion/vnic_set vmk1
vim-cmd hostsvc/advopt/update FT.VMknic string vmk1
```

7. You need to refresh to apply the changes by issuing the following command:

```
vim-cmd hostsvc/net/refresh
```

# Creating VMkernel interfaces on a vSphere Standard Switch

Much like vNIC is a network interface for a virtual machine, a VMkernel interface acts as a network interface for VMkernel. The very first VMkernel interface—vmk0 is created during the installation of ESXi. This interface is the management interface for the ESXi host. VMware allows you to create a maximum of 256 (vmk0—vmk255) VMkernel interfaces on an ESXi host. ESXi uses VMkernel interfaces for management traffic, VMotion traffic, FT traffic, virtual SAN traffic, iSCSI, and NAS interfaces. Since each interface acts as a network node point, it will need an IP configuration and a MAC address. The first VMkernel interface (vmk0) will procure the MAC address of the physical NIC it is connected to. The remaining interfaces pick up the VMware OUI MAC address generated by the ESXi host. In this section, we will learn how to create VMkernel interfaces.

## Getting ready

You will need the following data handy before you can create a VMkernel interface:

- Name of the port group for the VMkernel interface—most organizations follow a naming standard. It is essential to arrive at an accepted naming format.
- Physical uplinks—not all uplinks are configured to pass all traffic. It important to make sure you identify the correct uplinks. For example, it is possible that only a fixed number of VLANs are trunked to a port the uplink is cabled to.
- VLAN ID and the IP configuration for the interface.

## How to do it...

The following procedure will help you create VMkernel interfaces on vSphere Standard Switches:

1. Log in to the vSphere Web Client, navigate the vCenter inventory and select the ESXi host to create the vSphere Standard Switch on.

2. With the ESXi host selected, navigate to **Configure | Networking | VMkernel Adapters** to view the existing VMkernel interfaces on the host. Click on the icon to bring up the **Add Networking** wizard:

3. On the **Add Networking** wizard, select **VMkernel Network Adapter** and click **Next** to continue:

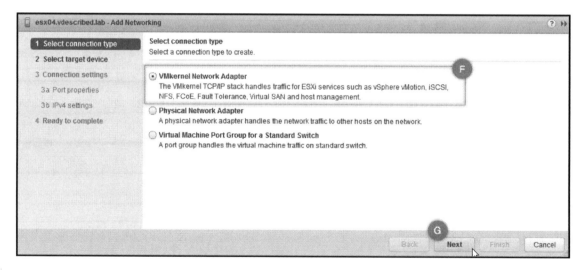

4. On the **Select target device** screen, you are allowed to **Select an existing standard switch** or create a new one for the VMkernel interface. In this case, we are using an existing standard switch. Click **Next** to continue:

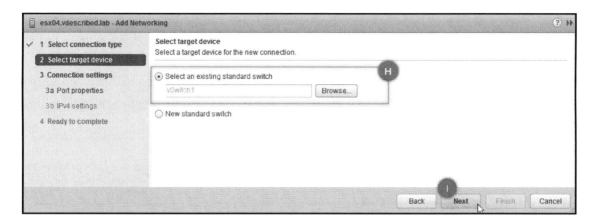

5. On the **Port properties** screen, supply a network label (this is nothing but the name of the port group that will be created to house the VMkernel interface), a **VLAN ID**, a **TCP/IP stack** and the services you would like to enable:

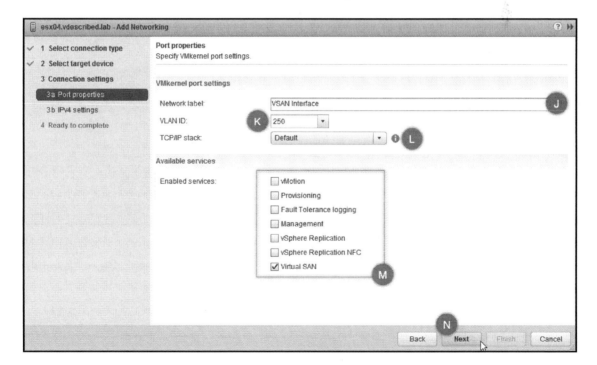

ESXi has three system TCP/IP stacks—one for VMotion traffic, a stack for provisioning traffic and a default stack for other services. Read the recipe, *Configuring VMkernel TCP/IP Stacks* for more information.

6. On the IPv4 settings screen, you can choose to obtain the IPv4 configuration from a DHCP server or create a static configuration. It is always recommended you set a static configuration for your VMkernel interfaces. Select the option **Use static IPv4 settings**, supply an IP address and its subnet mask:

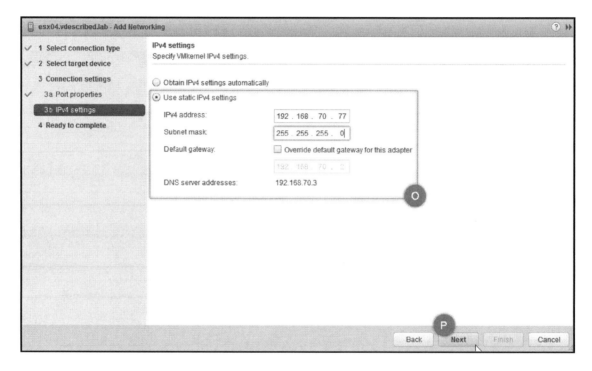

The gateway and DNS settings are inherited from the TCP/IP stack in use. Read the recipe, *Configuring VMkernel TCP/IP Stacks* for more information.

7. On the **Ready to complete** screen, review the settings and click **Finish**:

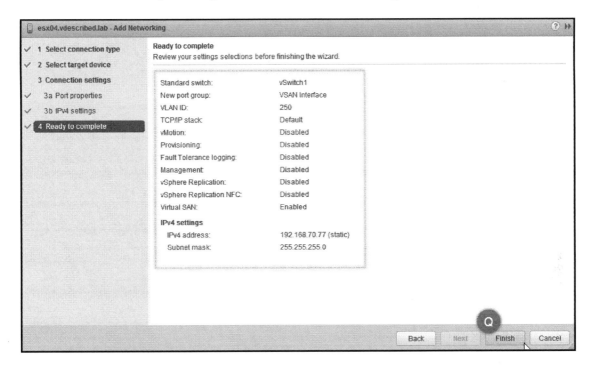

8. The **Recent Tasks** pane should show an **Update network configuration** screen completed successfully.

9. The newly create VMkernel interface will be listed under **Configure** | **Networking** | **VMkernel** adapters:

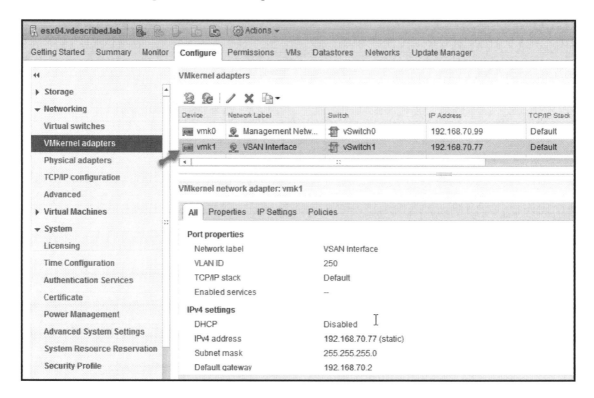

10. The virtual switch should show a new port group housing the interface. Note that the port group's name is the network label value that was supplied during the wizard:

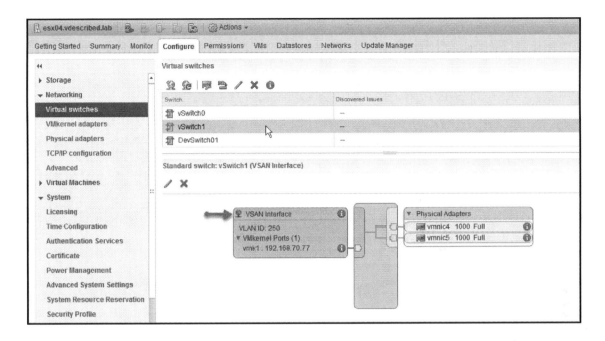

# There is more...

VMkernel adapters can also be created, using the ESXi CLI. The following procedure will help achieve the same:

1.  Connect to the ESXi host via SSH or via a server remote console access method.

2.  Use the following  command syntax to create a port group:

    ```
    # esxcli network vswitch standard portgroup add -p <Port Group
    Name> -v <Name of an existing vSwitch>
    ```

3.  Use any of the following command syntaxes to create a VMkernel interface and map it to the port group:

    ```
    # esxcfg-vmknic -a -i <IP Address> -n <Net Mask> -p <Name of the
    Port Group>
    # esxcfg-vmknic -a -i DHCP -p <Name of the Port Group>
    ```

4. Issuing the command `esxcfg-vmknic -l` should list the newly created VMkernel interface:

# Creating custom VMkernel TCP/IP stacks

A VMkernel includes more than one TCP/IP stack. There are three system stacks—VMotion, provisioning, and default. However, you are also allowed to create custom TCP/IP stacks. In this recipe, we will learn how to set up and use custom TCP/IP stacks.

## Getting ready

To be able to create custom TCP/IP stacks you need the following data handy:

- Name of the TCP/IP stack
- DNS addresses
- Gateway address of the subnet the TCP/IP stack will be a part of. You will only be able to set a default gateway address after you map a VMkernel interface to the custom stack.

# How to do it...

The following procedure will help you create a custom TCP/IP stack and configure it for use with a VMkernel interface.

1. Connect to the ESXi host via SSH or via a server remote console access method.
2. Use the following two-command syntax to create a custom TCP/IP stack:

```
# esxcli network ip netstack add -N <Custom Name of the Network
Stack>
```

There is no GUI method to create a custom TCP/IP stack as of vSphere 6.5:

1. Issue the following command to list the network stacks created:

```
# esxcli network ip netstack list
```

```
esx04.vdescribed.lab - PuTTY
[root@esx04:~]
[root@esx04:~]
[root@esx04:~] esxcli network ip netstack add -N DevNetwork  (A)
[root@esx04:~]
[root@esx04:~] esxcli network ip netstack list  (B)
defaultTcpipStack
    Key: defaultTcpipStack
    Name: defaultTcpipStack
    State: 4660

DevNetwork
    Key: DevNetwork
    Name: DevNetwork
    State: 4660
[root@esx04:~]
```

2. Select the ESXi host from the vCenter inventory and navigate to **Configure** | **Networking** | **TCP/IP configuration** | **Custom stacks** to view the newly created custom TCP/IP stack:

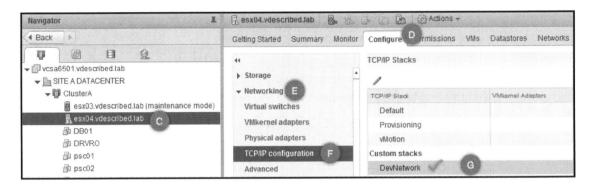

3. The next step will be to create a VMkernel interface and map it to the newly created TCP/IP stack. To learn how to create VMkernel interfaces, read the recipe *Creating VMkernel interfaces on a vSphere Standard Switch*:

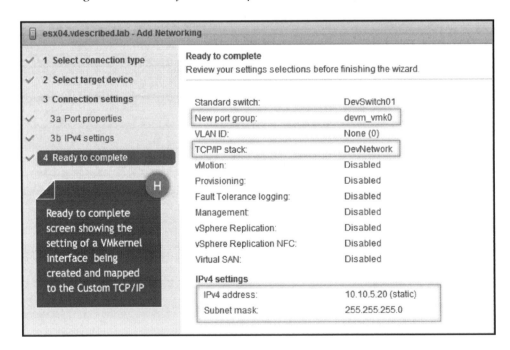

This is an important step, because without a VMkernel interface mapped to the TCP/IP stack you will not be allowed to configure a default gateway on it.

The stack mapping to a VMkernel interface cannot be changed after the interface has been created. If such a change is required then you will need to recreate the VMkernel interface:

1. Now, click on the pencil icon ✎ to edit the stack configuration:

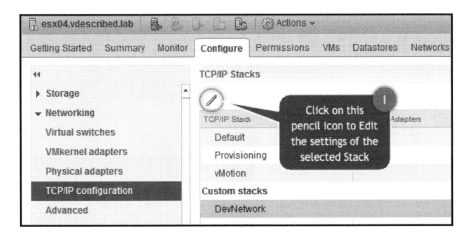

2. On the **Edit TCP/IP Stack Configuration** window, go to the **DNS configuration** screen and supply the DNS server IP addresses and search domains information:

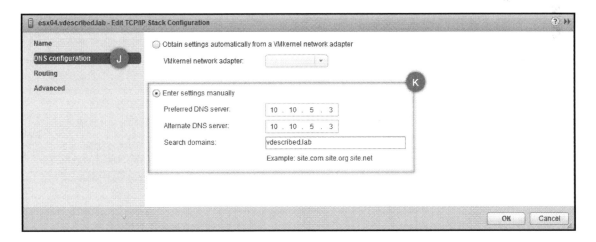

3. Go to the **Routing** screen and supply the **VMkernel gateway** address for this stack:

4. The **Advanced** screen will allow you to choose a **Congestion control algorithm** and the **Max. number of connections**. However, in most cases, you are not required to modify these settings. Click **OK** to close the **Edit TCP/IP Stack Configuration** window:

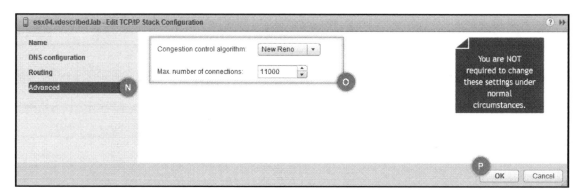

# How it works...

As mentioned before, although you are allowed to create custom TCP/IP stacks, VMkernel includes three system stacks and those are default, VMotion and provisioning. Multiple stacks enable the use of separate default gateways, thereby allowing VMkernel interfaces to be on separate physical network segments. Each TCP/IP stack enabled or created will maintain its own memory heap, ARP tables, routing tables and default gateway:

- The default stack will be the only stack used if you do not explicitly assign a different stack while creating a VMkernel interface

- The VMotion stack will, if used, allow the isolation of VMotion traffic handling to a separate gateway, removing the dependency on the management stack or network
- The provisioning stack is used to isolate cloning, cold migration and long distance NFC traffic to a separate gateway, thereby removing the dependency on the management stack or network
- The custom stacks can be used to isolate traffic onto separate VMkernel gateways, if required

# Creating virtual machine port groups on a vSphere Standard Switch

As we learned in the beginning of the chapter, the virtual machine interface cards or vNICs will be to connect to the vSwitch with the help of a port group. Since the standard vSwitch ports are not exposed individually for configuration, one or more port groups have to be used to supply the configuration.

## Getting ready

You will need the following data handy before you can create a VMkernel interface:

- Name of the port group (**Network label**)—most organizations follow a naming standard. It is essential to arrive at an accepted naming format.
- Physical uplinks—not all uplinks are configured to pass all traffic. It important to make sure you identify the correct uplinks. For example, it is possible that only a fixed number of VLANs are trunked to a port the uplink is cabled to.
- An optional VLAN ID.

## How to do it...

The following procedure will help you create virtual machine port groups on a standard vSwitch:

1. Log in to the vSphere Web Client, navigate the vCenter inventory and select the ESXi host to create the vSphere Standard Switch on.

2. With the ESXi host selected, navigate to **Configure** | **Networking** | **Virtual switches** to view the existing VMkernel interfaces on the host. Click on the icon to bring up the **Add Networking** wizard:

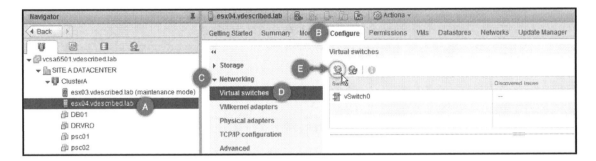

3. On the **Add Networking** wizard screen, select the option **Virtual Machine Port Group for a Standard Switch** and click **Next** to continue:

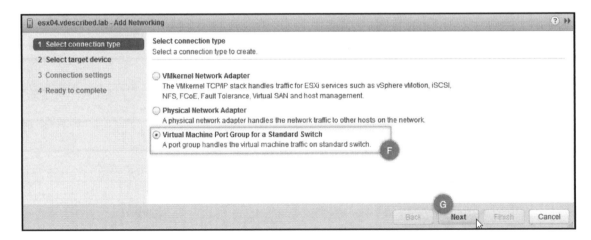

4. On the **Select target device** screen, choose the option named **Select an existing standard switch** or create a new one for the VMkernel interface. In this case, we are using an existing standard switch. Click **Next** to continue:

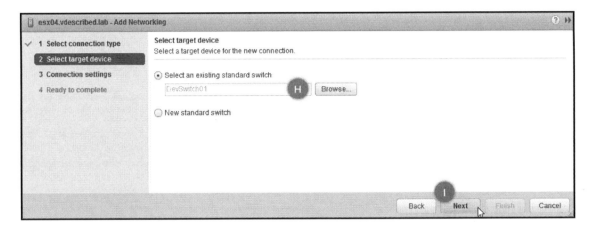

5. On the **Connection settings** screen, supply a **Network label** and an optional **VLAN ID** and click **Next** to continue:

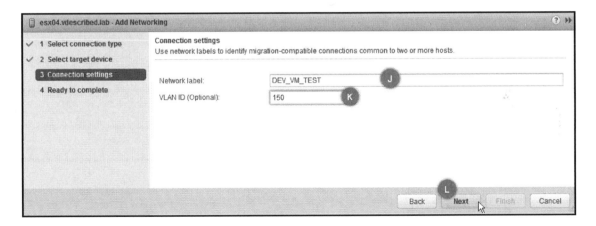

6. On the **Ready to complete** screen, review the setting and click **Finish** to create the port group:

7. The vSwitch the port group was created on, should now list the newly created port group:

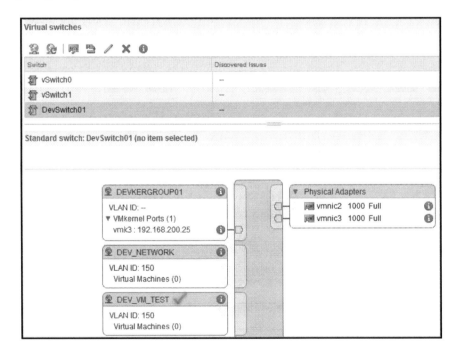

# There is more...

A virtual machine port group can also be created using the ESXi CLI. This skill would come in handy when you have no access to the GUI. Let us now look at how this is done:

1.  SSH into the ESXi host as `root` use a direct console access method such as HP ILO or DRAC and log in as `root`.

2.  Use the following command syntax to create a virtual machine port group:

    ```
    # esxcli network vswitch standard portgroup add -p <Name of the
    Port Group> -v <Name of an existing vSwitch>
    ```

3.  Use the following command syntax to assign a VLAN ID to the port group:

    ```
    # esxcli network vswitch standard portgroup set -p <Name of an
    existing port group> --vlan-id <VLAN Number>
    ```

4.  Issue the following command to list all the port groups on the host:

    ```
    # esxcli network vswitch standard portgroup list
    ```

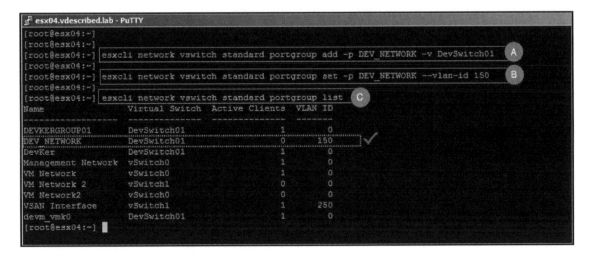

# Managing the physical uplinks of a vSwitch

There can be situations where you would need to add additional uplinks (physical NICs) for a vSphere Standard Switch. Such an addition is generally done with the intention of enabling the use of teaming and load balancing features. There are different GUI methods to achieve this. You could either use the **Add Networking** wizard or the **Manage Physical Network Adapters** option. For both methods, you start at different places in the GUI. In this recipe, we will use the manage physical network adapters method:

1. Log in to the vSphere Web Client, navigate the vCenter inventory and select the ESXi host to create the vSphere Standard Switch on.
2. With the ESXi host selected, navigate to **Configure** | **Networking** | **Virtual switches** to view the existing vSphere Standard Switched on the host.
3. Select the vSwitch you would like to manage physical adapters for and click on
   icon to bring up the **Manage Physical Network Adapters** window:

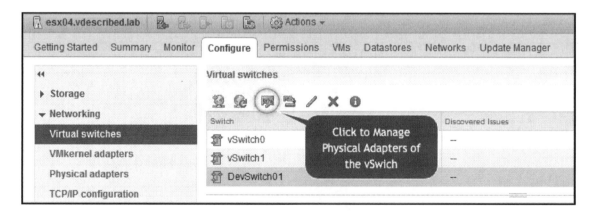

4. On the **Manage Physical Network Adapters** window, the up and down arrow keys can be used to change the order of physical adapters and also to move them to **Standby adapters** or **Unused adapters** sections:

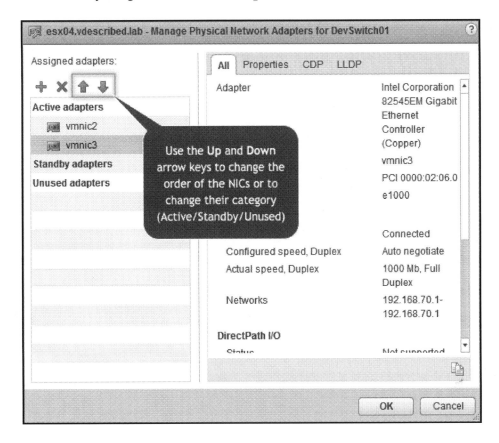

5. To map a new physical adapter to the NIC, click on the 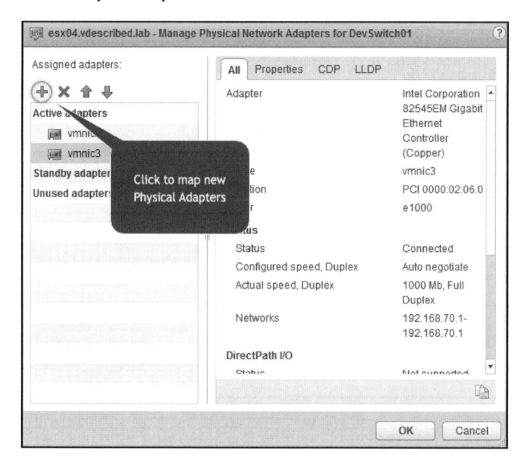 icon to bring up the **Add Physical Adapters to the Switch** window:

6. On the **Add Physical Adapters to the Switch** window, select the required adapters and click **OK**:

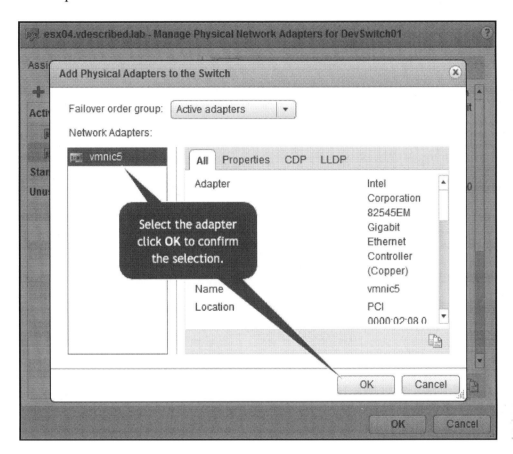

7. On the **Manage Physical Network Adapters** screen, click **OK** to confirm the settings and close the window:

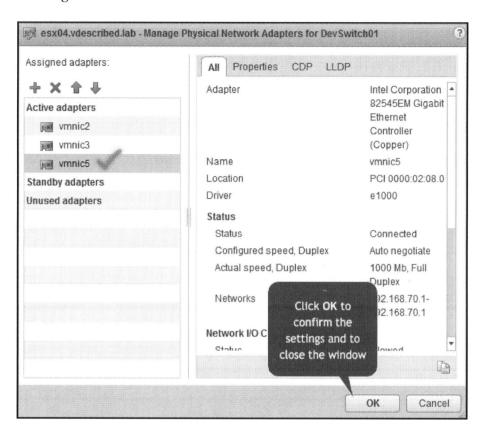

# There is more...

The standard vSwitch physical network adapters can also be managed using the ESXi CLI:

1. SSH into the ESXi host as `root` use a direct console access method such as HP ILO or DRAC and login as `root`.

2. Use the following command syntax to verify the current configuration of the vSwitch you would like to manage the adapters of:

```
# esxcli network vswitch standard list -v <Name of the vSwitch>
```

3. Use the following command syntaxes to add/remove uplinks:

```
# esxcli network vswitch standard uplink add -u <vmnic> -v <Name of
the vSwitch>
# esxcli network vswitch standard uplink remove -u <vmnic> -v <Name
of the vSwitch>
```

4. Issue the command from the second step to verify the changes:

# Configuring security, traffic shaping, teaming, and failover on a vSphere Standard Switch

The security, traffic shaping, teaming, and failover settings function in the same manner for a standard vSwitch and a **vSphere Distributed Switch** (**VDS** or **dvSwitch**), with a couple of exceptions regarding traffic shaping and load balancing methods. Unlike a standard vSwitch, a VDS can handle both ingress and egress traffic shaping. VDS also has a load balancing method called route based on physical NIC load. We learn more about dvSwitch in the next chapter. In this section, we will learn how to configure security, traffic shaping, team and failover on a vSphere Standard Switch.

## How to do it...

The following procedure will help you configure security, traffic shaping, teaming, and failover on vSwitch:

1. Log in to the vSphere web client, navigate the vCenter inventory and select the ESXi host to create the vSphere Standard Switch on.
2. With the ESXi host selected, navigate to **Configure** | **Networking** | **Virtual switches** to view the existing vSphere Standard Switched on the host.
3. Select the vSwitch you would like to configure the settings on and click on the pencil ✏ icon to bring up the **Edit Settings** window:

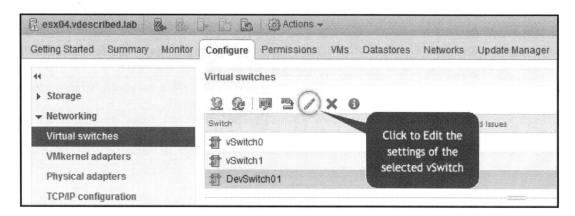

4. On the **Edit Settings** window, go to the **Security** screen and select options **Accept/Reject Promiscuous mode, MAC address changes**, and **Forged transmits**:

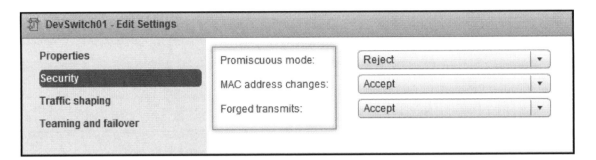

5. Go to the **Traffic shaping** screen, to enable it and configure average and peak bandwidth and burst size:

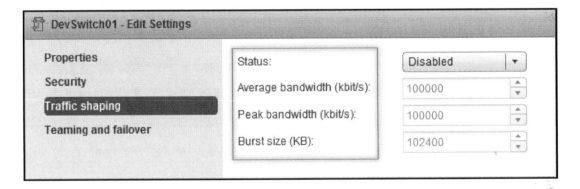

6. Go to the **Teaming and failover** screen, to configure **Load balancing**, **Network failure detection**, **Notify switches**, and **Failback**. Once done, click **OK** to confirm the settings and to close the **Edit Settings** window:

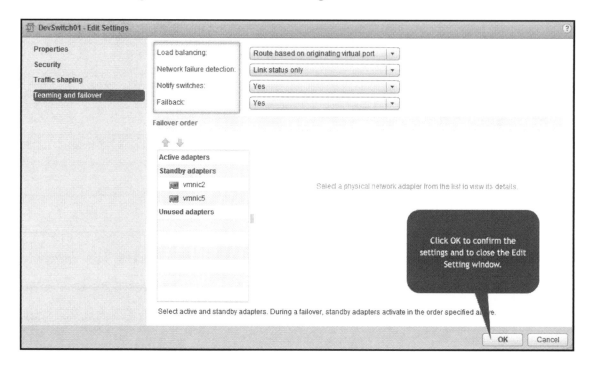

# 7
# Using vSphere Distributed Switches

In this chapter, we will cover the following topics:

- Creating a vSphere Distributed Switch
- Connecting hosts to a vSphere Distributed Switch
- Creating a vSphere Distributed port group
- Managing physical adapter (vmnic) to dvUplink mappings
- Migrating a virtual machine network from a vSphere Standard Switch (vSwitch) to a vSphere Distributed Switch (dvSwitch)
- Migrating VMkernel interfaces between vSphere Standard (vSwitch) and vSphere Distributed Switches (dvSwitch)
- Creating additional VMKernel interfaces on a vSphere Distributed Switch (dvSwitch)
- Creating a vSphere Distributed Switch backup
- Restoring dvSwitch from a backup
- Creating or importing a dvSwitch from a backup
- Configuring security, traffic shaping, teaming, and failover on a dvSwitch
- Configuring VLANs on a vSphere Standard or Distributed Switch
- Configuring private VLANs on a vSphere Distributed Switch
- Configuring LAGs on a vSphere Distributed Switch
- Creating user-defined network resource pools
- Using port mirroring on a vSphere Distributed Switch
- Enabling NetFlow on a vSphere Distributed Switch

# Introduction

A **vSphere Distributed Switch** (**dvSwitch** or **vDS**) is the second type of software switch solution created by VMware. Although it does not change the way ESXi handles network connections and traffic, it allows for a drastic improvement in how the software switch configuration and management are done in a vSphere environment. One of the administrative challenges with the Standard vSwitch was that it could only be configured/managed on a per-host level. A very common misconception is that dvSwitch is a single switch that spans over multiple ESXi hosts. The fact is that it is not. All it does is offer a single management plane for all the host data planes (hidden software switches) distributed on the ESXi hosts, hence the name distributed switch:

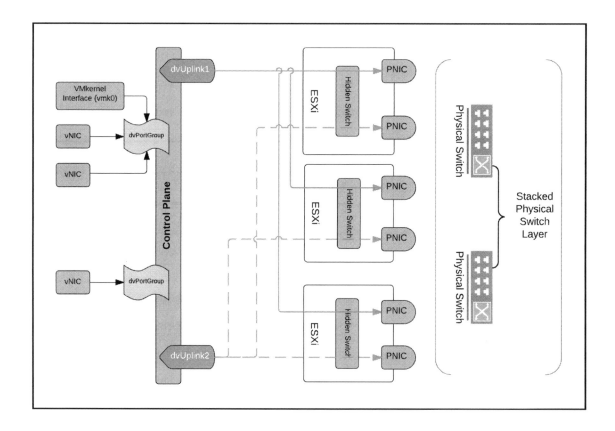

- **Distributed Port Group**: This is a method to group dvPorts under a common configuration umbrella. Unlike the port groups on a standard virtual switch, there is only a single common type of Distributed Port Group. A Distributed Port Group is sometimes referred to as a **dvPortGroup**, and that will be the terminology that we will use throughout this book. A single dvPortGroup can serve both virtual machine and VMkernel traffic.

- **dvUplink**: With dvSwitch, you can no longer apply teaming, load balancing, or failover policies directly for physical NICs. Instead, we now have an additional layer of abstraction called a **dvUplink**, which can be mapped to a physical NIC. The dvUplink count dictates the number of physical NICs from each host that can participate in the network configuration. dvSwitch provides advanced functionalities such as NetFlow, port mirroring, and ingress/egress traffic shaping, making a very feature-rich software switch.

# Creating a vSphere Distributed Switch

A vSphere Distributed Switch cannot be created on an ESXi host directly. You need to be connected to the vCenter Server, either by using the vSphere Client or by using the vSphere Web Client. Also, keep in mind that a dvSwitch can only be created at the data center level in the vCenter inventory.

# Getting ready

The ESXi hosts managed by the vCenter Server and it should be the vSphere Enterprise Plus licensed.

# How to do it...

The following procedure will guide you through the steps involved in creating a dvSwitch:

1. Log in to the **vSphere Web Client,** and use its inventory menu to go to **Networking**:

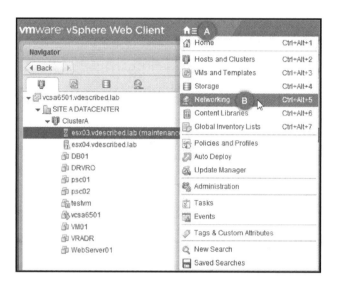

2. Right-click on the data center you intend to create the dvSwitch on and go to **Distributed Switch | New Distributed Switch...**:

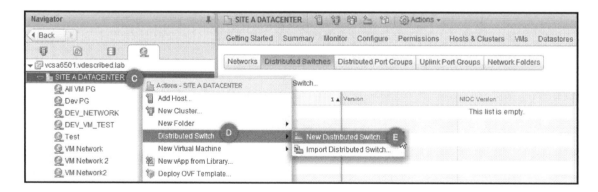

3. On the **New Distributed Switch** wizard screen, supply a **Name** for the dvSwitch and click **Next** to continue:

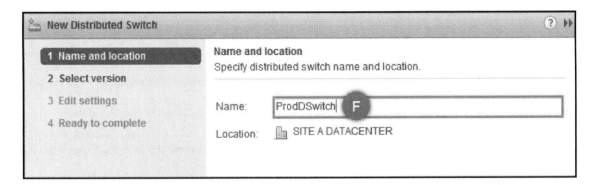

4. On the **Select version** screen, choose an intended dvSwitch version and click **Next** to continue:

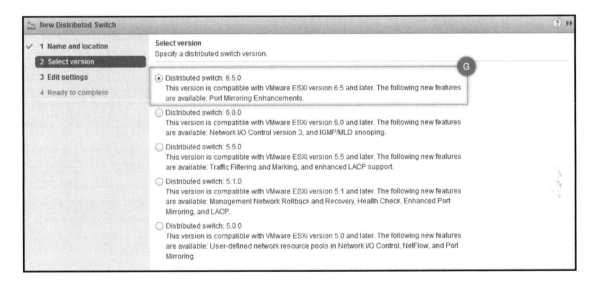

5. On the **Edit settings** screen, set the **Number of uplinks**, select **Enabled** or **Disabled** on the **Network I/O Control** option, and choose to either create or not create a default dvPortGroup. Click **Next** to continue:

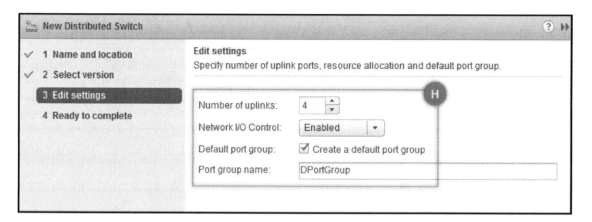

6. On the **Ready to complete** screen, review the settings and click **Finish**:

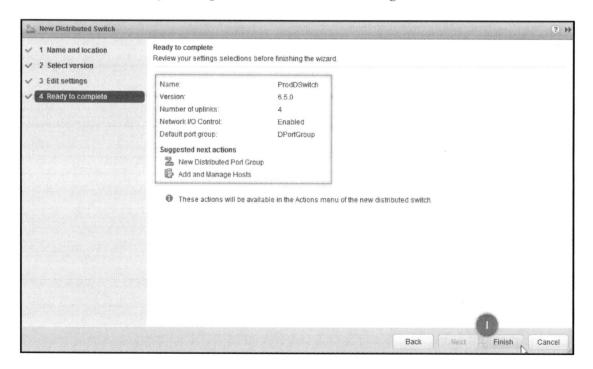

# How it works...

A vSphere Distributed Switch is created at the data center level and spans across multiple participating hosts or clusters. Therefore, it can only be created by using a vCenter Server. The vCenter's data center inventory object is the boundary for dvSwitches.

A dvSwitch will have a single control plane and multiple data planes. The control plane is at the vCenter Server and is used to create and manage the dvSwitch. There will be a data plane created on each of the participating ESXi hosts. This means that all the packet switching will happen at the ESXi hosts. The use of a dvSwitch reduces the administrative complexity of configuring vSphere Standard Switches on individual ESXi hosts in a large environment.

Five different versions of vSphere Distributed Switches were available in this example: 5.0, 5.1.0, 5.5, 6.0, and 6.5. Choosing version 6.5 will make the vSphere Distributed Switch incompatible with older versions of the ESXi hosts (if they are managed using the same vCenter Server).

A dvUplink is another layer of abstraction added to reduce the administrative complexity. Every dvSwitch with dvUplink/s will have a dvUplinks port group. Every dvPortGroup created will increase the network count by one. Additional ports will always be consumed by the number of dvUplinks in the dvUplinks port group. This is true regardless of whether or not a dvUplink is backed by a vmnic from the participating ESXi servers.

dvSwitch configuration is saved in the vCenter Server database; however, a local host copy is maintained on every participating ESXi host at the `/etc/vmware/dvsdata.db`. The host copy is synced every 300 seconds. The `dvsdata.db` file being binary can only be viewed using the `net-dvs` CLI command.

The `dvsdata.db` is only created after you connect an ESXi host to the dvSwitch. Running the `net-dvs` command without any ESXi hosts connected to the dvSwitch will yield no output.

# Connecting hosts to a vSphere Distributed Switch

Once you have created a dvSwitch at the vCenter Server, the next step is to connect ESXi hosts to the dvSwitch. ESXi hosts are ideally connected to a dvSwitch by mapping its physical network adapters to dvUplinks of the dvSwitch, but it is not mandatory though. ESXi hosts can be added to dvSwitch without really mapping any physical adapters to it, but you couldn't call that an act of connecting to a dvSwitch, as moving any VM to the dvSwitch will lose its network connectivity. Hence, it is recommended to always connect a host to a dvSwitch by mapping adapters.

The number of physical adapters that can be mapped to a dvSwitch from an ESXi host will depend on the number of dvUplinks configured on the dvSwitch created.

## How to do it...

The following procedure will help you connect ESXi host(s) to a dvSwitch:

1. Bring up the **Networking** inventory using the vSphere Web Client by using the key combination *Ctrl + Alt + 5*.
2. Right-click on the dvSwitch and select **Add and Manage Hosts...**:

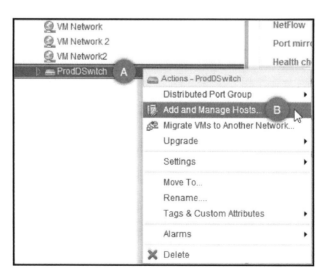

3. In the **Add and Manage Hosts** wizard, select the task as **Add hosts** and proceed:

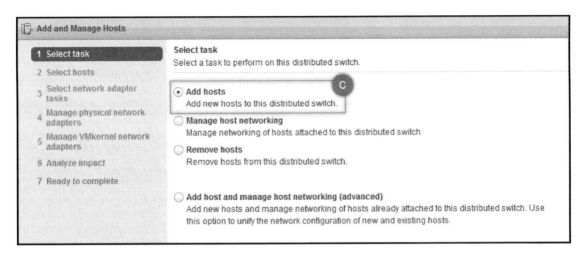

4. In the **Select hosts** screen, click on **New hosts...** to bring up a list of hosts managed by the vCenter Server:

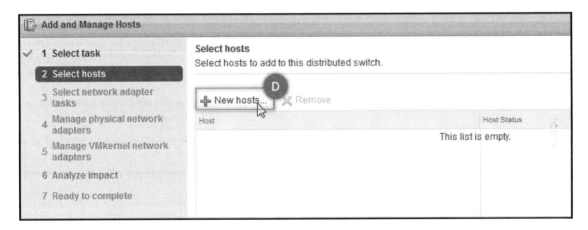

5. In the **Select new hosts** window, select the ESXi hosts you intend to add to the dvSwitch and click **OK**:

6. Back at the **Select hosts** wizard screen, select the checkbox **Configure identical network settings on multiple hosts (template mode)** and click **Next**:

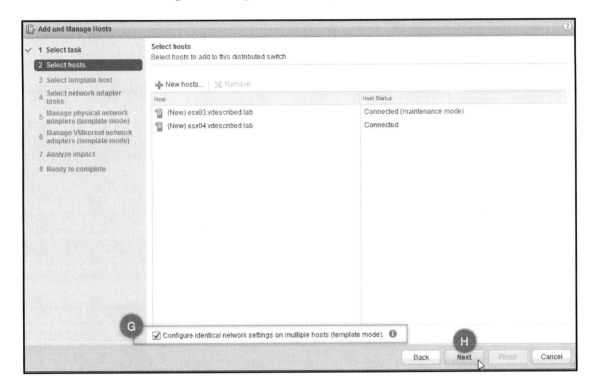

The template mode will allow you configure a chosen ESXi host and then apply the same configuration to the remaining selected hosts. This is a very handy feature when you are dealing with a large set of ESXi hosts.

7. In the **Select template host** wizard, choose a host and click **Next** to continue:

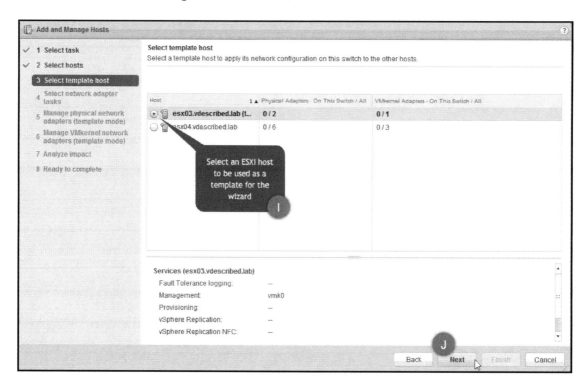

8. On the **Select network adapter tasks** screen, select the checkbox **Manage physical adapters (template mode)** and click **Next** to continue:

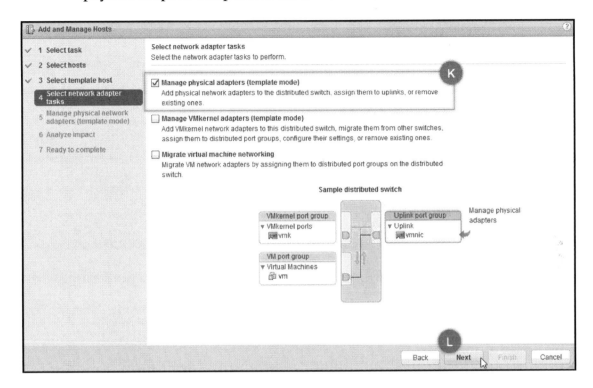

9. In the **Manage physical network adapters (template mode)** screen, use the top pane to assign vmnics to dvUplinks. This is done by selecting an unused vmnic and clicking the **Assign uplink** option at the top-left of the pane to bring up a list of dvUplinks on the dvSwitch:

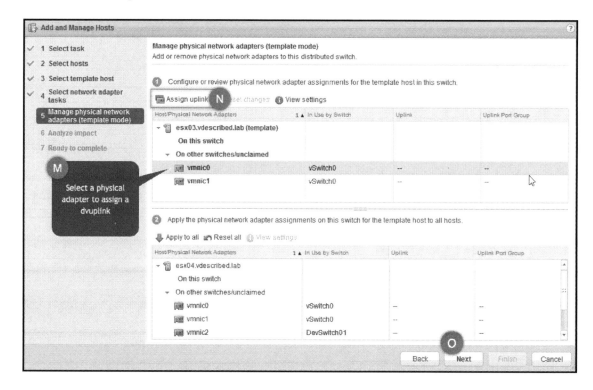

10. On the **Select an Uplink** window, choose an uplink for the vmnic and click **OK** to return to the wizard screen:

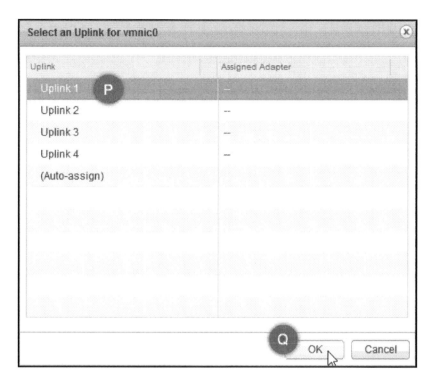

11. Repeat the procedures of steps 9 and 10 to map all the needed vmnics to dvUplinks.

12. Once all the vmnics to dvUplink mappings are done, click on the **Apply to all** option in the bottom pane to push a similar configuration to the remaining hosts. It will use the exact vmnics to dvUplink mapping on all the hosts. Click **Next** to proceed:

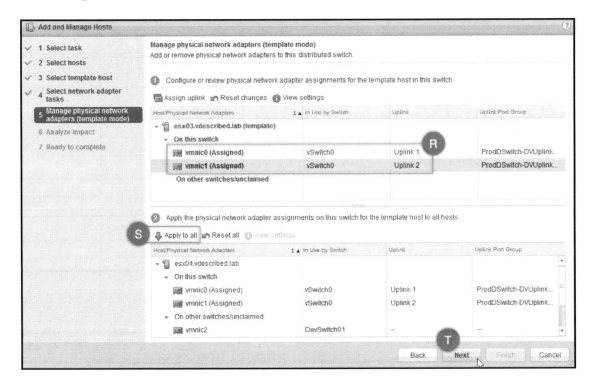

While in template mode, you will not be allowed to proceed further without applying the settings to the remaining hosts that were selected to be connected to the dvSwitch.

13. Review the **Analyze impact** screen for any possible impact detected by the wizard. Click **Next** to proceed further if there is no impact:

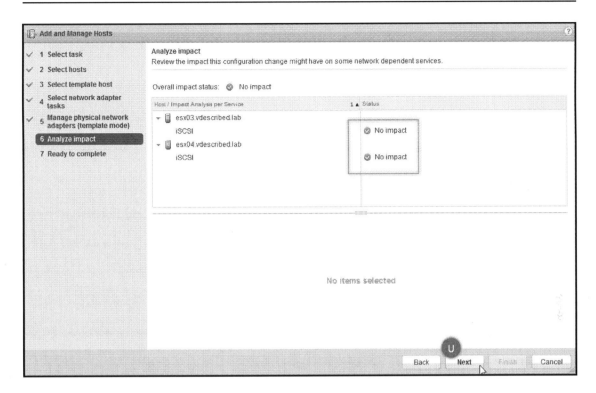

14. Review the summary of settings in the **Ready to complete** screen and click **Finish** to connect the ESXi hosts to the dvSwitch:

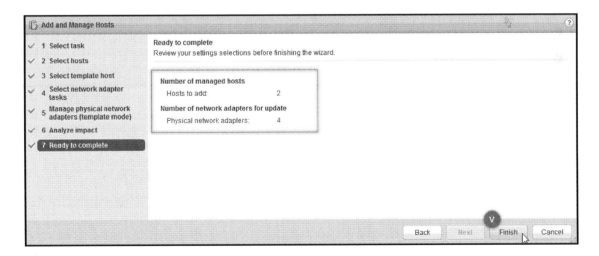

# Creating a vSphere Distributed port group

A **Distributed Port Group (dvPortGroup)** can only be created from the vCenter Server. Every dvPortGroup created has a default of 8 available ports. Port allocation is elastic, which means that the port count will automatically increase or decrease as needed.

## How to do it...

The following procedure will help you create a dvPortGroup:

1. Bring up the **Networking** inventory using the vSphere Web Client by using the key combination *Ctrl + Alt + 5*.

2. Right-click on the dvSwitch you intend to create the port group on and navigate to **Distributed Port Group** | **New Distributed Port Group...**:

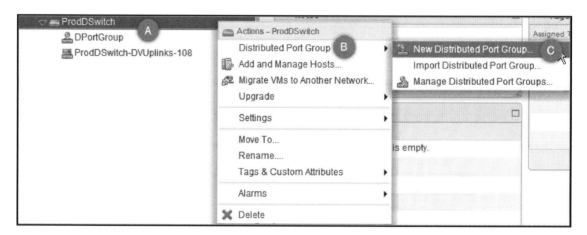

3. On the **New Distributed Port Group** screen, supply a name for the port group and click **Next** to continue:

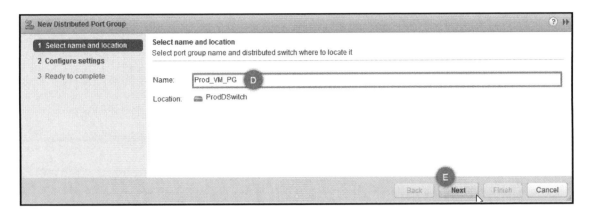

4. On the **Configure settings** screen, set the **Port binding, Port allocation, Number of ports, Network resource pool**, and **VLAN type**. You can also choose to override the dvSwitch settings by selecting the option, **Customize default policies configuration**.

5. On the **Security** screen, configure **Promiscuous mode, MAC address changes**, and **Forged transmits**:

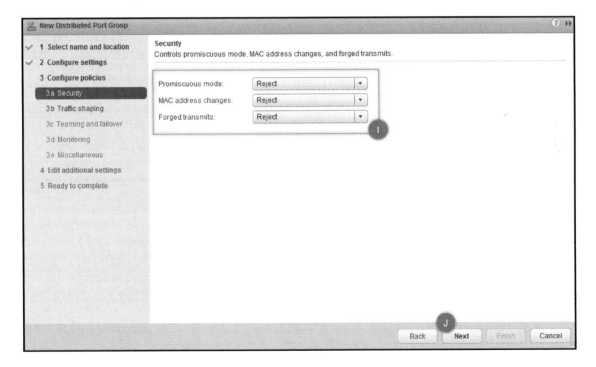

6. On the **Traffic shaping** screen, you can configure **Ingress** and **Egress** settings.

7. On **Teaming and failover** screen configure **Load balancing, Network failure detection, Notify switches,** and **Failback.**

8. On the **Monitoring** screen, you can choose to **Enabled** or **Disabled** the **Netflow** option:

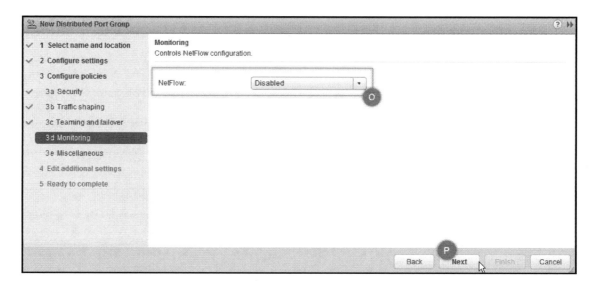

The use of Netflow requires additional configuration, which is covered in a later section of this chapter.

9. On the **Miscellaneous** screen, you have an option to disable all the ports on the dvPortGroup. It is, however, not an obvious practice to disable an entire port group so there is no change required on this screen. Click **Next** to continue.

10. On the **Edit additional settings** screen, you can override various port policies:

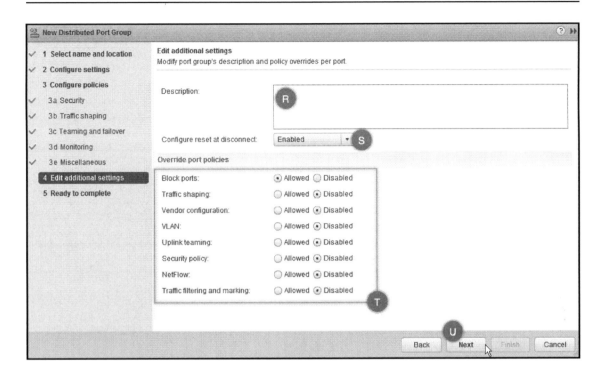

The **Configure Reset at disconnect** option (**Enabled** by default) will reset dvPort setting overrides to dvPort group settings after a virtual machine's vNIC is disconnected from a dvPort.

11. On the **Ready to complete** screen, review the settings and click **Finish** to create the dvPortGroup.

12. The **Networks | Distributed Port Groups** tab of the dvSwitch should list the newly created dvPortGroup:

# How it works...

Every dvPortGroup created will increase the network count by one and also increase the number of available ports on the dvSwitch. The increase in the number of available ports (referred to as the capacity of the dvSwitch) depends on the number of ports allocated to the dvPortGroup. The dvUplinks port group will also increase the network count by one. The following screenshot explains the summary of the new dvPortGroup created:

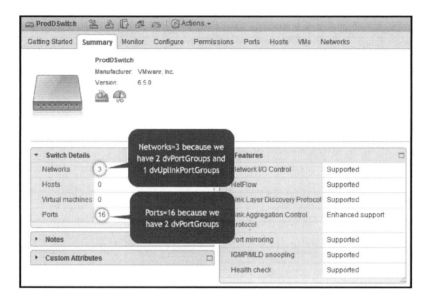

# Port binding

Port binding refers to the concept of associating a port of a dvSwitch (dvPort) to a virtual machine's NIC (vNIC).

There are different port binding methods available on a dvSwitch:

- Static binding
- Dynamic binding
- Ephemeral (no binding)

Static binding is the default method of port binding. vCenter assigns a dvPort to a virtual machine NIC when it is connected to the dvPortGroup for the first time. The assigned dvPort will remain reserved for the virtual machine until the virtual machine is removed from the port group. Temporarily disconnecting the vNIC will not remove the reservation. This type of binding has several advantages over the other types of binding methods because it retains the port statistics, which is essential if you want to monitor a virtual machine's traffic.

Dynamic binding is a method that will not be included in the future versions of vSphere. It is deprecated as of vSphere 5. The way it works is, when a virtual machine is powered on, a dvPort is dynamically allocated to a vNIC of the virtual machine that is connected to the dvPortGroup. The dvPort allocated in this manner will not be reserved. The moment the vNIC is disconnected, or if the virtual machine is vMotioned or powered off, the dvPort is unallocated and made available for any other virtual machine to procure.

Ephemeral binding, although categorized as a binding method, does no real binding. Ports are created and deleted on demand. A dvPort is created and allocated to a vNIC of a powered on virtual machine connected to the dvPortGroup. The dvPort is deleted if the vNIC is disconnected or if the VM is vMotioned or powered off. There is no reliance on vCenter for the port allocation.

# Port allocation

The port allocation method determines how the pool of available dvPorts on a dvPortGroup is managed. There are two types of port allocation method:

- Elastic
- Fixed

Elastic is the default port allocation method for a dvPortGroup. As with vSphere 5.5, an elastic dvPortGroup has eight dvPorts by default. However, if there is a need for more dvPorts, let's say you connected more than eight vNICs to the dvPortGroup, then the port allocation is expanded automatically by the number of ports needed. When the ports are no longer needed the port allocation is reduced, but no lower than what was configured on the dvPortGroup.

Fixed allocation will configure the set value for the number of ports as the limit to the dvPortGroup. For instance, if you set the allocation method to fixed and set the number of ports to five, then you will not be able to connect more than five vNICs to the dvPortGroup.

## Network resource pools

The network resource pool option available during the dvPortGroup creation wizard will allow you to select a user-defined network resource pool. If no user-defined resource pools are available, it will default to the system network resource pool Virtual Machine Traffic, although this is not explicitly indicated in the user interface.

# Managing physical adapter (vmnic) to dvUplink mappings

You can manage (add/change/remove) vmnic-to-dvUplink mappings using the Add Networking wizard. This is done on a per host basis, but you could use Add Networking wizard's template mode to push similar changes to multiple hosts if required.

Refer to step 12 of the Connecting hosts to a vSphere Distributed Switch recipe to learn how to push changes while in template mode.

## How to do it...

The following procedure will help you assign/remove vmnic-to-dvUplinks mappings on a dvSwitch:

1. Bring up the **Networking** inventory using the vSphere Web Client by using the key combination *Ctrl + Alt + 5*.
2. Right-click on the dvSwitch and select **Add and Manage Hosts...**:

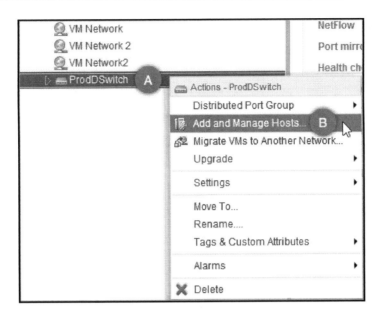

3. In the **Add and Manage Hosts** wizard, select the task **Manage host networking** and click **Next** to continue:

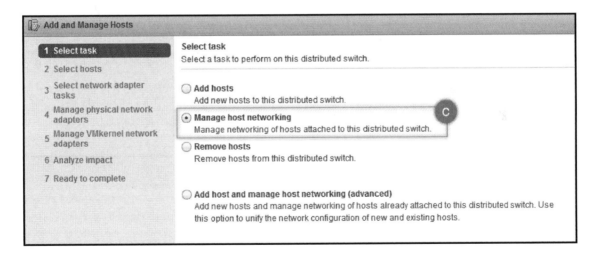

4. On the **Select hosts** screen, click on **Attached hosts...** to bring up the **Select member hosts** window:

5. On the **Select member hosts** window, select the ESXi host(s) to manage and click **OK** to confirm the selection and return to the **Select hosts** screen:

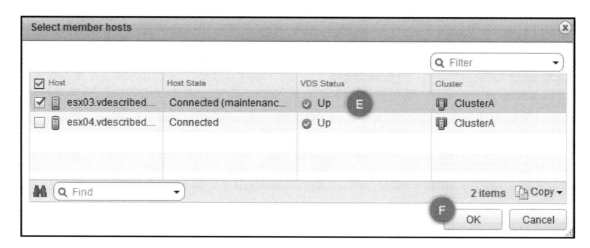

6. With the desired hosts selected, click **Next** on the **Select hosts** window:

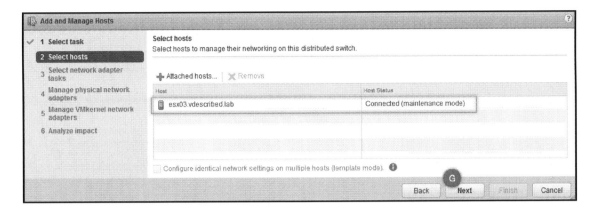

Template mode will be enabled only if you select more than one host to manage.

7. On the **Select network adapter tasks** screen, make sure only **Manage physical adapters** is selected:

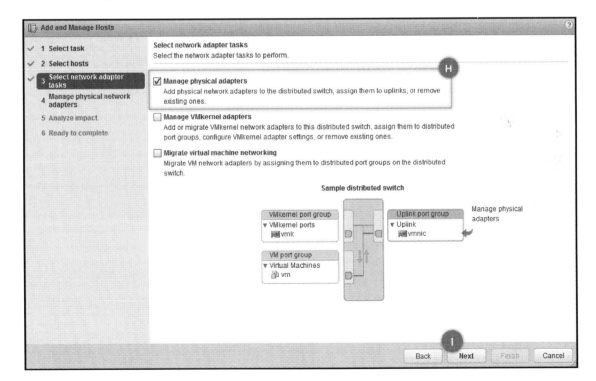

Deselecting **Manage VMkernel adapters** is not a requirement but is only done to focus on the intended activity.

8. On the **Manage physical network adapters** screen, you can select the physical adapter (vmnic) and choose to **Assign uplink** to a physical adapter or **Unassign adapter** from an uplink. Once done, click **Next** to continue:

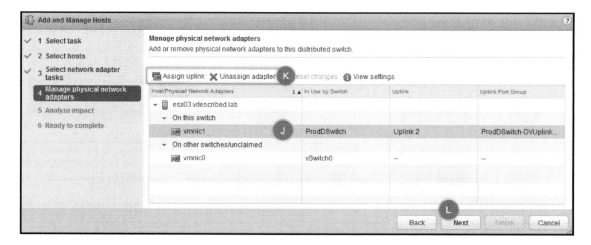

Assign uplink can also be used to change an existing vmnic-to-dvUplink mapping.

9. On the **Analyze impact** screen, review the impact. If it indicates **No impact**, then click **Next** to continue:

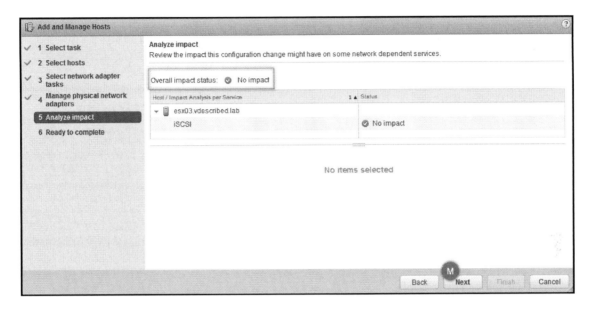

10. On the **Ready to complete** screen, review the settings and click **Finish** to make the changes:

# Migrating a virtual machine network from a vSphere Standard Switch (vSwitch ) to a vSphere Distributed Switch (dvSwitch)

Once you have laid the distributed switch foundation by creating dvSwitches, dvPortGroups, and by mapping physical adapters the next step is to migrate the virtual machines connected to a port group on a vSwitch to dvPortGroup on the dvSwitches.

## Getting ready

To ensure that the virtual machines do not lose network connectivity when they are migrated to the dvSwitch, verify that at least one or more physical adapters backing the virtual machine network have already been mapped to an uplink on the dvSwitch and is an active uplink on the destination dvPortGroup. The dvPortGroup should also be configured to use the same VLAN, MTU, and link aggregation (if any) settings.

Aspects such as cabling and VLAN trunking should be done correctly on the physical switches as well.

## How to do it...

The following procedure will help you migrate virtual machines that are currently connected to port groups on a vSphere Standard Switch to dvPortGroup on a vSphere Distributed Switch:

1. Bring up the **Networking** inventory using the vSphere Web Client by using the key combination *Ctrl + Alt + 5*.
2. Right-click on the desired dvSwitch and click on the menu item **Migrate VMs to Another Network...**:

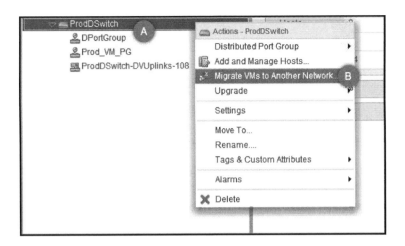

3. On the **Migrate VMs to Another Network** wizard screen, browse and select source and destination networks. Source network will be the virtual machine port group on a standard vSwitch, and the **Destination network** will be a dvPort group:

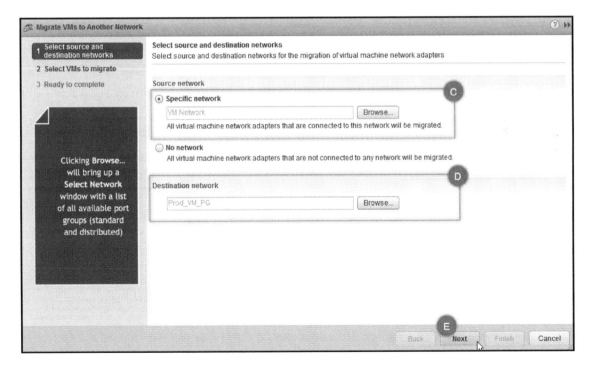

The wizard can be used to migrate virtual machines between two port groups regardless of their type (standard or distributed).

4. On the **Select VMs to migrate** screen, use the checkboxes to select the desired VMs and click **Next** to continue:

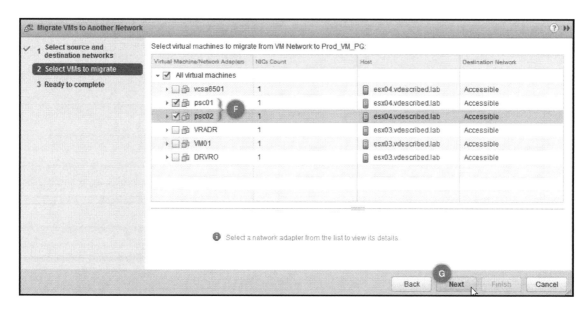

5. The **Ready to complete** screen will summarize the number of VMs and vNICs to migrate. If this matches with what you intended then click **Finish** to initiate the migration:

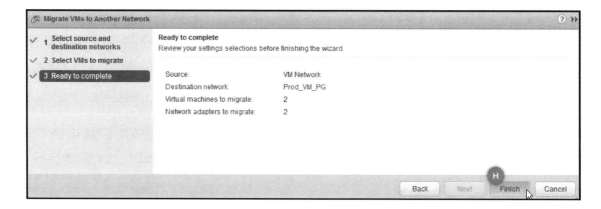

6. The **Recent Tasks** pane should list a **Reconfigure virtual machine** task for each of the VMs that are being migrated:

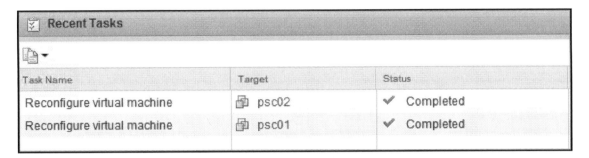

## How it works...

When you migrate a virtual machine network from a vSphere Standard Switch to a vSphere Distributed Switch, it changes the network label (port group) mapping for the selected vNICs to match the dvPortGroup's name. As long as the destination dvPortGroup has uplinks that support the virtual machine network traffic (for example, it is on the same VLAN), the network connectivity for the VMs will remain unaffected.

# Migrating VMkernel interfaces between vSphere Standard (vSwitch) and vSphere Distributed Switches (dvSwitch)

VMkernel interfaces can also be migrated from a vSwitch to dvSwitch. The process can be achieved using the Add and Manage Hosts wizard.

# Getting ready

Before you begin migrating the VMkernel interfaces from a vSwitch to dvSwitch, it is important to make sure you have a dvPortGroup configured with the necessary dvUplinks and ensure the other settings such as VLAN, MTU, and LACP (if required) are configured correctly:

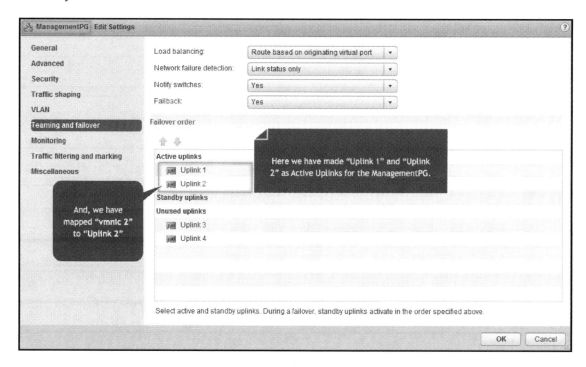

If you are to use the same vmnics currently mapped to the Standard vSwitch, then unmap one of those vmnics, assign a dvUplink to it, and mark it as the active uplink for the dvPortGroup configured for management interfaces.

# How to do it...

The following procedure will help you migrate VMkernel interfaces from a vSphere Standard Switch to a vSphere Distributed Switch:

1. Bring up the Networking inventory using the vSphere Web Client by using the key combination *Ctrl + Alt + 5*.

2. Right-click on the dvSwitch and select **Add and Manage Hosts...**:

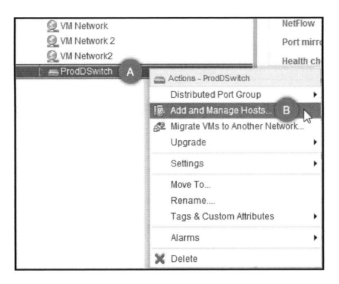

3. In the **Add and Manage Hosts** wizard, select the task **Manage host networking** and click **Next** to continue:

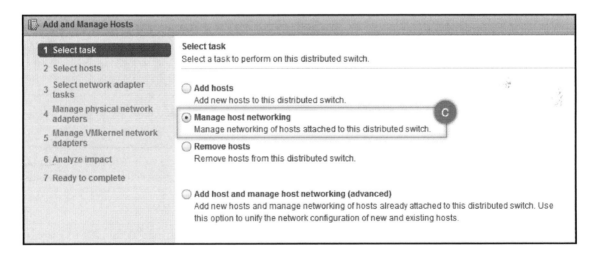

4. On the **Select hosts** screen, click on **Attached hosts...** to bring up the **Select member hosts** window:

5. On the **Select member hosts** window, select the ESXi host(s) to manage and click **OK** to confirm the selection and return to the **Select hosts** screen:

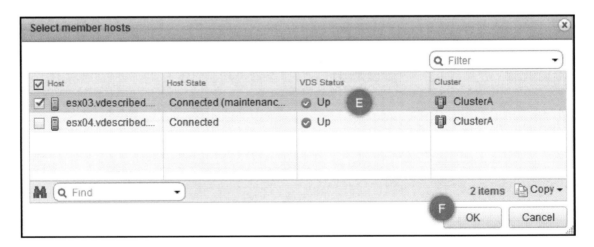

6. With the desired hosts selected, click **Next** on the **Select hosts** window:

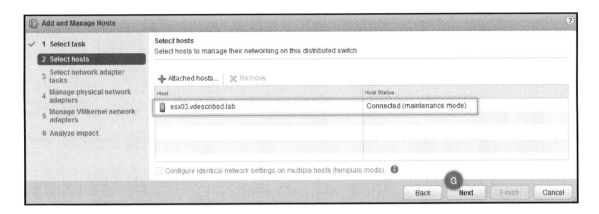

Template mode will be enabled only if you select more than one host to manage.

7. On the **Select network adapter tasks** screen, make sure that both **Manage physical adapters** and **Manage VMkernel adapters** are selected. Click **Next** to continue:

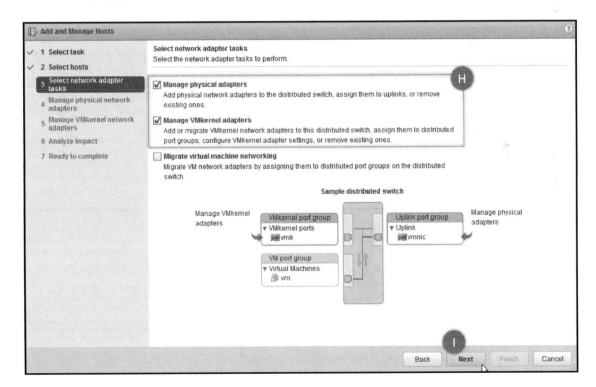

8. On **Manage physical network adapters** screen, verify/assign the correct physical adapter to a dvUplink that has been configured as an active uplink on the dvPortGroup created for the management of VMkernel interfaces. Once done, click **Next** to continue:

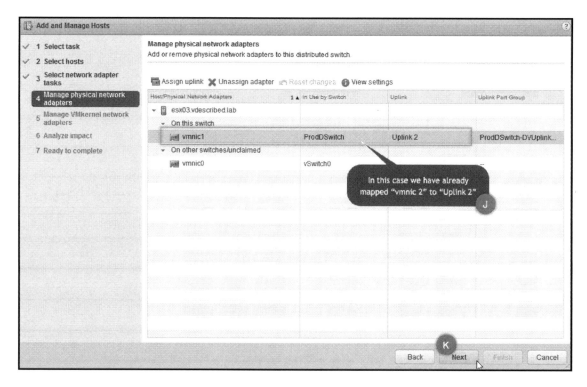

9. On the **Manage VMkernel network adapters** screen, select the VMkernel interface and click on **Assign port group**:

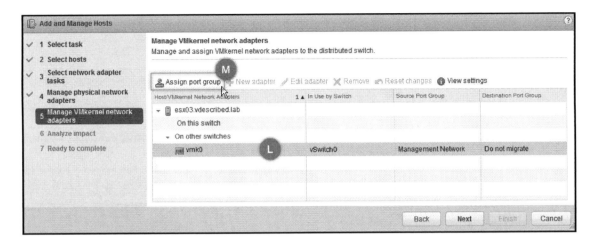

10. On the **Assign destination port group** window, select the dvPortGroup for the VMkernel interface and click **OK**:

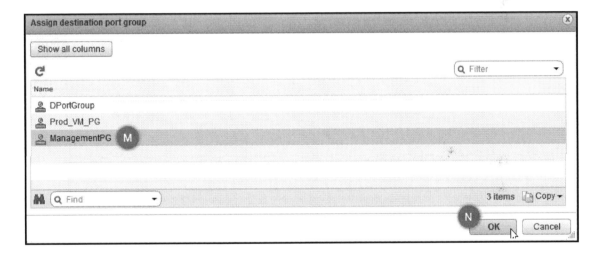

11. The **Manage VMkernel network adapters** screen will now list the destination port group. Click **Next** to continue:

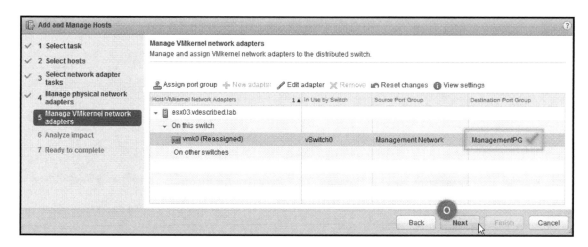

12. On the **Analyze impact** screen, review the impact. If it indicates **No impact**, then click **Next** to continue:

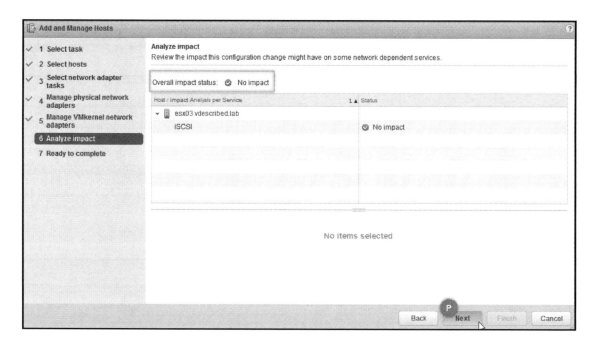

13. On the **Ready to complete** screen, review the settings and click **Finish** to migrate the VMkernel interfaces:

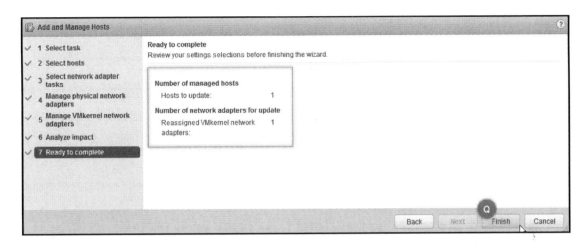

14. Switch to the **Hosts and Clusters** view using the key combination *Ctrl + Alt + 2*, select the ESXi host, and navigate to **Configure | VMkernel adapters** to view the migrated VMkernel interface:

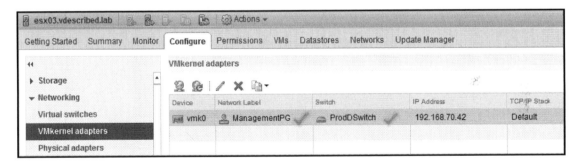

# How it works...

During the migration of the VMkernel interface, the communication over these resources will remain unaffected. However, if for any reason you end up migrating the management VMkernel interface to a dvPortGroup without the necessary configuration to support the traffic for the interfaces, then you will lose connectivity to the ESXi host. To recover from this, you will need to get to the console of the ESXi host via the host's IPMI console, such as the DRAC, ILO, or KVM and use the DCUI to restore the standard vSwitch or use the CLI to modify the configuration of the dvPortGroup.

More information on migrating a VMkernel interface used for the management network between standard vSwitches (VMware Knowledge Base article *2037654*) is available at: `http://kb.vmware.com/kb/2037654`.

# Creating additional VMkernel interfaces on a vSphere Distributed Switch (dvSwitch)

The default VMkernel management interface is not the only VMkernel interface that you will need in a vSphere environment. Features such as VMotion, iSCSI, NFS, and vSphere replication will also mandate the presence of a VMkernel interface. If these were already created on your vSphere Standard Switch, then they can be migrated using the instructions in the Migrating VMkernel interfaces between vSphere Standard Switch (vSwitch) and vSphere Distributed Switch (dvSwitch) recipe.

In this section, we will learn how to create these additional VMkernel interfaces on a dvSwitch.

# Getting ready

VMkernel interfaces are communication end points that VMkernel presents to the data center network. Hence these would require unique IP configuration:

- A dvPortGroup can house more than one VMkernel interface. However, it may not be a common practice to put all of them into the management port group. Your organization's infrastructure policy might require you to create a separate dvPortGroup for these interfaces. Perform what is required before you proceed with creating VMkernel interfaces. Also, not every uplink is configured to pass all traffic. It is important to make sure the correct uplinks are identified and made active. For example, it is possible that only a fixed number of VLANs are trunked to a port the uplink is cabled to. In this example, we have created a dvPortGroup called the StoragePG:

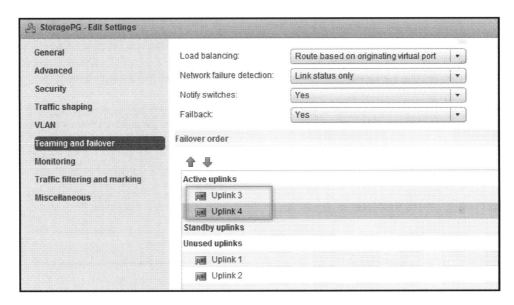

- You will need a VLAN type, VLAN ID, and the IP configuration for the VMkernel interface.

# How to do it...

The following procedure will help create new VMkernel interfaces on a dvSwitch:

1. Bring up the **Networking** inventory using the vSphere Web Client by using the key combination *Ctrl + Alt + 5*.

2. Right-click on the dvSwitch and select **Add and Manage Hosts…**:

3. In the **Add and Manage Hosts** wizard, select the task **Manage host networking** and click **Next** to continue:

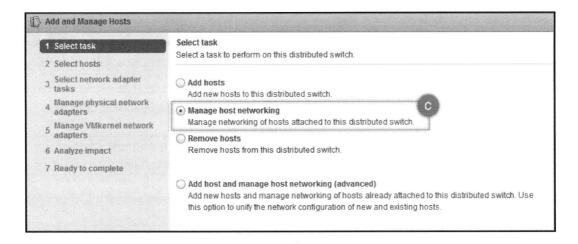

4. On the **Select hosts** screen, click on **Attached hosts...** to bring up the **Select member hosts** window:

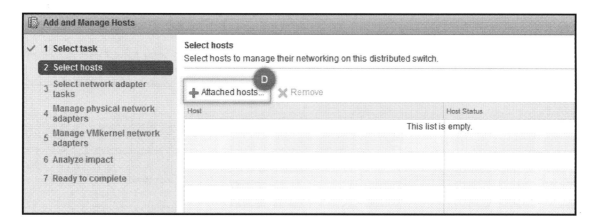

5. On the **Select member hosts** window, select the ESXi host(s) to manage, and click **OK** to confirm the selection and return to the **Select hosts** screen:

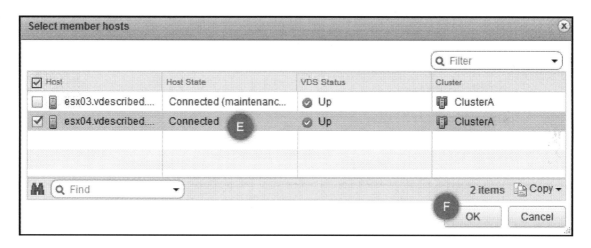

6. With the desired hosts selected, click **Next** in the **Select hosts** window:

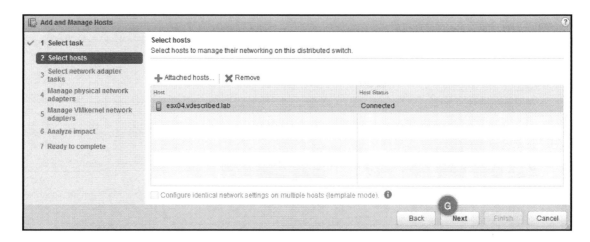

7. On the **Select network adapter tasks** screen, make sure that both **Manage physical adapters** and **Manage VMkernel adapters** are selected. Click **Next** to continue:

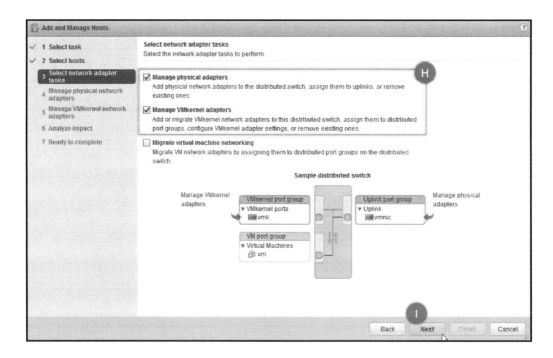

8. On the **Manage physical network adapters** screen, verify/assign the correct physical adapters to dvUplinks that have been configured as active uplinks on the dvPortGroup created for the VMkernel interface. Clicking on **Assign uplink** brings up a list of dvUplinks to choose from. Make the selection and click **OK** to return to the **Manage physical network adapters** screen. Once done, click **Next** to continue:

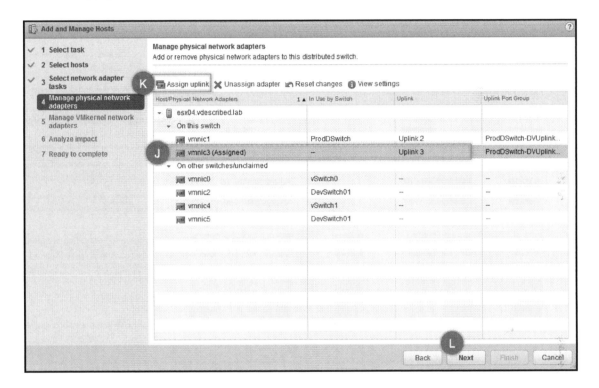

9. On the **Manage VMkernel network adapters** screen, select the ESXi host and click on **New** adapter:

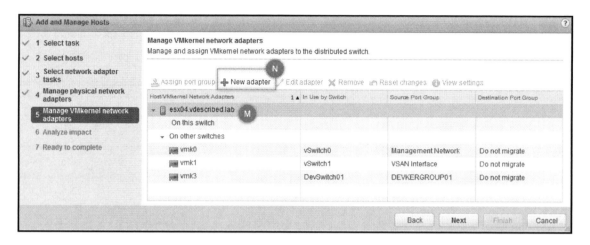

10. On the **Add Networking** wizard, browse and select the dvPortGroup pre-created for the VMkernel interface and click **Next** to continue:

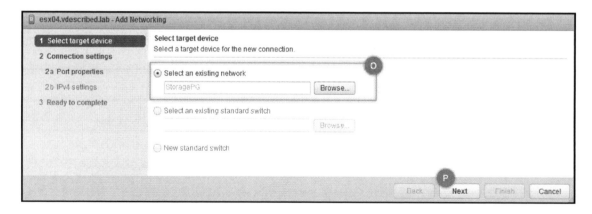

11. On the **Port properties** screen, enable a service (traffic type) for the VMkernel interface. In this case, we have selected **Virtual SAN**. Once you have made the desired selection click **Next** to continue:

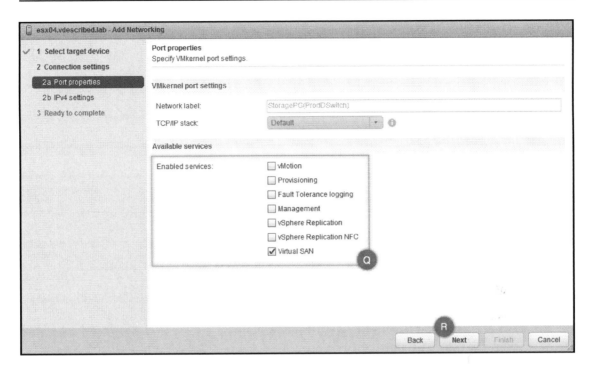

12. On the IPv4 settings screen, supply the IP configuration and click **Next** to continue:

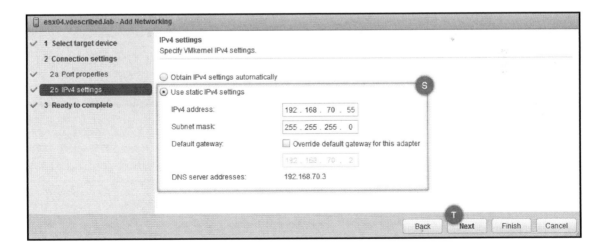

13. On the **Ready to complete** screen, review the settings and click **Finish** to create the interface:

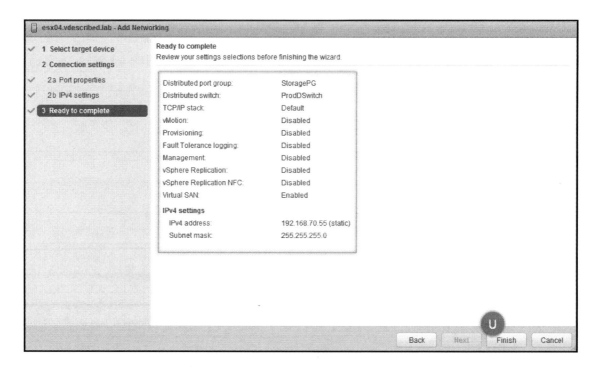

14. The **Manage VMkernel network adapters** screen should now list the newly created VMkernel (vmk) interface. Click **Next** to continue:

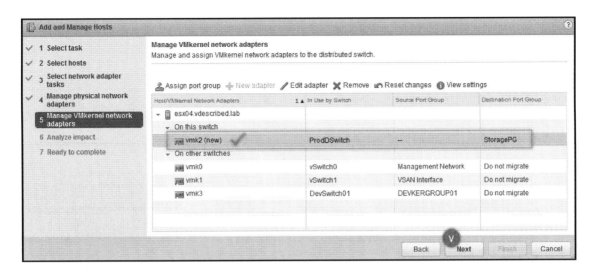

15. On the **Analyze impact** screen, review the impact. If it indicates **No impact**, then click **Next** to continue:

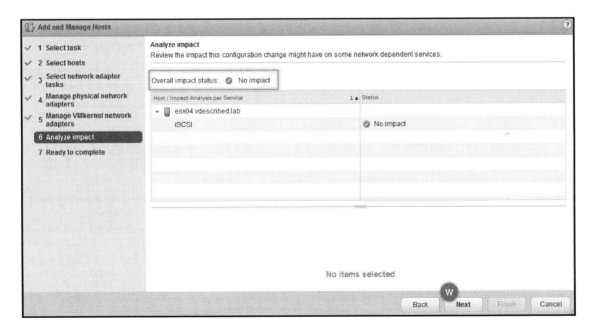

16. On the **Ready to complete** screen, review the settings and click **Finish**.

17. Switch to the **Hosts and Clusters** view using the key combination *Ctrl + Alt + 2*, select the ESXi host the VMkernel interface was created on, and navigate to **Configure | VMkernel adapters** to view the newly created interface:

18. To verify whether the VMkernel interface has been configured correctly, try pinging its gateway using the following command syntax:

```
vmkping -I <vmk adapter> <Gateway IP Address>
```

# Creating a vSphere Distributed Switch backup

It may become necessary to back up your dvSwitch configuration so that it can be restored when required. One of most common use cases is to back up (export) dvSwitch configuration before implementing a change. Backing up and restoring a dvSwitch is quick and easy and saves time that would otherwise be spent in the back up/restore of the vCenter or its database.

## How to do it...

The following procedure will help you back up/export the configuration of a dvSwitch:

1. Bring up the **Networking** inventory using the vSphere Web Client by using the key combination *Ctrl + Alt + 5*.

2. Right-click on the desired dvSwitch, go to **Settings**, and click on **Export Configuration...**:

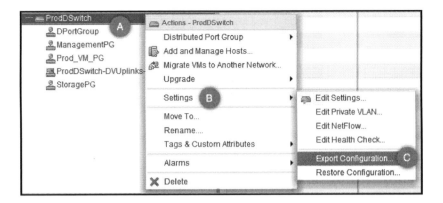

3. In the **Export Configuration** window, you are allowed to either export dvSwitch along with the port groups or just the dvSwitch. Choose the desired option, supply an optional description, and click **OK.**:

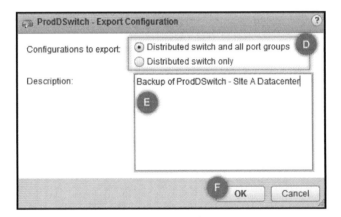

4. On the **Confirm Configuration Export** dialog, click **Yes** to confirm the action:

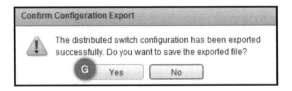

5. Choose a hard disk location on the client machine to save the backup file and click **Save**:

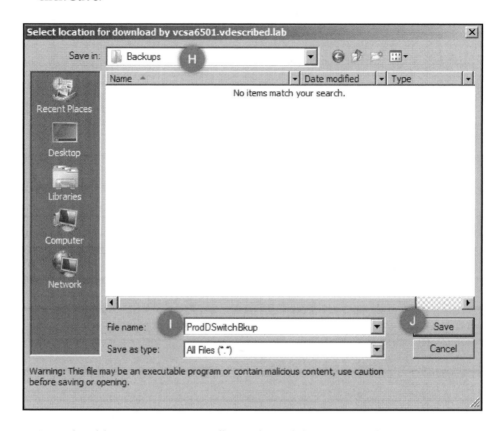

6. You should see an **Export configuration** of the entity task complete successfully in the **Recent Tasks** pane.

# How it works...

The backup taken is a snapshot of the current dvSwitch configuration. The ZIP archive created will contain the dvSwitch data in binary format. However, the ZIP archive does contain a data.xml file with dvSwitch metadata:

```
<?xml version="1.0" encoding="UTF-8" standalone="yes" ?>
<ns1:Envelope xmlns:ns1="http://vmware.com/vds/envelope/1">
  - <ns1:References>
      <ns1:File ns1:id="file0" ns1:href="data/50 0b 18 c0 ec 3c 42 ce-53 06 4d 04 2c ad 7a f5.bak" />
      <ns1:File ns1:id="file1" ns1:href="data/dvportgroup-123.bak" />
      <ns1:File ns1:id="file2" ns1:href="data/dvportgroup-122.bak" />
      <ns1:File ns1:id="file3" ns1:href="data/dvportgroup-109.bak" />
      <ns1:File ns1:id="file4" ns1:href="data/dvportgroup-110.bak" />
      <ns1:File ns1:id="file5" ns1:href="data/dvportgroup-121.bak" />
    </ns1:References>
  - <ns1:AnnotationSection>
      <ns1:Annotation>Backup of ProdDSwitch - Site A Datacenter</ns1:Annotation>
      <ns1:CreateTime>2017-05-06T17:41:08.825Z</ns1:CreateTime>
    </ns1:AnnotationSection>
  - <ns1:DistributedSwitchSection>
      <ns1:DistributedSwitch ns1:id="dvs-108" ns1:fileRef="file0" ns1:name="ProdDSwitch" ns1:uuid="50 0b 18 c0 ec 3c 42 ce 53 06 4d 04 2c ad 7a f5" ns1:configVersion="11"
        ns1:numberOfUplinks="4" ns1:numberOfResourcePools="0" ns1:version="6.5.0" />
    </ns1:DistributedSwitchSection>
  - <ns1:VlanSection>
      <ns1:VlanAccess ns1:id="access_0" ns1:vlan="0" />
    - <ns1:VlanTrunk ns1:id="trunk_0-4094_">
        <ns1:VlanTrunkRange ns1:start="0" ns1:end="4094" />
      </ns1:VlanTrunk>
    </ns1:VlanSection>
  - <ns1:DistributedPortGroupSection>
      <ns1:DistributedPortGroup ns1:id="dvportgroup-123" ns1:name="StoragePG" ns1:configVersion="1" ns1:fileRef="file1" ns1:type="standard" ns1:binding="static" ns1:allocation="elastic"
        ns1:vlanRef="access_0" />
      <ns1:DistributedPortGroup ns1:id="dvportgroup-122" ns1:name="ManagementPG" ns1:configVersion="2" ns1:fileRef="file2" ns1:type="standard" ns1:binding="static" ns1:allocation="elastic"
        ns1:vlanRef="access_0" />
      <ns1:DistributedPortGroup ns1:id="dvportgroup-109" ns1:name="ProdDSwitch-DVUplinks-108" ns1:configVersion="2" ns1:fileRef="file3" ns1:type="uplink" ns1:binding="static"
        ns1:allocation="fixed" ns1:vlanRef="trunk_0-4094_" />
      <ns1:DistributedPortGroup ns1:id="dvportgroup-110" ns1:name="DPortGroup" ns1:configVersion="0" ns1:fileRef="file4" ns1:type="standard" ns1:binding="static" ns1:allocation="elastic"
        ns1:vlanRef="access_0" />
      <ns1:DistributedPortGroup ns1:id="dvportgroup-121" ns1:name="Prod_VM_PG" ns1:configVersion="1" ns1:fileRef="file5" ns1:type="standard" ns1:binding="static" ns1:allocation="elastic"
        ns1:vlanRef="access_0" />
    </ns1:DistributedPortGroupSection>
</ns1:Envelope>
```

Contents of the
data.xml file

This backup ZIP archive can be used to restore the dvSwitch configuration or to create a dvSwitch in a new data center.

# Restoring dvSwitch from a backup

The fact that we can create a backup of a dvSwitch enables the ability to restore its configuration from a backup. The restore functionality is particularly useful when the changes made to a dvSwitch have yielded undesired results.

# How to do it...

The following procedure will help you restore dvSwitch from a backup:

1. Bring up the **Networking** inventory using the vSphere Web Client by using the key combination *Ctrl + Alt + 5*.

2. Right-click on the desired dvSwitch, go to **Settings**, and click on **Restore Configuration...**:

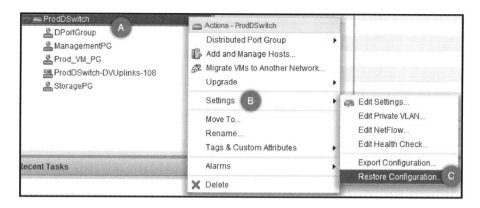

3. In the **Restore Configuration** window, browse and select the backup file to restore from and choose to either restore dvSwitch and its port group settings or just the port group. Once you have made the desired choice, click **Next** to continue:

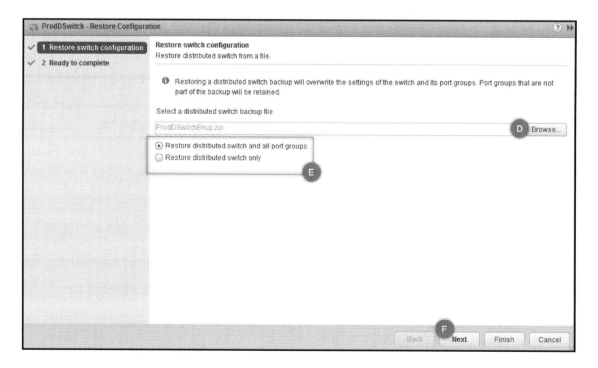

4. On the **Ready to complete** screen, review the **Import settings** and click **Finish** to perform the restore:

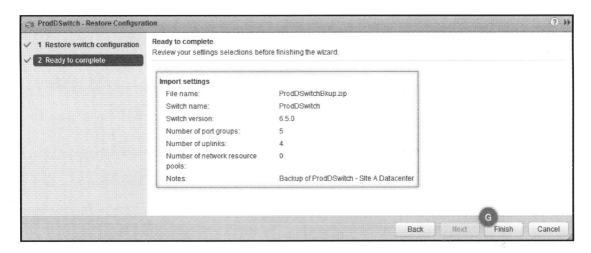

5. You should see an **Import configuration** of the entity task complete successfully in the **Recent Tasks** pane.

# Creating or importing a dvSwitch from a backup

It is possible to import a dvSwitch into a data center from a configuration backup. Unlike the restore operation, which can only be done on a dvSwitch, the import operation can be performed on a data center with or without existing Distributed Switches in them. This functionality comes in handy if you want to create a similar dvSwitch in a different data center.

Refer to the Creating vSphere Distributed Switch backup recipe to learn how to back up a dvSwitch.

# How to do it...

The following procedure will help you create or import a dvSwitch from a backup. It can be done from any of the inventory views listing the data centers:

1. Right-click on the desired data center, go to **Distributed Switch,** and click on **Import Distributed Switch...**:

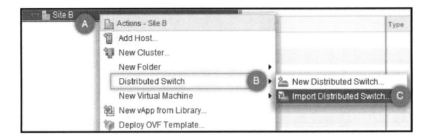

2. In the **Import Distributed Switch** wizard, select **Browse...** and select the backup (`.zip`) file and click **Next** to continue. You may choose to **Preserve original distributed switch and port group identifiers** if required:

 Read the *How it works...* section of this recipe to learn more about the preserve option.

3. On the Ready to complete screen, review the **Import settings** and click **Finish** to perform the import:

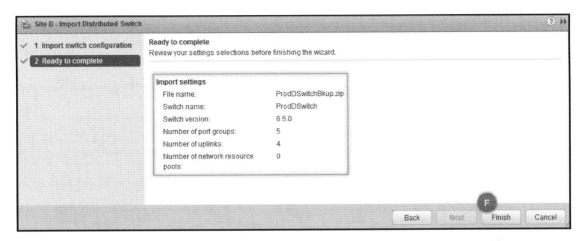

4. You should see an **Import configuration** of the entity task complete successfully in the **Recent Tasks** pane.

# How it works...

If we select the Preserve original distributed switch and port group identifiers option and the vCenter managing the data center that the dvSwitch is being imported to has a dvSwitch with the same name, then that dvSwitch or its port groups are not deleted. Instead, the information from the backup file is merged and updated with the existing dvSwitch.

If we do not select the Preserve original distributed switch and port group identifiers option and the vCenter managing the data center that the dvSwitch is being imported into has a dvSwitch with the same name, then that dvSwitch or its port groups are not deleted, but a new dvSwitch with the configuration from the backup file is created. For example, if the data center had a dvSwitch with the name ProdDSwitch, then the new dvSwitch will be called ProdDSwitch (1).

# Configuring security, traffic shaping, teaming, and failover on a dvSwitch

As discussed in the previous chapter, the security, traffic shaping, teaming, and failover mechanisms function identically on both types of switches—standard or distributed. However, the Distributed Switch offers enhancements to traffic shaping and teaming methods. In this recipe, we will learn to configure all these settings on a dvSwitch. We will also learn how these settings impact network traffic.

## Getting ready

Before you decide on the required setting, it is essential to understand how they work. Hence, I would recommend reading the How it works... section of this recipe before you start to configure them. Also, keep in mind that these settings cannot be configured directly on a dvSwitch, it can only be done on a dvPortGroup or a dvPort.

## How to do it...

The following procedure will help you configure the security, traffic shaping, teaming, and failover on a vSphere Distributed Switch:

1. Bring up the **Networking** inventory using the vSphere Web Client by using the key combination *Ctrl + Alt + 5*.
2. Right-click on the desired dvPortGroup and click on **Edit Settings...**:

3. In the **Edit Settings** window:

    1. Use the **Security** screen to accept or reject **Promiscuous mode, MAC address changes**, and **Forged transmits**:

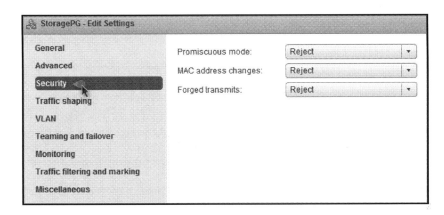

    2. Use the **Traffic shaping** screen to configure ingress and egress traffic shaping settings:

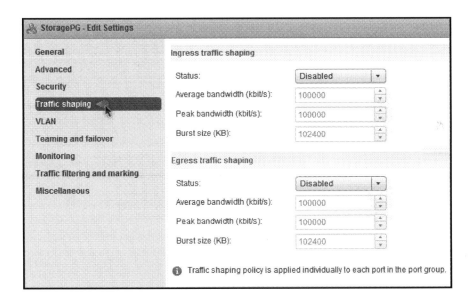

3. Use the **Teaming and failover** screen to configure **Load balancing** policies, **Network failure detection** method, enable or disable **Notify switches**, choose a **Failback** method, and configure the failover order:

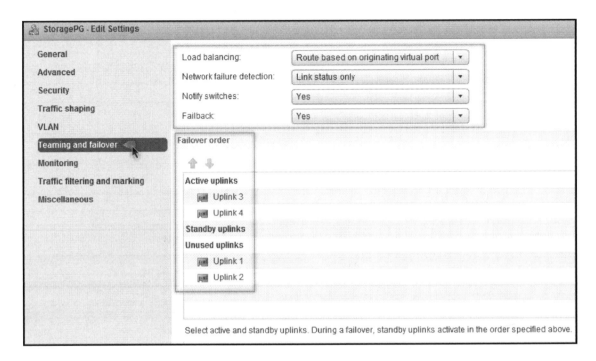

4. Once the desired settings have been configured, click **OK** to apply the changes and to close the **Edit Settings** window.

# How it works...

Before we delve deeper into each of the settings, let's compare and contrast them for both vSphere Standard and Distributed Switches:

| Category | vSwitch | dvSwitch |
|---|---|---|
| **Security** | • Promiscuous mode <br> • MAC address changes <br> • Forged transmits | • Promiscuous mode <br> • MAC address changes <br> • Forged transmits |
| **Traffic shaping** | • Outbound (egress) traffic only <br> • Average bandwidth <br> • Burst size <br> • Peak bandwidth | • Both inbound (ingress) and outbound (egress) traffic <br> • Average bandwidth <br> • Burst size <br> • Peak bandwidth |
| **Teaming and failover** | • Load balancing <br> • Route based on originating virtual port <br> • Route based on IP hash <br> • Route based on source MAC hash <br> • Use explicit failover order <br> • Failover detection <br> • Failover order | • Load balancing <br> • Route based on originating virtual port <br> • Route based on IP hash <br> • Route based on source MAC hash <br> • Route based on physical NIC load <br> • Use explicit failover order <br> • Failover detection <br> • Failover order |

# Security

The security policies behave the same on both switch types. The vSphere Distributed Switch allows for an additional level of granularity by making the same settings configurable at the dvPort level. For this to work, the dvPortGroup should be configured to allow dvPort level policy overrides. With a vSphere Standard Switch, security settings can only be applied at the port group level.

There are three security settings that can be either set to Accept/Reject:

- Promiscuous mode
- MAC address changes
- Forged transmits

All three settings are set to Reject by default and we will learn why.

## Promiscuous mode

Promiscuous mode, if configured to Accept on a port group, will allow all the virtual machine vNICs connected to that port group to see all the traffic on the vSwitch or dvSwitch. Since this is not an advisable configuration, it is set to Reject by default. When set to Reject, the vNICs can only see traffic destined to their MAC address. This mode is usually enabled on a port group with one or more network monitoring VMs, so that they can analyze the traffic on the vSwitch or dvSwitch. Such VMs are configured in a separate port group that sees traffic from a particular subnet it needs to monitor. By doing so, you are enabling promiscuousness on only those network monitoring VMs.

With a dvSwitch, the need for a separated port group can be avoided by overriding the dvPortGroup settings at the dvPort to which the analyzer VM's vNIC is connected.

## MAC address changes and forged transmits

Every virtual machine has two MAC addresses by definition. The MAC address that is assigned to the vNIC of a virtual machine when the vNIC gets created is called the initial MAC address. The MAC address that a guest operating system configures for the network interface it detects is called the effective MAC address. The effective MAC address should generally match the initial MAC address (which is actual MAC on NIC):

- MAC address changes apply to the traffic entering a virtual machine from the virtual switch. If MAC address changes are set to Accept, then it means that you allow the virtual machine to receive traffic originally intended for another VM, by impersonating the other VM's MAC address. For example, if VM-A wanted to receive traffic intended for VM-B, then VM-A will need to present itself with a MAC address belonging to VM-B. This is usually achieved by changing the effective MAC address (OS level). Such a VM's initial MAC address will remain unchanged. With MAC address changes set to Accept, the virtual switch will allow the effective MAC address to be different from the initial MAC address. With MAC address changes set to Reject, the port/dvPort to which the vNIC is connected will be blocked, consequently the VM will stop receiving any traffic.
- The Forged transmits setting applies to the traffic leaving a virtual machine and entering a virtual switch. If set to Accept, it allows source MAC address spoofing, meaning, a virtual machine will be allowed to send out frames with a source MAC address that is different from the initial/effective MAC address. With the option set to Reject, the virtual switch will drop the frame with a MAC address that does not match the initial/effective MAC address.

Both **MAC address changes** and **Forged transmits** are set to **Reject** by default.

# Traffic shaping

Both virtual switches (vSwitch or dvSwitch) include a traffic shaper that enables control of network transfer rates. The only difference is that the traffic shaper on the vSphere Standard Switch can only handle the egress traffic, but the vSphere Distributed Switch can handle both ingress and egress.

Anything that leaves a virtual switch (standard or dvSwitch) is egress, and anything that enters a virtual switch (vSwitch or dvSwitch) is ingress. The ingress source can either be a vNIC or a VMK interface.

VMware cannot control what happens beyond the host's physical network adapter boundaries. Hence, the traffic flow that the traffic shaper can control is the flow (ingress/egress) between the virtual machines/VMkernel interfaces and the virtual switch:

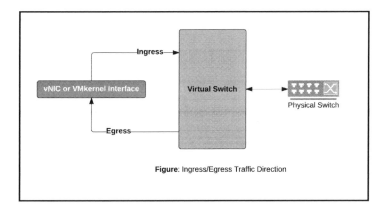

**Figure**: Ingress/Egress Traffic Direction

The traffic shaper does its job by controlling three parameters that affect any network traffic:

- Average bandwidth
- Peak bandwidth
- Burst size

Now, let us go through each of the preceding points:

- The average bandwidth is the average transfer rate at which the virtual switch can send traffic. It is measured in kilobits per second (kbps). The value is normalized over time.
- The peak bandwidth is the maximum transfer rate that the virtual switch is allowed to perform at. It is measured in kbps. This limit cannot be breached.

- Burst size is a tricky concept to understand. Although specified in kilobytes (KB), it is actually the effective amount of time (measured in seconds) that the virtual switch is allowed to perform at the maximum transfer rate.
- The effective amount of burst time is calculated using the following formula:

*Effective burst time = (Burst size in kilobits)/(Peak bandwidth value in kbps)*

- Let's take an example so as to better understand how the effective burst time is arrived at. If you were to set the peak bandwidth value to 4,000 kbps, the average bandwidth to 2,000 kbps, and the burst size to 2,000 KB then you are allowing the virtual switch to perform at the maximum transfer rate of 4,000 kbps lasting no more than 4 seconds in time.
- Here is how the value is arrived at:
    - Burst size in KB to be converted to kbits by multiplying the value by 8. In this case, it is *2,000 KB * 8 = 16,000 kbits.*
    - Now, by applying the formula *16,000 kbits/4,000 kbps = 4 seconds.*

# Teaming and failover

Virtual machine workloads share not only the compute and storage resources on an ESXi server, but the physical network interfaces as well. There are physical limits on how well these network interfaces can serve the bandwidth needs of the virtual machines using them. More importantly, not every virtual machine has the same network workload characteristics. Hence, it becomes extremely critical for the virtual switches to have network load distribution, load balancing, and failover capabilities.

Let's begin by comparing the teaming and failover capabilities of both the switch types:

| Teaming methods | vSwitch | dvSwitch |
|---|---|---|
| Route based on originating virtual port ID | Yes | Yes |
| Route based on source MAC hash | Yes | Yes |
| Route based on IP hash | Yes | Yes |
| Load based teaming | No | Yes |

| Failover methods | vSwitch | dvSwitch |
|---|---|---|
| Use Explicit failover order | Yes | Yes |

**Route based on the originating virtual port**, With this mechanism, every virtual port to which a vNIC connects is associated with an uplink (vmnic) in a round-robin fashion. This means that, if there were only two physical uplinks—vmnic-A/dvUplink-A and vmnic-B/dvuplink-B, and four virtual ports—Port1, Port2, Port3, and Port4, then Port1, and Port3 will be associated with vmnic-A/dvUplink-A and Port2, and Port4 will be associated with vmnic-B/dvUplink-B:

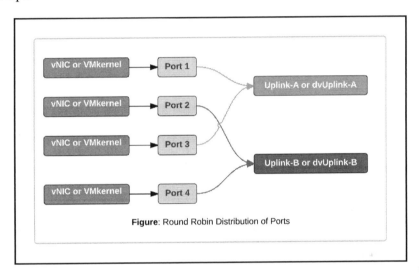

**Figure**: Round Robin Distribution of Ports

Once associated, the uplinks will be used for traffic unless there is an uplink failure, a VMotion, or a power-cycle of the VM. This is the default load balancing mechanism chosen for both vSwitch and dvSwitch:

- **Route based on source MAC Hash**: This is a deprecated method of load balancing. An uplink is chosen based on the source MAC address of the frames that enter the virtual switch.

- **Route based on IP Hash**: This method uses the combined hash value of the source and destination IP addresses to choose an uplink. The physical NICs must be in the same link aggregation group. If the physical NICs are cabled to different switches then those switches should be stacked. The route based on the IP hash is particularly useful if there are multiple source and destination IP addresses to calculate hashes from. For instance, if you have a web server virtual machine with clients from a different subnet then such a combination is an ideal candidate for the route based on the IP hash algorithm.
- **Load Based Teaming (LBT)**: This load balancing mechanism is only available on a dvSwitch. Unlike the other methods, this offers true load balancing. The other methods only offer the distribution of the physical adapter assignments based on their algorithms. With LBT, the initial assignment is done in a round-robin fashion, but from then on, the physical adapters are monitored for load saturation. If any of the physical adapters hit a saturation threshold of 75% that persists for over 30 seconds, then some of the traffic is relocated to another unsaturated physical adapter.
- **Use explicit failover**: This is not a load balancing or distribution method; instead, it uses a pre-defined failover order to use the active, available physical adapters in the event of a failure. When you set load balancing to use explicit failover order, all the traffic is traversed through a single physical adapter at any point in time. If there is more than one active physical adapter, then it will choose the adapter that has been up and active for the longest time. For instance, if vmnic1, vmnic2, and vmnic3 are the three active uplinks, and have an uptime of 48 hours, 32 hours, and 5 minutes respectively, then vmnic1 with 48 hours of uptime is chosen. The logic behind such a choice is to select the most stable among the available adapters.

## Network failure detection

This is used to determine the liveliness of a physical uplink. There are two mechanisms that are used for this, and they are link status only and beacon probing. Link status only is used to determine the connectivity status of the physical uplink, which could have encountered a NIC failure, a cable disconnect, and so on. Beacon probing is used to determine the following:

- **Link status only**: This is used to determine the connectivity status of the physical uplink, which could encounter a NIC failure, a cable disconnect, and so on.
- **Beacon probing**: This is used to determine upstream failure. For more information on beacon probing, read the VMware KB article *1005577* at: https://kb.vmware.com/s/article/1005577.

# Notify switches

Layer-2 physical switches have the ability to maintain a MAC address table, lookup table, or CAM table. The table maps MAC addresses to switch port numbers. If there is no corresponding entry for a frame's destination MAC address in the lookup table, the switch will flood the frame via every switch port, other than the source port. To reduce the occurrence of such flooding, the switch has a mechanism to learn the MAC addresses and maintain a mapping table. It does so by reading the source MAC address information from the frames that enter the switch. Now, when you cable the physical NICs of an ESXi host to the physical switch ports, the switch is expected to see the MAC addresses of a number of vNICs. The switch will only be able to add an entry into the lookup table if the VMs start to communicate. VMware ESXi, however, can proactively notify the physical switch of the virtual machine's MAC addresses so that its lookup table is up to date even before a VM begins to communicate. It achieves this by sending a gratuitous ARP (seen as a RARP frame by the switch) with vNIC's effective address as the source MAC of the RARP frame. The RARP will have the destination MAC address set to the broadcast address—FF:FF:FF:FF:FF:FF.

ESXi will send out an RARP under the following circumstances:

- **When a virtual machine is powered-on**: The vNIC on the VM has to be bound to a physical NIC. The NIC chosen would depend on the load balancing policy used. To learn more about the load balancing policies, read the load balancing and failover section. When vSwitch assigns a physical NIC to a vNIC, ESXi will need to send an RARP frame to enable the switch to update its lookup table with a new physical port number mapping for the vNIC's MAC address. This is necessary because every time a virtual machine is powered-on, it is not guaranteed the same vNIC to PNIC mapping.
- **When a virtual machine is migrated from one host to another**: The vNICs of the corresponding VM will now be mapped to a physical NIC of the destination host. Hence, it becomes a proactive necessity to let the physical switch update its lookup table with a new port number for the vNIC's MAC address.
- **When a physical NIC fails over**: The vNIC will be re-distributed among the available active adapters. Again, it becomes necessary for the physical switch to be notified of the new port numbers for the vNIC MAC addresses.
- **LBT automatically rebinds the vNICs to different PNICs**: Based on the physical NIC load saturation levels. Since the vNIC to PNIC assignment is bound to change, the physical switch will need to be notified of the new port numbers of the vNIC MAC addresses.

### Failback

Setting **Failback** to **Yes** (default) will let a recovered uplink resume its active role. In other words, a failed active uplink, when returned to normalcy, will be redesignated as the active uplink. The impact of this configuration is dependent on the Failover Order configured.

### Failover order

Uplinks to a virtual switch (vSwitch or dvSwitch) can be teamed up to control their participation in a failover configuration, by designating them as active, standby, or unused uplinks. This is done to provide for failover, performance, and redundancy:

- Active adapters are available for use in any configuration and will carry traffic
- Standby adapters act as the backup to active adapters and will be made active only if any of the active adapters fail
- Unused adapters cannot be used in any configuration of the virtual switch construct (vSwitch, standard port group, dvPortGroup, or dvPort)

# Configuring VLANs on a vSphere Standard or Distributed Switch

VLANs or Virtual LANs are a method to further divide your physical network subnet into unique broadcast domains. It is not uncommon in a modern day IT infrastructure to host your business workload on different VLANs. Both the Standard and Distributed Virtual Switches support the use of VLANs. However, they cannot be configured directly on the switches, but only on port groups, dvPortGroup, or dvPorts.

# Getting ready

Before you learn how to configure VLANs on a Standard or Distributed Switch it is important to know that there are four supported types:

- **External Switch Tagging (EST)**: Requires no VLAN ID to be configured on the port group (Standard or Distributed).
- **Virtual Switch Tagging (VST)**: Requires setting a VLAN ID on the port group (Standard or Distributed) or dvPort.

- **Virtual Guest Tagging (VGT)**: Requires setting a VLAN ID of 4095 on a vSphere Standard Switch. A dvSwitch allows you to specify a VLAN ID or a range of VLAN IDs to be trunked by the dvSwitch.
- **Private VLANs**: Requires configuration of Private VLANs on the dvSwitch. Read the Configuring private VLANs on a dvSwitch recipe.

# How to do it...

The following procedure will help you configure a VLAN on a Standard or Distributed Switch:

1. To be able to configure VLAN on a vSphere Standard Switch, open the **Edit Settings** of the desired standard port group on a Standard vSwitch and specify a VLAN ID:
   - **None (0)**: For external switch tagging:

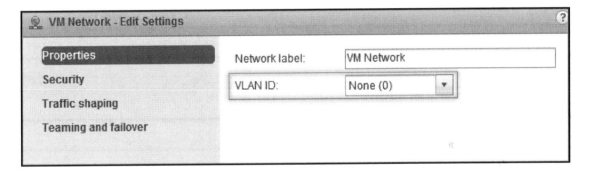

   - **VLAN number**: For virtual switch tagging
   - 4095: For virtual guest tagging

2. To be able to configure VLAN on a vSphere Distributed Switch, switch to **Edit Settings** of the desired dvPortGroup and go to the VLAN screen to choose a **VLAN type**:

- **None**: For external switch tagging:

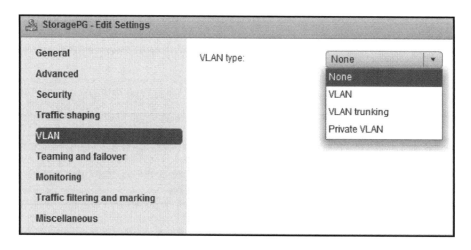

- **VLAN**: For virtual switch tagging
- **VLAN trunking**: For Virtual guest tagging
- **Private VLAN**: For using a Private VLAN type

# How it works...

We learned where and how to configure the VLAN settings on both Standard and Distributed Switches. Now, lets review the VLAN types in detail.

## External switch tagging

The physical switch, to which the ESXi host physical NICs are cabled will do the tagging/untagging of the layer-2 frames. The physical switch port will need to be configured as an access port for this to work. One of the major drawbacks to this type of implementation is that the entire vSwitch (all the port groups on it) will only handle traffic from a single layer-2 subnet:

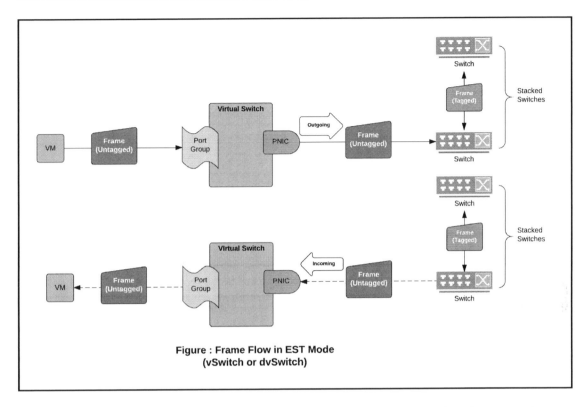

**Figure : Frame Flow in EST Mode**
**(vSwitch or dvSwitch)**

In EST mode, when a virtual machine's layer-2 frame enters the vSwitch, it hits an active uplink, which then carries the frame onto the physical switch. The physical switch's access port will then assign a VLAN ID to it and handle the traffic switching. When a frame tries to flow back into the vSwitch, the access port will untag the frame and send the traffic into the vSwitch, then back to the virtual machine's vNIC.

# Virtual Switch Tagging

With **Virtual Switch Tagging (VST)**, Ethernet layer-2 frames are tagged at the virtual switch layer. For this implementation to work, the physical NIC carrying the traffic should be connected to a physical switch port, which is configured to trunk the necessary VLANs. The virtual machine or VMkernel port groups created on the vSwitch will then need to be configured with the VLAN IDs of their respective subnets.

This is the most common and favored implementation in most large/medium/small environments, not just because of the flexibility it offers but also because of the fact that most modern day blade system environments have reduced the number of physical NIC ports on the server hardware, owing to the advent of 10 Gbps Ethernet:

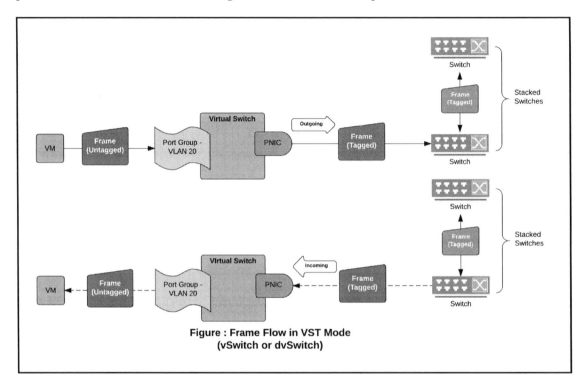

**Figure : Frame Flow in VST Mode**
**(vSwitch or dvSwitch)**

In VST mode, when a frame from a virtual machine enters a virtual switch, it is assigned a VLAN number. The VLAN number should already be configured on the port group the virtual machine is connected to. The VLAN tag will then be carried over from the active physical NIC to the trunk port on the physical switch. When a frame enters a virtual switch from the physical switch, it will untag the frame and then switch the frame to the virtual machine.

# Virtual Guest Tagging (VGT)

With VGT, it becomes the guest operating system's responsibility to assign VLAN tags to its outbound traffic. The port group to which such a virtual machine is connected should be configured with VLANID 4095 (meaning to trunk):

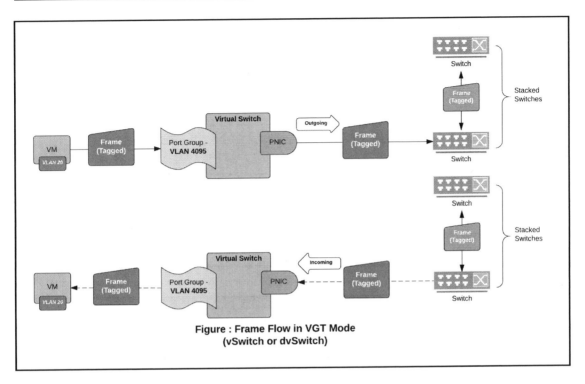

**Figure : Frame Flow in VGT Mode
(vSwitch or dvSwitch)**

In VGT mode, the VLAN-tagged traffic will flow unmodified through the virtual switch and to the physical switch. The guest operating system is solely responsible for tagging and untagging on the frames.

# Configuring private VLANs on a dvSwitch

VLANs provide logical segmentation of a network into different broadcast domains. Private VLANs (PVLANs) provide a method to further segment a VLAN into different private groups. We can add and configure PVLANs on a vSphere Distributed Switch. For private VLANs to work, the physical switches backing your environment should be PVLAN-aware.

# Getting ready

Private VLANs should be configured on the physical switches for the configuration to work. Contact your network administrator for the primary, community, and isolated VLAN numbers. Here is an example of how it is configured on a physical switch. So we will configure a primary VLAN 25, a secondary VLAN 100 in community mode, and another secondary VLAN 50 in isolated mode:

```
vdescribed-labSW1(config)#vtp mode transparent
Device mode already VTP TRANSPARENT
vdescribed-labSW1(config-vlan)#vlan 25
vdescribed-labSW1(config-vlan)#private-vlan primary
vdescribed-labSW1(config-vlan)#private-vlan association 100,50
vdescribed-labSW1(config-vlan)#
vdescribed-labSW1(config-vlan)#
vdescribed-labSW1(config-vlan)#vlan 100
vdescribed-labSW1(config-vlan)#private-vlan community
vdescribed-labSW1(config-vlan)#
vdescribed-labSW1(config-vlan)#vlan 50
vdescribed-labSW1(config-vlan)#private-vlan isolated
vdescribed-labSW1(config-vlan)#
vdescribed-labSW1(config-vlan)#
vdescribed-labSW1(config-vlan)#int fa 0/1
vdescribed-labSW1(config-if)#switchport mode private-vlan promiscuous
vdescribed-labSW1(config-if)#switchport private-vlan mapping 25 100,50
vdescribed-labSW1(config-if)#
vdescribed-labSW1(config-if)#
vdescribed-labSW1(config-if)#int fa0/4
vdescribed-labSW1(config-if)#switchport mode private-vlan host
vdescribed-labSW1(config-if)#switchport private-vlan mapping 25 100
vdescribed-labSW1(config-if)#
vdescribed-labSW1(config-if)#
vdescribed-labSW1(config-if)#int fa0/6
vdescribed-labSW1(config-if)#switchport mode private-vlan host
vdescribed-labSW1(config-if)#switchport private-vlan mapping 25 50
vdescribed-labSW1c(config-if)#
```

> **VLAN 25** being configured as Primary. **100** and **50** being associated as Secondary VLANs

> **VLAN 100** being configured as **Community** and **VLAN 50** as **Isolated**

> **Port 0/1** - Promiscuous ; Mapped Primary and Secondary VLANs to the port

> **Port 0/4** - host mode ; Mapped Secondary VLAN 100 to the port

> **Port 0/6** - host mode ; Mapped Secondary VLAN 50 to the port

# How to do it...

The following procedure will help you configure private VLANs on a vSphere Distributed Switch:

1. Bring up the **Networking** inventory using the vSphere Web Client by using the key combination *Ctrl + Alt + 5*.

2. Right-click on the desired dvSwitch and navigate to **Settings** | **Edit Private VLAN...**:

3. In the **Edit Private VLAN Settings** window, click **Add** under the **Primary VLAN ID** section to add a primary VLAN ID. Click **Add** under the **Secondary VLAN ID** section to add secondary VLANs of the **Community** or **Isolated** type. Once done click **OK** to confirm the settings:

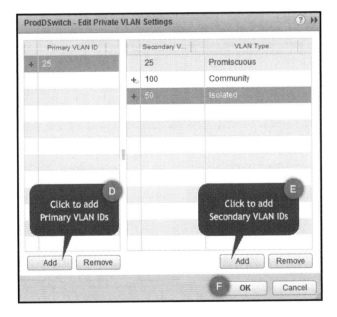

4. Private VLANs, once configured, can be used with port groups. The port groups can be configured to use any of the secondary PVLANs created. This is done in the **Edit Settings** window for a port group. The VLAN section will allow you to set VLAN type to Private VLAN ID, and let you choose the secondary PVLAN IDs:

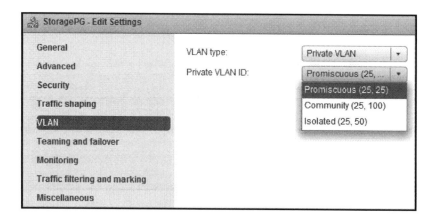

# How it works...

Now that we have learned how to configure them, let's try and understand how they work. Private VLANs are not a VMware concept, but a switching concept that is in use in various environments. For private VLANs to work, you will need to create the primary and secondary VLANs on the physical switch and associate them.

A primary VLAN is a VLAN that is configured as a primary private VLAN on the physical switch interface in promiscuous mode.

Secondary VLANs are VLANs that are associated to a primary VLAN. There are three types of secondary private VLANs:

- **Promiscuous PVLAN**: VMs in a promiscuous PVLAN can communicate with any VM belonging to any of its secondary PVLANs. The promiscuous PVLAN will act as a gateway for other secondary PVLANs.
- **Community PVLAN**: VMs in a community PVLAN can only talk among VMs in the same community PVLAN or the promiscuous PVLAN. It cannot communicate with VMs in any other secondary PVLAN.

- **Isolated PVLAN**: VMs in an isolated PVLAN are isolated from every other VM in the same isolated PVLAN. It can only communicate with the VMs in a promiscuous PVLAN. There can only be a single isolated PVLAN per primary PVLAN:

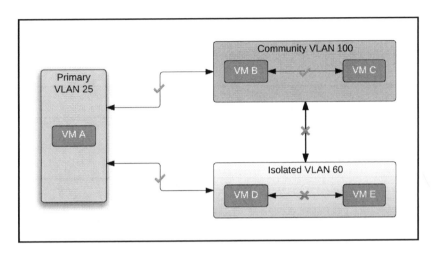

# Configuring LAGs on a vSphere Distributed Switch

The **Link Aggregation Control Protocol** (**LACP**) allows the grouping of host physical adapters and physical switch ports to form a bigger communication pipeline, increasing availability and bandwidth. Such a pipeline is referred to as an EtherChannel. The grouping of physical adapters or physical switch ports is called a **Link Aggregation Group** (**LAG**).

# Getting ready

Creating LAGs involves physical switch configuration as well. Hence it is important to understand the high-level procedure before learning how to create LAGs on a vSphere Distributed Switch:

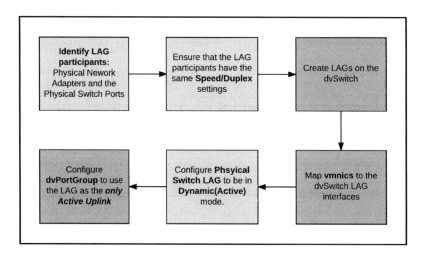

# How to do it...

The following procedure will help you configure LAG on a vSphere Distributed Switch:

1. Bring up the **Networking** inventory using the vSphere Web Client by using the key combination *Ctrl + Alt + 5*.

2. Select the desired dvSwitch and navigate to **Configure | LACP** and click on the icon ✚ to bring up the **New Link Aggregation Group** window:

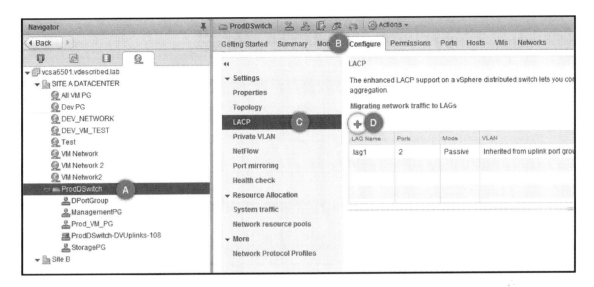

3. On the **New Link Aggregation Group** window, supply a **Name** for the LAG, configure the **Number of ports** to be used, set a LAG **Mode**, and choose a **Load balancing mode**. With the desired settings in place, click **OK** to confirm the settings:

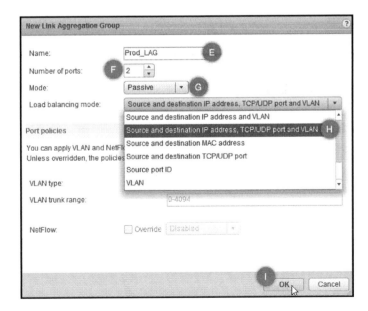

4. The LACP page should now list the newly created LAG. Click on **Migrating network traffic to LAGs**:

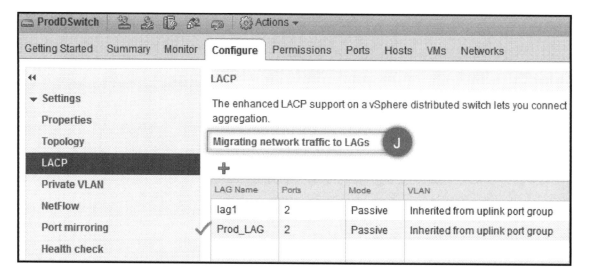

5. Follow the instructions on the **Migrate Network Traffic to Link Aggregation Groups** window to unobtrusively migrate the traffic to the LAG interfaces. The window provides direct links to the **Manage Distributed Port Groups** and the **Add and Manage Hosts** wizards:
   - Make the LAG a standby uplink for the dvPortGroup:

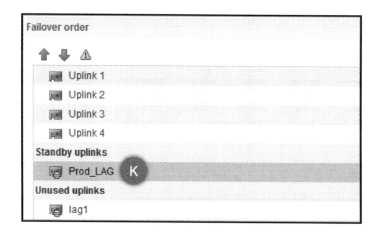

- Assign correct physical adapters (vmnics) to the LAG interfaces:

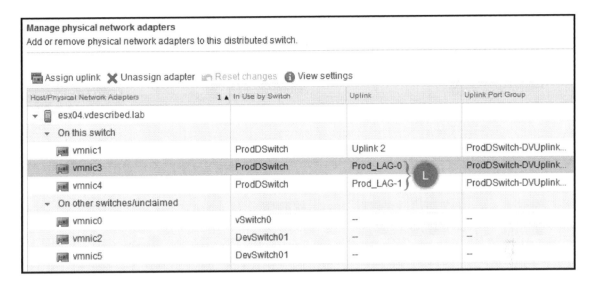

- Set the LAG as the only Active uplink for the dvPortGroup:

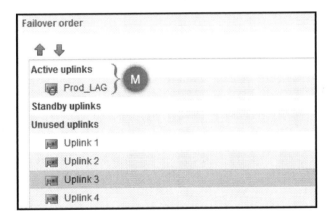

6. You have now successfully configured the use of LAG on your vSphere Distributed Switch.

# How it works...

We learned how to create and use a LAG on a vSphere Distributed Switch. Keep in mind that configuring LAGs on the dvSwitch alone will not create an Etherchannel. It would require you to configure LAGs on both the dvSwitch and the physical switch to form an EtherChannel:

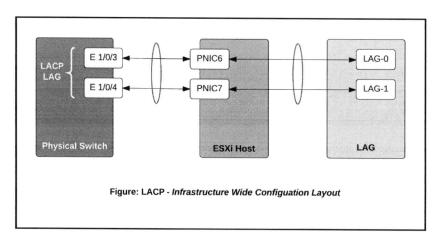

Figure: LACP - *Infrastructure Wide Configuation Layout*

You can configure up to a maximum of 64 LAGs on a dvSwitch of version 5.5 and above. Prior to dvSwitch 5.5, we were allowed to create only a single LAG per dvSwitch.

As with vSphere 6.5, each LAG can have up to 32 LAG ports, meaning, from a dvSwitch's perspective, every participating ESXi can have up to 32 physical NICs mapped to a single LAG.

LACP LAGs operate in two modes—active (dynamic) and passive (static). In dynamic mode, the LAG is in an active mode sending LACP PDUs negotiating LACP status and configuration. In static mode, the LAG is in passive mode waiting on LACP PDUs from the active LAG. At least one of the LAGs in an EtherChannel should be in active mode for the LACP to work.

Prior to dvSwitch 5.5, VMware supported the use of LACP (static mode), but starting with dvSwitch 5.5, support for the dynamic link aggregation group was enabled.

# Creating user-defined network resource pools

**Network I/O Control (NIOC)** has the ability to detect system traffic type and control its bandwidth usage based on shares, reservations, and limits.

There are nine system traffic types as shown in the following list:

- Fault tolerance traffic
- Management traffic
- NFS traffic
- Virtual machine traffic (this needs to be enabled)
- Virtual SAN traffic
- iSCSI traffic
- vMotion traffic
- vSphere data protection backup traffic
- vSphere replication traffic

System traffic types don't have any reservations by default. However, we are allowed to set a reservation on each of the traffic types by editing their settings.

User-defined network resource pools allow further segregation and control over the VM traffic detected by the NIOC. In this recipe, we will learn how to create one.

# Getting ready

**Network I/O Control** is **Enabled** by default when you create a dvSwitch. If you had chosen to disable it at the time of creation, then you should enable NIOC to make use of the network pools. NIOC can be enabled from the **Edit Settings** page of a dvSwitch:

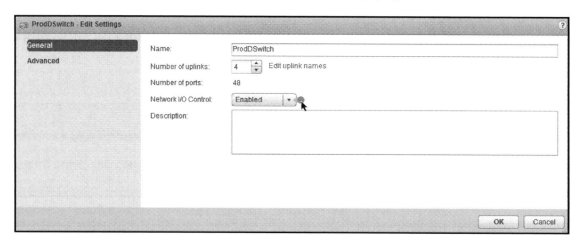

# How to do it...

The following procedure will help you create User-defined Network Resource Pools:

1. Bring up the **Networking** inventory using the **vSphere Web Client** by using the key combination *Ctrl + Alt + 5*.
2. Select the desired dvSwitch and navigate to **Configure | Network resource pools** and click on **Reserve Bandwidth for virtual machine system traffic...**:

3. On the **Edit Resource Settings for Virtual Machine Traffic** window, leave the **Shares** value at **High** and set a **Reservation**. This reservation is a bandwidth reservation per physical NIC. In this case, it is being set to 500 Mbps:

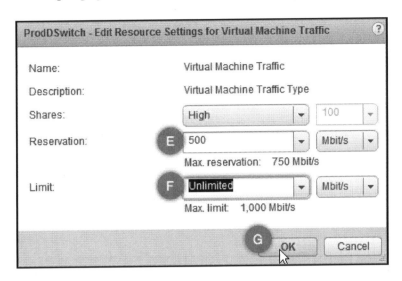

4. The **Configured reservation** will now be equivalent to the total number of participating physical NICs multiplied by the bandwidth reservation per NIC. (In this case, *500 Mbps x 4 vmnics = 2 Gbps*). It is from this unused reservation quota that you can further divide the reservation among the network resource pools. Click on the ✚ icon to bring up the **New Network Resource Pool** window:

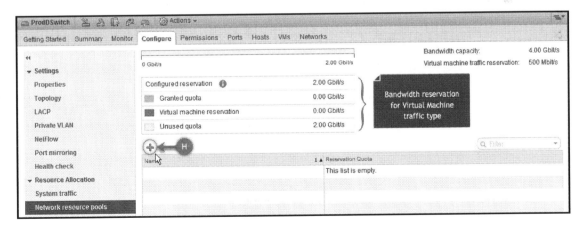

5. On the **New Network Resource Pool** window, supply a **Name**, an optional **Description**, and the **Reservation quota** in Mbps or Gbps. Here we have reserved 1 Gbps (1,000 Mbps):

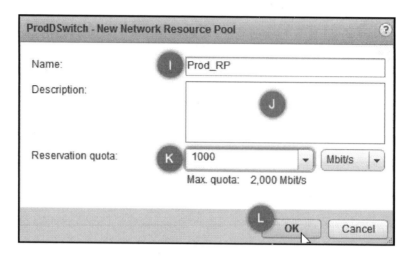

6. Now you could assign the NRP to the desired dvPortGroup. Click **Edit Settings** of the desired dvPortGroup and choose the **Network resource pool** to be used:

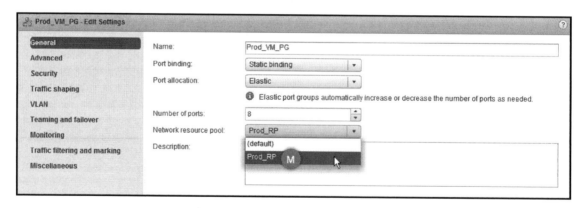

With this configuration, the dvPortGroup is guaranteed to receive the reserved bandwidth regardless of the bandwidth needs of other virtual machine traffic.

# How it works...

These user-defined network resource pools can be associated with any dvPortGroups with virtual machines mapped to them. Such custom resource pools can only be used to set bandwidth reservations in Mbps. Reservations are always met, and any leftover bandwidth is allocated to different traffic types based on the relative share values.

# There's more...

The configuration of NetIOC has been hugely simplified with the introduction of reservations. However, shares also play a very critical role in allocating unreserved bandwidth among the contenders based on the share values.

We will try to understand how shares work by way of an example.

For instance, the default share value configuration of medium (50) for the traffic types vMotion, management, and vSphere replication assumes the following:

- All three traffic types have to be configured to use an uplink that has a bandwidth of 10 Gbps
- Since each of the traffic types has a share value of 50, the cumulative share value for all three traffic types is 150 on the uplink
- During contention, each of the traffic types will get *(50/150) \*100 = 33%* of the total bandwidth
- That translates to 33% of 5,000 Mbps, which is approximately 1.6 Gbps for each traffic type

# Using port mirroring on a vSphere Distributed Switch

Port mirroring is a functionality that allows cloning of vNIC network traffic to another port or uplink (destination) on the dvSwitch. This is particularly useful when you have a packet analyzer or **Intrusion Detection System (IDS)** deployed on the network. Port mirroring can only be enabled on a vSphere Distributed Switch and not on a vSphere Standard Switch.

# Getting ready

Before you learn how to configure port mirroring it is important to have an good understanding of the mirroring methods and the supported source/destinations.

The following table compares the select source/destination options available based on the mirror session types, which will help you decide on the correct type of mirror session required:

| Mirroring session type | Available sources type | Available destination type |
|---|---|---|
| Distributed port mirroring | dvPorts | dvPorts |
| Remote mirroring source | dvPorts | Uplinks |
| Remote mirroring destination | VLAN ID | dvPorts |
| Encapsulated remote mirroring (L3) source | dvPorts | IP Address |
| Distributed port mirroring (legacy) | dvPorts | dvPorts and Uplinks |

# How to do it...

The following procedure will help you configure port mirroring on a dvSwitch:

1. Bring up the **Networking** inventory using the **vSphere Web Client** by using the key combination *Ctrl + Alt + 5*.
2. Select the desired dvSwitch and navigate to **Configure** | **Port mirroring** and click **New...** to bring up the **Add Port Mirroring Session** window:

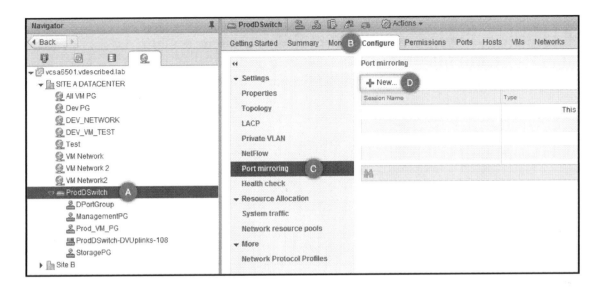

3. On the **Add Port Mirroring Session** window, select the desired session type and click **Next** to continue:

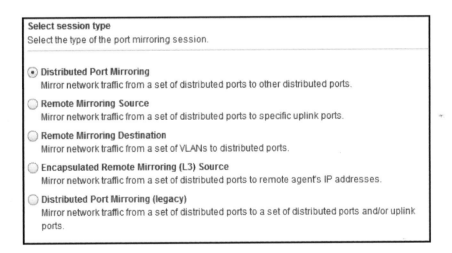

4. On the **Edit Properties** screen configure the following settings:

- **Name**: A string used to identify the session defined.
- **Status**: This can be set to either **Enabled/Disabled**.
- **Normal I/O on destination ports**: This will let you choose whether or not to allow regular traffic along with the mirrored traffic on the destination port. For instance, if the destination vNIC-assigned dvPort is the only port in use by the VM, then you might want to allow regular traffic on that as well.
- **Mirrored packet length (Bytes)**: This is used to set a limit of the mirror packet length in bytes. Leave this untouched unless you have not configured your destination monitoring tool to breakdown the packet per its requirement.
- **Sampling rate**: This is used to define the number of packets to be mirrored. The default value of 1 will mirror every packet in the traffic. If you set it to **5**, then every fifth packet is mirrored.
- **Description**: This is an optional field unless you want to use it for notes.
- **Encapsulation VLAN ID**: This is made available only for the remote mirroring source session type. Since the destinations of this mirroring type are uplinks, it is quite possible that the uplinks are trunked for a different VLAN. Therefore, it becomes necessary to encapsulate the frames using the uplink VLAN ID. If the source dvPorts are on a different VLAN themselves then you could choose the **Preserve original VLAN** option to doubly encapsulate the frames that are being mirrored:

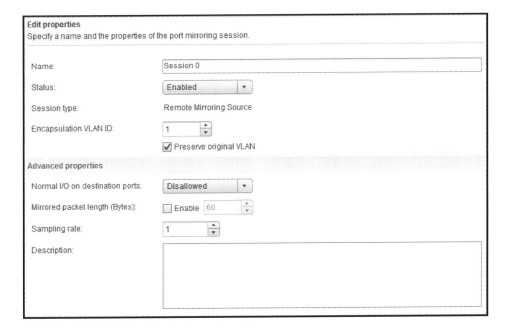

5. The options presented to you in the **Edit Sources** and **Edit Destinations** screens vary depending on the type of mirroring session. Refer to the *Getting ready* section of this recipe to learn about the available source and destination for each session type.

6. On the **Ready to complete** screen review the settings and click **Finish**.

# How it works...

Once **Port mirroring** is **Enabled**, all the traffic that arrives at the chosen source is mirrored (replicated) to the desired destination.

The source can be distributed ports or VLANs. The destination can be distributed ports, uplinks, or IP addresses of machines running the traffic monitoring application.

There are five mirroring session types, as follows:

- **Distributed port mirroring**: This is used for replicating network traffic from one or more distributed ports to distributed port(s), to which the vNIC(s) of the VM(s) running the packet monitoring software are attached. This session type will work only if the source and destination VMs are on the same ESXi host.

- **Remote mirroring source**: This is used when the traffic analyzer is a machine connected to one of the ports on the physical switch. This would require a configuration change on the physical switch to mirror the traffic received on a physical port to another physical port on the same switch to which the packet analyzer machine is connected, or to a port on a different switch (with the help of RSPAN VLAN).
- **Remote mirroring destination**: This is used when you want to monitor traffic in a particular VLAN by mirroring the traffic to a VM connected to a distributed port.
- **Encapsulated remote mirroring (L3) source**: This is used when the packet analyzer is on a machine on a different L3 subnet. In this case, the source will be the distributed ports and the destination will be the IP address of the packet analyzer machine.
- **Distributed port mirroring (legacy)**: This is used when we need uplinks and distributed ports as the destination.

You can also control the maximum packet size and the sampling rate of a mirroring session using the following:

- **Maximum packet length (bytes)**: This is the maximum size of a packet that will be allowed to be mirrored. The remainder of the packet will be truncated. The default size is 60 bytes.
- **Sampling rate**: This determines the rate at which the packets are mirrored. The default value of 1 will allow you to capture every single packet. If you increase the value to 3, then every third packet will be mirrored.

# Enabling NetFlow on a vSphere Distributed Switch

NetFlow is an industry standard for network traffic monitoring. Although originally developed by Cisco, it has since become an industry standard. Once enabled, it can be used to capture IP traffic statistics on all the interfaces where NetFlow is enabled, and send them as records to the NetFlow collector software. VMware supports NetFlow version 10.

# How to do it...

The following procedure will help you enable Netflow on a vSphere Distributed Switch:

1. Bring up the **Networking** inventory using the **vSphere Web Client** by using the key combination *Ctrl + Alt + 5*.

2. Select the desired dvSwitch and navigate to **Configure** | **NetFlow** and click **Edit**:

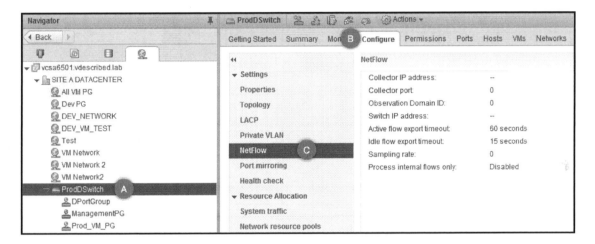

3. In the **Edit NetFlow Settings** window, supply a **Collector IP address**, **Collector port**, **Observation Domain ID**, and **Switch IP address**. Modify the **Advanced settings** if necessary. Click **OK** to save the settings:

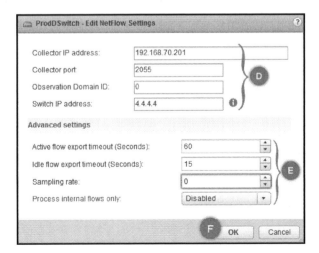

4. The **NetFlow** screen should now show the applied settings:

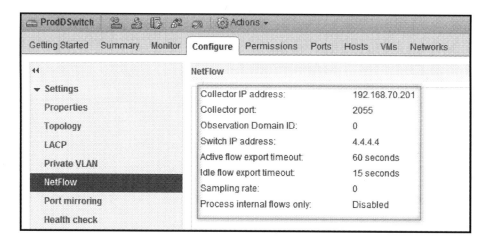

5. Once done, you can **Enable** NetFlow on individual dvPortGroups:

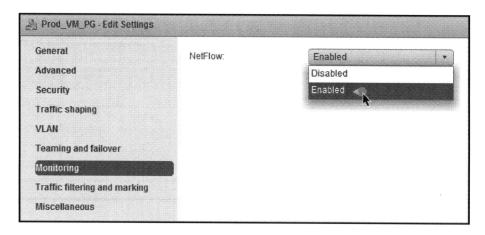

# How it works...

NetFlow, once configured on the dvSwitch, will allow the NetFlow collector software to capture and analyze statistics for the dvSwitch. The dvSwitch is identified by the NetFlow collector software using the IP address that we assigned to the dvSwitch while configuring NetFlow on it. The IP assigned to the dvSwitch doesn't give it a network identity. It is only used by the NetFlow collector to uniquely identify the dvSwitch. If you do not specify an IP, then you will see a separate session for the ESXi host that is a member of the dvSwitch.

Now, let's review the NetFlow settings in detail:

- **Collector IP address**: This is the IP address of the NetFlow collector machine in your environment.
- **Collector port**: UDP port 2055 is the most widely used NetFlow collector port number.
- **Observation Domain ID**: This is the observation ID of the NetFlow collector. This information can be obtained from the NetFlow collector machine.
- **Switch IP address**: This is just a representative IP address and not the real one. This doesn't make up the VDS part of any network. It only provides a unique ID to the VDS in the NetFlow monitoring software.
- **Active flow export timeout**: The amount of time measured in seconds that the VDS will wait before it begins to fragment an active traffic flow and send the data to the NetFlow monitor.
- **Idle flow export timeout**: The amount of time measured in seconds that VDS will wait before it begins to fragment an idle flow and send the data to the NetFlow monitor.
- **Sampling rate**: This value determines the number and frequency of the packet collection. The default 0 will collect every packet. If the value is set to 5, then it collects every fifth packet.
- **Process internal flows only**: This is used to collect data from traffic that never leaves an ESXi host. For instance, traffic between two VMs in the same VLAN and the same host does not have to leave the host.

# 8

# Creating and Managing VMFS Datastore

In this chapter, we will cover the following topics:

- Viewing the LUNs presented to an ESXi host
- Viewing the datastores seen by the ESXi hosts
- Creating a VMFS datastore
- Managing the multipathing configuration of a VMFS datastore
- Expanding a VMFS datastore
- Extending a VMFS datastore
- Unmounting and detaching a VMFS datastore
- Mounting a VMFS datastore
- Deleting a VMFS datastore
- Upgrading from VMFS 5 to VMFS 6
- Managing VMFS volumes detected as Snapshots
- Masking paths to a LUN
- Unmasking paths to a LUN

# Introduction

Storage is an integral part of any infrastructure. It is used to store the files backing your virtual machines. There are different types of storage that can be incorporated into a vSphere infrastructure, and these types are determined based on a variety of factors, such as the type of disks used, the type of storage protocol used, and the type of connectivity used. The most common way to refer to a type of storage presented to a VMware environment is based on the protocol used and the connection type.

VMware supports the following types of storage based on the protocol and connection type in use:

- **Fiber Channel (FC) storage**: This connects over the FC SAN fabric network. It uses the FC protocol to encapsulate the SCSI commands. Hosts connect to the FC network using an **FC Host Bus Adapter (FC-HBA)**. At the core of the FC network are the fabric switches that enable connecting the hosts and storage arrays to the fiber channel network.
- **FC over Ethernet (FCoE)**: This connects over an Ethernet network. Hosts connect using a **Converged Network Adapter (CNA)**. FC frames are encapsulated in Ethernet frames. FCoE does not use TCP/IP for transporting FC frames. FCoE is gaining prominence in most modern data centers implementing a converged infrastructure.
- **Network Attached Storage (NAS)**: This connects over the IP network and hence is easier to implement in an existing infrastructure. Unlike FC and FCoE, this is not a lossless implementation. As the SCSI commands are sent over the TCP/IP network, they are prone to experience packet loss due to various reasons. Although this behavior does not break anything, it will have an impact on the performance when compared to FC or FCoE.
- **iSCSI**: Internet SCSI allows you to send SCSI commands over an IP network to a storage system that supports the use of this protocol.
- **Network File System (NFS)**: NFS is a distributed filesystem protocol that allows you to share access to files over the IP network. Unlike iSCSI, FC, FCoE, or DAS, this is not block storage protocol. VMware supports NFS version 3.
- **Direct Attached Storage (DAS)**: This is used for local storage.

Keep in mind that FC, FCoE, and iSCSI are used to present block storage devices to ESXi, whereas NFS presents file storage. The key difference here is that the block storage can be presented in a raw format with no filesystem on it; file storage is nothing but a network folder mount on an already existing filesystem.

There are four other common terms that we use when dealing with storage in a VMware environment, namely LUN, datastore, VMFS, and NFS. The following points will introduce you to these terms and what they represent in a VMware environment:

- **LUN**: When storage is presented to an ESXi host, the space for it is carved from a pool in the storage array. Each of the carved-up containers of disk blocks is called a logical unit and is uniquely represented by a **Logical Unit Number** (**LUN**). The concept of a LUN is used when you present block storage. It is on this LUN that you create a filesystem, such as VMFS. vSphere 6.5 supports up to 512 LUNs per ESXi host which is 2 x more than what was supported with the previous version. Also, the highest possible LUN ID is now 16383 as compared to 1023 with vSphere 6.0. However, the supported maximum size of a LUN is still capped at 64 TB.

- **Datastore**: This is the vSphere term used to refer to a storage volume presented to an ESXi. The volume can be a VMFS volume on a LUN or an NFS mount. All files that make up a virtual machine are stored in a datastore. With the datastore being a managed object, most common file operations such as create, delete, upload, and download is possible. Keep in mind that you can't edit a configuration file directly from the datastore browser as it doesn't integrate with a text editor. For instance, if you are required to edit a configuration file like the .vmx, then the file should be downloaded, edited, and re-uploaded. You can create up to 512 VMFS datastores and 256 NFS datastores (mounts) per ESXi host.

- **VMFS volume**: A block LUN presented from an FC/iSCSI/DAS array can be formatted using the VMware's proprietary filesystem called **VMFS**. VMFS stands for **Virtual Machine File System**. The current version of VMFS is version 6. VMFS will let more than one host have simultaneous read/write access to the volume. To make sure that a VM or its files are not simultaneously accessed by more than one ESXi host, VMFS uses an on-disk locking mechanism called **distributed locking**. To place a lock on a VMFS volume, vSphere will either have to use an SCSI-2 reservation or if the array supports VAAI, it can use an **Atomic Test and Set** (**ATS**) primitive.

Like the previous version, VMFS version 6 supports the following:

- A maximum volume size of 64 TB
- A uniform block size of 1 MB
- Smaller subblocks of 8 KB

An interesting improvement in VMFS 6, is automatic space reclamation using VAAI UNMAP. This can be configured any VMFS 6 datastore.

- **NFS volume**: Unlike a VMFS volume, the NFS volume is not created by formatting a raw LUN with VMFS. NFS volumes are just mounts created to access the shared folders on an NFS server. The filesystems on these volumes are dependent on the type of NFS server. You can configure up to 256 NFS mounts per ESXi host.

# Viewing the LUNs presented to an ESXi host

During the initial phase of adding shared storage to an ESXi host, LUN devices are presented to the ESXi host. The presentation is achieved at the storage and fabric levels. We will not get into the details of how a LUN is presented using the storage or fabric management software as that is beyond the scope of this book.

Once the LUNs are made available to the ESXi hosts, you can then format them with VMFS to host the virtual machine files. The LUNs can also be presented as RAW volumes to the virtual machines, in which case they are called **Raw Device Mappings (RDMs)**. For more information on RDMs, refer to the recipe *Attaching RDM to a virtual machine* in *Chapter 11, Creating and Managing Virtual Machines*.

In this recipe, we will learn how to view the LUNs that are already presented to an ESXi host.

# How to do it...

The following procedure will help you view all the storage devices seen by an ESXi host:

1. Log in to the vCenter Server using the vSphere web client and use the key combination *Ctrl + Alt + 2* to bring up the hosts and clusters inventory view, as shown.

2. Select the desired host and navigate to **Configure** | **Storage Devices** to view all the LUN devices seen by the ESXi host. The LUN devices could be local or remote storage (FC, iSCSI, NAS, FCoE):

Alternatively, you can issue the commands `esxcfg-scsidevs -u` and `esxcli storage core device list` at the ESXi CLI to list the storage devices.

# Viewing datastores available on an ESXi host

ESXi requires the use of datastore(s) for storing files that back a virtual machine. A datastore is nothing but a storage LUN with a VMFS filesystem on it or an NFS mount from an NAS server. Each ESXi host maintains a list of datastores that it has access to. In this recipe, we will learn how to pull this list.

## How to do it...

The following procedure will help you view all the datastores by an ESXi host:

1. Log in to the vCenter Server using the vSphere web client and use the key combination *Ctrl + Alt + 2* to bring up the hosts and clusters inventory view, as shown.

2. Select the desired host and navigate to the **Datastores** tab to view a list of all datastores the ESXi host has access to:

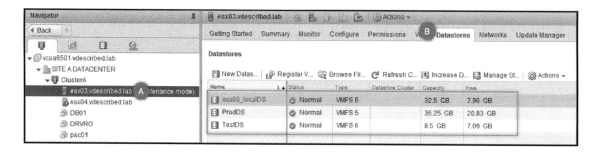

# Creating a VMFS datastore

Once we have presented raw LUNs to an ESXi host, for it to be used as a storage container for virtual machine files, the LUN has to be formatted using VMFS. This is achieved by creating a VMFS datastore using the LUN.

# Getting ready

You will need the NAA ID, LUN ID and the size of the desired LUN handy to ensure that you use the correct LUN to create the VMFS volume on. For the LUN discovery to work, the LUN should be presented correctly to the ESXi host at the storage array. If the ESXi host does not see the intended LUN, issue a rescan on the storage adapters to discover the presented LUN device.

# How to do it...

The following procedure will help you to create a VMFS volume:

1. Present or map a LUN of ESXi hosts. This activity is performed at the **Storage** array. Refer to the Storage Array vendor documentation for instructions:https://pubs.vmware.com/vsphere-50/index.jsp?topic=%2Fcom.vmware.vsphere.storage.doc_50%2FGUID-15A7E014-6189-4F65-A26F-8F409CA74338.html.

2. Log in to the vCenter Server using the vSphere web client and use the key combination *Ctrl + Alt + 2* to bring up the hosts and clusters inventory view.

3. Right-click on one of the ESXi hosts the LUN was mapped to and navigate to **Storage | Rescan Storage...**:

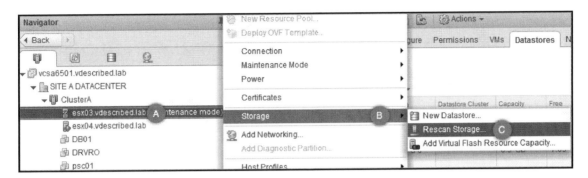

4. On the **Rescan Storage** dialog box, click **OK** to initiate the rescan operation. You choose to rescan for new VMFS volumes if in case you are trying to discover VMFS volumes:

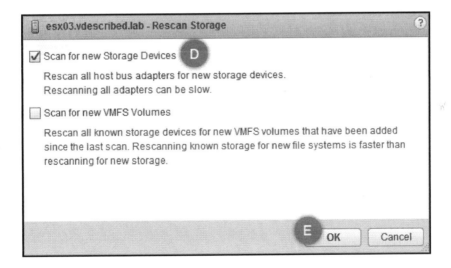

5. Right-click on one of the ESXi hosts the LUN was mapped to and navigate to **Storage** | **New Datastore...**:

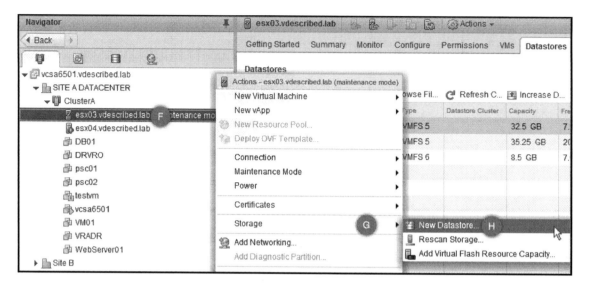

6. In the **New Datastore** wizard screen, select **VMFS** as the datastore type and click **Next** to continue:

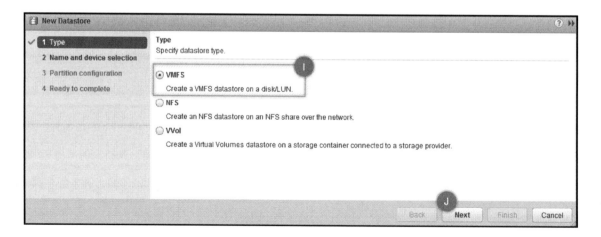

7. On the **Name and device selection section** screen, supply a **Datastore name** for the VMFS volume and select the LUN device to create the filesystem on, and click **Next** to continue:

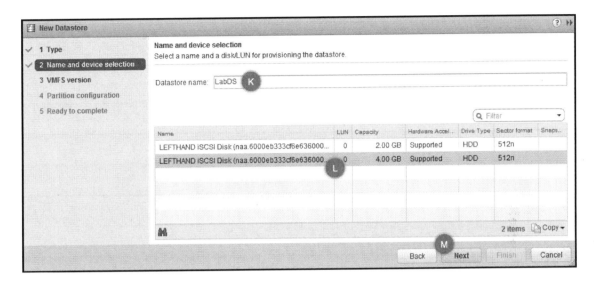

8. On the **VMFS version** screen, you can choose between VMFS 5 or VMFS 6. In this case, we will select **VMFS 6** and click **Next** to continue.

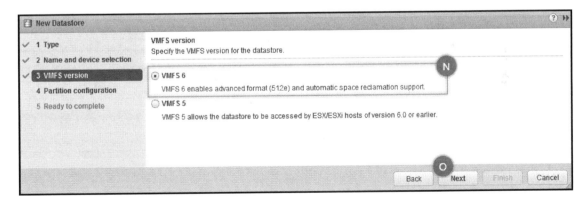

9. On the **Partition configuration** screen, choose to **Use all available partitions** or use the slider to adjust the size of the VMFS partition and set the **Space Reclamation Priority** to either **None** or **Low**. Setting it to **None** will disable *automatic space reclamation* using VAAI's UNMAP primitive:

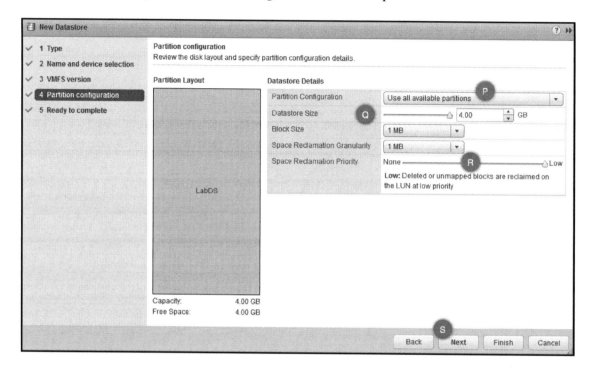

10. On the **Ready to complete** screen review the setting and click **Finish** to create the VMFS volume:

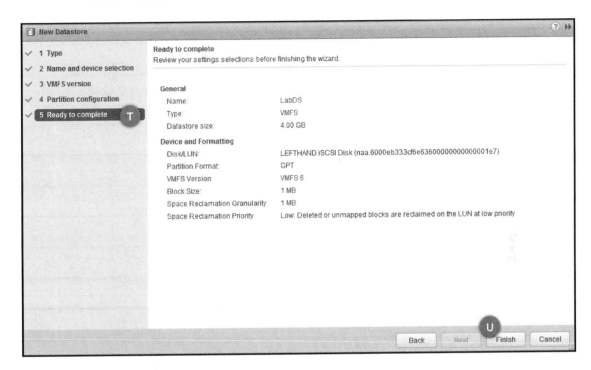

# Managing multipathing configuration of a VMFS datastore

Storage LUNs presented to the ESXi hosts preferably need to be made highly available. This is achieved by enabling multiple connectivity paths between the ESXi hosts and the SAN storage. Once configured correctly, these paths can then be used either to failover or load balance the I/O activity.

In this section, we will learn how to view the current multipathing configuration for a particular LUN.

# How to do it...

The following procedure will help you view and manage multipathing configuration:

1. Log in to the vCenter Server using the vSphere web client and use the key combination *Ctrl+Alt+4* to switch to the storage view.

2. Select the desired datastore, navigate **Configure | Connectivity and Multipathing,** select any of the ESXi hosts that the datastore is currently mounted to, to view its multipathing configuration. In this case, the LUN presented from an iSCSI storage array has only a single path which is not an ideal configuration in a production environment:

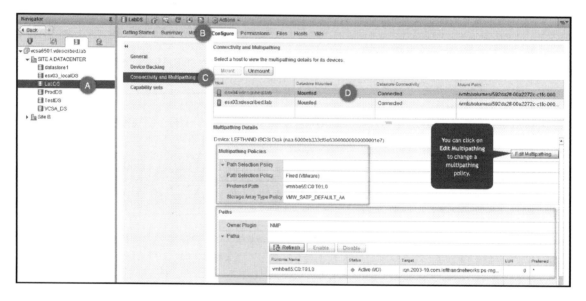

3. You can click on **Edit Multipathing...** if you choose to modify the multipathing configuration.

4. In the **Edit Multipathing Policies** window, choose the desired policy and click **OK** to confirm the change:

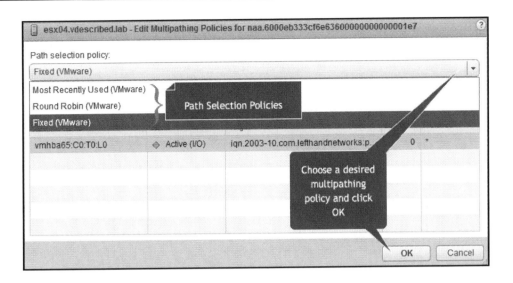

# How it works...

A path to a LUN includes the **Host Bus Adapter** (**HBA**) or **initiator**, the fabric/network switches, and the storage controllers in the array. The availability of a path will be affected if any of these hardware components along the path fail or stop functioning. Multipathing is a method to configure and maintain multiple paths between the host and the storage array. Although redundant fabric switches will be used to achieve this, the multipathing information available at ESXi will not show the switches involved.

Storage multipathing on an ESXi host is achieved with the help of a framework of APIs called **Pluggable Storage Architecture** (**PSA**). The APIs can be used by the storage vendors to write their own **Multipathing Plugins** (**MPP**), thus enabling a closer integration of their storage devices. Some examples for available third-party MPPs are as follows:

- EMC PowerPath.
- Dell EqualLogic MEM for iSCSI multipathing.
- VERITAS dynamic multipathing for VMware.
- The default multipathing plugin on an ESXi host is called **Native Multipathing Plugin** (**NMP**). The NMP adds support for all the supported storage arrays in the VMware compatibility list.

The NMP has two sub plugins known as **Storage Array Type Plugin (SATP)** and **Path Selection Plugin (PSP)**. VMware includes the SATP and PSP associations for all tested and supported storage arrays in the form of claim rules.

SATP detects the path state and handles path failover, whereas PSP determines which available physical path should be used to send the I/O.

VMware supports the following path selection plugins:

- **Most Recently Used (MRU):** In the event of a path failover, this would continue to use the path even if the original path becomes accessible again. Its initial path selection happens during the boot up of ESXi, where it selects the first-discovered path as the active path. MRU is the preferred PSP for active/passive arrays and ALUA-based arrays.
- **Fixed:** One of the multiple paths available is marked as the preferred path. So, in the event of a preferred path becoming accessible again, it will failback to the preferred path. This is most commonly used with active/active and ALUA-based arrays.
- **Round Robin (RR):** This distributes I/O to all the active paths. By default, it distributes 1,000 IOs on an active path before it sends the next 1,000 IOs down the next active path.

We discussed choosing a PSP depending on the array type, so it is important to understand different array types from the multipathing perspective. The array type is determined by the mode in which it operates. There are three such types from a multipathing perspective:

- **Active/active array:** This supports the simultaneous ownership of a LUN by more than one storage processor.
- **Active/passive array:** This supports only one storage processor owning a particular LUN. A storage processor that owns a LUN or a set of LUNs becomes the active controller for those LUNs.
- **Asymmetric Logical Unit Access (ALUA) based array:** Similar to an active/active array, but uses the concept of optimized and unoptimized paths. Here, an unoptimized path is a data path to the LUN via the interconnect to the other controller.

# Expanding or growing a VMFS datastore

It is likely that you would run out of free space on a VMFS volume over time as you end up deploying more and more VMs on it, especially in a growing environment. Fortunately, accommodating additional free space on a VMFS volume is possible. However, this requires that the LUN either has free space left on it or it has been expanded/resized in the storage array.

The procedure to resize/expand the LUN in the storage array differs from vendor to vendor, and as this is beyond the scope of this book, we assume that the LUN either has free space on it or has already been expanded.

The following flowchart provides a high-level overview of the procedure:

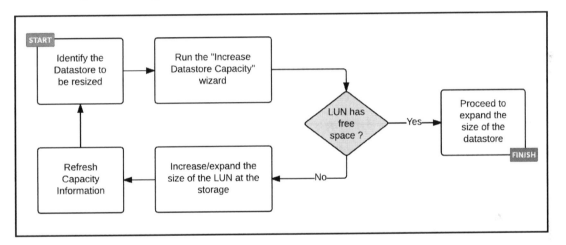

# Getting ready

If there is no free space on the LUN, then contact your storage administrator to increase the size of the LUN. Once done, right-click on the datastore again and select **Refresh Capacity Information**:

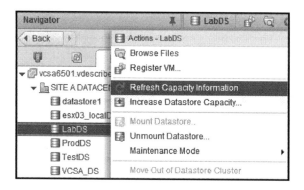

# How to do it...

The following procedure will help you expand the size of a VMFS datastore:

1. Log in to the vCenter Server using the vSphere web client and use the key combination *Ctrl + Alt + 4* to switch to the storage view.

2. Right-click on the desired datastore and click **Increase Datastore Capacity...**:

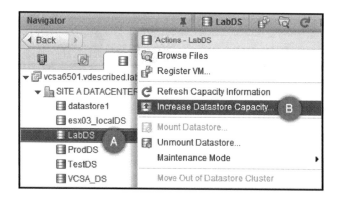

3. On the **Increase Datastore Capacity** wizard screen, select the LUN corresponding to the datastore you wish to expand. You will not see the LUN listed, if there is no free space on the LUN:

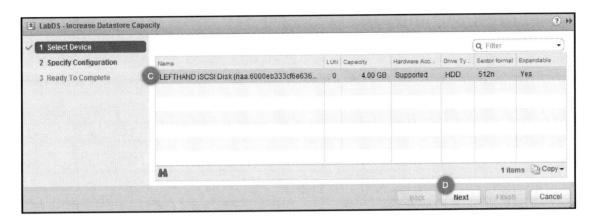

4. On the **Specify Configuration** screen, you can either choose to use up all the available free space or use the slider to adjust the amount of free space to up:

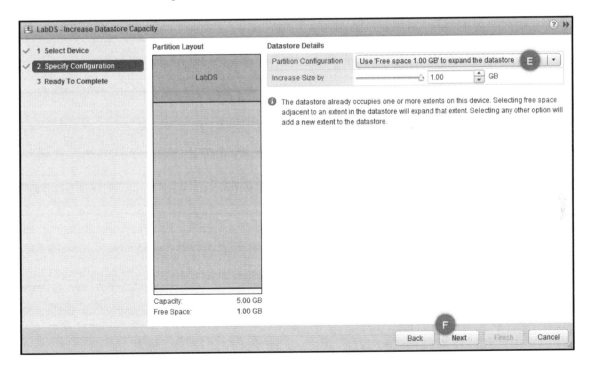

5. On the **Ready to Complete** screen, verify the settings and click **Finish** to initiate the expand operation.
6. You will see an **Expand VMFS datastore** complete successfully in the **Recent Tasks** pane.

# Extending a VMFS datastore

In the *Expanding or growing a VMFS datastore* recipe, we discussed the procedure involved in increasing the size of a datastore on the same LUN backing the VMFS volume, and that was possible only if the LUN has unused free space on it or was expanded.

You can run into a situation where there is no unused space on the LUN backing the VMFS volume, but your datastore runs out of space. Fortunately, vSphere supports the spanning of a VMFS volume onto multiple LUNs. This means you can span the VMFS volume onto a new LUN so that it can use the free space on it. This process of spanning a VMFS volume onto another LUN is called **extending a VMFS datastore**.

# Getting ready

Present a blank LUN to all the ESXi hosts which have the VMFS volume mounted. Make a note of the NAA ID, LUN ID and the size of the blank LUN. Issue a rescan on the storage adapters on any one of the ESXi hosts.

# How to do it...

The following procedure will help you extend a VMFS volume:

1. Log in to the vCenter Server using the vSphere web client and use the key combination *Ctrl + Alt + 4* to switch to the storage view. Right-click on the desired datastore and click **Increase Datastore Capacity...**:

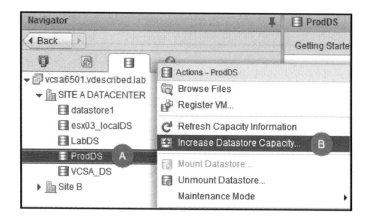

2. On the **Increase Datastore Capacity** wizard screen, select the LUN that will be used as the extent and click **Next** to continue:

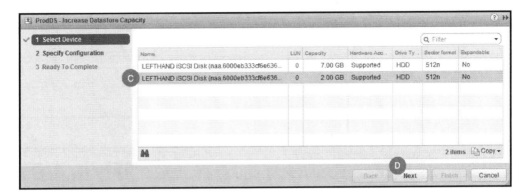

3. On the **Specify Configuration** screen, you can either choose to use up all the available free space or use the slider to adjust the amount of free space to up:

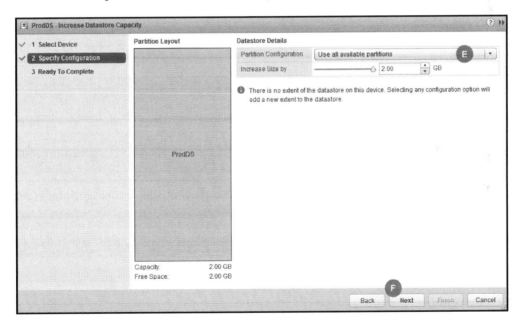

4. On the **Ready to Complete** screen, review the settings and click **Finish** to perform the extend operation.

5. The **Recent Tasks** pane, will show an **Extend datastore operation** complete successfully.

# Unmounting and detaching VMFS volumes

Unmounting a datastore is done when you intend to preserve the data on a VMFS volume, but still remove access to the volume. Detaching is performed on a LUN device and it is done to make sure that the access to the LUN is gracefully removed. It is recommended you unmount a VMFS datastore and detach its corresponding LUN device, before the LUN backing it is unpresented from an ESXi host.

# Getting ready

Make a note of the NAA ID of the LUN corresponding to the VMFS volume. This can be done by selecting the datastore and navigating to **Configure** | **Device Backing**:

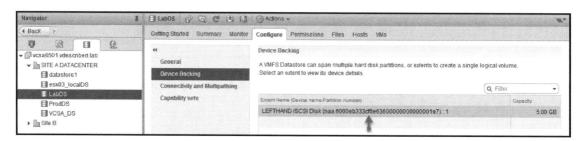

Alternatively, you can issue the command `esxcli storage vmfs extent list`:

It is advised that you take care of the following before you proceed with the unmount operation:

- All the VMs should be migrated off to a different datastore
- The datastore should be removed from a datastore cluster
- The datastore should remain unmanaged by **Storage DRS (SDRS)**
- **Storage I/O Control (SIOC)** should be disabled for the datastore
- Should not be in use as a vSphere HA heartbeat datastore

# How to do it...

The following procedure will help unmount a VMFS volume and detach its corresponding LUN device:

1. Log in to the vCenter Server using the vSphere web client and use the key combination *Ctrl + Alt + 4* to switch to the storage view.

2. Right-click on the desired datastore and click **Unmount Datastore...**:

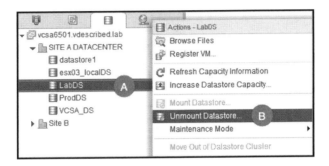

3. On the **Unmount Datastore...** window, select all the ESXi hosts to unmount the datastores from, and click **OK**:

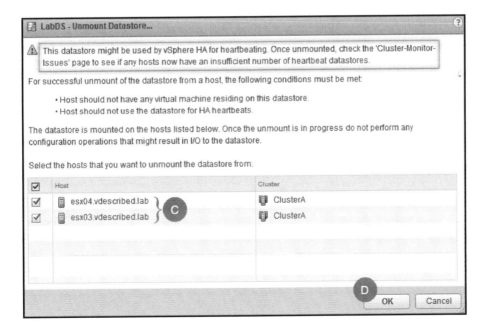

4. The **Recent Tasks** pane should list an **Unmount Datastore** task complete successfully for each of the ESXi hosts. And the VMFS datastore will be marked as **Inactive**.

5. Use the key combination *Ctrl + Alt + 2* to switch to the **Host and Clusters** view.

6. Select an ESXi host, navigate to **Configure | Storage Devices**, select the LUN corresponding to the unmounted datastore and click on the icon [icon] to detach the LUN:

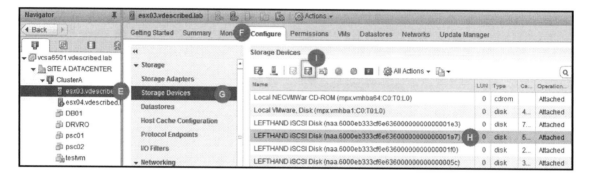

7. On the **Detach Device** dialog box, click **OK** to confirm the operation:

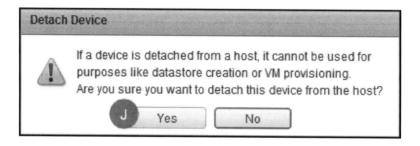

8. The **Recent Tasks** pane should list a **Detach SCSI LUN** task complete successfully. Also, the LUN device should now be listed as **Detached**:

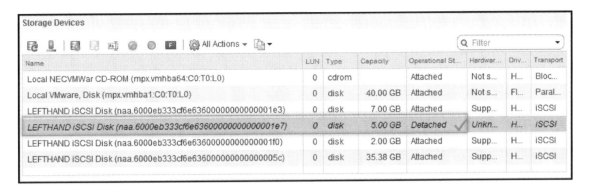

# Re-mounting a VMFS datastore

A previously unmounted VMFS datastore can be re-mounted to the ESXi host. Doing so will make the datastore available for I/O operations.

## Getting ready

Make sure the LUN backing the volume is presented to the ESXi hosts. Issue a rescan on the storage adapters to discover the LUN.

## How to do it...

The following procedure will help mount a VMFS datastore to the ESXi host:

1. Log in to the vCenter Server using the vSphere web client and use the key combination *Ctrl + Alt + 2* to switch to the **Host and Clusters** view.

2. Select an ESXi host, navigate to Configure | Storage Devices, select the LUN corresponding to the unmounted datastore and click on the icon 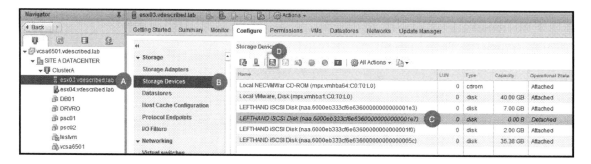 to attach the LUN:

3. The **Recent Tasks** pane should list an **Attach SCSI LUN** task complete successfully.

4. Now that you have re-attached the LUN, switch to the datastore view using the key combination *Ctrl + Alt + 4*.

5. The unmounted datastore will appear as **inactive**. Right-click on it and select **Mount Datastore...**:

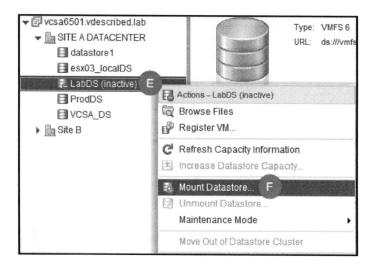

6. On the **Mount Datastore...** window, select the ESXi host to mount the datastore to, and click **OK**:

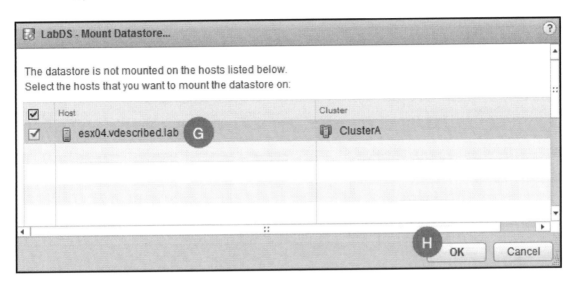

7. The **Recent Tasks** pane, should show a **Mount VMFS volume** task complete successfully.

# Deleting VMFS datastores

Unlike the unmount operation, a delete operation will destroy all the data on the datastore. Once done, you cannot revert this operation. Hence, ensure that you move all the virtual machine data that is currently on the datastore to another datastore.

# Getting ready

Migrate all the virtual machines (regardless of their power state) and their data onto a different datastore. Examine the datastore to make sure that it is empty.

# How to do it...

The following procedure will help you delete a VMFS volume:

1. Log in to the vCenter Server using the vSphere web client and use the key combination *Ctrl + Alt + 4* to switch to the storage view.

2. Right-click on the desired datastore and click **Delete Datastore**:

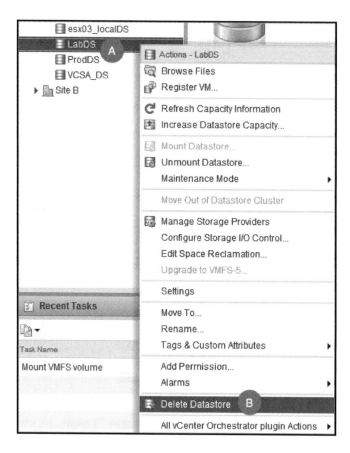

3. On the **Confirm Delete Datastore** window, click **Yes** to confirm the action:

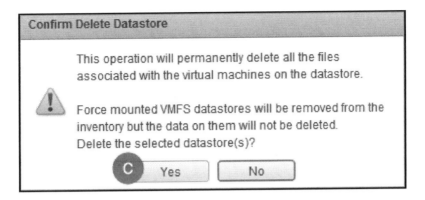

4. The **Recent Tasks** pane should list a **Remove datastore** task complete successfully.

# Upgrading from VMFS 5 to VMFS 6

Unlike the previous VMFS upgrade, there is no method to perform an in-place upgrade of a VMFS 5 volume to VMFS 6. As per VMware, this is due to the changes done to the structure of VMFS metadata to make compatible with 4K alignment. In this recipe, we will provide you with a high-level overview to migrate your workload to VMFS 6.

# How to do it...

The following high-level procedure will help you host all your VM workload on VMFS 6 volumes:

1. Make an inventory of all your datastores and their current utilization.
2. Now, depending on the amount of free space available in the storage array, you can choose to create LUNs of the same size as the existing datastores or create a set of larger LUNs to temporarily migrate the VMs onto them.
3. Once the datastores have been created, use storage vMotion to migrate the VM data on the datastores.
4. If you have created larger temporary LUNs, then select one or more datastores in batches, migrate VM data off of them, delete the empty VMFS 5 volumes, create a new VMFS 6 volume on their LUNs and migrate the VMs back to them.

# There is more...

Since not every environment is identical, there are several factors that would constrain your methods. VMware has put together a great Knowledge Base article *Migrating VMFS 5 datastore to VMFS 6 datastore (2147824)* at `https://kb.vmware.com/kb/2147824`.

# Managing VMFS volumes detected as snapshots

Some environments maintain copies of the production LUNs as a backup, by replicating them. These replicas are exact copies of the LUNs that were already presented to the ESXi hosts. If for any reason a replicated LUN is presented to an ESXi host, then the host will not mount the VMFS volume on the LUN. This is a precaution to prevent data corruption.

ESXi identifies each VMFS volume using its signature denoted by a **UUID** (**Universally Unique Identifier**). The UUID is generated when the volume is first created or resignatured and is stored in the LVM header of the VMFS volume.

When an ESXi host scans for new LUN; devices and VMFS volumes on it, it compares the physical device ID (NAA ID) of the LUN with the device ID (NAA ID) value stored in the VMFS volumes LVM header. If it finds a mismatch, then it flags the volume as a snapshot volume.

Volumes detected as snapshots are not mounted by default. There are two ways to mount such volumes/datastore:

- **Mount by keeping the existing signature intact**: This is used when you are attempting to temporarily mount the snapshot volume on an ESXi that doesn't see the original volume. If you were to attempt mounting the VMFS volume by keeping the existing signature and if the host sees the original volume, then you will not be allowed to mount the volume and will be warned about the presence of another VMFS volume with the same UUID.

- **Mount by generating a new VMFS signature**: This has to be used if you are mounting a clone or a snapshot of an existing VMFS datastore to the same host(s). The process of assigning a new signature will not only update the LVM header with the newly generated UUID, but all the physical device ID (NAA ID) of the snapshot LUN. Here, the VMFS volume/datastore will be renamed by prefixing the word snap followed by a random number and the name of the original datastore:

| Name | Status | Type | Datastore Cluster | Capacity | Free |
|------|--------|------|-------------------|----------|------|
| datastore1 | Normal | VMFS 5 | | 32.5 GB | 31.55 GB |
| VCSA_DS | Normal | VMFS 6 | | 299.75 GB | 249.71 GB |
| snap-78e9b26a-LABDS | Normal | VMFS 6 | | 4.75 GB | 3.34 GB |

# Getting ready

Make sure that the original datastore and its LUN is no longer seen by the ESXi host the snapshot is being mounted to.

# How to do it...

The following procedure will help mount a VMFS volume from a LUN detected as a snapshot:

1. Log in to the vCenter Server using the vSphere web client and use the key combination *Ctrl + Alt + 2* to switch to the **Host and Clusters** view.
2. Right click on the ESXi host the snapshot LUN is mapped to and go to **Storage** | **New Datastore**.
3. On the **New Datastore** wizard, select **VMFS** as the filesystem type and click **Next** to continue.

4. On the **Name and device selection** screen, select the LUN detected as a snapshot and click **Next** to continue:

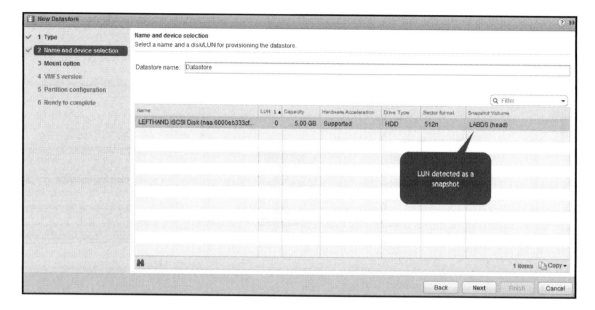

5. On the **Mount option** screen, choose to either mount by assigning a new signature or by keeping the existing signature, and click **Next** to continue:

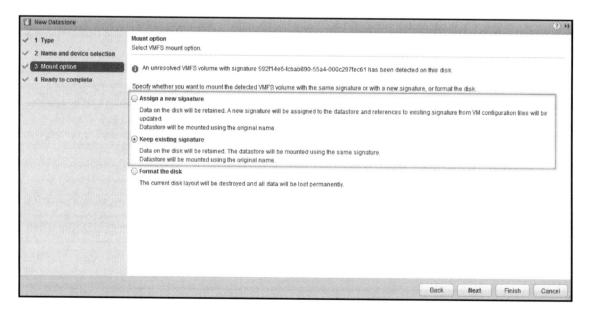

6. On the **Ready to complete** screen, review the setting and click **Finish** to initiate the operation.

# Masking paths to a LUN

You can remove access to a LUN by masking all of its paths to the ESXi host. This can be used when troubleshooting storage issues. This is achieved by using the MASK_PATH PSA plugin to claim the paths corresponding to the intended LUN.

The following flowchart depicts a high-level overview of the process:

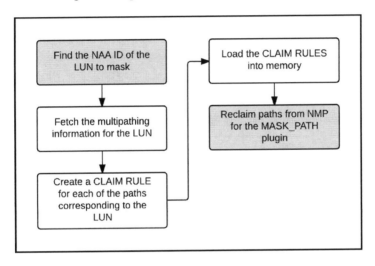

# How to do it...

The following procedure will help you mask paths to a LUN:

1. Get the NAA ID of the LUN, which needs to be masked, by issuing the following command. The following command will list all the NAA IDs seen by the ESXi:

```
esxcfg-scsidevs -u
```

2. Get the multipathing information of the LUN by issuing the following command syntax:

```
esxcfg-mpath -l -d <naa-id of the LUN>
```

```
~ # esxcfg-mpath -l -d naa.6000eb30adde4c1b0000000000000112
iqn.1998-01.com.vmware:localhost-6ec490dc-00023d000002,iqn.   -10.com.lefthandnetwo
   Runtime Name: vmhba33 C1:T2:L0
   Device: naa.6000eb30adde4c1b0000000000000112
   Device Display Name: LEFTHAND iSCSI Disk (naa.6000eb30adde4c1b0000000000000112)
   Adapter: vmhba33 Channel: 1 Target: 2 LUN: 0
   Adapter Identifier: iqn.1998-01.com.vmware:localhost-6ec490dc
   Target Identifier: 00023d000002,iqn.2003-10.com.lefthandnetworks:labmainstroage:2
   Plugin: NMP
   State: active
   Transport: iscsi
   Adapter Transport Details: iqn.1998-01.com.vmware:localhost-6ec490dc
   Target Transport Details: IQN=iqn.2003-10.com.lefthandnetworks:labmainstroage:274

iqn.1998-01.com.vmware:localhost-6ec490dc-00023d000001,iqn.2003-10.com.lefthandnetwo
   Runtime Name: vmhba33 C0:T2:L0
   Device: naa.6000eb30adde4c1b0000000000000112
   Device Display Name: LEFTHAND iSCSI Disk (naa.6000eb30adde4c1b0000000000000112)
   Adapter: vmhba33 Channel: 0 Target: 2 LUN: 0
   Adapter Identifier: iqn.1998-01.com.vmware:localhost-6ec490dc
   Target Identifier: 00023d000001,iqn.2003-10.com.lefthandnetworks:labmainstroage:2
   Plugin: NMP
   State: active
   Transport: iscsi
   Adapter Transport Details: iqn.1998-01.com.vmware:localhost-6ec490dc
   Target Transport Details: IQN=iqn.2003-10.com.lefthandnetworks:labmainstroage:274
```

3. Create a claim rule for each of the paths to the LUN by issuing the following command syntax:

```
esxcli storage core claimrule add -r <rule number> -t location -A
<hba> -C <channel number> -L <LUN Number> -P MASK_PATH
```

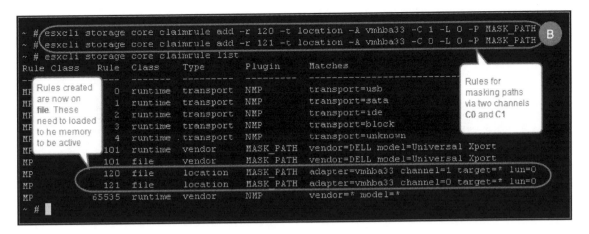

4. Load the rules on the file into the memory by issuing the following command:

```
esxcli storage core claimrule load
```

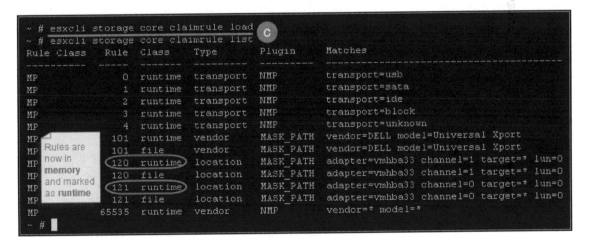

5. Reclaim the paths for MASK_PATH for NMP by using the following command syntax:

```
esxcli storage core claiming reclaim –d <NAA ID of the LUN>
```

# Unmasking paths to a LUN

It is possible to unmask paths to a LUN. Deleting the claim rules, which were created to assign the ownership of the paths to the MASK_PATH plugin, and unclaiming the paths from the plugin, does this. Understanding how the paths to a LUN are masked will be a good starting point for this task. Read the recipe *Masking paths to a LUN* before you begin.

The following flowchart provides a high-level overview of the unmasking procedure.

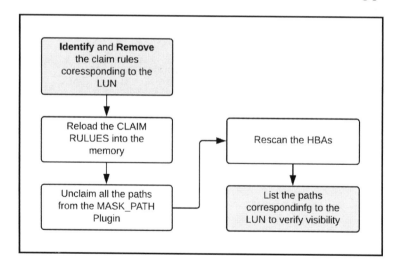

# How to do it...

The following procedure will help you unmask paths to a LUN:

1. Identify the claim rules corresponding to the LUN and remove them:

   ```
   esxcli storage claimrule remove -r <rule ID>
   ```

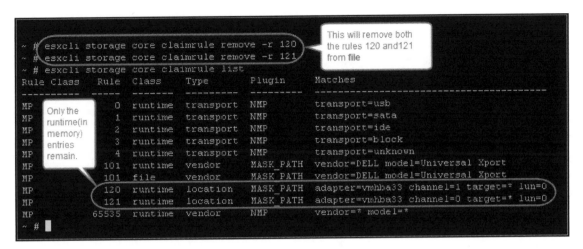

2. Now that the rules have been deleted from the file, reload the claim rules to the memory to remove the runtime entries. Issue the following command to load the rules in the memory:

   ```
   esxcli storage core claimrule load
   ```

3. The runtime entries for `120` and `121` will be removed from the memory because they don't have a corresponding file entry.

4. Unclaim all the paths for the LUN from the `MASK_PATH` plugin by using the following command syntax:

   ```
   esxcli storage core claiming unclaim -t location -A <HBA> -C
   <Channel> -L <LUN ID> -P MASK_PATH
   Examples:
   esxcli storage core claiming unclaim -t location -A vmhba33 -C 0 -L
   0 -P MASK_PATH
   esxcli storage core claiming unclaim -t location -A vmhba33 -C 1 -L
   0 -P MASK_PATH
   ```

5. Issue a rescan on the HBAs using the following syntax:

```
esxcfg-rescan <HBA>
Example:
esxcfg-rescan vmhba33
```

6. Verify the LUN's visibility by listing all the paths corresponding to it, using the following command syntax:

```
esxcfg-mpath -l -d <naa-id of the LUN>
Example:
esxcfg-mpath -l -d naa.6000eb30adde4c1b0000000000000112
```

# 9

# Managing Access to the iSCSI and NFS Storage

In this chapter, we will cover the following topics:

- Adding the software iSCSI adapter
- Configuring iSCSI multipathing using port binding
- Configuring access to an iSCSI Target Server
- Creating NFSv3 datastores
- Creating NFSv4 datastores with Kerberos authentication

## Introduction

Both iSCSI and NFS are storage solutions that can leverage the existing TCP/IP network infrastructure. Hence, they are referred to as *IP-based storage*. Before we start learning how to configure them, let's delve into some iSCSI and NFS fundamentals.

## iSCSI fundamentals

The **Internet Small Computer Systems Interface (iSCSI)** is a protocol used to transport SCSI commands over a TCP/IP network. In an iSCSI environment, the client machine (in this case, an ESXi host) uses iSCSI initiators (hardware/software) to connect to iSCSI targets on an iSCSI storage system.

Let's review some of the iSCSI terminology that you will need to be aware of before you learn how to configure and manage access to iSCSI storage:

- **iSCSI initiator:** This is a software/hardware adapter that resides on an ESXi host and has the ability to connect to an iSCSI target. The software iSCSI adapter is built into the VMkernel and can be enabled when intended. The hardware iSCSI adapter can be of two types: *dependent* and *independent*. While the dependent iSCSI adapter handles the packet processing, it is still reliant on ESXi for its network configuration and management. The independent iSCSI adapter provides for both configuration and packet processing.
- **iSCSI target:** This is a network interface on the iSCSI array or on a LUN. Some arrays, such as Dell EqualLogic and HP StoreVirual, present each LUN as a target.

 With vSphere 6.5, unlike the previous versions, the iSCSI initiator and the iSCSI target can now be on two different layer-2 subnets.

- **iSCSI portal:** This is a combination of the iSCSI target's IP address and the listening port (default: 3260). An iSCSI portal at the initiator is the IP address of the VMkernel interface.
- **iSCSI session:** This is a TCP/IP session established between an iSCSI initiator and an iSCSI target. Each session can have one more connection to the target. In the case of software iSCSI, a session is established between each bound VMkernel interface and an iSCSI target. For example, if there are two VMkernel interfaces bound to the iSCSI initiator, then the initiator will establish two separate sessions for each target it discovers.
- **iSCSI connection:** Each iSCSI session can have multiple connections to the iSCSI target portal.
- **CHAP:** The **Challenge Handshake Authentication Protocol (CHAP)** is used by iSCSI to make sure that the initiator and target establish a trusted and secure connection.
- **Dynamic Discovery:** This is a commonly used target discovery mechanism, which comes in handy when the iSCSI server has made a large number of LUNs/targets via its target portal.
- **Static Discovery:** Unlike the Dynamic Discovery mechanism, static discovery does not see every LUN/target exposed via the target portal. Instead, it only sees the specified targets.

# NFS fundamentals

**Network File System** (**NFS**) is a protocol used to process shared access to a filesystem location, such as a folder, over the TCP/IP network. VMware added support for NFS 4.1 with vSphere 6.0 and with vSphere 6.5 is now supported for use with vSphere Host Profiles. vSphere 6.5 supports both the NFS versions.

NFS exports—are folder shares created on the NFS server's local filesystem to be used by the NFS client; which in this case is an ESXi host.

NFS datastore—an NFS mount that connects to an export on the NFS server. In this way, the NFS server allows the ESXi host to access its filesystem, but the access is restricted to the NFS export.

# Adding the software iSCSI adapter

For an ESXi host to be able to access iSCSI targets, it needs to be configured with an iSCSI initiator (adapter). For cases where you do not have hardware iSCSI initiators available, VMkernel has a software iSCSI adapter built into it; however, it is not enabled by default.

# Getting ready

The software iSCSI adapter will use the VMkernel network stack to establish sessions with the iSCSI targets. Hence, by default, it will use the management network's VMkernel interface (vmk0). It is recommended that you create a different VMkernel interface for iSCSI. This will become essential when the management network is in a different subnet than the IP storage network.

# How to do it...

The following procedure will help you enable the software iSCSI adapter:

1. Log in to the vCenter Server, using the vSphere Web Client and use the key combination *Ctrl + Alt + 2* to switch to the **Host and Clusters** view.

2. Select the desired ESXi host, navigate **Configure** | **Storage** | **Storage Adapters**, click on the ✚ icon ,and select **Software iSCSI adapter**:

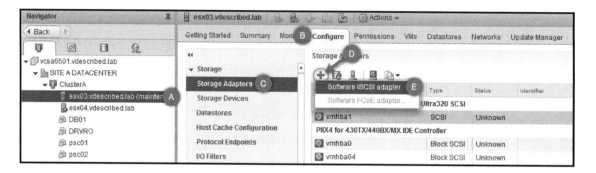

3. In the **Add Software iSCSI Adapter** dialog box, click **OK** to add the adapter:

4. The **Recent Tasks** pane should show two tasks—**Change Software Internet SCSI Status** and **Open firewall ports**—completed successfully:

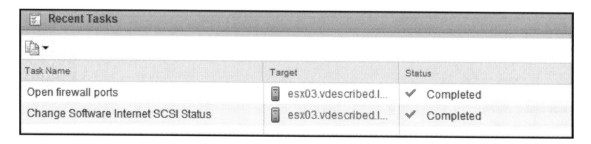

5. The **Storage Adapters** section should now list an **iSCSI Software Adapter**:

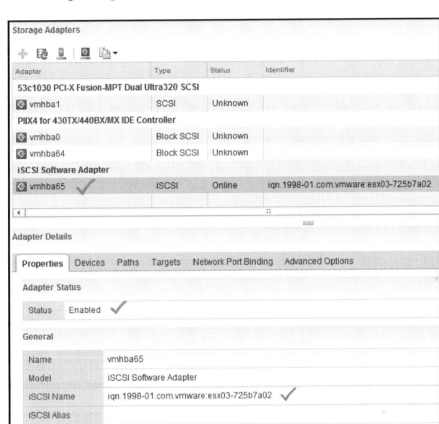

## How it works...

When you add a software iSCSI adapter, all it does is enable the adapter and open all outgoing connections for TCP port 3260 in the ESXi firewall.

To view the firewall rule for Software iSCSI, select the ESXi host, navigate to **Configure** | **System** | **Security Profile**, and review the **Outgoing Connections** section:

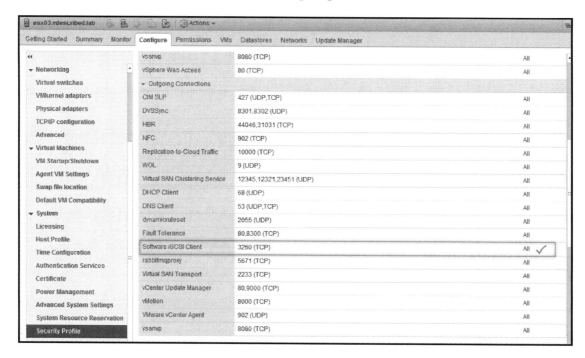

# Configuring iSCSI multipathing using port binding

By default, ESXi generates a single path between the software iSCSI adapter and the iSCSI targets, unless the iSCSI array is a multi-portal array allowing target access via more than one network interface. To enable load balancing or redundancy for iSCSI traffic egressing an ESXi host, you will need to bind multiple VMkernel interfaces (vmk) to the software iSCSI adapter. There is an important catch to this type of configuration though, that is that the Vmkernel interfaces and the iSCSI target portals cannot be on disparate network subnets. In other words, they should be in the same broadcast domain (VLAN). This does not mean that iSCSI does not support routing; it is only a limitation with the port binding.

Port binding is only done with the software iSCSI adapter and dependent hardware iSCSI adapters.

# Getting ready

Create two VMkernel interfaces on two separate distributed port groups, with IP addresses in the same subnet as the iSCSI target portal:

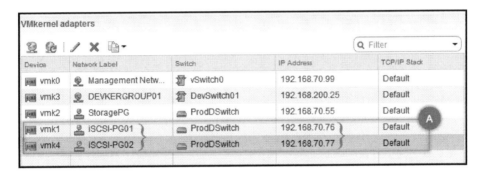

Configure the NIC teaming on the distributed port groups, in such a way that there is only a single active adapter and the other adapters are unused:

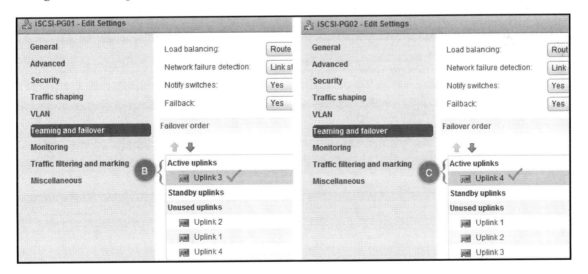

# How to do it...

The following procedure will help you bind VMkernel adapters to the iSCSI adapter:

1. Once you are done with creating the VMkernel interfaces and distributed port groups as instructed in the *Getting ready* section, go to *step 2*.

2. Use the key combination *Ctrl + Alt + 2* to switch to the **Host and Clusters** view, select the ESXi host and navigate to **Configure** I **Storage** I **Storage Adapters**, and select the iSCSI adapter:

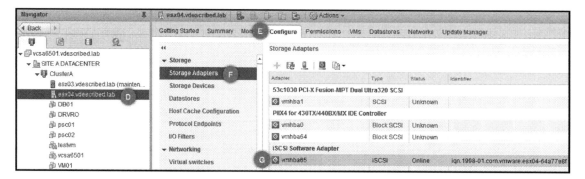

3. With the iSCSI adapter selected, navigate to its **Network Port Binding** tab and click on the ✚ icon to bring up the **Bind vmhbaXX with VMkernel Adapter** window:

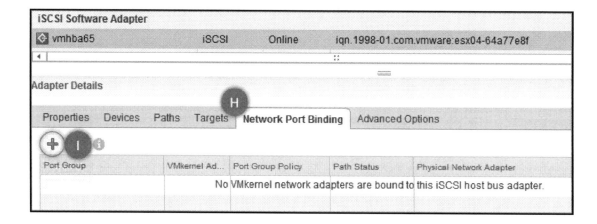

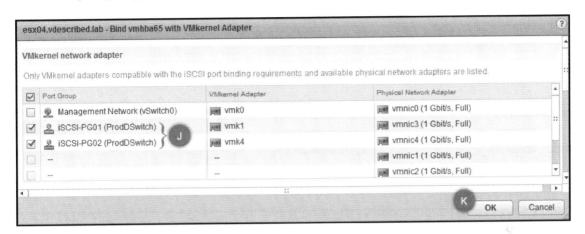

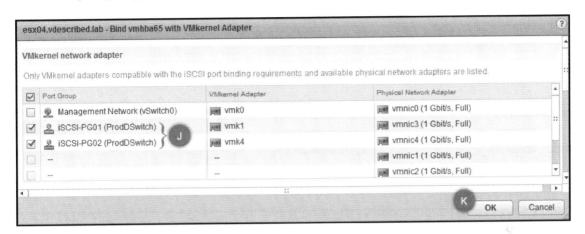

4. On the **Bind vmhbaXX with VMkernel Adapter** window, select the distributed port groups that were created for binding and click **OK:**

5. Once this is done, you will see the VMkernel adapters listed under the **Network Port Binding**. The **Path Status** is **Not used** because we have not configured any iSCSI targets yet. It also recommends a rescan, which again is not required at this point in time, because we don't have targets configured:

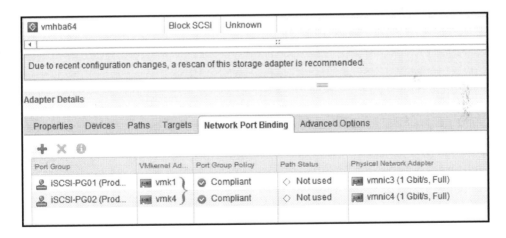

 The next step is to configure access to an iSCSI target, which is covered in the next recipe *Configuring Access to an iSCSI Target Server.*

6. Once you have configured access to a target server, you should see the **Path Status** for each of bound interface change to **Active**:

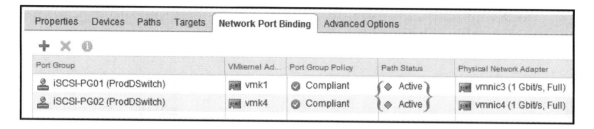

# How it works...

The number of paths made available for the iSCSI initiator will depend upon the type of iSCSI storage array.

With single portal arrays, the storage array exposes a single portal to be discovered by the source (initiator). Hence, the number of paths to such an array will depend on the number of VMkernel interfaces associated with the iSCSI initiator. The process of associating VMkernel interfaces with an iSCSI initiator is called **port binding**. We will learn more about port binding in the *Configuring iSCSI multipathing using port binding* section of this chapter. Arrays such as the HP's HPE StoreVirtual and Dell EqualLogic are examples of single portal arrays.

With multi-portal arrays, the storage array exposes multiple portals to be discovered by the iSCSI initiator. Therefore, the number of paths to the array will not only depend on the number of VMkernel ports bound to the iSCSI initiator but also the number of portals exposed. For instance, if two VMkernel ports are bound to the iSCSI initiator discovering four target portals, then the number of paths to the iSCSI target is eight.

With multi-target arrays, the storage array can have more than one iSCSI targets, with one or more portals associated with them.

The formula for calculating the number of paths possible is dependent on the number of sources (VMkernel port) and target portals and not the number of targets:

*Total number of paths = (Number of Source Portals) x (Number of target portals).*

Here, the source portal is nothing but the VMkernel interfaces bound to the iSCSI initiator.

When you view the multipathing information for single/multi-portal arrays from the vCenter GUI, every discovery portal will be listed as a target. These targets will have the same IQN, but different portal IP addresses associated with them. However, for multi-target arrays, you will see targets with different IQNs as well.

> There are cases when port binding should not be used to achieve multipathing. The *When not to use port binding* section of the VMware Knowledge Base article—*2038869* (`https://kb.vmware.com/s/article/ 2038869`) has more details.

# Configuring access to an iSCSI target server

For the ESXi server to be able to see iSCSI targets/LUNs, the iSCSI adapter needs to be configured with the details of the iSCSI target server. The target server is nothing but an iSCSI array. Here, the term *target* can refer to the network interfaces on the iSCSI array or individual LUNs. The definition changes depending on the type of array being used. For example, a Dell EqualLogic array will present its LUNs as targets.

## Getting ready

To configure the access to an iSCSI target server, we'll need following setup in place:

- Discoverable IP address of the iSCSI target server and the port number to use.
- CHAP authentication details (if any).
- The iSCSI array should be configured to allow access to the iSCSI initiator. You will need the iSCSI adapter IQN handy for this activity.
- The iSCSI array has to be configured to allow the necessary LUNs to be discovered.

# How to do it...

The following procedure will help you configure access to an iSCSI target server:

1. Log in to the vCenter Server using the vSphere Web Client, use the key combination *Ctrl + Alt + 2* to switch to the host and clusters view, select the ESXi host, navigate to **Configure** | - | **Storage Adapters**, and select the iSCSI adapter:

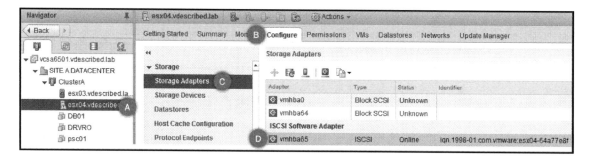

2. With the iSCSI adapter selected, navigate to **Targets** | **Dynamic Discovery** and click on **Add...** to bring up the **Add Send Target Server** window:

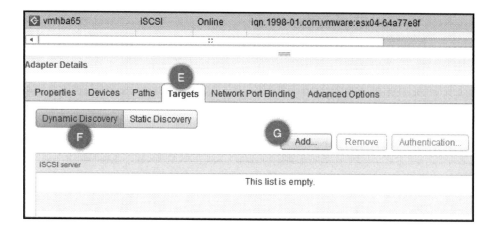

3. On the **Add Send Target Server** window, supply the IP address and the port number of the target portal and click **OK**:

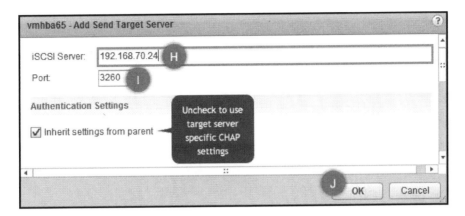

4. The **Targets** tab of the initiator will now list the iSCSI target server. Issue a rescan to discover LUN presented to the ESXi host:

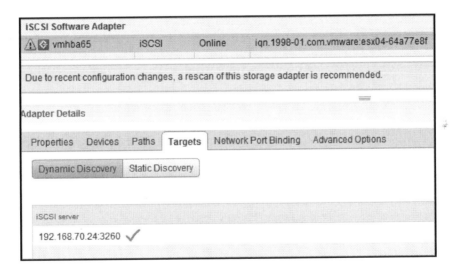

# How it works...

Once an iSCSI target server is added, a `SEND TARGETS` command is sent to the target server from each of the bound VMkernel (vmk) interfaces. In response, the target server will send a list of targets presented to the iSCSI initiator. The target list received from the array will be listed in the **Static Discovery** tab, as shown in the following screenshot:

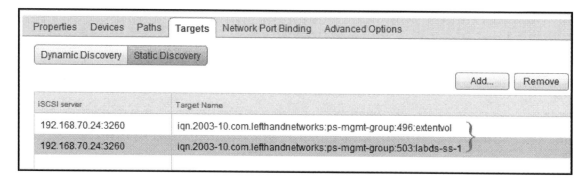

In the **Devices** tab, all of the LUN devices discovered will be listed:

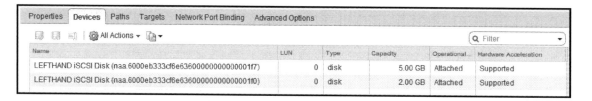

If you review a full list of all paths to all the discovered targets (LUNS) then, in this case, you should see two paths for each target. This is because we bound two VMkernel interfaces to the iSCSI initiator and HPE StoreVirtual is a single portal array:

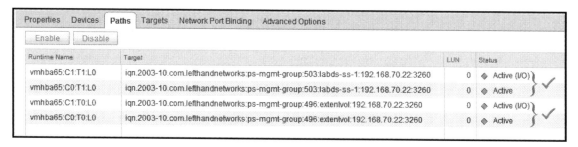

# Creating NFSv3 datastores

NFS Storage is network attached like the iSCSI storage. However, unlike the iSCSI storage, NFS does not provide access to block storage. NFS Server's operating system maintains its own filesystem and exports filesystem locations (folders in most cases) for access from an NFS client. Hence, ESXi cannot format an NFS export to put VMFS on it, instead, they are simply mounted. In this recipe, we will learn how to create NFS datastores (mounts).

## Getting ready

You will need the FQDN/IP address of the NFS server and the folder path (export) information handy before you proceed. Your storage admin can provide you with this information. NFS will also require a VMkernel interface to connect to the storage. Hence, you should make sure that one is already created for this purpose.

> At the NFS server, configure to allow root access to your shares. It is commonly referred to as `no_rootsquash`.

## How to do it...

The following procedure will help you create an NFS datastore:

1.  Log in to the vCenter Server using the vSphere Web Client, use the key combination *Ctrl + Alt + 2* to switch to the host and clusters view, right-click on the desired ESXi host, and go to **Storage | New Datastore...**:

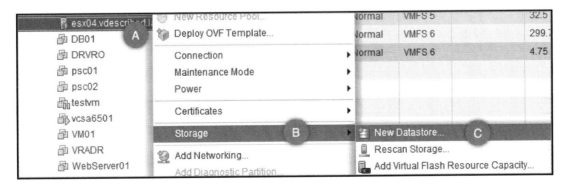

2. On the **New Datastore** wizard, set the **Type** as **NFS** and click **Next** to continue:

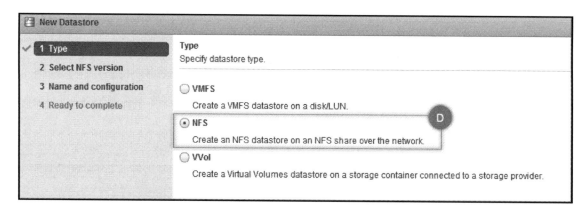

3. On the **Select NFS version** screen, select **NFS 3** and click **Next** to continue. Keep in mind that it is not recommended to mount an NFS export using both NFS 3 and NFS 4.1 client:

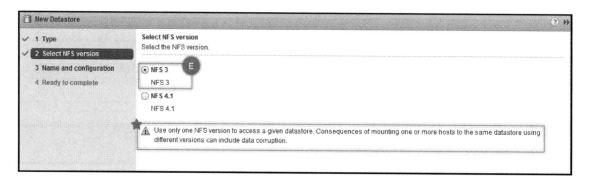

4. On the **Name and configuration** screen, supply a **Datastore name** for the datastore, the NFS export folder path, and NFS server's IP address or FQDN. You can also choose to mount the share as read-only, if desired:

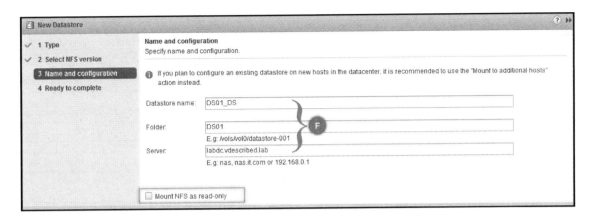

5. On the **Ready to complete** screen review the setting and click **Finish** to mount the NFS export:

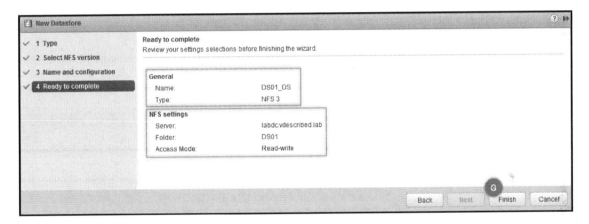

6. Once done, you should see the NFS mount listed as one of the datastores:

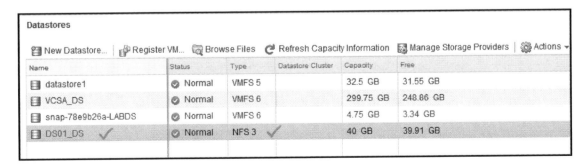

# How it works...

By default, you can only create *eight* NFS mounts per ESXi server. Although this limit can be increased up to 256 by using the advanced setting NFS.MaxVolumes, increasing this limit would generally require an increase in the minimum amount of VMkernel TCP/IP heap memory. The minimum heap memory value can be specified using the advanced setting Net.TcpipHeapSize. You can also set the maximum amount of heap size using the advanced setting Net.TcpipHeapMax. Most vendor documentation will have guidelines regarding the configuration of these parameters. Make sure you refer to them before you modify the defaults.

For more information regarding the TCP/IP heap size value, read the VMware Knowledge Base article—2239 (https://kb.vmware.com/kb/2239).

# Creating NFSv4.1 datastores with Kerberos authentication

VMware introduced support for NFS 4.1 with vSphere 6.0. vSphere 6.5 added several enhancements:

- It now supports AES encryption
- Support for IPv6
- Support Kerberos integrity checking mechanism

In this recipe, we will learn how to create NFS 4.1 datastores. Although the procedure is similar to NFSv3, there are a few additional steps that needs to be performed.

# Getting ready

The following setup is required for Creating NFSv4.1 datastores with Kerberos authentication:

- For Kerberos authentication to work, you need to make sure that the ESXi hosts and the NFS server are joined to the Active Directory domain
- Create a new or select an existing AD user for NFS Kerberos authentication
- Configure the NFS server/share to allow access to the AD user chosen for NFS Kerberos authentication

# How to do it...

The following procedure will help you mount an NFS datastore using the NFSv4.1 client with Kerberos authentication enabled:

1. Log in to the vCenter Server using the vSphere Web Client, use the key combination *Ctrl + Alt + 2* to switch to the host and clusters view, select the desired ESXi host, navigate to its **Configure** | **System** | **Authentication Services** section, and supply the credentials of the Active Directory user that was chosen for NFS Kerberos authentication (Read the *Getting ready* section of this recipe):

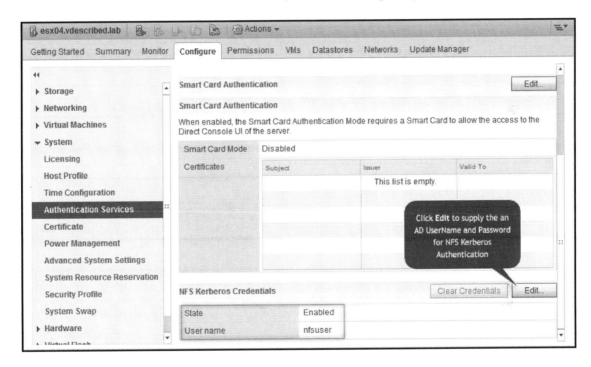

2. Right-click on the desired ESXi host and go to **Storage** | **New Datastore** to bring-up the **Add Storage** wizard.
3. On the **New Datastore** wizard, set the **Type** as **NFS** and click **Next** to continue.
4. On the **Select NFS version** screen, select **NFS 4.1** and click **Next** to continue. Keep in mind that it is not recommended to mount an NFS export using both NFS 3 and NFS 4.1 client.

5. On the **Name and configuration** screen, supply a name for the datastore, the NFS export's folder path, and the NFS server's IP address or FQDN. You can also choose to mount the share as read-only, if desired:

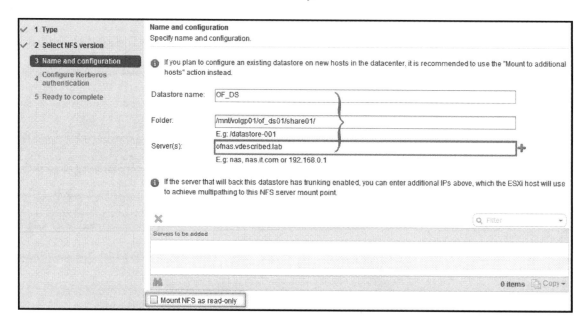

6. On the **Configure Kerberos authentication** screen, check the **Enable Kerberos-based authentication** box, choose the type of authentication required, and click **Next** to continue:

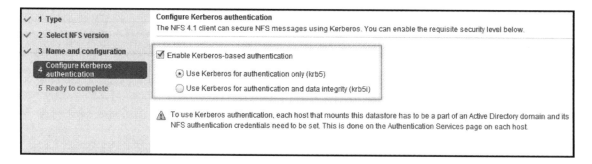

7. On the **Ready to complete** screen, review the settings and click **Finish** to mount the NFS export.

# 10

# Storage IO Control, Storage DRS, and Profile Driven Storage

Storage IO Control, Storage DRS, and Profile Driven Storage. In this chapter, we will cover the following recipes:

- Setting disk shares on virtual machines disks
- Enabling Storage I/O Control (SIOC)
- Using storage DRS
- Integrating a VASA provider with the vCenter Server
- Using vCenter tags to define storage capabilities
- Creating VM storage policies
- Assigning VM storage policies

## Introduction

In the previous two chapters, we learned how to configure and manage access to FC, iSCSI, and NFS storage devices. Once we present storage devices to the ESXi host or a cluster of ESXi hosts, the business would start using them by hosting live virtual machine data on them.

As time progresses, more and more virtual machines are added to the mix and consume storage capacity in terms of space and throughput. Hence it becomes important to, not only fine-tune the process of placing the VMs on datastores backed by the correct type of storage tier, but also control the space and bandwidth utilization among all the virtual machines.

Storage I/O Control is one of the mechanisms to use ensure a fair share of storage bandwidth allocation to all VMs running on shared storage, regardless of the ESXi host the virtual machines are running on.

Storage DRS monitors datastore space utilization and SIOC metrics to redistribute VM files among datastores in a datastore cluster. It also provides initial placement recommendations when deploying virtual machines into the datastore cluster.

**Storage Policy Based Management (SPBM)** helps a vSphere administrator create virtual machine storage policies, to enable selection of datastores based on their storage characteristics, which are either user defined or learned using a VASA provider.

# Settings disk shares on virtual machine disks

Every ESXi host runs a local scheduler to monitor and balance the I/O between the virtual machines. If there are virtual machines generating a considerable amount of I/O (more than normal), then it is important to make sure that the other virtual machines running on the same datastore remain unaffected, in a manner that they should be allowed to issue I/O to the device with performance expected. This can be achieved by setting per-disk (vmdk) shares thereby controlling the volume of I/O each participating virtual machines can generate, during contention. Disk shares works pretty much like the CPU or memory shares and would only kick-in during contention. The default virtual disk share value is 1,000, high being 2,000 and low being 500. The disk with a relatively higher share value will get to issue a larger volume of I/O to the device.

## How to do it...

Every virtual disk (VMDK) will have a normal (1,000) share value set on it, by default. The following procedure will help you modify disk shares on a virtual machine:

1. Connect to the vCenter Server using the web client and switch to the **Virtual Machines and Templates** view using the key combination *Ctrl + Alt + 3*.
2. Right-click on the desired VM and go to **Edit Settings...**:

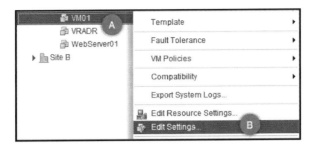

3. In the **Edit Settings** window, click on the hard disk you intend to modify the shares and use the shares drop-down box to choose between, **High** (2,000), **Normal** (1,000), **Low** (500) or **Custom** (user-defined share value). Once you have set the desired shares value, click **OK** to confirm and exit:

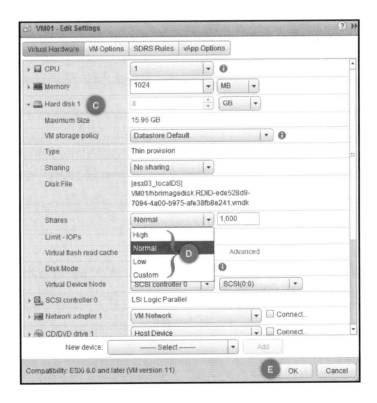

# Enabling Storage I/O Control (SIOC)

The use of disk shares will work just fine as long as the datastore is seen by a single ESXi host. Unfortunately, that is not a common case. Datastores are often shared among multiple ESXi hosts. When datastores are shared, you bring in more than one local host scheduler into the process of balancing the I/O among the virtual machines. However, these lost host schedules cannot talk to each other and their visibility is limited to the ESXi hosts they are running on. This easily contributes to a serious problem called the noisy neighbor situation:

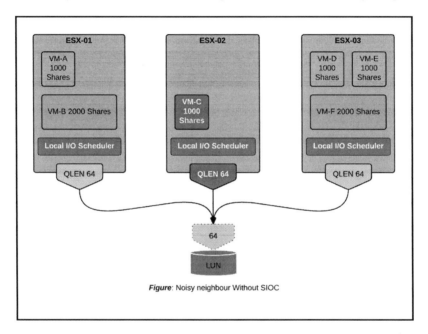

**Figure**: Noisy neighbour Without SIOC

The job of SIOC is to enable some form of communication between local host schedulers so that I/O can be balanced between virtual machines running on separate hosts. We will learn more about how SIOC functions in the *How it works...* section of this recipe. Before that, we will learn how to *enable SIOC*.

# How to do it...

The following procedure will help you enable SIOC on a datastore:

1. Connect to the vCenter Server using the web client and switch to the **Storage** view using the key combination *Ctrl + Alt + 4*.

2. Right-click on the desired datastore and go to **Configure Storage I/O Control...**:

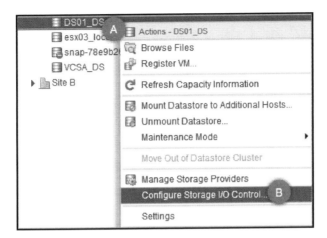

3. On the **Configure Storage I/O Control** window, select the checkbox **Enable Storage I/O Control**, set a custom **Congestion Threshold** (only if needed) and click **OK** to confirm the settings:

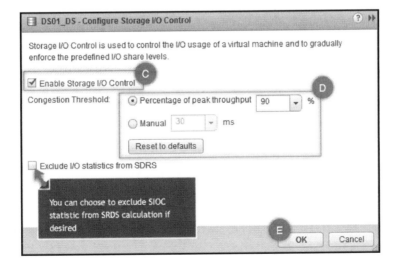

4. With the virtual machine selected from the inventory, navigate to its **Configure | General** tab and review its **Datastore Capabilities** settings to ensure that SIOC **Status** shows **Enabled**:

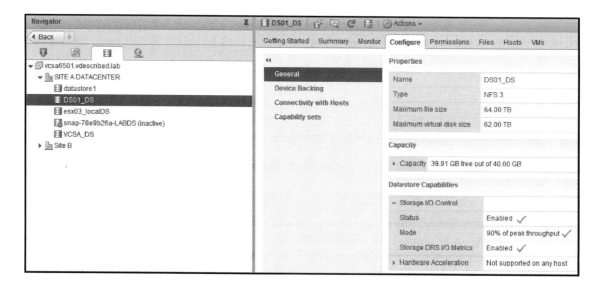

# How it works...

As mentioned earlier, SIOC enables communication between these local host schedulers so that I/O can be balanced between virtual machines running on separate hosts. It does so by maintaining a shared file in the datastore that all hosts can read/write/update. When SIOC is enabled on a datastore, it starts monitoring the device latency on the LUN backing the datastore. If the latency crosses the threshold, it throttles the LUN's queue depth on each of the ESXi hosts in an attempt to distribute a fair share of access to the LUN for all the virtual machines issuing the I/O.

The local scheduler on each of the ESXi hosts maintains an `iostats` file to keep its companion hosts aware of the device I/O statistics observed on the LUN. The file is placed in a directory (`naa.xxxxxxxxx`) on the same datastore.

For example, if there are six virtual machines running on three different ESXi hosts, accessing a shared LUN. Among the six VMs, four of them have a normal share value of **1,000** and the remaining two have high (**2,000**) disk share value set on them. These virtual machines have only a single VMDK attached to them. **VM-C** on host **ESX-02** is issuing a large number of I/O operations. Since that is the only VM accessing the shared LUN from that host, it gets the entire queue's bandwidth. This can induce latency on the I/O operations performed by the other VMs: **ESX-01** and **ESX-03**. If the SIOC detects the latency value to be greater than the dynamic threshold, then it will start throttling the queue depth:

| Hosts | ESX-01 | | ESX-02 | ESX-03 | | | How to arrive at the ratio (portion value) ? | |
|---|---|---|---|---|---|---|---|---|
| VMs | VM-A | VM-B | VM-C | VM-D | VM-E | VM-F | | |
| Disk Shares | 1000 | 2000 | 1000 | 1000 | 1000 | 2000 | Ratio | (VM Share Value) / (Total Share Value) |
| VM's portion of the shares | 1/8 | 1/4 | 1/8 | 1/4 | 1/8 | 1/8 | 1/8 | 1000/8000 |
| | | | | | | | 1/4 | 2000/8000 |
| VM's Percent of Shares | 12.5 | 25 | 12.5 | 25 | 12.5 | 12.5 | | |
| DQLEN for the VM | 8 | 16 | 8 | 16 | 8 | 8 | | |
| DQLEN for the Host | 24 | | 8 | 32 | | | | |

The throttled DQLEN for a VM is calculated as follows:

*DQLEN for the VM = (VM's Percent of Shares) of (Queue Depth)*

*Example: 12.5 % of 64 = (12.5 \* 64)/100 = 8*

The throttled DQLEN per host is calculated as follows:

*DQLEN of the Host = Sum of the DQLEN of the VMs on it*

*Example: VM-A (8) + VM-B(16) = 24*

The following diagram shows the effect of SIOC throttling the queue depth:

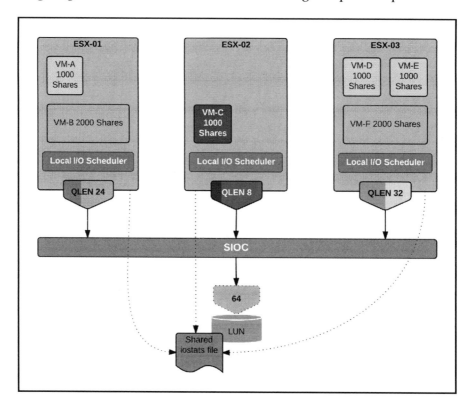

# Integrating a VASA provider with the vCenter Server

If you have a VASA capable array, then you can add a VASA provider to the vCenter Server so that it can generate array capabilities for each LUN or datastore. A capability generated by the provider is called a **system storage capability**.

# Getting ready

Since we are using an HPE StoreVirtual VSA, you will need a storage provider server configured with HP's HPE OneView installed. HPE OneView will have the VASA provider module. Since the installation instructions are beyond the scope of this book, we assume that the insight control for storage is installed and configured correctly. For instructions specific to the storage provider, refer to the vendor documentation.

# How to do it...

The following procedure will help you add a VASA storage provider to the vCenter Server:

1. Connect to the vCenter Server using the web client and switch to the **Host and Clusters** view using the key combination *Ctrl + Alt + 2*. (You can switch to any view since this activity is performed on the vCenter object).
2. Select the desired vCenter and navigate to its **Configure** | **More** | **Storage Providers** and click on the ➕ icon to bring up the **New Storage Provider** window:

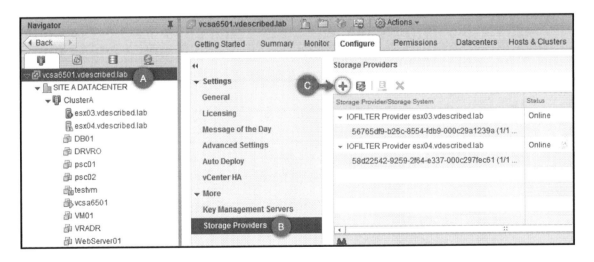

3. On the **New Storage Provider** window, supply a **Name**, a provider **URL** and credentials to connect to the VASA provider and click **OK**:

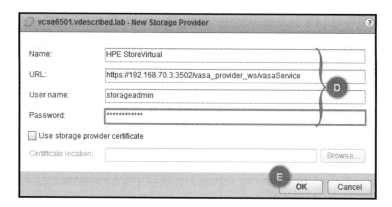

4. A **Security Alert** will prompt you to confirm the provider certificate, click **Yes**:

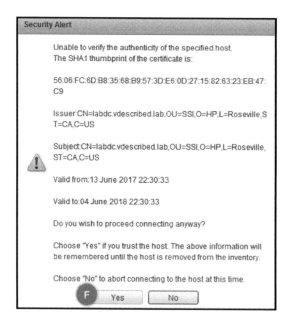

# How it works...

Once done, the newly added VASA provider should be listed in the **Storage Providers** screen:

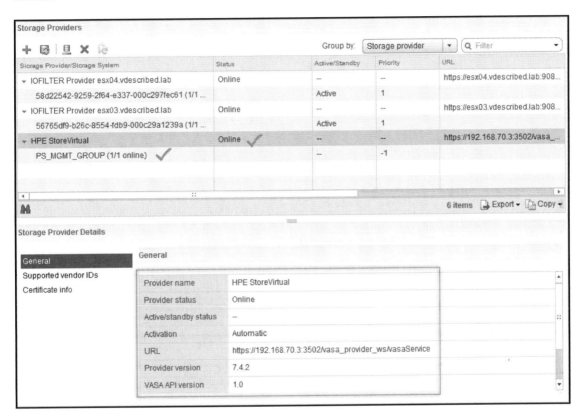

# Using vCenter tags to define storage capabilities

You can use the vCenter's tagging mechanism to create and associate tags to datastores. The tags are user defined and can have any name and category that the user would define. The tags can then be included in a storage policy to aid in the placement of VMs on them.

# How to do it...

The following procedure will help you use vCenter tags to create and assign custom capabilities to datastore objects for their use with virtual machine storage policies:

1. Connect to the vCenter Server using the web client and use the inventory menu to go to **Tags & Custom Attributes**:

2. In the **Tags & Custom Attributes** page, go to the **Categories** tab and click on the icon to create a **New Category** for datastores:

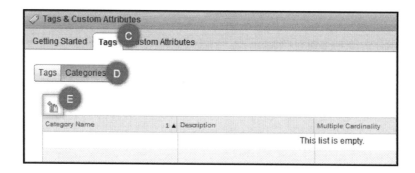

3. On the **New Category** window, supply the **Category Name** as Datastores, leave the **Cardinality** at **One tag per object**, select **Datastore** as the object to associate with and click **OK** to create the category:

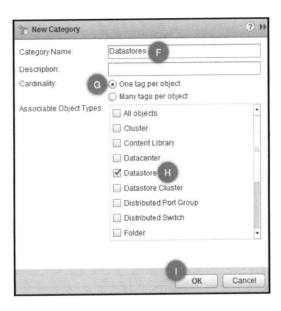

4. Once done you should see the **Datastores** category listed:

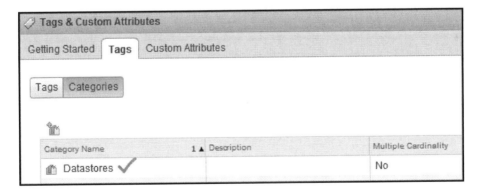

5. Now, go to the **Tags** tab and click on 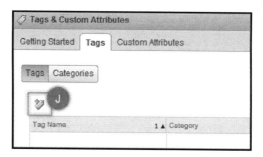 icon to create the new tag:

6. On the **New Tag** window, supply a **Name**, an optional **Description** and choose the **Category** as **Datastores**. In this case, we are creating a tag to denote local datastores. Click **OK** to create the tag:

7. Once done you should see the newly created vCenter tag as demonstrated here:

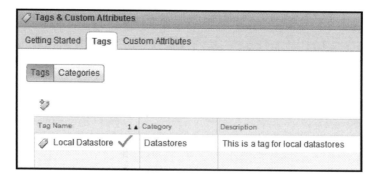

8. Now that you have the tag created, switch to storage view, right-click on the desired datastore and navigate to **Tags & Custom Attributes** | **Assign Tag...**:

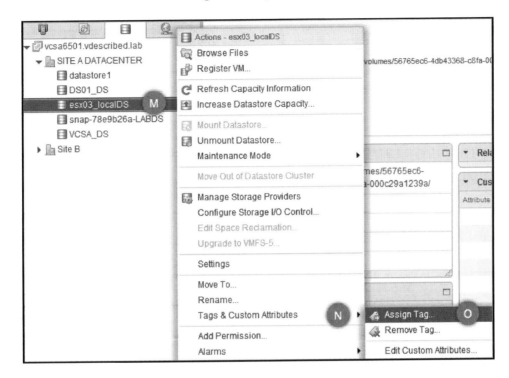

9. On the **Assign Tag** window, select the desired tag and click on **Assign**:

10. Now, if you review the **Summary** of the datastore, you will see a tag associated with it:

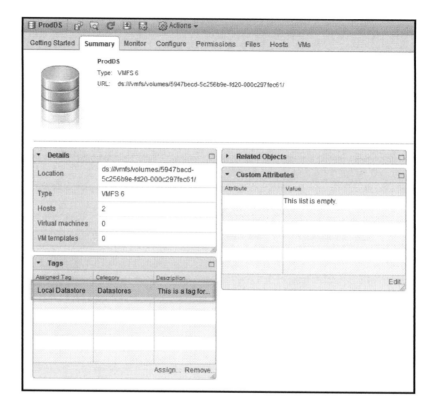

# Creating VM storage policies

Once you have the VASA provider added or the user-defined datastore tags created, you can create storage policies to define VM placement guidelines. For example, LUNs thin-provisioned volume, wherein a thin-provisioned volume, being a capability, can be categorized so that VMs running applications that do not demand first-write performance can be placed on these datastores. The first write performance could be impacted on a thin-provisioned volume because the volume should be increased in size before the data is first written to it.

# How to do it...

The following procedure will help you create VM storage policies:

1. Connect to the vCenter Server using the web client, navigate to the inventory home and click on **VM Storage Policies**:

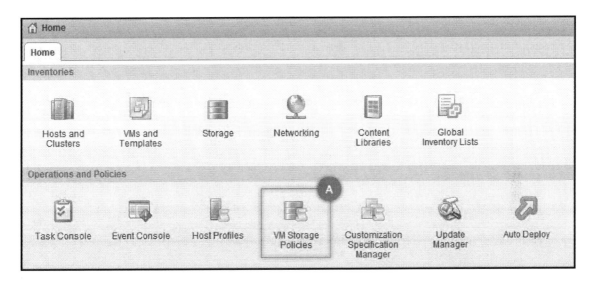

2. On the **VM Storage Policies** page, click on **Create VM Storage Policy...**:

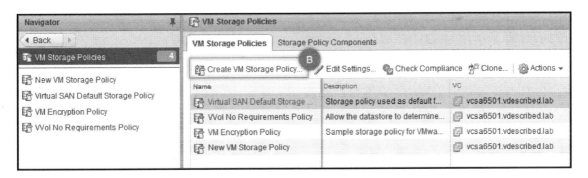

3. On the **Create New VM Storage Policy** wizard screen, supply a **Name** and optional **Description** and click **Next** to continue:

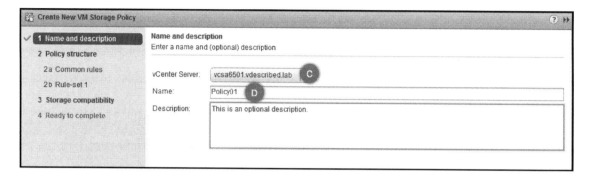

4. On the **Policy structure** page, click **Next** to continue:

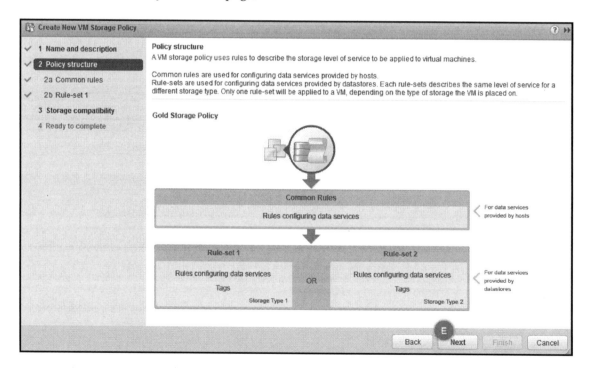

5. On the **2a Common rules** page, you can choose to include vSphere data services such as SIOC and encryption into the rule, by selecting the checkbox **Use common rules in the VM storage policy** and adding the service component to the rule:

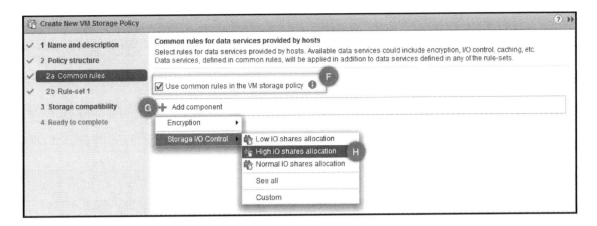

6. In this case, we have chosen to apply SIOC–high IO shares. Click **Next** to continue:

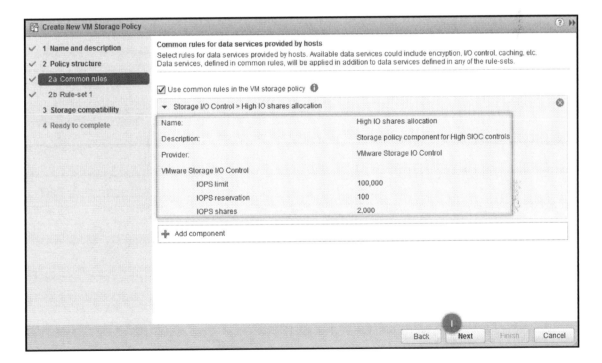

7. On the **2b Rule-set 1** page, select the **Storage Type** (which can be storage provider or a vCenter tag) and click on **<Add rule>** to add a system label:

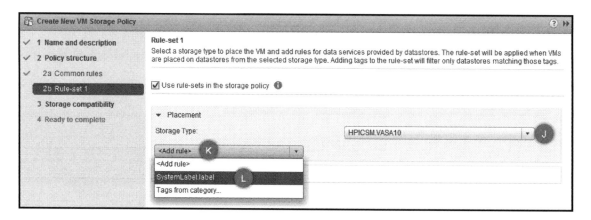

8. Choose a system label, which is nothing but a storage property as learned by the VASA provider. Click **Next** to continue:

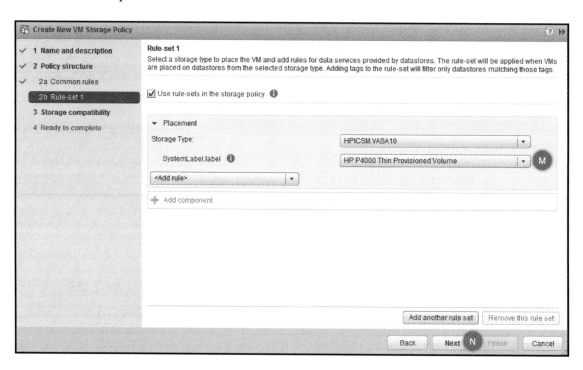

9. The **Storage compatibility** screen will display a filtered list of **Compatible** and **Incompatible** datastores. Review the list and click **Next** to continue:

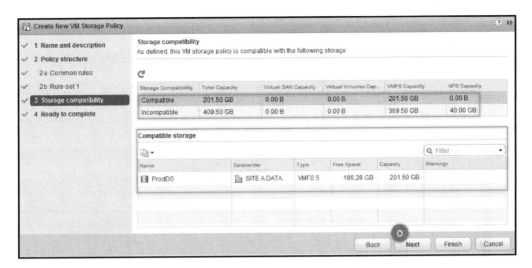

10. On the **Ready to complete** screen review the settings and click **Finish** to create the policy:

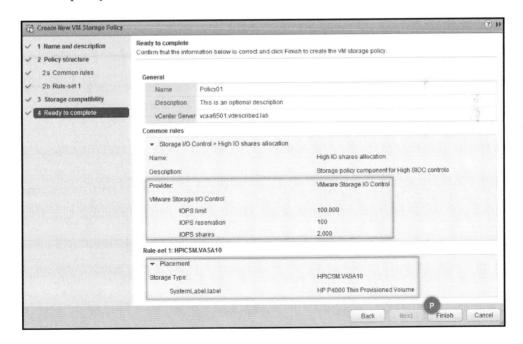

# How it works...

VM storage policies once created can then be used to filter and choose the desired datastore during various virtual disk (vmdk) placement scenarios.

For instance, if you were to create a new virtual machine, then you can choose to place its VMDKs on a datastore that matches a VM storage policy:

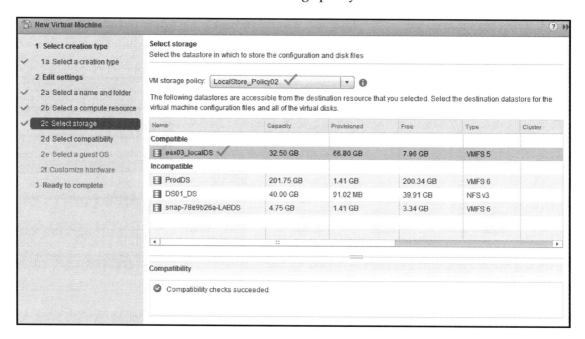

You can also manually associate VM storage policy to existing VMDKs. Read the next recipe *Assigning VM storage policies* to learn how.

# Assigning VM storage policies

As indicated in the previous recipe, you can assign/edit VM storage policies to/of existing virtual machines. This will help associate virtual machines with desired storage tiers.

The policy can be applied even to the virtual machines home directory, in case you want virtual disks to be stored in a different storage tier.

# How to do it...

The following procedure will help you to edit the VM storage policies of a VM:

1. Connect to the vCenter Server using the web client and switch to the **Host and Clusters** view using the key combination *Ctrl + Alt + 2* (since this activity is performed on a VM, you can use the **VMs and Templates** view as well, using the key combination *Ctrl + Alt + 3*).

2. Right-click on the desired VM and navigate to **VM Policies** and **Edit VM Storage Policies...**:

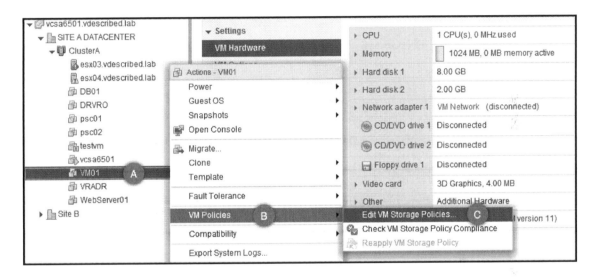

3. In the **Edit VM Storage Policies** window, choose a **VM storage policy** to apply to all the associated files or assign individual VM storage policies to each of the items. Click **OK** to confirm the settings:

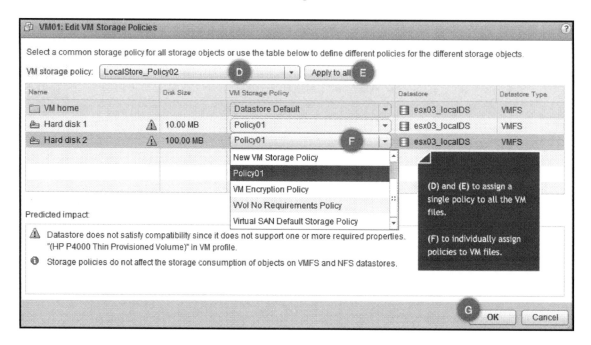

4. Once done, select the VM and navigate to its **Monitor | Policies** tab to view its policy compliance status:

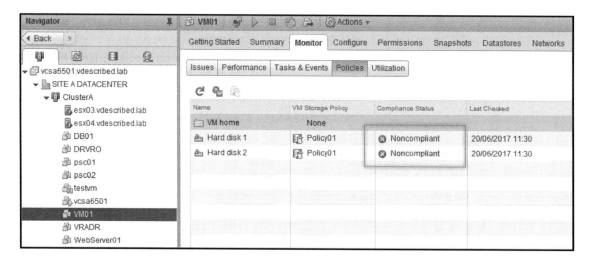

# How it works...

Once VM storage policies are assigned to a VM and its VMDKs, its profile compliance status will remain non-compliant unless they are moved to a datastore matching the VM storage policy. The VM can be moved using the migration wizard. In the migration wizard, the intended VM storage policy can be selected to list the compliant datastores so that the VMs and its files can be moved to one of them.

# 11

# Creating and Managing Virtual Machines

In this chapter we shall cover:

- Creating a virtual machine
- Creating a new hard disk for a virtual machine
- Adding an existing hard disk to a virtual machine
- Attaching a Raw Device Mapping to a virtual machine
- Mapping a virtual machine's vNIC to a different port group
- Adding a new virtual network adapter to a virtual machine
- Creating virtual machine snapshot
- Deleting a virtual machine snapshot
- Restoring a snapshot in the linear snapshot tree
- Switching to an arbitrary virtual machine snapshot
- Consolidating snapshots
- Converting a virtual machine to a template
- Cloning a virtual machine to a template
- Exporting to an OVF template
- Deploying a virtual machine from an OVF template
- Exporting a virtual machine
- Creating a local content library
- Creating a subscribed content library

# Introduction

The heart of the **Software-Defined Data Center (SDDC)** lies in the virtual machine. The virtual machine provides the skeletal structure within which a guest operating system is installed. In the previous chapters, we have gone over building the vSphere environment that serves as the platform, now we shall delve into effectively creating and managing these VMs.

# Virtual machine components

Let us briefly touch upon what a virtual machine truly comprises. A virtual machine exists in an abstract form as a set of files. The files themselves are directly, or indirectly, representative of the virtual hardware components and configuration settings that the guest operating system will need at runtime. We shall discuss the files that make up the virtual machine and their respective uses later in the chapter. In simpler words, a virtual machine can be created, copied, or destroyed with basic file manipulation operations. This very attribute of the virtual machine enables a plethora of features, such as agility, availability, security, and portability.

A virtual machine is initially populated with the following default virtual hardware:

- Memory, CPUs, a SCSI controller, hard disks, and network adapters
- Video card, VMCI device, CD/DVD drive, and floppy drive

Components can be added or modified at the end of the virtual machine creation wizard, or by using the **Edit Settings** wizard at any time during the life cycle of the VM. The wizard presents the following components:

- Hard disk (new/existing/RDM)
- Network adapter
- CD/DVD drive
- Floppy drive
- Serial port, parallel port, host USB device, and USB controller
- SCSI device, PCI device, and shared PCI device
- SCSI controller, NVMe controller, and SATA controller

# Files that make up a virtual machine

The following table outlines a list of key files that make up a virtual machine along with their description and use:

| File | Description | Use |
|------|-------------|-----|
| `.vmx` | Virtual machine configuration file | Comprises all configuration related details associated with the virtual machine |
| `.vmxf` | Additional virtual machine configuration files | Comprises additional/extended configuration information |
| `.vmdk` | Virtual machine descriptor file | Comprises description and layout of the virtual machine disk |
| `-flat.vmdk` | Virtual machine data disk file | Comprises the actual data of the virtual machine disk |
| `.nvram` | Virtual machine BIOS or EFI configuration file | Comprises BIOS or EFI specific information |
| `.vmsd` | Virtual machine snapshot descriptor file | Comprises description and layout of the snapshots associated with the virtual machine |
| `.vmsn` | Virtual machine snapshot memory state file | Stores the memory sate of the virtual machine's snapshot |
| `.vswp` | Virtual machine swap file | Serves as a backing store for virtual machine's memory content |
| `.vmss` | Virtual machine suspend file | Stores the memory state of a suspended virtual machine |
| `.log` | Current virtual machine log file | Stores current logs of the virtual machine |
| `-#.log` | Old virtual machine log entries | Historical log information of the virtual machine |

# Creating a virtual machine

It's important to note that starting with vSphere 6.5 onwards, the legacy C#/thick/vSphere client has been retired and can no longer be used to manage ESXi hosts or vCenter. The vSphere Web Client will be the primary utility to manage the environment and alongside this, a new HTML5-based client has been introduced with a subset of the features of the vSphere Web Client. More details of this are covered in a knowledge base article KB—2147929: `https://kb.vmware.com/s/article/2147929`.

# Getting ready

Let's start by defining the means by which a virtual machine can be deployed, we can follow four methodologies:

1. Create through the standard **New Virtual Machine** wizard.
2. Deploy from a virtual machine template or clone from a VM that was preconfigured/precreated.
3. Deploy from an OVF template, from an internal or external repository.
4. Deploy virtual machine from a content library.

In this recipe, we will create a virtual machine following the standard *new virtual machine* workflow through the vSphere Web Client.

# How to do it...

1. Connect to the vCenter Server as an administrator or a user with relevant privileges by using the vSphere Web Client.
2. Navigate to the **VMs and Templates** view from the inventory home as shown in the following screenshot:

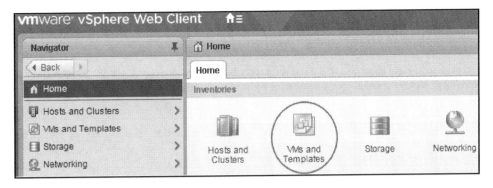

3. Navigate to the datacenter object and right-click to traverse to **New Virtual Machine** and click on the **New Virtual Machine...** option as depicted in the following screenshot:

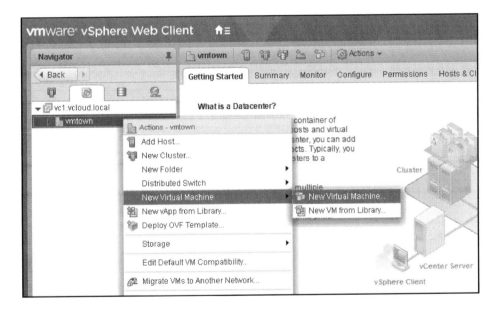

4. Choose the **Create a new virtual machine** option and click on **Next** as indicated in the following screenshot:

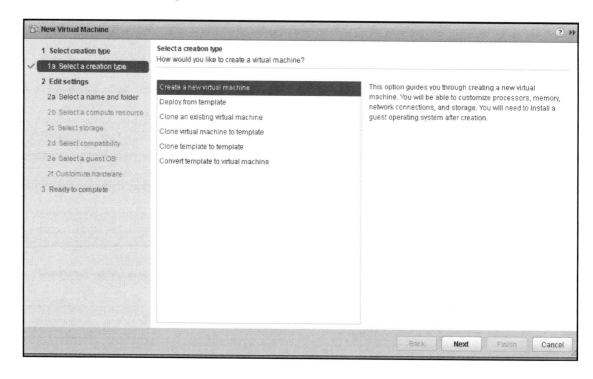

5. Provide a name for the virtual machine, choose an inventory location, and then click on **Next**, as demonstrated in the following screenshot:

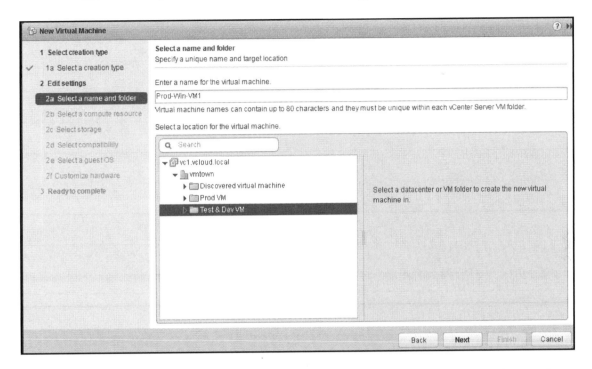

 It's a best practice to standardize virtual machine naming conventions and conform to a nomenclature.

6. Navigate to **Select a compute resource** (you can choose a host, DRS enabled cluster, vApp, or resource pool), and click on **Next** as shown in the following screenshot:

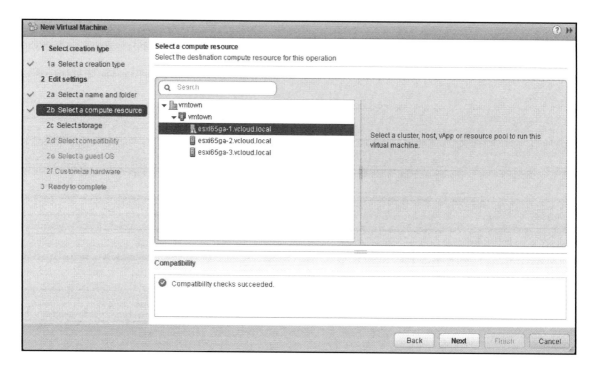

7. Choose a datastore to store the virtual machine and then click on **Next**. You can choose to leverage a **VM storage policy** to cater to specific requirements, such as security, redundancy, and performance or leave it at the default as shown in the following screenshot:

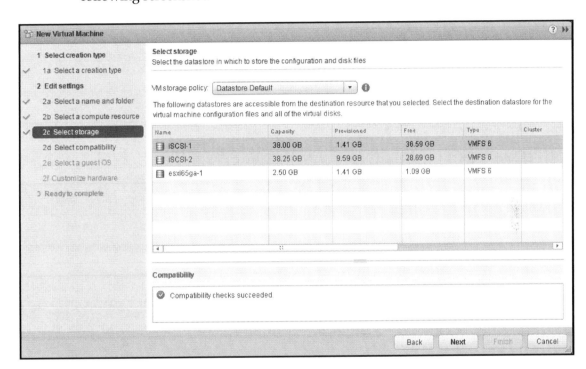

 Learn more about VM storage policies in `Chapter 10`, *Storage IO Control, Storage DRS, and Profile Driven Storage.*

8. Select a virtual machine compatibility mode by clicking on the **Select compatibility** option and then selecting from the listed options as shown in the following screenshot:

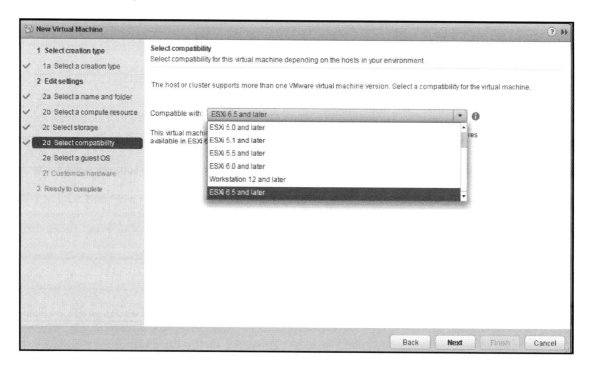

 Ideally, you would choose a compatibility with the latest and greatest version, unless there are specific reasons such as backward compatibility.

9. Select the **Guest OS Family** and **Guest OS Version** details, and then click on **Next**:

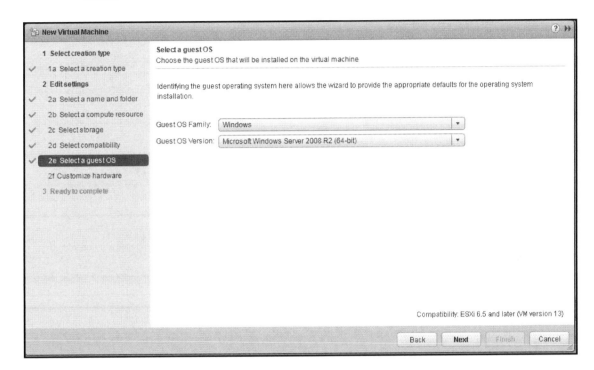

Selecting the appropriate **Guest OS Version** ensures that certain recommended and supported hardware is mapped to the virtual machine, and also maps the correct version of VMware tools to be installed.

10. Any amendments or additions to the virtual machine can be made in the **Customize hardware** screen, click **Next** to continue:

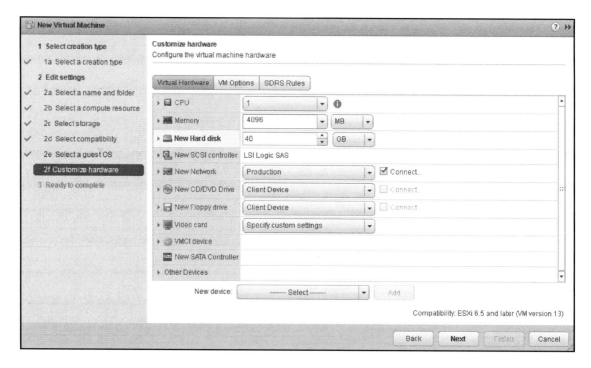

11. On the **Ready to complete** screen, review the information and click **Finish** to create the virtual machine.

# How it works...

Once you hit **Finish**, all of the settings and configuration details are consolidated and passed onto the ESXi host in the cluster to create the actual virtual machine. In essence, the set of files described earlier in this chapter get created and a virtual server hardware is carved out and abstracted from the physical hardware. The virtual machine administrator can now install a guest operating system following any of the traditional methods, such as mapping an ISO file, CD drive, or PXE based installation.

# Creating a new hard disk for a virtual machine

A virtual machine typically may or may not require additional hard disks in its life cycle. However, at the least, it is a best practice to segregate an operating system disk from the data disk. In the following recipe we will append an additional hard disk to the virtual machine we have created to enable such use cases.

# How to do it...

1. Navigate to the newly-created virtual machine, right-click on the VM, and click on **Edit Settings**, as demonstrated in the following screenshot:

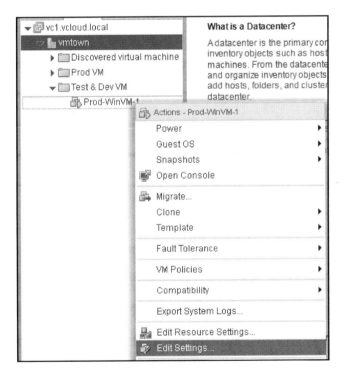

2. Click on the drop-down menu adjacent to the **New device** option, select **New Hard Disk,** and click **Add**:

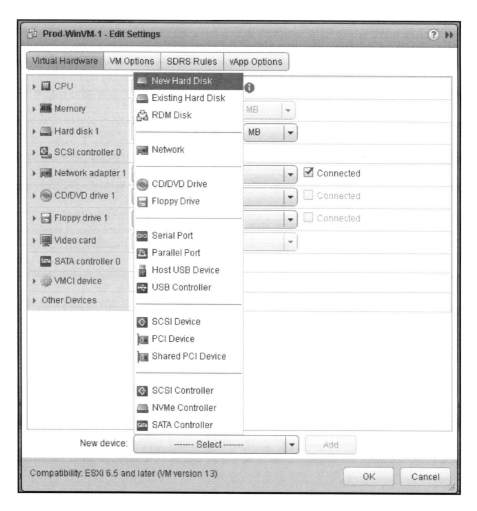

3. Now we see a new addition to the virtual hardware list. Collapse the drop-down menu adjacent to the newly-added hard disk to complete the configuration.

4. Populate the appropriate disk size within the **Maximum Size**:

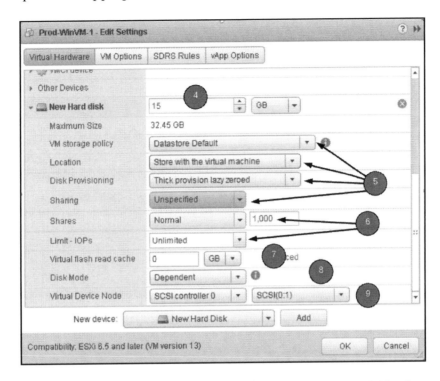

5. Leave **VM storage policy**, **Location**, **Disk Provisioning**, and **Sharing** at default; these are typically not modified unless there are specific performance and redundancy requirements.

6. **Shares** and **Limit - IOPs** enable IOPS prioritization and disk bandwidth control, leave at the default—**Normal**-1000 and **Limit - IOPs** to **Unlimited**, a misconfiguration here could lead to performance issues and is best managed by the host.

7. **Virtual flash read cache** can be left at default. This is applicable only for certain types of read-intensive workloads and only if the hosts are equipped with flash devices to serve the purpose.

8. Leave **Disk Mode** at default—**Dependent**. This setting emulates typical physical hardware, however in VDI backed environments and certain use cases of test, dev, lab, or setup, one may choose independent disk modes.

9. The SCSI controller is automatically allocated by host based on the existing hard disks that have been provisioned.

10. Click **OK** to complete the process.

# How it works...

The virtual machine disk plays a crucial role in the performance and availability of a guest operating system or its applications. Let's look at how the configuration choices actually work and influence the guest OS behavior:

- **Maximum Size**: This parameter provides the current estimate of storage space available on the datastore location that is chosen.
- **VM storage policy**: This allows for greater control and compliance of the *type* of storage a virtual machine disk gets in its life cycle. A policy can be configured to ensure the application requirements are satisfied, such as caching and replication.
- **Location**: By default, the virtual machine disk files are stored in the same location as the VM. This is much simpler in terms of file management and troubleshooting. If there are requirements for specific disks such as database VM or any latency sensitive applications, it would be ideal to define and attach an appropriate VM storage policy.
- **Disk Provisioning**: There are three formats to choose from:
    - **Thick provision lazy zeroed**: This option reserves and allocates storage space on the datastore. The disk would gradually be zeroed out on-demand at first write. This is the default and preferred option on a generic note.
    - **Thick provision eager zeroed**: This option reserves, allocates, and zeroes out the storage space on the datastore. This option offers better performance since the overhead of zeroing on-demand IOPs is reduced. This is also a requirement for certain clustering features, such as **fault tolerance** and **latency sensitive applications**.
    - **Thin provision**: This option grows the file as data is being written, hence it's used for space conservation. This does imply that there will a performance penalty in comparison to the thick provisioning options.
- **Sharing**: This feature is a natively available security and control mechanism to ensure that a virtual machine disk is written by the owning virtual machine or process. However, for clustering purposes or other use cases, a virtual machine disk may permit being accessed by another virtual machine. In such cases, we have the following options to choose from based on the requirement:
    - **Physical**: Share disk with VMs across hosts
    - **Virtual**: Share disk with VMs on the same hosts
    - **None**: Virtual disks are not shared with other virtual machines

- **Shares**: This feature allows for I/O prioritization of one VM over another.
- **Limit - IOPs**: This feature provides the capability to control IOPs from a certain workload. It is more often than not used to restrict rather than unleash. It may typically be used to avoid *noisy neighbor* situations and also most often leads to performance issues if not configured according to application requirements. This is yet another setting best left to default and for the host to manage.
- **Disk Mode**: There are three types of disk mode to choose from:
    - **Dependent**: Standard hard disk that writes changes permanently to disk and can be used and included with snapshot feature
    - **Independent-Persistent**: Same as dependent except that it's excluded when a snapshot is taken
    - **Independent-Nonpersistent**: Changes are discarded when you power-off or reset the virtual machine

On clicking **OK**, the configuration settings are processed through the preceding set of conditions and the virtual machine is reconfigured and disk creation and placement is complete.

# Adding an existing disk to a virtual machine

You may find it a necessity to add an existing disk (vmdk) to a virtual machine in certain use cases. This is again done through the **Edit Settings** wizard for the virtual machine. This task can be performed while the VM is powered-on or off.

# How to do it...

1. Navigate to the **VMs and Templates** inventory view, select and right-click on the VM to which you intend to add an existing virtual hard disk (VMDK), and then click on **Edit Settings**:

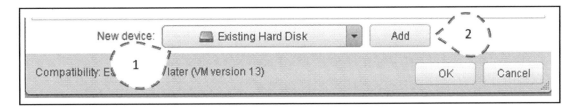

2. Use the **New device** option available in the **Edit Settings** window, select **Existing Hard Disk** as the device option, and then click on **Add**.

3. Navigate to the location of the VMDK, select the appropriate VMDK file, and then click on **OK** to confirm the selection, as shown in the following screenshot:

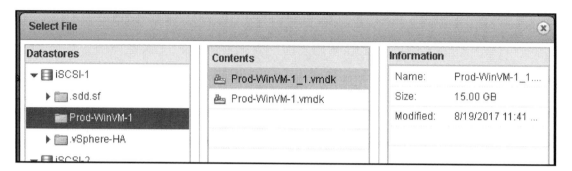

Prior to clicking **OK**, you can choose to modify a virtual device node or disk mode if necessary.

# Attaching a Raw Device Mapping to a virtual machine

A **Raw Device Mapping** (**RDM**) may be required in special cases where an application or guest operating system requires access to a device directly, or with a native filesystem on the device, unlike the normal methodology of the disk residing on a VMFS backed datastore. To enable this, a LUN can be directly provisioned to a virtual machine through the use of RDMs.

# Getting ready

Present the LUN to all the ESXi hosts in the cluster, this is imperative to ensure virtual machine mobility. In a cluster, it's quite typical for a virtual machine to restart or migrate on other hosts, the LUN can be continuously accessed by the virtual machine.

Needless to state, this is a prerequisite for features such as vMotion and HA with
**Distributed Resource Scheduler** (**DRS**) so they work on the virtual machine in question.

# How to do it...

The following procedure demonstrates attaching an RDM to a virtual machine:

1. Navigate to the **VMs and Templates** inventory view, select and right-click on the
   VM to which you intend to map an RDM, and then click on **Edit Settings**.
2. Use the **New device** option and select **RDM Disk** and click on **Add** as indicated
   in the following screenshot:

3. Navigate to the LUN presented and verify the NAA ID to ensure that the correct
   device is added:

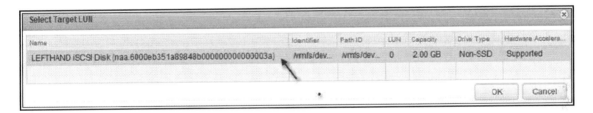

4. A new hard disk entry for the RDM should now be visible on the settings page,
   click on it to expand the advanced/additional settings for the hard disk. Change
   the **Location**, **Virtual Device Node**, and **RDM Compatibility Mode** if required
   and click **OK** to complete the process.

# How it works...

A Raw Device Mapping operates in two compatibility modes, physical and virtual. Here we briefly compare the two:

- **Physical compatibility** mode is also known as pass-through mode. In this mode a guest operating system directly accesses the hardware. All the SCSI commands except the REPORT LUN command are directly sent to the device. Due to this, certain key features, such as cloning and snapshot features cannot be used. This also implies that standard virtual machine backup methodologies cannot be used to back up the physical RDM hard disk, it would require SAN-based back up methods.
- **Virtual compatibility** mode allows only the *read* and *write* commands to be sent directly to the device and intercepts the rest of the I/O through the VMkernel. This interception and tracking allows for features such as snapshots to be used on the disk.

Leaving aside specific use cases, the virtual compatibility mode strikes a balance between device control and ownership with vSphere features, hence is preferred wherever feasible.

A common use case for RDM is MSCS clustering. There are certain guidelines on supportability and compatibility at the VMware Knowledge Base article KB *1037959 at:* https://kb.vmware.com/s/article/1037959.

# Mapping a virtual machine's vNIC to a different port group

One of the basic requirements for a virtual machine is network connectivity across other virtual machines and/or physical machines residing in the internal/external network. A virtual machine connects to the network through its **Virtual Network Interface Controller (VNIC)**. The VNIC is mapped to a port group, which is in turn associated with physical uplinks, that is, **Network Interface Cards (NICs)**.

It's not mandatory to have a physical uplink, a port group can remain an internal only port group.

# Getting ready

Prior to mapping a virtual machine network adapter to its appropriate network, the host needs to have the vSphere Standard Switch and vSphere Distributed Switches configured and ready. Extensive discussion around this has been covered in Chapter 6, *Using vSphere Standard Switches* and Chapter 7, *Using vSphere Distributed Switches*.

# How to do it...

The following procedure outlines the steps to map a vNIC to a different port group,

1. Navigate to the **VMs and Templates** inventory view, select and right-click on the VM, and then click on **Edit Settings**.
2. Use the **New device** option available in the **Edit Settings** window, select **Network** adapter as the device option, and then click on the **Add** button to make the changes:

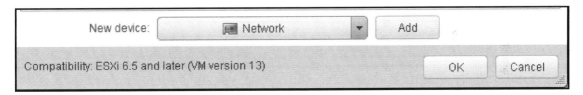

3. A **New Network** is added to the virtual hardware list as shown in the following screenshot:

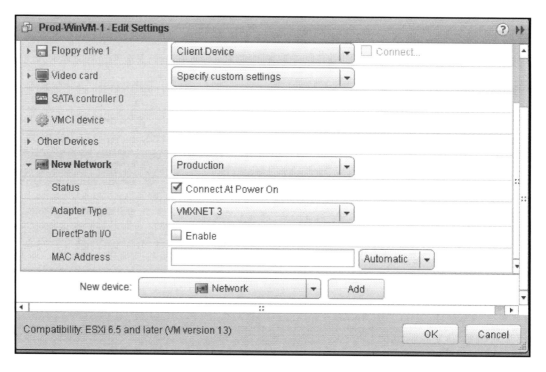

4. Choose the correct network port group that the virtual machine network adapter needs to connect to from the drop-down menu. In this case, we associate the network adapter to the **Production** network port group.

5. Leave the **Status** checked, this is similar to plugging/unplugging a network cable to the physical server.

6. Select an appropriate network adapter type, **VMXNET 3** is a recommended and optimized adapter type.

7. You may assign a MAC address manually or the host will assign one automatically and click **OK** to complete.

 **DirectPath I/O** is a unique feature to directly allow a PCI device access to the virtual machine. Prior to enabling this, the devices must be reserved for PCI pass-through on the host on which the virtual machine runs. Certain features such as vMotion, snapshot cannot be used alongside DirectPath I/O.

# How it works...

In very simple words, under the hood, vSwitches or dvSwitches are parts of the ESXi host code that logically connect a virtual network adapter to a physical network adapter by ensuring the configuration conditions are applied. By adding the network adapter to a virtual machine, we have created a **network identity** that conforms and complies with IETF standards.

Furthermore, the network adapter to port group mapping can be modified at any time in the virtual machine life cycle providing great levels of agility. In addition, the inherent nature of virtualization is that, virtual machines are mobile across the environment and the hosts need to explicitly advertise when there is a movement of the virtual machine.

While all the complexity is dealt with and abstracted by the ESXi hosts, there is very little configuration modification required on the underlying network fabric.

# Creating virtual machine snapshots

Often, we have situations where we need to preserve a specific state, virtual machine snapshots provide such a functionality. To be more precise, a snapshot can even preserve a running state of a virtual machine. This comes in handy in development use cases and in general, is a more reliable **known good configuration** state. Furthermore, the ability to take snapshots also aids in other extended features such as linked clones and enables backup capabilities for use with vSphere Data Protection or other third-party solutions.

# Getting ready

You will need to log in to vCenter with the relevant privileges to be able to take snapshots. Snapshots do not work with:

- Virtual machines with RDMs in physical mode
- Virtual machines with PCI vSphere Direct Path I/O devices attached
- Virtual machines with Bus sharing enabled

Most importantly, snapshot do not replace backups. While it's advantageous in the short term, snapshots should not be allowed to prolong more than 72 hours, else it may have severe performance degradation. Also, more than 32 levels of snapshots on a virtual machine is not supported.

# How to do it...

The following procedure guides you through the steps required to create a snapshot on a virtual machine:

1. Navigate to the **VMs and Templates** inventory view, select and right-click on the VM for which you intend to create a snapshot, select **Snapshots**, and then click on **Take Snapshot...**, as demonstrated in the following screenshot:

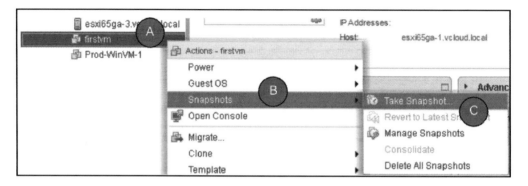

2. Provide a **Name** for the snapshot and an optional **Description**. The **Quiesce guest file system** option requires VMware tools to be installed on the guest operating system and **Snapshot the virtual machine's memory** option is selected by default for a powered-on virtual machine. Click on **OK** as depicted in the screenshot:

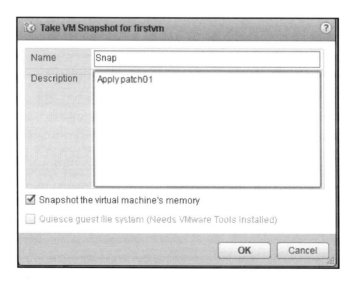

3. The progress of the task can be tracked in the **Recent Tasks** pane:

4. Once completed, navigate back to the virtual machine, right-click, and click on **Manage Snapshots**:

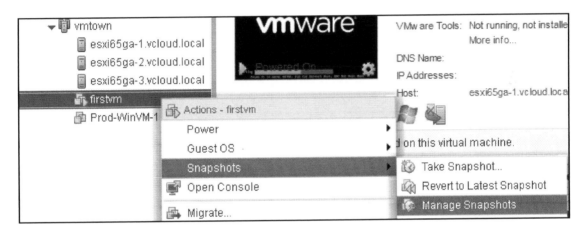

5. The snapshot manager for the virtual machine depicts the newly-created snapshot in a tree structure, along with details as shown in the following screenshot:

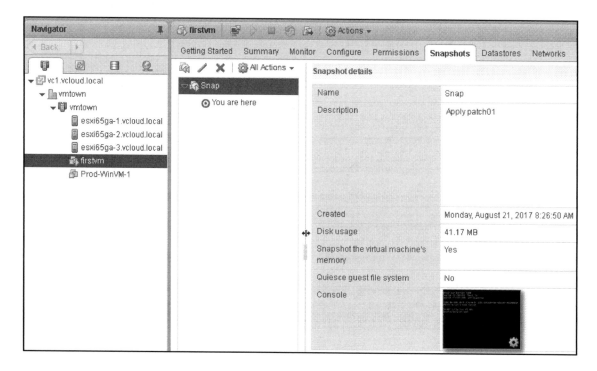

# How it works...

In simple terminology, we know that a virtual machine exists in an abstract form of files. The snapshot feature takes advantage of this and leverages file manipulation techniques to capture the current state in one set of files while a newer state (or delta from the present state) is redirected to a newer set of files. It does it in the following sequence of steps:

1. If the virtual machine memory is included, the ESXi host flushes the memory of the virtual machine to disk (*.vmem)

2. If the **Quiesce guest file system (Need VMware Tools Installed)** option is selected, the host invokes quiescing through the VMware tools.

3. File state changes are written to a *.vmsd file such that the snapshot manager UI populates the snapshot chain.

4. Any new writes are redirected to the snapshot disks created (`*-0000X.vmdk` and `*-0000X-sesparse.vmdk`).

The following screenshot is obtained through SSH access to the ESXi host, where the virtual machine currently runs. Note the files created and modified in the timestamp `Aug 21 15:19`, this reflects the effect of a typical snapshot operation:

```
[root@esxi65ga-1:/vmfs/volumes/584664ad-174480d8-cedd-00505601a712/firstvm] ls -altr
total 8548544
drwxr-xr-t     1 root     root            73728 Aug 16 14:14 ..
-rw-------     1 root     root         41943040 Aug 16 14:14 firstvm-flat.vmdk
-rw-r--r--     1 root     root              230 Aug 16 14:14 firstvm-5453e172.hlog
-rw-r--r--     1 root     root           177736 Aug 20 06:28 vmware-1.log
-rw-------     1 root     root              486 Aug 21 13:59 firstvm.vmdk
-rw-------     1 root     root        115343360 Aug 21 14:25 vmx-firstvm-4232710544-1.vswp
-rw-------     1 root     root                0 Aug 21 14:25 firstvm.vmx.lck
-rw-------     1 root     root       4294967296 Aug 21 14:25 firstvm-fc4a0990.vswp
-rw-r--r--     1 root     root               13 Aug 21 15:05 firstvm-aux.xml
-rw-------     1 root     root           629145 Aug 21 15:19 firstvm-000001-sesparse.vmdk
-rwxr-xr-x     1 root     root              250 Aug 21 15:19 firstvm.vmx~
-rwxr-xr-x     1 root     root              251 Aug 21 15:19 firstvm.vmx
-rw-r--r--     1 root     root               42 Aug 21 15:19 firstvm.vmsd
-rw-------     1 root     root               32 Aug 21 15:19 firstvm-000001.vmdk
drwxr-xr-x     1 root     root             7782 Aug 21 15:19 .
-rw-------     1 root     root             8684 Aug 21 15:19 firstvm.nvram
-rw-------     1 root     root       4294967296 Aug 21 15:19 firstvm-Snapshot4.vmem
-rw-r--r--     1 root     root            17155 Aug 21 15:19 vmware.log
-rw-------     1 root     root           122228 Aug 21 15:19 firstvm-Snapshot4.vmsn
```

# There's more...

A virtual machine snapshot file is a **growable file**, that is, it employs a **copy-on-write (COW)** mechanism, hence it starts small and with every write it can grow as much as the base disk. This also brings about an inherent performance penalty. A read has to traverse the entire snapshot chain to reference the correct block and a write has to get a block allocated and then write even if the parent/base disk is eager-zeroed thick format.

For best practices on creating virtual machine snapshots, read the VMware Knowledge Base article *1025279:* `https://kb.vmware.com/s/article/1025279`.

# Deleting a virtual machine snapshot

As previously discussed, snapshots are for temporary use only and would need to be removed subsequently. Deleting a snapshot is often misconceived as deleting data in the snapshot, however it is actually the process of committing (writing) the disk data into the immediate parent disk. This also implies the memory state (if taken) from the snapshot files are restored as well. The user can do this for every single snapshot or cumulatively for all the snapshots that exist.

## Getting ready

You will need to log in to the vSphere Web Client with the appropriate privileges to manage snapshots. All tasks are to be done through the virtual machines' snapshot manager. Manual modification of files requires significant expertise or may lead to data loss.

## How to do it...

A delete operation can be performed in the following two methods:

- **Delete Snapshot**: This operation will allow for a specific snapshot to be deleted. When this is done, the data held by its VMSN and the delta file are committed (written) to its immediate parent. The virtual machine's configuration file (vmx) will be amended to reflect the parent disk/base disk of the deleted snapshot.
- **Delete All Snapshots**: This operation will allow for all snapshots to be deleted. When this is done, the data held by its VMSN and the delta file are committed (written) to its base disk. The virtual machine's configuration file (vmx) will be amended to reflect the base disk of the deleted snapshot.

The following procedure walks through the process of deleting a snapshot:

1. Right-click on the VM and select **Manage Snapshots**.
2. Select the snapshot to be deleted, and then click on **Delete Snapshot** as indicated in the following screenshot:

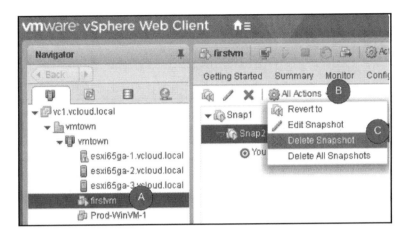

3. Confirm the snapshot deletion, as depicted in the following screenshot:

# How it works...

We shall walk through this with a typical use case of testing a patch.

In a hypothetical situation, an administrator needs to deploy a patch on Windows 2012/R2 systems across the data center. As a rule of thumb, these have to be tested in the test and dev cluster VMs and observed for stability before implementing in production:

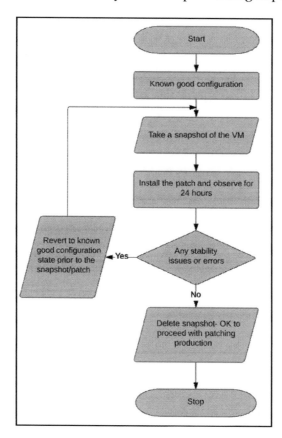

Here would be the typical workflow:

1. Virtual machine is at a known good configuration state.
2. Admin takes a snapshot of the virtual machine.
3. Installs the patch on the guest OS and observes the VM for 24 hours for stability.
4. Are there application crashes, errors, or warnings in the event logs or user reported issues?
   - If no (no issues found), commit the patch, that is, delete the snapshot taken in the first step and proceed to patch production VMs
   - If yes (issues observed), go back to the previous state, that is, revert to the state prior to applying the patch

Under the hood, the patch applied is held in the snapshot file. If the patch is proven to be stable, we commit the snapshot to the base disk, that is, preserve and save the stable state. If the patch is found to cause stability issues it is discarded by reverting back to the previous state.

# Restoring a snapshot in linear snapshot tree

Creating a snapshot typically leaves us with a decision making process of whether to commit the changes or discard the changes. The **Revert to the Latest Snapshot** achieves the latter, by discarding the subsequent changes. When we revert to a snapshot, we restore the state of the virtual machine to the original state when the snapshot was taken.

# How to do it...

Let's walk through the procedure to revert to the current state:

1. Right-click on the VM and click on **Snapshots** | **Revert to Latest Snapshot**, as depicted in the following screenshot:

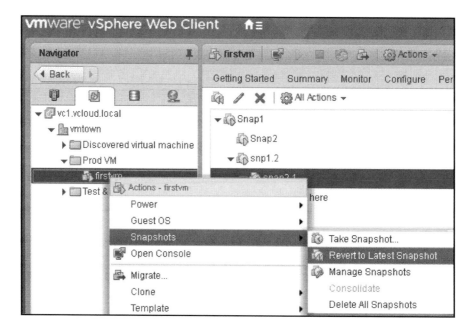

2. Confirm the revert operation as depicted here, you may choose to suspend the virtual machine in the process:

## How it works...

Reverting to a latest snapshot will discard its delta contents and moves one level up in the current snapshot hierarchy. The contents of the delta file are permanently lost. As demonstrated in our example, we go back in time to the state prior to installing the patch.

# Switching to an arbitrary virtual machine snapshot

In complex use cases, one may require having multiple levels and hierarchies in a snapshot tree. This is specifically applicable in a development life cycle, wherein each change may need to be backtracked to ascertain which change triggered an issue. This is done through the **Revert to** option.

This methodology allows granular control over switching to any arbitrary snapshot in a snapshot tree, as opposed to moving up one level at a time with the **Revert to the Latest Snapshot** option. The virtual machine returns to the original state at which the snapshot was taken.

## How to do it...

The following procedure outlines the steps to reverting or switching to a specific snapshot:

1. Right-click the virtual machine and select **Manage Snapshots**:

2. Select a snapshot and click **Revert to** to restore the virtual machine to the snapshot.

3. Click **Yes** to complete the process:

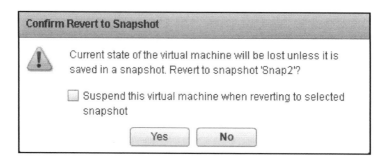

## How it works...

The **Revert to** option restores the selected snapshot in the snapshot tree and makes that snapshot the parent snapshot of the current state of the virtual machine. Newer snapshots taken from this point onward create a new branch of the snapshot tree.

## Consolidating snapshots

Snapshot consolidation is a process of committing the content of snapshots to the base disk. Traditionally, snapshots that were managed by third-party backup solutions were prone to mismanagement. This lead to stale snapshot files and other residual files left in the virtual machine directory, and skewed information displayed in the snapshot manager UI. This option eases the troubleshooting and snapshot management effort by ascertaining the virtual machine disk that requires consolidation and providing a UI to consolidate the files.

# How to do it...

The following procedure outlines the steps to consolidate the snapshot:

1. Right-click on the VM, select **Snapshots**, and click on **Consolidate**.
2. Click **Yes** to complete the process and consolidate the residual data:

# How it works

During a **Delete Snapshot** or **Delete All Snapshots** task, the process initiated removes the snapshot from the snapshot manager and subsequently works in the backend consolidating the files. At this juncture, if there are communication issues between host and vCenter or there are multiple levels of snapshots or large snapshots being consolidated, there will be a mismatch of information. In such cases, the **Needs Consolidation** feature scans the virtual machine datastore and provides a mechanism to correct the skew.

# Converting a virtual machine to a template

General datacenter practice is to have standardized IT approved OS images that will be used for deployment, as opposed to building and installing a guest OS from scratch at every instance. This is addressed by using either virtual machine templates that are native to vSphere or leveraging open virtual machine standard OVF/OVA.

# How to do it...

In the following recipe, we shall discuss converting/cloning a virtual machine to a template/OVF for reuse:

1. Right-click on a VM and navigate to **Template** | **Convert to Template**:

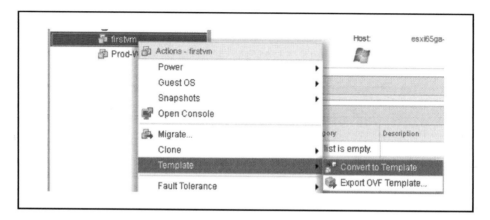

2. Confirm from the **Recent Tasks** pane that the task is completed as shown in the screenshot:

# How it works...

The **Convert to Template** option simply marks a virtual machine as a template. The underlying file extension of a virtual machine configuration file (.vmx) changes to a virtual machine template file (.vmtx). This ensures that typical virtual machine-specific tasks such as power-on or reset can no longer be executed against the template.

# Cloning a virtual machine to template

Often, the use case for storing virtual machine images is done through cloning the virtual machine to a template. This method creates a copy of the original virtual machine, whereas previous methods *mark* the source VM as a template. In addition, the cloning process also allows an additional option to modify the disk storage type. This helps conserve storage space by allowing any disk format to be changed to a thin provision format.

## How to do it...

In this recipe, let's walk through the steps to clone a VM to template:

1. Right-click on the VM and navigate to **Clone | Clone to Template**.
2. Choose an appropriate **Name**, **Folder**, **Compute Resource**, and **Storage Resource** and click **Finish**:

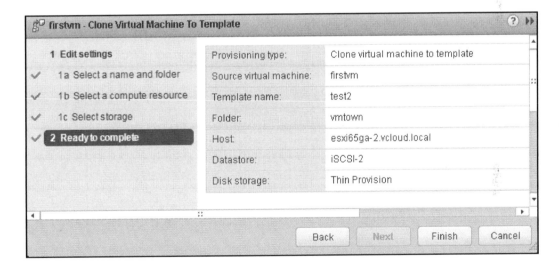

# Exporting to an OVF template

A virtual machine is highly portable. This moved a notch higher with the coming together of key vendors in standardizing the virtual machine format. The standardization effort lead to **Distributed Management Task Force (DMTF)** and the outcome of this is the **Open Virtualization Format (OVF)**.

# How to do it...

In the following recipe, we will demonstrate exporting a Virtual Machine to OVF template for portability across a supported virtualization platform:

1. Right-click on a VM and navigate to **Template | Export to OVF Template...**:

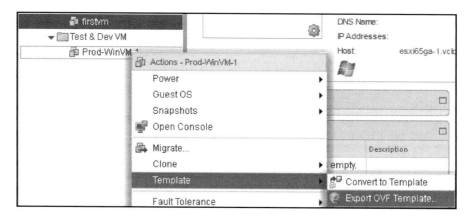

2. Provide additional details required—**Name, Annotation** and leave the **Advanced** option unchecked:

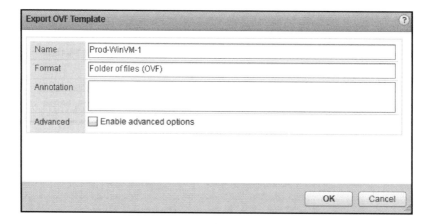

3. Confirm from the **Recent Tasks** pane that the task is completed.

# How it works...

In the backend, the virtual machine is copied and converted into an OVF format that conforms to the format prescribed and agreed upon by the **Distributed Management Task Force (DMTF)**.

While the advanced option allows for additional configuration settings to be incorporated, it drastically affects the portability across other virtualization platforms and should be avoided unless required.

# Deploying a virtual machine from an OVF template

Deploying virtual machines from OVF templates has become a defacto standard. This is due to the obvious reasons of faster deployment, easier management, and compliance to standards. In this recipe, we will walk through deploying a virtual machine from an OVF that was sourced from an external repository.

# Getting ready

Determine a source URL from where an OVF can be downloaded. If the network connectivity is unstable or flaky, it is preferred to download the OVF files. Ensure file integrity through checksum mechanisms and store in a repository accessible to the vSphere environment.

# How to do it...

The following procedure outlines the steps to deploy a VM from an OVF template:

1. Connect to the vCenter Server as an administrator or a user with relevant privileges by using the vSphere Web Client.
2. Navigate to the **VMs and Templates** view from the inventory home.

3. Right-click on the datacenter object and click on **Deploy OVF Template...** as shown in the following screenshot:

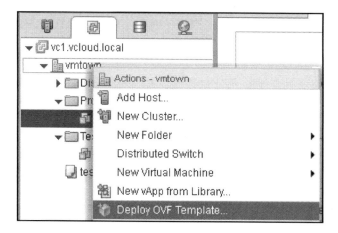

4. Click on **Local file** (or point to the URL) and click **Next**, as depicted here:

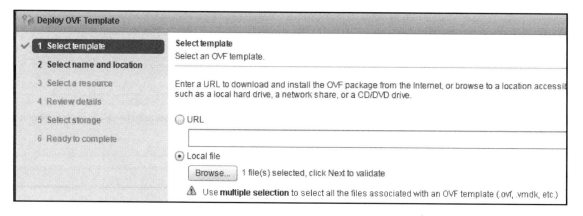

5. Populate the **Name, Location,** and **Compute Resource**.

6. Choose an appropriate datastore and disk format, and click **Next** as depicted here:

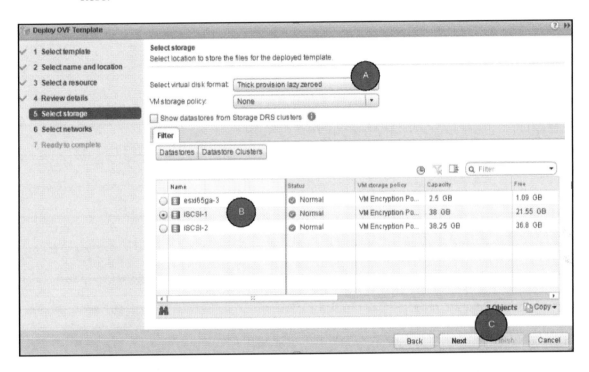

7. Select the appropriate network, review the details, and click **Finish**.

# How it works...

As part of the **Deploy from Template** wizard, an OVF file is imported and is validated. Once the file integrity is verified in the import process, a virtual machine creation process with the respective inputs is passed to the host very similar to the standard virtual machine.

# There is more...

For a deeper understanding and the specifications of OVF, see the resources published by DMTF, called *Open Virtualization Format White Paper - DSP2017*: https://www.dmtf.org/sites/default/files/standards/documents/DSP2017_2.0.0.pdf.

# Creating a local content library

A content library is a repository for VM templates or other files that can span across vCenter instances within or across locations. This further enhances the consistency, compliance, and efficiency in managing virtual machines. Content libraries are primarily of two kinds:

- Local library
- Subscribed library

A **Local library** is intended to service a single vCenter Server instance, however one can choose to publish it for users from other vCenter Server instances to subscribe and use. A **Subscribed library** is carved out of subscribing from a published library.

## How to do it...

In the following recipe, we shall create a local content library and upload contents:

1. Log in to vCenter Server with the relevant privileges.
2. Navigate to **Home** | **Content Libraries** as shown here:

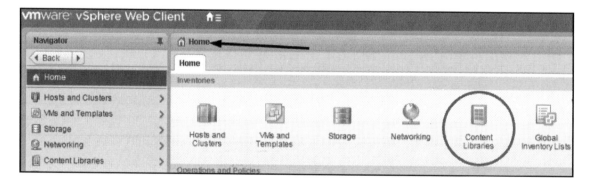

3. Select **Local content library** and check **Publish externally**, you may choose to have an authentication enabled by selecting the **Enable authentication** checkbox:

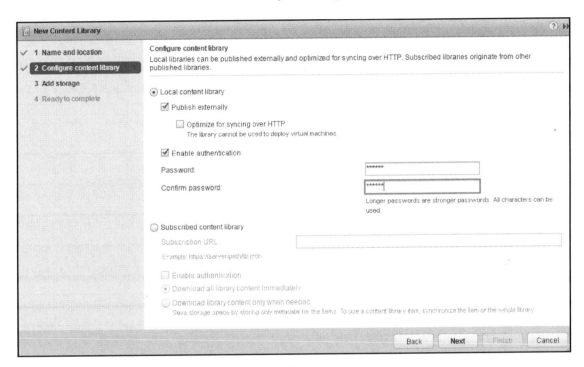

4. Choose an appropriate datastore and click **Finish**. Review the **Recent Tasks** to confirm that library creation is complete:

5. Navigate to the newly created content library, home, and then content library | library name:

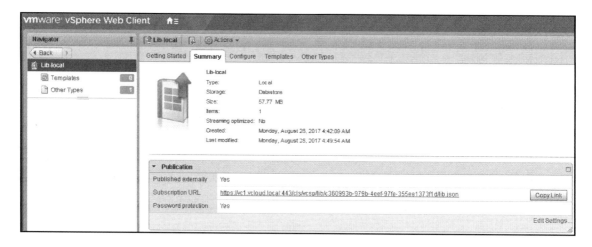

6. Note down the **Subscription URL** depicted under **Summary** | **Publication** for future reference.

7. Click on **Actions** | **Import Item...**:

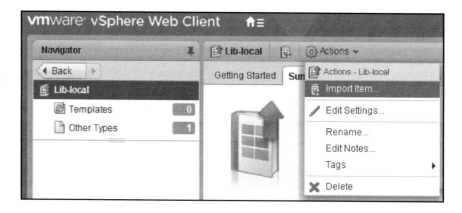

8. Provide the location of the file to be imported in the section named **Source file** through any of the two available options: **URL** or **Local file** as shown here:

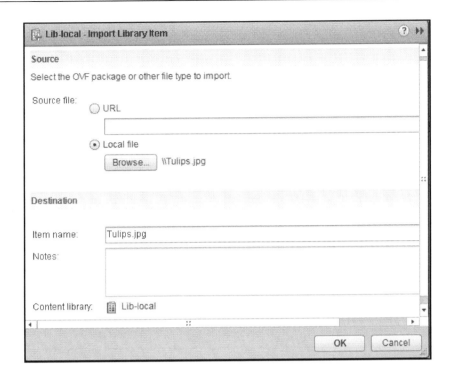

## How it works...

Prior to the content library, virtual machine templates or ISO files were typically shared through an NFS datastore as a common practice. There were also other archaic techniques to move files through external/portable storage to share data around using third-party solutions. A content library simplifies this portability and enables this as a native feature. Any valid datastore available in vCenter is exposed as a repository for commonly used files. Furthermore, if the datastore is connected directly to participating ESXi hosts, the data transmission operations can leverage **vSphere Storage APIs for Array Integration (VAAI)** to greatly reduce the file transfers.

## Creating a subscribed content library

A subscribed library primarily piggybacks on an existing content library by subscribing to it. It also optimizes storage space by synchronizing only the metadata, and does not copy over all the library items from the local published library unless required.

# Getting ready

In order to create a subscribed library, we need the source local content library on which the content is published externally. You will also need the following details:

- Subscription URL of the source content library
- Authentication credentials to access the library

# How to do it...

The following procedure outlines the steps to create a subscribed content library,

1. Log in to vCenter Server with the relevant privileges.
2. Navigate to **Home** | **Content Libraries** as show here:

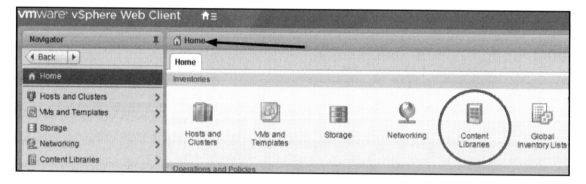

3. Select **Subscribed content library** and provide the **Subscription URL** local.
4. If authentication was enabled on the source local content library, choose **Enable authentication** and provide the credentials.
5. Select **Download library content only when needed**:

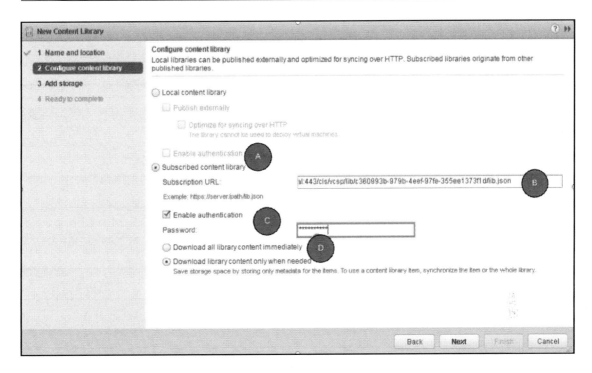

6. Choose the appropriate datastore to host the subscribed library items.
7. Review the chosen configuration details and click **Finish** as depicted here:

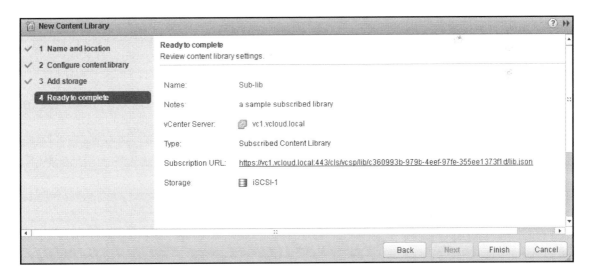

# How it works...

A subscribed library synchronizes the content from the source local content library that is published. We have two options available while creating a subscribed library:

- **Download all library content immediately**
- **Download library content only when needed**

The **Download all library content immediately** option initiates a synchronization process from the source library datastore to the destination library datastore. This process copies the entire content once the library creation task is complete.

The **Download library content only when needed** option creates a catalog of the library items of the source library, in other words it creates a catalog or metadata of information available in the source library.

You may choose to download only necessary content when required and subsequently delete the item from the subscribed library to conserve storage space.

# 12
# Configuring vSphere 6.5 High Availability

In this chapter, we shall cover the following recipes:

- Enabling vSphere HA on a cluster
- Configuring vSphere HA Admission Control
- Setting the host isolation response for a HA cluster
- Setting the VM restart priority for a HA cluster
- Configuring VM monitoring
- Configuring datastore heartbeating
- Disabling host monitoring
- Configuring vCenter Native High Availability

# Introduction

VMware vSphere **High Availability (HA)** is a functionality that is used to prepare a cluster of hosts to handle failure gracefully. vSphere HA has several mechanism and failure tolerance levels that can be set on the workloads, and can minimize or, in specific cases, also nullify downtime. In essence, any IT organization has to deliver and adhere to a set of SLAs and vSphere HA is a critical feature that aids in meeting these business-driven SLAs. Starting with vSphere 6.5, one key addition has been made to the vSphere HA optimization by enabling a native High Availability for vCenter.

The key aspect of the feature is that it's *native* unlike the previous clustering and back up methodologies that were used to safeguard vCenter as an application. On the other hand, **vSphere AppHA** is no longer available in vSphere 6.0 onwards. In this chapter, we will learn the configuration steps and nuances of High Availability.

# Enabling vSphere HA on a cluster

The fundamental principle of HA is to be able to recover virtual machines from a host that has failed to another. That implies that other hosts in the cluster are capable of providing compute, storage, and network identity for the virtual machine similar to the failed host.

vSphere HA is not enabled by default on a host cluster. It has to be manually enabled. In this recipe, we will understand the requirements of a HA cluster, how it is enabled, and how it works.

## Getting ready

Although the actual process of enabling HA is as simple as a click of the checkbox, in order to successfully host the VMs from a failed host, the following prerequisites need to be met:

1. All hosts must be licensed for vSphere HA.
2. All hosts should access the same shared storage, that is, access to the datastore containing the virtual machine files.
3. All hosts should have access to the same virtual machine networks.
4. All hosts should be configured to have a common **Management Network**.
5. Sufficient compute resources (CPU and memory) to meet the virtual machine resource requirements to support a failover event.

# How to do it...

1. Log in to vSphere Web Client with the relevant privileges.
2. Navigate to the specific cluster | **Configuration** | **vSphere Availability** as depicted in the following screenshot:

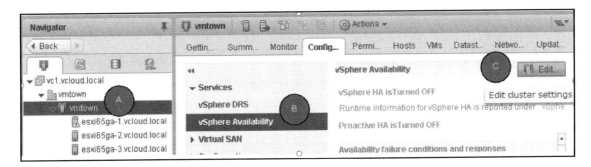

3. Click on **Edit...** and click the checkbox **Turn ON vSphere HA** and click **OK**:

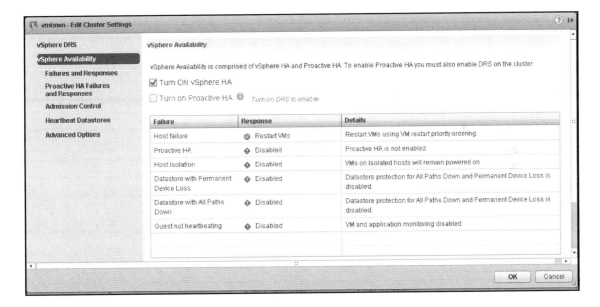

4. You may also verify that vSphere HA has been successfully configured and enabled from the **Tasks** and **Events** pane:

| Task Name | Target | Status |
|---|---|---|
| ▾ Reconfigure cluster | 📇 vmtown | ✔ Completed |
| Configuring vSphere HA | 📇 esxi65ga-1.vcloud.local | ✔ Completed |
| Configuring vSphere HA | 📇 esxi65ga-3.vcloud.local | ✔ Completed |
| Configuring vSphere HA | 📇 esxi65ga-2.vcloud.local | ✔ Completed |

# How it works...

Under the hood, vSphere HA is a **Fault Domain Manager** (**FDM**). FDM leverages the concept of master and slave, that is, in a given cluster, there is an elected master that monitors the health of the other hosts in the cluster and also communicates the status with the vCenter. When the enable HA operation is initiated, each host in the cluster goes through a preparation state of activating an agent and enabling communication across the agents. The host that has the most numbers of datastores accessible wins the race to be the master.

Once the master is elected, its key responsibilities are to:

1. Monitor the hosts in terms of availability and maintain an inventory of the protected VMs and their power state from all the hosts.
2. Restart the VMs known to be running on a given host when they fail to alternate hosts.
3. Reflect the state of health of the cluster through vCenter.

The master host leverages the management network to detect host heartbeats from every host each second. If at any given instance a heartbeat is not received, a secondary validation is done by checking if the datastore in the cluster has received the heartbeat. If the host is neither heartbeating to the host over a management network nor to the datastore, it is deemed failed. If the host stops heartbeating to the master but continues to heartbeat to the datastore then the host is deemed as isolated or network partitioned.

In other words, there is likely to be a problem in the management network connectivity alone and the virtual machines by themselves are unaffected. With host isolation/network partition, there is also a likelihood of the virtual machine network connectivity getting affected. For instance, if the host network cards fail or if the uplink switch manifests a problem, particularly in a converged infrastructure, the impact can be widespread and affect the virtual machine network as well. In almost all scenarios, a VM with impaired network connectivity is as bad as any other outage. Nonetheless, vSphere HA is fairly capable of handling these scenarios well, depending on the stability and redundancy available on the physical network, one can design a graceful response to isolation/network partition as well.

# Configuring vSphere HA Admission Control

As with any environment, not all workloads are the same and we will need to be selective about the virtual machines that need to be restarted, and more importantly the sequence of restart. Admission control configuration plays a key role in ensuring that the right virtual machines are restarted in a specific order and ensuring that it does not do so at the cost of performance degradation of the other running VMs.

There are three admission control policies:

- Cluster resource percentage
- Slot Capacity
- Specify dedicated failover hosts

In this recipe, we will discuss configuring admission control and its nuances.

# Getting ready

Needless to say; ensure vSphere HA is *configured*. At a high level, have a *categorization of workloads* based on their criticality. In addition, remember that failover capacity is a key attribute in your original design, that is, how much headroom you have in your cluster in the event of failure in terms of **capacity** or the **number of hosts failures** you can afford to tolerate.

# How to do it...

The admission control configuration is available as a subset of vSphere HA settings described earlier in the chapter:

1. Navigate to **Cluster** | **Configuration** | **vSphere Availability** | **Edit**. Click on **Admission Control** as depicted here:

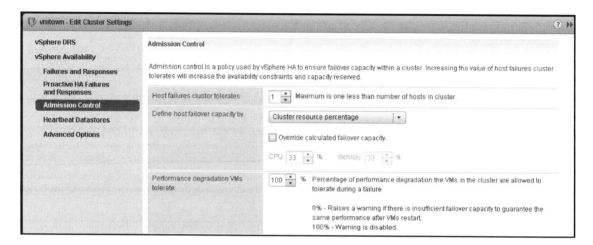

2. Select **Cluster resource percentage**.
3. Click **OK** to accept the default values.

# How it works...

Admission control can be set to tolerate a maximum of *N-1* number of host failures in a cluster.

With the **Cluster resource percentage** option, a computed or user defined failover capacity is reserved in the cluster. Any operation violating this constraint is disallowed. This is enforced as follows:

1. Computes the total resource requirements for all powered-on virtual machines in the cluster.
2. In parallel, it calculates the total host resources available for virtual machines.
3. Calculates the **Current CPU Failover Capacity** and **Current Memory Failover Capacity** for the cluster.

If either the Current CPU Failover Capacity or Current Memory Failover Capacity is less than the corresponding *configured failover capacity* then the operation is disallowed. vSphere HA by default uses the actual reservations of the virtual machines. If a virtual machine does not have reservations, a default of 0 MB memory and 32 MHz CPU is applied.

With the **Slot capacity** option, a placeholder slot is derived at. Each slot acts as a placeholder for a virtual machine, that is, a slot can satisfy resource requirements of any given powered-on virtual machine in the cluster:

1. Compute **Slot capacity**.
2. Determines how many slots each host in the cluster can hold.
3. Determines the current failover capacity of the cluster.
4. This is the number of hosts that can fail and still leave enough slots to satisfy all of the powered-on virtual machines.
5. Determines whether the current failover capacity is less than the configured failover capacity (user-defined). If it is, Admission Control disallows the operation.

With the **Dedicated failover hosts** option, specific targeted hosts are intended for restarting the virtual machines. These hosts play the role of *spares*. You can neither vMotion nor power-on virtual machines to the dedicated **Failover Hosts**:

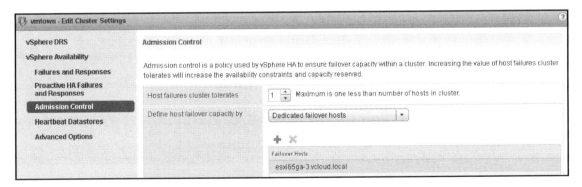

# Setting the host isolation response for a HA cluster

Getting into the nitty-gritties of HA, a host failure may not be as straightforward as a going hard down/crash. There are situations when the host may fail partially, for instance, let's presume a set of network cards have failed. If the NICs were associated with the management network, the host gets isolated from the other hosts. At this juncture, the host has not truly failed and all of the virtual machines are in a pristine functioning state. vSphere HA could restart these VMs, causing an outage to the application/end user, or it could choose to have additional validations and trigger a more appropriate response.

In this recipe, we will discuss configuring host isolation response.

## Getting ready

Similar to previous recipes of availability, understand the criticality of your virtual machines as well as their SLAs. This information is key to configuring HA right.

## How to do it...

1. Log in vSphere Web Client with the relevant privileges.
2. Navigate to the specific cluster | **Configuration** | **vSphere Availability**.
3. Click on **Failures and Responses**.
4. Click on the expand the drop-down list for **Response for Host Isolation** response.
5. The default option is to leave **Disabled**, leave it unchanged as depicted in the following screenshot:

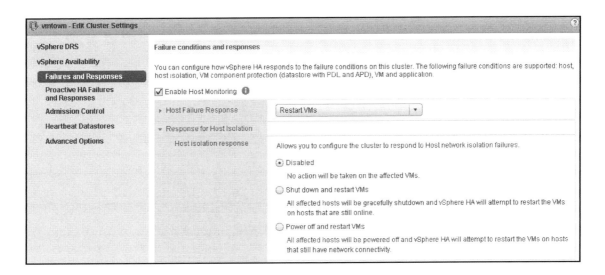

# How it works...

Once a host is determined to be isolated, we have the following three options:

- **Disabled**: Do not take any action, running VMs continue to run
- **Shut down and restart VMs**: The running virtual machines will be shut down (provided VMware tools are installed) and vSphere HA will restart the VMs on other hosts in the cluster
- **Power off and restart VMs**: The running virtual machine will be abruptly powered-off, vSphere HA will restart the VMs on other hosts in the cluster

The key question is when to choose what. The answer to this is subjective to certain conditions. If we know that the network is flaky, not highly redundant, or prone to intermittent outages, a host isolation perhaps is a common phenomenon. In such cases, it's best to leave this option disabled. As an evasive option as shutdown or restart can increase the outage time. On the other hand, if the network is known to be fairly stable and workloads are critical, its best to choose to shut down the VMs.

The choice between shutdown and power off are straightforward. For critical workloads it's best to save in-memory data through a graceful shutdown.

# Setting the VM restart priority for a HA cluster

VM restart priority, in conjunction with the previous configuration settings, ensure that critical workloads get precedence over other workloads. This can be fairly important in terms of how quickly a workload resumes and is of particular importance when admission control is enabled. Given a situation wherein you have 10 VMs to be restarted, 3 of them being critical workloads, by setting higher restart priority for the 3 VMs, we ensure that they get restarted first and they have a better probability of obtaining the reserved capacity of failover.

## Getting ready

The restart priority is relative, hence it is important to differentiate the critical workloads from the rest. Unless explicitly overridden, all VMs adhere to the global settings at the cluster and are deemed equal.

## How to do it...

1. Log in to the vSphere Web Client with the relevant privileges. Navigate to the specific cluster | **Configuration** | **VM Overrides**:

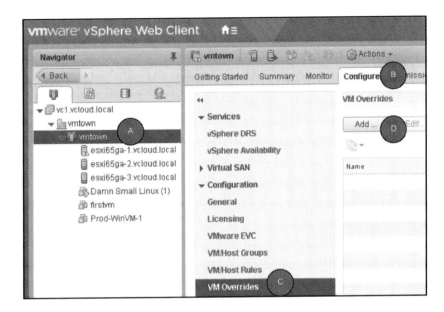

2.  Click on **Add...** | + sign to select one or more VMs as shown. Choose from varying degrees of criticality from **Lowest** to **Highest**:

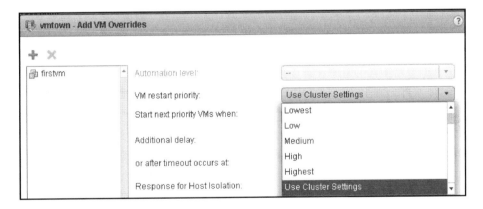

3.  Click **OK** to complete.

# How it works...

Each VM level setting overrides the cluster level global setting in the event of host failure. VM specific settings are assessed and addressed, followed by the default setting applied at the cluster level. The outcome of having varied restart priorities across a workload is that vSphere HA will now have an inventory of VMs that ought to be restarted in a very sequential fashion.

# Configuring VM monitoring

vSphere HA can be configured to monitor virtual machines, so that unresponsive VMs can be restarted (reset). This is achieved by enabling VM monitoring on the HA cluster. You can also enable application monitoring. This will restart a VM if the **VMware Tools** application heartbeats are not received within a predefined timeout value. This is not to be confused with the host monitoring itself and is independent. This feature helps in cases where a virtual machine has hung and typically requires being restarted.

# How to do it...

The following procedure outlines how VM monitoring can be configured:

1. Log in to the vSphere Web Client with the relevant privileges. Navigate to the specific cluster | **Configuration** | **vSphere Availability**.
2. Click on **Failures and Responses** | **VM Monitoring** shown in the following screenshot:

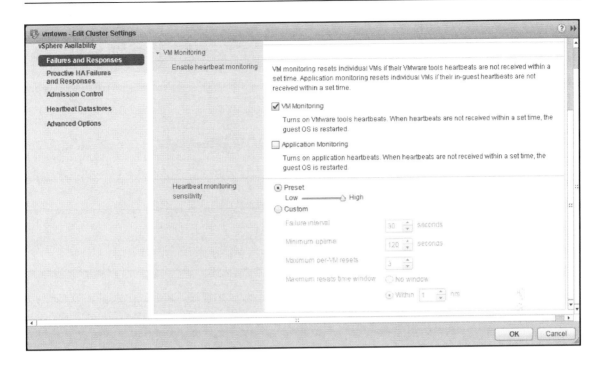

# How it works...

Virtual machine monitoring uses VMware Tools to send heartbeats to the host its running on. If a heartbeat is not received within the configured threshold, then the VM is deemed as unresponsive/hung and then subsequently restarted. The threshold/sensitivity for heartbeating is configurable:

- **High**: Checks for a heartbeat every 30 seconds and reset every 1 hour
- **Medium**: Checks for a heartbeat every 60 seconds and reset every 24 hour
- **Low**: Checks for a heartbeat every 120 seconds and reset every 7 days

In order to avoid repetitive restarts and false positives, for any level of sensitivity three resets can be initiated per VM in a given reset period. Another key aspect is while heartbeats are not received, the network and storage activity of the VM is validated prior to initiating a reset. If any storage or network activity has been observed in the last 120 seconds, the VM will not be reset. This is done to ensure that the issue is not specific to VMware tools but the actual guest OS.

While the previous predefined configurations can be chosen from, a user is also at liberty to set his own criterion for VM monitoring. The same logic applies to **application monitoring**, however specific SDKs need to be configured to monitor application heartbeats instead of VMware tool heartbeats.

# Configuring datastore heartbeating

vSphere HA uses datastore heartbeating to check the liveliness of a host if it cannot be reached over the management network. This is enabled by default and cluster datastores are automatically chosen, this can also be user configured.

## How to do it...

1. Log in to the vSphere Web Client with the relevant privileges. Navigate to the specific cluster | **Configuration** | **vSphere Availability**.
2. Click on **Heartbeat Datastores** shown in the following screenshot:

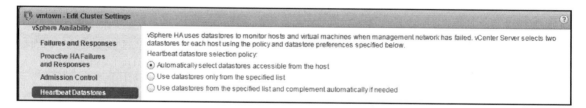

3. Click on **Automatically select datastores accessible from the host**.

## How it works...

vCenter automatically chooses two heartbeat datastores per host (can have an overlap between hosts). When the host is network isolated or partitioned, the datastore acts as a witness to rule if the host has truly failed or is network impaired. This setting may seldom require to be changed, if there is datastore known to be more resilient then the user can override vCenter's choice and configure the heartbeat datastore manually. An even safer option would be to prescribe a heartbeat datastore and complement it with an automatic choice, which is the third option available.

# Disabling host monitoring

Host monitoring is generally disabled during network maintenance activities that would affect the host's management network connectivity. This is done to prevent unnecessary triggering of the host isolation response configured for the HA cluster. Host monitoring can be disabled by editing the cluster settings.

## How to do it...

1. Log in to the vSphere Web Client with the relevant privileges. Navigate to the specific cluster | **Configuration** | **vSphere Availability**.
2. Click on **Failures and Responses** and uncheck **Enable Host Monitoring**:

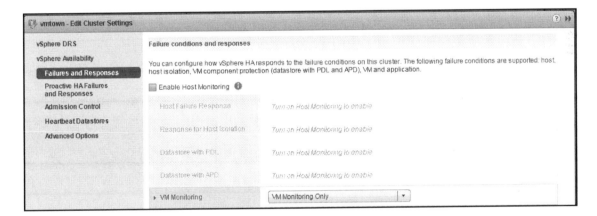

## How it works...

All HA activity is disabled until the setting is enabled again. But why do this when you can just disable HA? This setting reflects a transient state and conserves the effort to completely unconfigure HA across the cluster and essentially saves some cycles.

# Configuring vCenter Native High Availability

**vCenter Native High Availability (vCHA)** is certainly one of the most awaited features of vSphere 6.5. Until now, there have been a slew of features that were enabled by the vCenter but not for the vCenter. In this recipe, we shall discuss configuring vCHA.

## Getting ready

This feature works with a standard vCenter license and work with vCenter Server Appliance 6.5 embedded or external PSC. A minimum of three ESXi hosts are needed. You will also need to configure a separate network/portgroup that is different from the management network to configure the vCHA network.

## How to do it...

1. Log in to vCenter with the appropriate privileges. Navigate to **Home** | **Host and Clusters**.
2. Click on your specific vCenter | **vCenter HA**. Click on **Configure** as depicted in the following screenshot:

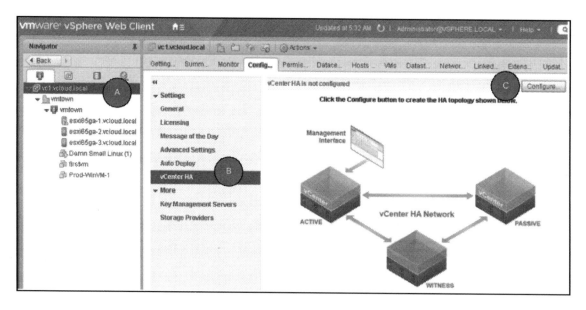

3. Choose the **Basic** option.

4. Provide a unique IP address for the **Passive Node** and the **Witness Node**, and click **Next** as depicted in the following screenshot:

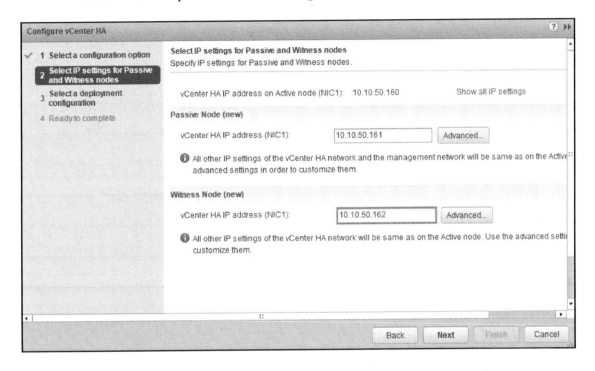

5. **Select a deployment configuration** by providing distinct target hosts and datastores for the three nodes and click **Next** as depicted here:

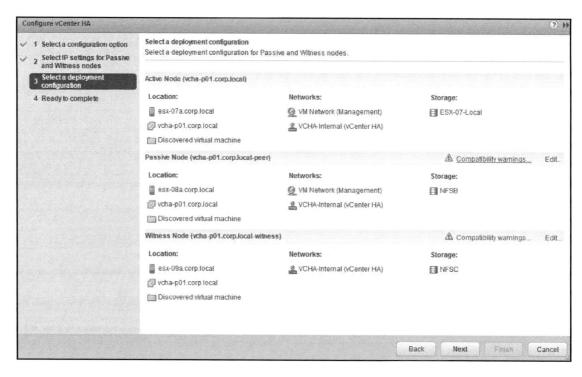

6. Review configuration on the **Ready to complete** and click **Finish** to complete.

# How it works...

On completion of the wizard, two cloned copies of the vCenter are created, one is designated as the passive node and the other a witness node. Each node also has an additional network adapter with the network configuration details provided. This network is leveraged for the following tasks:

- Synchronously replicate the PostgreSQL database from **Active Node** to **Passive Node**
- Asynchronously replicate flat files (configuration state)

To replicate the PostgreSQL database, a PostgreSQL native replication mechanism is leveraged, whereas the flat files are replicated through the native Linux utility rsync.

The passive node maintains sync with the active node. On failure of the active node, the passive node promotes itself to an active node and activates itself on the network using the same network identity as the failed active node. The witness node comes into play as quorum to avoid a split brain state when the nodes seem isolated:

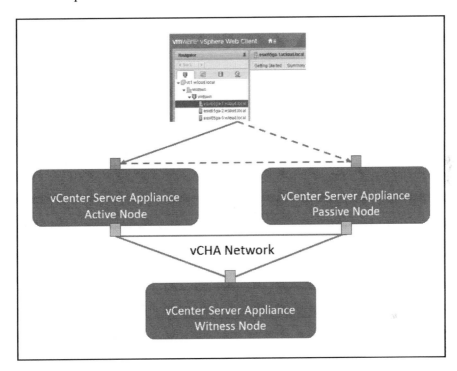

Possible failure scenarios:

- **Active node failure**: Passive node is still able to communicate with witness node and takes over as active node
- **Passive node failure**: No action is taken, however cluster enters a degraded state
- **Witness node failure**: No action, however cluster enters a degraded state
- **Two Node failure**: Availability is impacted

# See also

- An important FAQ on *vCenter High Availability* is documented at: `https://kb.vmware.com/s/article/2148003`.

# 13
## Configuring vSphere DRS, DPM, and VMware EVC

In this chapter, we will cover the following recipes:

- Enabling vSphere DRS on a cluster
- Configuring VMware Enhanced vMotion compatibility
- Choosing a DRS automation level
- Overriding the cluster automation level for a VM
- Setting a migration threshold
- Creating DRS VM or host groups
- Creating VMs to host affinity rules
- Creating VM affinity or anti-affinity rules
- Configuring vSphere Distributed Power Management
- Configuring Predictive DRS

# Introduction

vSphere **Distributed Resource Scheduler** (**DRS**) is a feature of vCenter that pools resources from a given cluster of hosts. It then efficiently organizes the running virtual machines across the ESXi to ensure optimal resource utilization at a cluster level. Furthermore, it also aids in initial placement of the virtual machine on the best-suited host. While the virtual machines are optimally placed, an administrator can impose certain rules and conditions to meet availability and application requirements.

DRS also enables a higher degree of automation for the purposes of host maintenance, upgrades/updates, and also to modify (increase/decrease) cluster capacity non-disruptively.

In addition to load balancing, DRS can also be extended to power management in conjunction with **Distributed Power Management (DPM)**.

# Enabling vSphere DRS on a cluster

The first step to unleash the plethora of DRS features is to enable it at the cluster level. In this recipe, we shall walk through the necessary steps.

## Getting ready

vSphere DRS is a licensed feature, hence ensure that sufficient licenses are available. vSphere DRS is directly dependent on VMotion feature to balance VMs across hosts, hence the prerequisites of VMotion are applicable and need to be satisfied for DRS to function.

## How to do it...

1. Log in to vCenter and navigate to the desired cluster, **Configure** | **vSphere DRS**, then click on **Edit**.
2. Click on the checkbox **Turn ON vSphere DRS,** as depicted in the following screenshot:

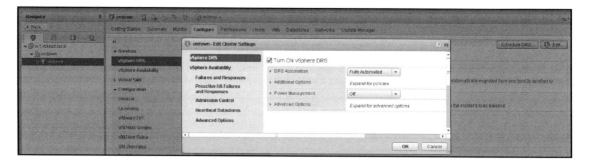

3. Choose the **DRS Automation** level; leave it at default values.

# How it works

DRS, once enabled, will aggregate the resources from the participating ESXi hosts as cluster resources. Its job is to load balance the DRS cluster for better utilization of the cluster resources. It does so by migrating or generating migration recommendations for VMs whenever needed. It also provides initial placement for the VMs. Migration recommendations will be generated by vSphere DRS only when it identifies a resource imbalance in the cluster. A resource imbalance is determined on a per-ESXi-host basis. It does so by considering the resource reservations for all of the VMs on the ESXi host, comparing these against the total capacity of the host, and then checking whether the host can or cannot meet the cumulative resource reservations of the VMs. The result will become a deviation metric, which is then compared against the migration threshold set on the cluster. DRS does this imbalance check on every ESXi host in the DRS cluster every 5 minutes.

After DRS detects a cluster imbalance, it will check the migration threshold value set on the cluster. If the deviation calculated is more than the migration threshold, then DRS will generate a migration recommendation. DRS generates a migration recommendation by simulating the migration of each VM on the ESXi host in order to recalculate the cluster imbalance metric. It will then choose a VM that will best serve in reducing the resource crunch on the host.

# Configuring VMware Enhanced vMotion compatibility

EVC features enable a user-configurable setting of a common CPU feature baseline across a cluster. This ensures that vMotion is seamless within a given family of CPU vendors—Intel or AMD.

# Getting ready

Ensure you look at the *VMware Compatibility Guide* to validate the EVC modes supported by the CPU make and model of your server hardware. You could also download a utility from the VMware portal, available at `https://www.vmware.com/support/shared_utilities.html`. This utility provides a detailed report of hardware compatibility and software configuration compatibility with advanced VMware features.

# How to do it...

The following procedure will help you configure EVC on an ESXi cluster:

1. Connect to vCenter Server with the appropriate privileges.
2. Ensure that there are no *powered-on virtual machines* (power-off or migrate VMs accordingly).
3. From the vCenter's inventory home, navigate to the **Hosts and Clusters** view.
4. Click on the **Configure** tab, select **VMware EVC**, and click on **Edit...,** as shown in the following screenshot:

5. In the **Change EVC Mode** window, select an EVC mode. Change from the default **Disable EVC** to either of the following two options:
   - **Enable EVC for AMD Hosts**
   - **Enable EVC for Intel® Hosts**
6. Based on the compatibility applicable to the CPU, select the appropriate mode.
7. Click on **OK** once the validation succeeds.
8. Power off the migrated VMs and move them back to the EVC cluster and power them back **ON**.

# How it work...

For vMotion to work, a very basic constraint is that the source and destination host should have a *similar* CPU if not identical. Let's extrapolate on the word *similar* in this context, and the relevance of EVC. A VM running on a given generation of CPU make and model runs with the features exposed by the CPU. EVC allows the vSphere administrator to set a common baseline of features that are exposed to the VMs, thus allowing for a newer CPU generation of hosts to be added to the cluster, and be able to readily migrate the VMs. Without EVC, such a task would present an error message that the host with the latest generation of CPU is incompatible.

# See also

- The Knowledge Base article comprises *EVC and CPU Compatibility FAQ (1005764)* at: `https://kb.vmware.com/kb/1005764`

# Choosing a DRS automation level

By default, DRS works at the **Fully automated** automation level. You can, however, choose to set it to **Manual** or **Partially automated**. Although the names of the automation levels are self-explanatory, there are a few additional differences:

- **Manual**: This displays the initial placement and the migration recommendations to the administrator; it requires the administrator's approval to be applied
- **Partially automated**: This carries out VM initial placements automatically, but migration recommendations are displayed to the administrator and are not performed until the administrator applies them
- **Fully automated**: This automatically carries out VM initial placements and migrations

# Getting ready

This function is available only on the DRS-enabled cluster; therefore, ensure the feature is enabled.

# How to do it...

1. Log in to vCenter and navigate to the desired cluster, **Configure | vSphere DRS**, and click on **Edit**.
2. Choose the DRS automation level:
   - **Manual**
   - **Partially automated**
   - **Fully automated**

# How it works...

The DRS automation level defines how DRS will react to cluster resource imbalances and whether it requires little or no manual intervention. DRS can choose to apply the generated migrations/placement recommendations or present them to the administrator to choose from. If there is more than one migration recommendation, then the administrator is provided with a prioritized list of recommendations to choose from. Initial placement refers to the process of choosing an ESXi host from a DRS cluster to power on or resume a VM. DRS generates these recommendations by choosing an ESXi host that has enough resources to run the VM being powered on or resumed.

The following table depicts how migration recommendations and initial placements are dealt with, based on the DRS automation level configured on the cluster:

| Automation level | Virtual machine migrations (vMotion) | Virtual machine initial placement |
|---|---|---|
| **Fully automated** | VMs are automatically migrated. | VM is powered on or resumed on a suitable ESXi host automatically. |
| **Partially automated** | Migration recommendations are displayed to the administrator. The administrator has to manually apply one of the migration recommendations. | VM is powered on or resumed on a suitable ESXi host automatically. |
| **Manual** | Migration recommendations are displayed to the administrator. The administrator has to manually apply one of the migration recommendations. | Initial placement recommendations are displayed to the administrator. The administrator has to manually apply one of the placement recommendations. |

# Overriding the cluster automation level for a VM

In the previous recipe, we learned how to set the cluster-wide automation levels. In this section, we will learn how to set an automation level on a per-VM basis. The cluster settings are overridden by creating VM overrides.

# Getting ready

Prepare the list of VMs that are sensitive to vMotion/DRS migrations.

# How to do it...

1. Log in to vCenter and navigate to the desired cluster, **Configure | VM Overrides**, and click on **Add...**, as depicted in the following screenshot:

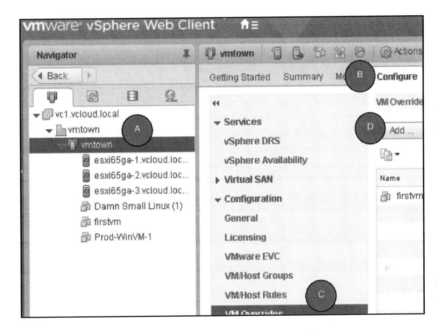

2. Click the (+) sign to choose from the list of available VMs.
3. Modify to the desired automation level, overriding the default defined at the cluster level.
4. Click **OK** to finish.

# Setting a migration threshold

Once DRS is enabled, several algorithms and metrics are continually evaluated to ascertain the optimal VM placement. However, the user may need to set the appropriate threshold to balance how aggressively or conservatively DRS should migrate VMs. This will ensure that, based on the criticality of the workload, it can be migrated when required. Another rationale behind this setting is to ensure that there is no negative impact, such as a frequent ping-pong of VMs across hosts.

## How to do it...

In this recipe, we shall increase the threshold value to migrate VMs if there could be moderate improvements made to the cluster's load balance:

1. Log in to vCenter and navigate to the desired cluster, **Configure** | **vSphere DRS**, and click on **Edit**. Expand the DRS automation.
2. Move the **Migration Threshold** slider toward **Aggressive** by 1 unit, as depicted in the following screenshot:

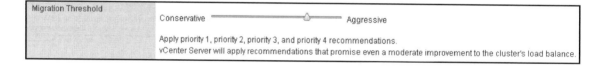

## How it works...

Let's start with asking the question, if DRS is aimed at distributing resources and ensuring a balance in the cluster, why should there be a setting to increase or decrease the effectiveness of DRS?

To answer that, we should understand what potential negative influence DRS could have. To be fair, DRS means no ill intent; however, when vMotion is initiated, there is an overhead cost on two accounts:

- The workload may experience a momentary freeze (a few pings drop)
- Additional task on vCenter

Both these are subjective to the sensitivity of the environment; that is, in a test and development environment, wherein a cluster is fully populated with VMs, you may reap very little benefit with a very aggressive setting of DRS. This would likely set off a ping-pong of VMs across the host, impacting both the workload and vCenter. On a similar note, in a production environment, a critical workload may benefit even with the slightest improvement in performance, thereby DRS can be set to be more aggressive than the default.

The threshold has five settings, ranging from 1 to 5, with 5 being most aggressive. The logic behind the settings is fairly simple. The recommendations at the backend have five levels of recommendation priority. With every level of DRS setting, the equivalent level of recommendations gets applied. For instance, at level 4, recommendations of one-four priorities are applied.

# Creating DRS VM or host groups

DRS provides an option to segregate VMs and ESXi hosts into their own groups. The groups are used with VM-host affinity rules. These rules do not address individual VMs/hosts. These groups are created using the **DRS Groups Manager**.

The creation of DRS hosts/VMs groups is a prerequisite for the creation of affinity rules. This recipe covers how to create DRS host groups.

# Getting ready

This is done on a DRS-enabled ESXi cluster. Ensure that you have access to a vCenter managing the intended DRS cluster and the relevant privileges.

# How to do it...

The following procedure will help you create DRS host groups:

1. From the vCenter's inventory home, navigate to the **Hosts and Clusters** view. Select a cluster, and navigate to **Configure** | **VM/Host Groups**.

2. Click on **Add...**, as depicted in the following screenshot:

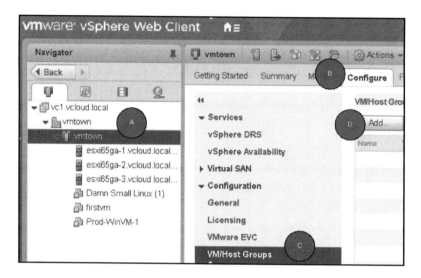

3. Provide a name for the group. Select if the group is a VM or host group from the drop-down menu.

4. Add member VMs or hosts to the group and click **OK,** as depicted here:

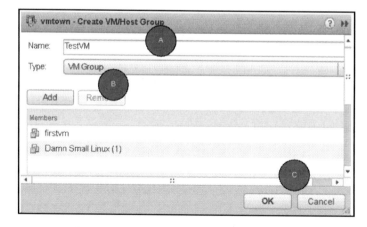

5. On completion, you will see the groups created on the landing page of **VM/Host Groups**.

# How it works...

DRS VM/host groups operate as containers. Once the containers are created, there could be rules that could either have affinity or anti-affinity with each other. In the upcoming recipes, we shall look at putting DRS groups to use effectively.

# Creating VMs to host affinity rules

In this recipe, the objective is to restrict the VMs to run on specific groups of hosts.

# Getting ready

A prerequisite to setting an affinity is creating the DRS groups for the respective VMs and hosts.

# How to do it...

1. Select a cluster, and navigate to **Configure** | **VM/Host Rules**. Provide a name for the rule and ensure it's enabled.
2. Choose the affinity **Type—Virtual Machines to Hosts**. Choose a **VM group** from the available groups.

3. Choose the rule from the drop-down menu—**Should run on hosts in group**. Choose the **Host Group** where the VMs ought to have the affinity, the setting should reflect the following screenshot:

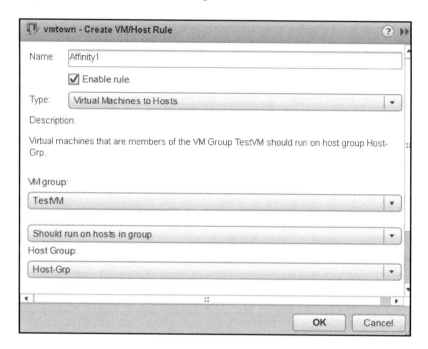

## How it works...

The following rules are available for the VM-host affinity rules:

- **Must run on hosts in a group**
- **Must not run on hosts in a group**
- **Should run on hosts in a group**
- **Should not run on hosts in a group**

The key difference is that for a must rule, it is mandatory to adhere to it, immaterial of the availability situation in the cluster. For instance, if a rule governs that a set of VMs must run on specific hosts and those hosts fail, the VMs would remain down.

A should rule preferentially keeps the VM based on the affinity or anti-affinity; however, it overrides the rules when there is a host failure and restarts the VM. This implies that availability overrides the affinity.

# Creating VM affinity or anti-affinity rules

VM affinity or anti-affinity rules go a level down from the group level affinity to a virtual machine level rule. The objective is to ensure that virtual machines are tied together or repel each other. This feature comes into play in situations where you may have two load balancer VMs that you want to keep apart, so that in the event of an underlying host failure the other instance is unaffected. Similarly, any clustering-based VMs would need to be kept separate to ensure both are not impacted by the same failures. In this recipe, we will walk through an example of ensuring that VMs run together.

## Getting ready

These rules are created for VMs that are in a DRS-enabled ESXi cluster. Ensure you have access to a vCenter managing the cluster. Also be sure to have a list of VMs that have dependencies for which the rules ought to be created.

## How to do it...

The following procedure will help you create an inter-VM affinity / anti-affinity rule:

1. From the vCenter's inventory home, navigate to the **Hosts and Clusters** view. Select the cluster, navigate to **Configure | VM/Host Rules**, and click on **Add** to bring up the **Create VM/Host Rule** window.

2. Provide a name for the rule and choose **Keep Virtual Machines Together** as the rule type, as shown in the following screenshot:

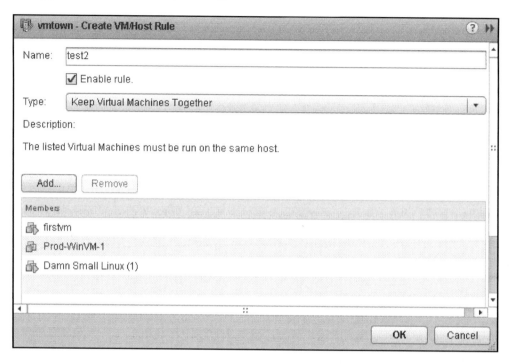

3. Add the VMs that need to be running together. Click **OK** to complete.

# How it works...

The affinity rules act as prerequisite conditions for DRS. The rules need to be adhered to prior to initiating an action. In essence, the rules are closely validated before a DRS recommended vMotion is triggered.

Also, if there are conflicts, the oldest DRS rule comes into effect and the subsequent conflicting rules are disabled.

# Configuring Distributed Power Management

A DRS cluster can be configured to change the power state of the selected hosts in order to reduce the power consumption by the cluster. It does this by evaluating overall resource requirements and available resources. If the cluster can sustain without the contributions of one or more hosts, it would move the host(s) to a standby state. It's also capable of performing vice-versa; that is, DPM would also restore hosts from a standby state to a powered-on state if the cluster resource demand increases. In the following recipe, we will go over the prerequisites and the procedure to enable the feature.

## Getting ready

While it's easy to move hosts to standby mode, to reverse the process DPM requires **Wake On LAN (WOL)** capability. In order to activate the capability, each host needs to be configured either with the iPMI or ILO setting:

This will need to be done on every host.

1. Navigate to **Configure | System**. Traverse to **IPMI/iLO Settings for Power Management** and click on **Edit**.
2. Populate the details of the IPMI/iLO settings as depicted here; this may need to be retrieved from the physical hardware settings:

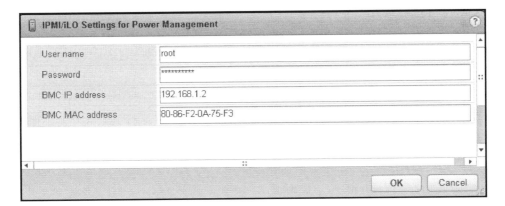

# How to do it...

1. From the vCenter's inventory **Home**, navigate to the **Hosts and Clusters** view. Select the cluster, navigate to **Configure | vSphere DRS**. Choose an appropriate option under **Power Management**.
2. Here we choose **Automatic** to allow vCenter to enable the feature:

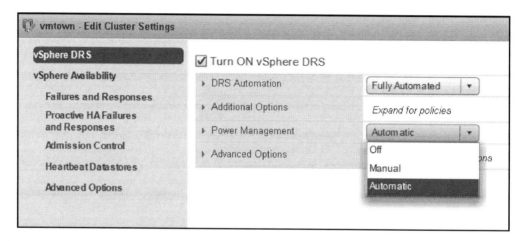

# How it works...

Once enabled, power management (vSphere DPM) will analyze the cumulative resource requirements (current usage and reservations), verify the HA requirements, and determine the number of hosts required to meet them. From then on, DPM will selectively put ESXi host/hosts into standby mode. Prior to putting an ESXi into standby mode, DPM will leverage DRS's ability to
distribute the VMs running on the selected ESXi host to the other ESXi hosts in the cluster.

DPM can operate in three modes:

- **Off**: In this mode, DPM is **Disabled**
- **Manual**: In this mode, the DPM recommendations are displayed for the administrator to choose and confirm
- **Automatic**: In this mode, the DPM recommendations are automatically executed

The DPM threshold, much like DRS's migration threshold, will display/apply recommendations based on the priority assigned to the recommendation.

# Configuring Predictive DRS

The traditional DRS feature is based upon the current state of affairs and pertains to real-time performance and utilization. Predictive DRS take this one notch higher by integrating with vRealize Operations Manager and balancing the cluster based on past trends. In this recipe, we shall enable the feature and understand its nuances.

# Getting ready

The Predictive DRS feature requires vRealize Operations Manager to supply the metric data to vCenter Server in order to function.
Ensure that the feature is enabled in vRealize Operations Manager and it is configured to send predictive data to the intended vCenter.

# How to do it...

1. From the vCenter's inventory **Home**, navigate to the **Hosts and Clusters** view. Select the cluster and navigate to **Configure | vSphere DRS**.

2. Click on the checkbox adjacent to **Predictive DRS,** as depicted in the following screenshot:

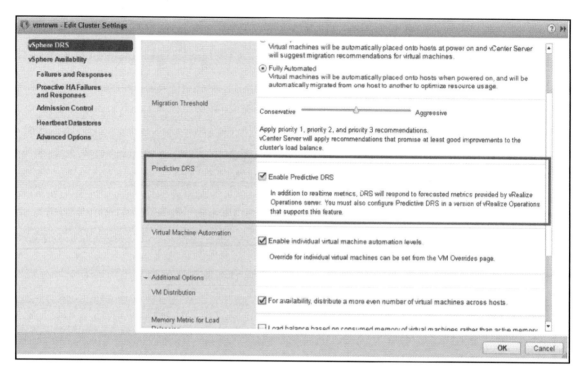

3. Click **OK** to complete the process.

# How it works...

**vRealize Operations Manager (vROPS)** is a phenomenal tool for performance monitoring, among various other capabilities that it has. The Predictive DRS feature taps into the intelligence of vROPS to smartly place the workloads proactively. This is done by retrieving key metrics of a workload and deducing a time-bound pattern. The pattern is then used to understand the upcoming resource requirements of the workload and moves them accordingly.

The data supplied by vROPS is ingested ahead of time and DRS balances the cluster forecasting the change in the resource requirement.

# See also

- The blog by the VMware technical marketing team delves into more detail with a real-time example at: `https://www.brianjgraf.com/2016/10/17/vsphere-6-5-drs-whats-new-part-2-predictive-drs/`

# 14
# Upgrading and Patching using vSphere Update Manager

In this chapter, we will cover the following recipes:

- Installing vSphere Update Manager on Windows
- Activating vSphere Update Manager in vCenter Server Appliance
- Installing the Update Manager download service
- Configuring VUM with a download source
- Creating a custom baseline
- Creating a baseline group
- Importing an ESXi image and updating a host
- Leverage a VM/VA baseline to remediate a VM/VA

# Introduction

**vSphere Update Manager** (**VUM**) aids with managing the life cycle of the vSphere environment by ensuring appropriate patches and updates are installed in the environment. With the vSphere 6.5 release, VUM has been integrated with vCenter Server Appliance and is also available for installation on a Windows instance. VUM integration with vCenter Server Appliance adds another reason why one should migrate to VCSA. In this chapter, we will discuss the workflow involved in setting up VUM on Windows as well as vCSA and typical recipes to configure VUM, download patches, and remediate hosts, tools, and virtual hardware for VMs, and update virtual appliances.

# Installing vSphere Update Manager on Windows

VUM in its legacy state had been only available as a Windows-based installation and this has carried on with vSphere 6.5 while adding an integrated version with the vCenter Server Appliance. We shall walk through a simple installation procedure in this recipe.

## Getting ready

VUM is a 64-bit application and requires a 64-bit OS on which it needs to be installed. VUM is packaged into the vCenter installation file. Download the vCenter installation binary onto the virtual machine/physical machine intended to host the VUM server instance. In addition, ensure that the minimum system requirements are met.

Also, note that a Windows-based installation of VUM cannot be integrated or used with the vCenter Server Appliance. Hence you would require the Windows-based vCenter server credentials to integrate with VUM during the installation process.

# How to do it...

1. Log in to the server hosting the VUM operating system. Click on `autorun.exe` with the appropriate privileges.
2. Click on the **Server** option beneath the **vSphere Update Manager** label. Navigate to the **Embedded Database Option** section and select **Use Microsoft SQL Server 2012 Express as the embedded database** and click on **Install,** as shown in the following screenshot:

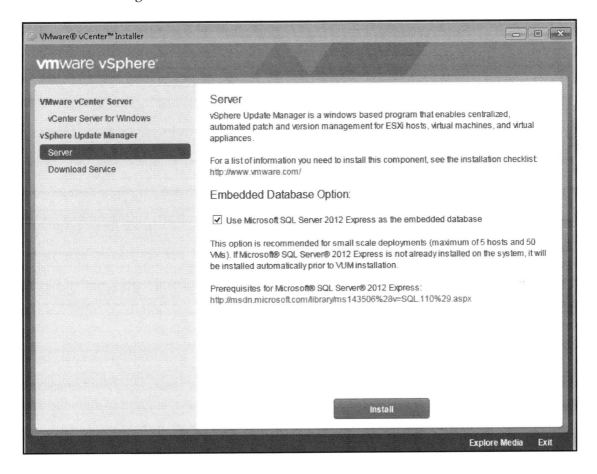

3. On completion, vSphere Update Manager workflow commences. Click on **Next** to proceed, as shown here:

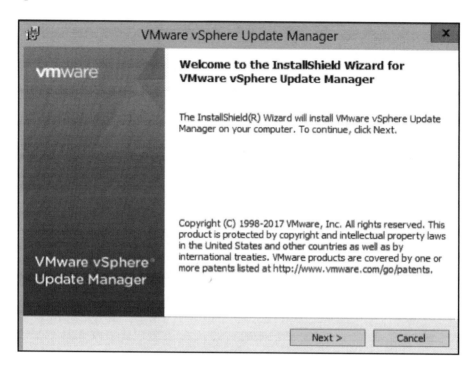

4. Read and accept the license agreement, and click **Next**.

5. Review the **Support Information** page, select whether to download updates from the default download sources immediately after installation, and click **Next**:

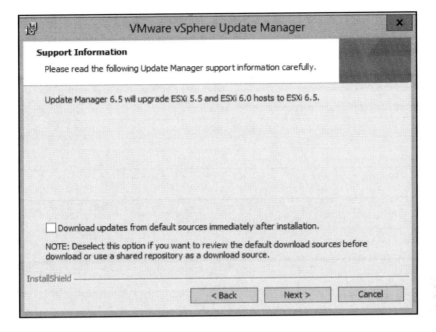

6. Provide the vCenter details and credentials for authentication:

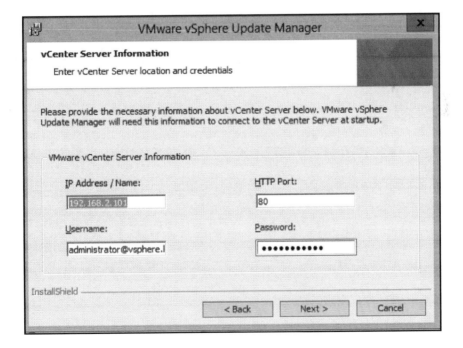

7. Provide the vSphere Update Manager network details, such as the IP address and ports for the firewall, as depicted in the following screenshot:

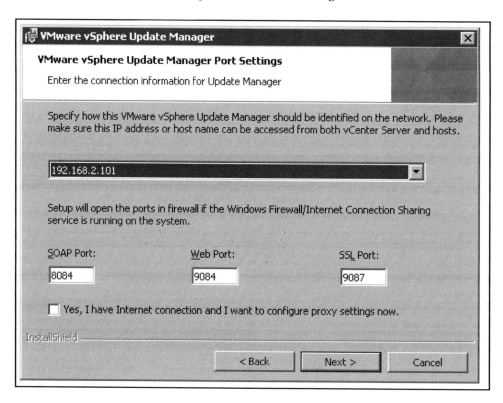

8. Confirm or modify the installation and repository path, if required:

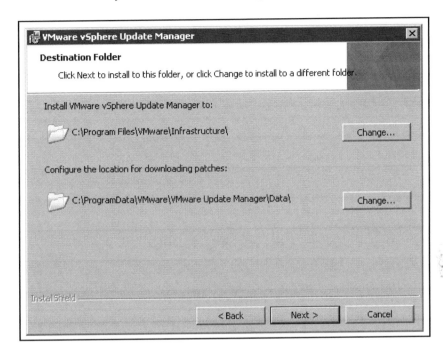

9. Click **Install** to proceed with the installation.

# Activating vSphere Update Manager in vCenter Server Appliance

vSphere Update Manager embedded with vCSA require fewer steps to get started. Typically, the vSphere Update Manager service is automatically started and uses the same PostgreSQL database that vCenter service uses but has a distinct database instance. In the following recipe, we ensure that the VUM service is started and activated to proceed with the subsequent patching/upgrade activities.

# Getting ready

Ensure that you have the appropriate privileges to access the vCenter and update the objects.

# How to do it...

1. Log in to the vCenter and navigate to the **Home** page. Click on **System Configuration,** as depicted in the following screenshot:

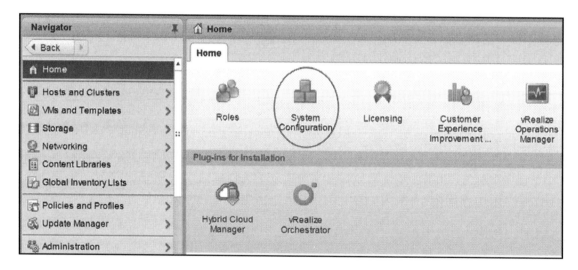

2. Click on **Services** and navigate to **VMware vSphere Update Manager,** as shown in the following screenshot:

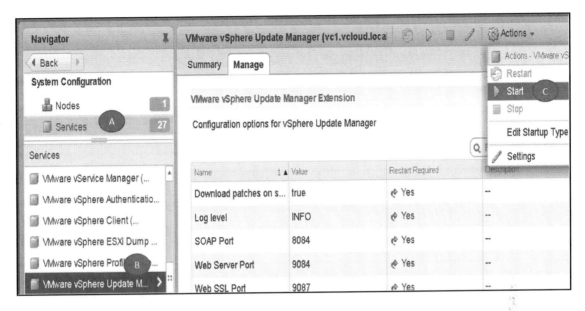

3. Navigate to the **Actions** drop-down menu and click on **Start**.

# How it works...

The VUM service starts and stops automatically with the vCenter. However, there may be situations that require the service to be started/stopped/restarted. This can be performed through the Web Client UI. The service is pre-configured and connected to a separate database instance on the embedded PostgreSQL; therefore, no additional steps or preparatory steps are required to set up the VUM on vCSA.

# Installing the Update Manager download service

In the event that VUM is installed in a secure environment and does not have internet access, you would need to install the **Update Manager Download Service (UMDS)**. The UMDS acts as an intermediary to connect to the internet and download a repository of relevant patches/updates from the VMware portal and services VUM with the repository securely. In the following recipe, we will walk through UMDS installation on a Windows Server.

# Getting ready

Ensure that the UMDS server has internet access; this is required to connect to the public VMware portal to retrieve patch/update related information.

# How to do it...

1. Log in to the server hosting the VUM operating system. Click on `autorun.exe` with the appropriate privileges.
2. Click on the `Download Service` option beneath the **vSphere Update Manager** label. On the **Embedded Database Option** section, select **Use Microsoft SQL Server 2012 Express as the embedded database** and click on **Install,** as shown in the following screenshot:

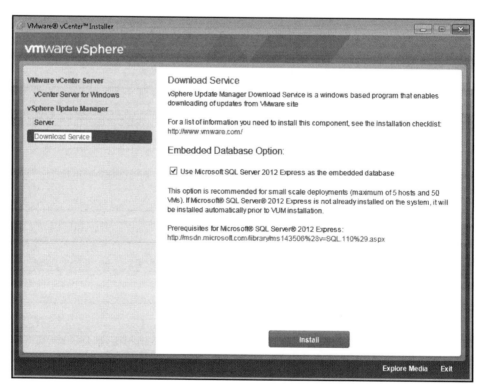

3. Review the welcome screen and click on **Next**:

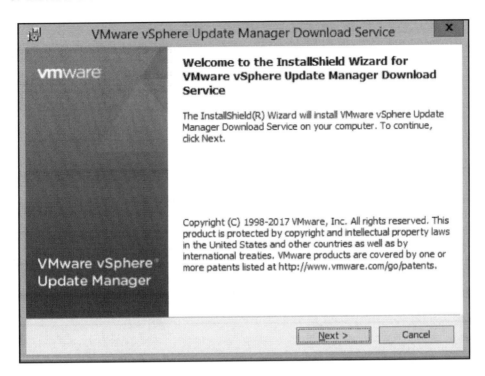

4. Accept the license agreement and click **Next**. Optionally, if the environment connects to the internet through a proxy server, enter the details; otherwise, skip this step.

5. Confirm or modify the installation location and patch download repository location and click **Next** to continue the installation:

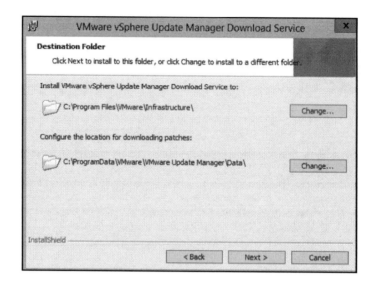

6. Click on **Install** to complete the process, as shown here:

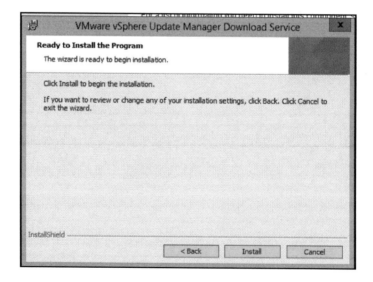

7. Click **Finish** to exit the wizard:

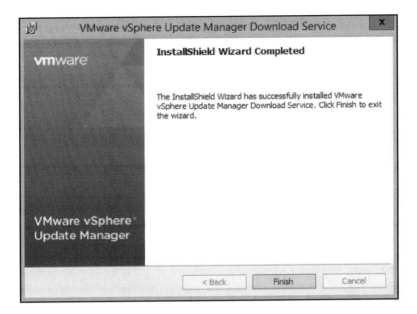

# Configuring VUM with a download source

The vSphere Update Manager that has internet connectivity can directly connect to the VMware portal or requires a shared repository from where content has been downloaded and stored. The latter is achieved by setting up a **vSphere Update Manager Download Service**. In the following recipe, we shall look at the process of configuring a download source for VUM.

# Getting ready

For direct internet ensure that the UMDS server has internet access. This is required to connect to the public VMware portal to retrieve patch/update- related information. If access to the internet is via a proxy, be sure to have the appropriate proxy server and port details.

# How to do it...

1. Login to vCenter and navigate to the **Home** page. Click on **Update Manager,** as depicted here:

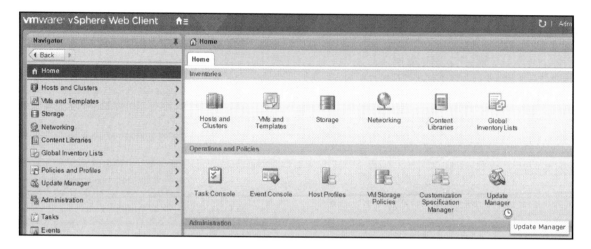

2. Click on the designated vCenter instance. Click on **Manage** tab and navigate to **Download Settings**.
3. Click on **Edit...** and select **Use direct connection to internet,** as depicted in the following screenshot:

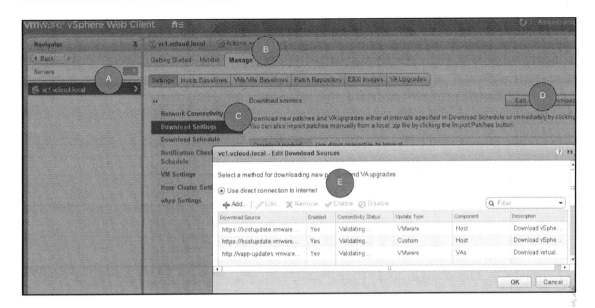

4. Alternatively, you can choose a shared repository for UMDS and provide the location, as outlined in the following screenshot:

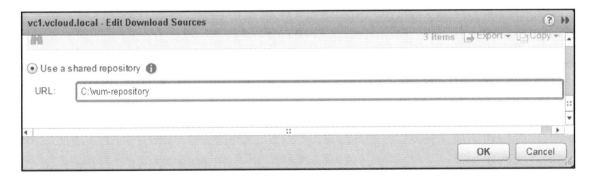

# How it works...

VUM interacts with the VMware portal or the shared repository to locate the appropriate patches/upgrades/extensions against the objects in the vSphere inventory.

# Creating a custom baseline

A baseline is a standard that you compare a vSphere object against for compliance. Certain baselines are created by default, that is, predefined; alternatively, a custom baseline can also be created, tailored to the requirements. In this recipe, we shall walk through creating a custom recipe.

## How to do it...

1. Log in to vCenter and navigate to the **Home** page. Click on the **Update Manager** icon, as shown here:

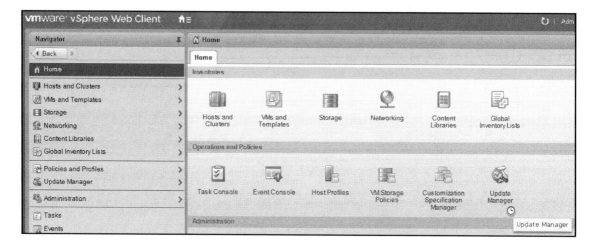

2. Click on the **Manage** tab. Click the **Hosts Baselines** tab, and then click on **New Baseline....**

3. Provide a name for the baseline and click on **Next** ,as depicted in the following screenshot:

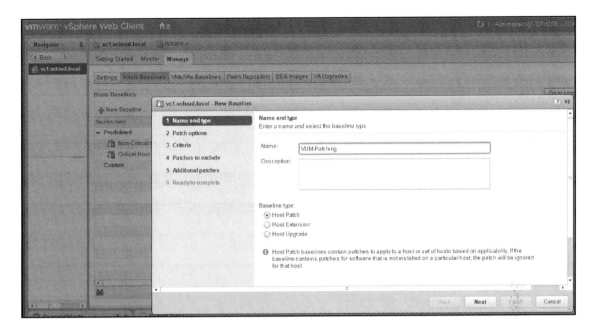

4. Click on the **Dynamic** baseline radio button:

5. Provide the relevant criterion, as demonstrated in the following screenshot. Here we select VMware Inc. patches that are of **Critical** severity and the **Security** category associated with **embeddedEsx 6.0.0** and click **Next**:

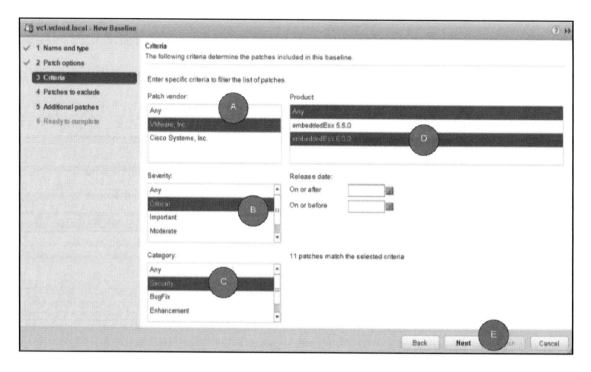

6. Leave at default, since we do not want to exclude any of the patches:

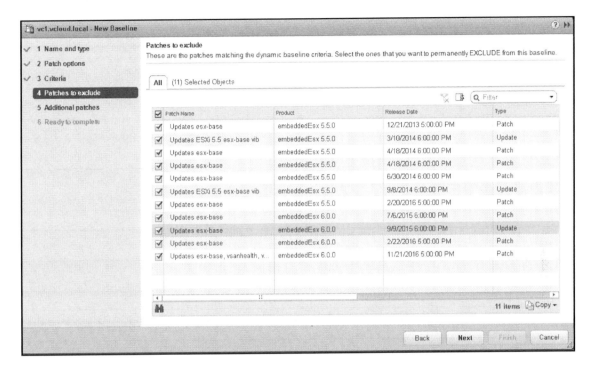

7. Click on **Finish** in the **Ready to complete** screen:

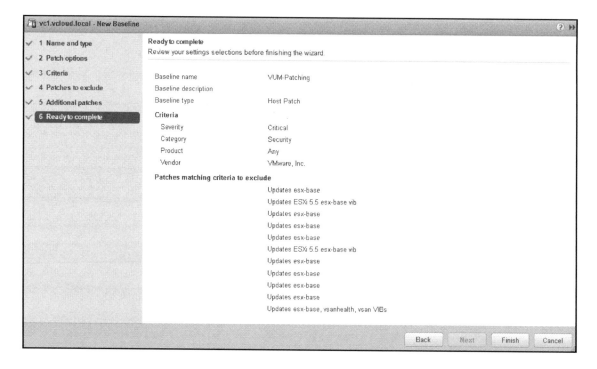

# How it works...

Base-lining is a method of creating a reference container for a set of patches or upgrades that you would like to have installed on a host, virtual machines, or virtual appliances. You can choose to leverage the predefined baselines or custom-created baselines. For instance, you may choose to have very aggressive security compliance for DMZ-based servers, whereas internal test or development servers may have a relaxed compliance. For such use cases, you may choose to have two different custom baselines with the relevant criterion. In the preceding recipe, we have targeted *critical—security* patches to be dynamically associated with a baseline. This would ensure that any new patches meeting the criterion are added to the baseline. Once the baseline is composed of the relevant patches, it would be validated against target hosts for compliance.

# Creating a baseline group

A baseline group comprises of a set of baselines, as the name may imply. Creating a baseline group enables us to associate multiple baselines to scan and remediate objects. In essence, you can build a singular workflow to orchestrate a host upgrade, along with patches and extension baselines.

# How to do it...

1. Log in to vCSA and traverse to **Home** I **Update Manager,** as shown in the following screenshot:

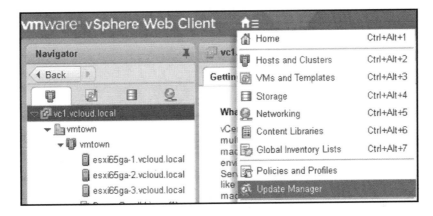

2. Navigate to **Manage** I **Hosts Baselines**:

3. Click on **New Baseline Group....** Complete the wizard by populating the appropriate **Upgrades**, **Patches**, and **Extensions** to be added to the baseline group.

4. Validate the information provided and click on **Finish,** as shown here:

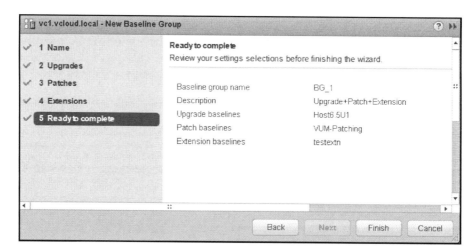

# How it works...

A baseline group, once created, helps orchestrate end-to-end upgrade activity. Typically, during the maintenance window, the upgrade, patches, and extensions required for a specific object are pre-populated in the baseline group. This allows an administrator to scan the baseline group against the object(s) for compliance, as opposed to leveraging the individual baselines. This is particularly useful in larger deployments. The backend functionality is similar to the single baseline creation discussed earlier, albeit that it's nested in a group with the baseline group feature.

# Importing an ESXi image and updating a host

VUM also enables the vSphere administrator to import ESXi images and update the hosts. In this workflow, we copy over an image file (*.iso) to the VUM server and import the image that could be applied on the host. This also works as a quick workaround if there are any network connectivity or firewall issues in the environment. In the following recipe, we walk through the necessary steps to import an image file and upgrade a host.

# Getting ready

Log in to My VMware portal with the appropriate privileges and download the ESXi image file.

# How to do it...

1. Log in to vCenter and navigate to the **Home** page. Click on the **Update Manager** icon:

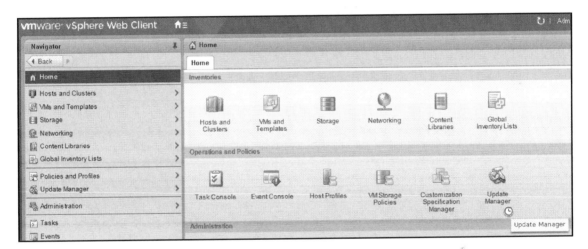

2. Click on the **Manage** tab | **ESXi Images** tab, and then click on **Import ESXi Image...,** as depicted in the following screenshot:

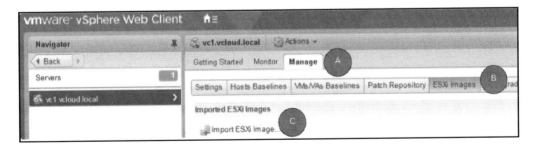

3. Click on **Browse** and navigate to the file on the local machine, as depicted in the following screenshot:

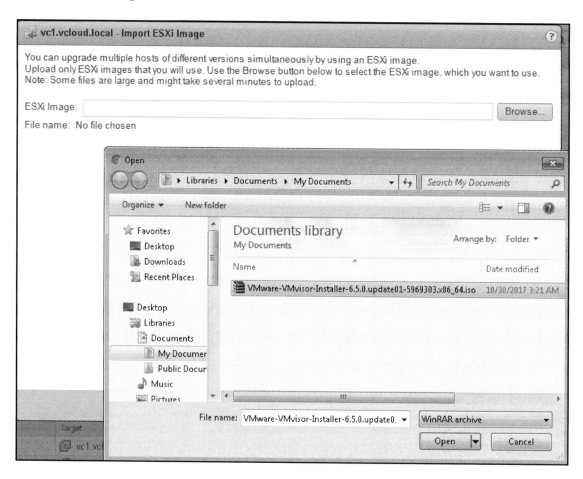

4. Provide a suitable name and click on the **Host Upgrade** radio button:

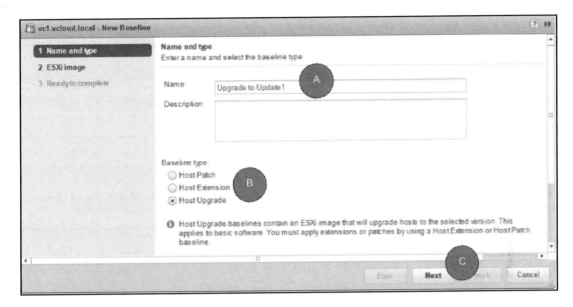

5. Select the appropriate ESXi image file earlier and click **Next**:

6. Review the settings and click on **Finish**:

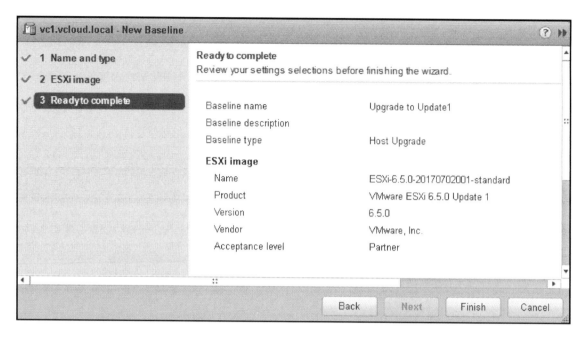

7. Select the specific baseline and click on **Create baseline,** as shown in the following screenshot:

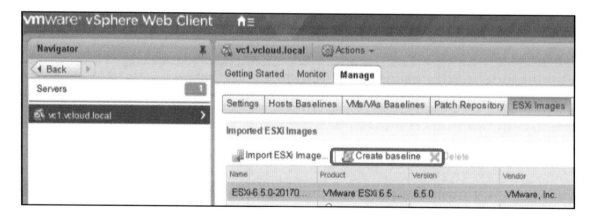

8. Provide an appropriate **Name** and **Description** and click **OK**:

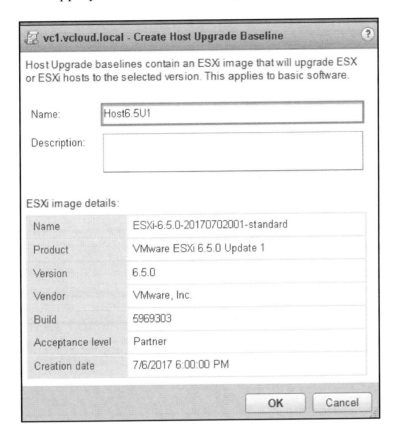

9. Navigate to the target host and click on the **Update Manager** tab. Click on **Attach Baseline** and associate with the newly created baseline, as depicted in the following screenshot:

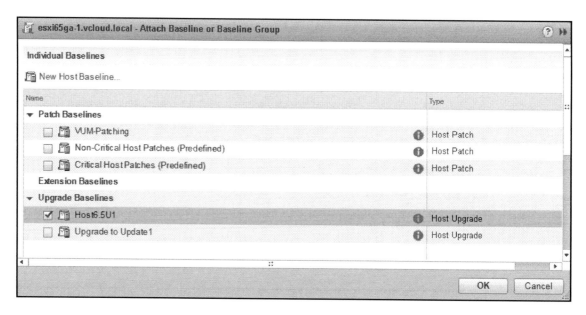

10. Click on **Scan for Updates...** and note that the host is marked as non-compliant:

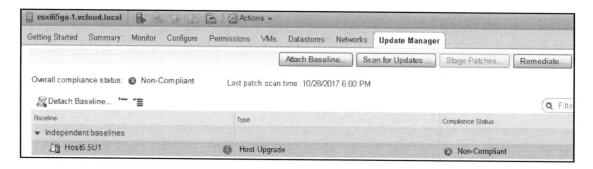

11. Click on **Remediate....** Select the baseline created for the upgrade, as shown in the following screenshot:

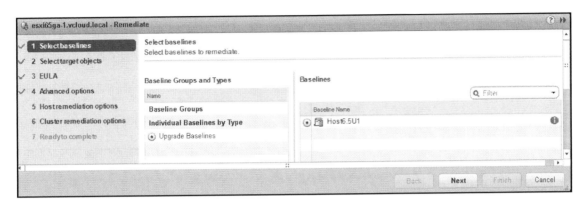

12. Select the target objects (in this case the ESXi host), as depicted in the following screenshot:

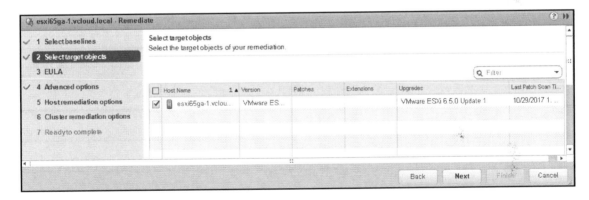

13. Accept EULA. **Advanced options**—you can choose to **Schedule this action to run later** or leave unchecked to execute immediately.

14. Leave at the defaults for **Host remediation options**. Leave at the defaults for cluster remediation options, since this recipe is intended for a single host upgrade.

15. Review the **Ready to complete** screen and click **Finish** to initiate the upgrade:

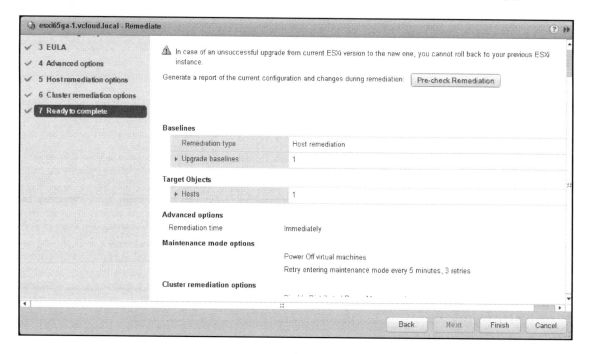

# How it works...

In this recipe, we cover in entirety the following steps:

1. Upload an ESXi image profile to the VUM server.
2. Create a baseline from the uploaded image.
3. Attach the baseline to a target host.
4. Scan the host against the baseline for compliance.
5. Remediate (upgrade/patch) the host that was non-compliant;

These steps form the crux of VUM capability and workflow with slight variations when performed against different objects and different download sources.

# Leveraging a VM/VA baseline to remediate a VM/VA

In this recipe, we will walk through the steps to leverage a VM/VA baseline and use it to upgrade virtual hardware of a virtual machine.

## How to do it...

1. Log in to vCenter and navigate to the target VM. Click on the **Update Manager** tab. Click on **Attach Baseline...** and then click on **VM Hardware Upgrade to Match Host** and **OK** to complete, as shown here:

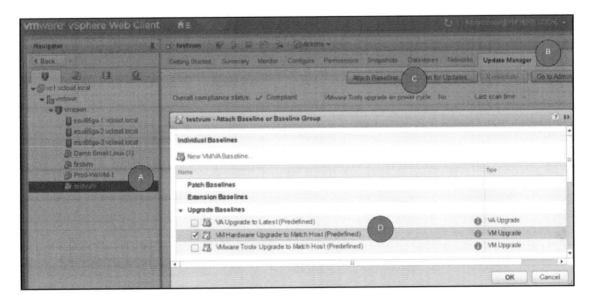

2. Click on **Scan for Updates...** and note that object is marked as non-compliant, as shown here:

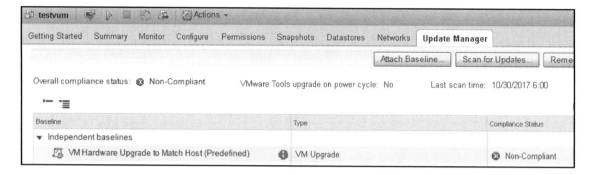

3. Click on **Remediate** and complete the wizard with default values.
4. Review the **Ready to complete** screen and click on **Finish,** as shown in the following screenshot:

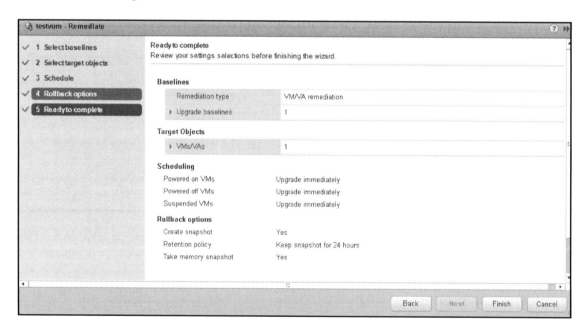

5. Once the task is complete, notice that now the target VM is compliant:

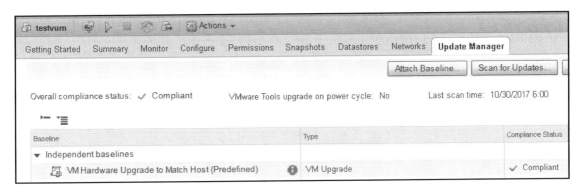

# How it works...

VUM allows for virtual machine hardware, tools, and virtual appliance upgrade by creating the relevant baselines. In the previous recipe, a VM that was imported from a vSphere 5.x hardware had an older virtual hardware. The predefined baseline validates the virtual hardware of the virtual machine against the latest available on the host it's currently registered on. In the previous case, the virtual hardware associated with vSphere 6.x, virtual hardware version 13 was available. On remediating the VM, we see that the virtual hardware was upgraded to vHW 13. The workflow also allows for snapshots of the VM to be taken as a rollback measure. In addition, the task can be scheduled depending on business requirements.

# 15

# Using vSphere Certificate Manager Utility

In this chapter, we will cover the following topics:

- Regenerating a new VMCA Root Certificate and replacing all certificates
- Generating certificate signing requests with vSphere Certificate Manager
- Replacing all certificates with a custom certificate
- Reverting the last performed operation by republishing old certificates
- Resetting all certificates

## Introduction

vSphere components securely communicate through SSL. This ensures security, compliance, and integrity of the data exchanged across the components. With vSphere 6.x onwards, most of the certificate management tasks have been natively integrated in the vSphere Certificate Manager utility, thereby greatly reducing external dependency to manage certificates. In this chapter, we will discuss the different capabilities and workflows associated with managing vSphere certificates.

# Regenerating a new VMCA Root Certificate and replacing all certificates

Typically a new deployment of vCSA incorporates a VMCA-signed certificate for all its components. In the event that this certificate needs to be replaced/regenerated, perhaps due to expiry, we will need to initiate the process described in this recipe. Here, we shall regenerate the VMCA Root Certificate, replace the local machine SSL certificate, and the local solution user certificates with VMCA-signed certificates.

## Getting ready

All the steps in this recipe would be carried out from either an embedded deployment or on a **Platform Services Controller (PSC)**. Ensure that you have the appropriate access credentials to the respective systems. In the following recipe, we will perform the steps from the vCenter Server Appliance with Embedded PSC.

## How to do it...

1. Log in to the vCSA. Key in the command `shell` when prompted, to access the shell, as shown in the following console output :

   ```
   Command> shell
   Shell access is granted to root
   root@vc1 [ ~ ]#
   ```

2. The vSphere Certificate Manager utility can be invoked by the `/usr/lib/vmware-vmca/bin/certificate-manager` command, as shown in the following command window:

```
root@vc1 [ ~ ]# /usr/lib/vmware-vmca/bin/certificate-manager

                *** Welcome to the vSphere 6.0 Certificate Manager  ***

                        -- Select Operation --

            1. Replace Machine SSL certificate with Custom Certificate

            2. Replace VMCA Root certificate with Custom Signing
               Certificate and replace all Certificates

            3. Replace Machine SSL certificate with VMCA Certificate

            4. Regenerate a new VMCA Root Certificate and
               replace all certificates

            5. Replace Solution user certificates with
               Custom Certificate

            6. Replace Solution user certificates with VMCA certificates

            7. Revert last performed operation by re-publishing old
               certificates

            8. Reset all Certificates

Note : Use Ctrl-D to exit.
Option[1 to 8]:
```

3. Type in option 4 to `Regenerate a new VMCA Root Certificate and replace all certificates`.

4. Type in N to accept user input to generate the certificates. Provide the username and credentials, similar to the following screenshot:

```
Option[1 to 8]: 4
Do you wish to generate all certificates using configuration file : Option[Y/N] ? : N  Ⓐ

Please provide valid SSO and VC priviledged user credential to perform certificate operations.
Enter username [Administrator@vsphere.local]:  Ⓑ
Enter password:  Ⓒ

Please configure root.cfg with proper values before proceeding to next step.

Press Enter key to skip optional parameters or use Default value.

Enter proper value for 'Country' [Default value : US] :
```

5. Provide the appropriate input or accept default values as per the requirements for the organization details and location; here we have proceeded with the default values:

```
Please configure root.cfg with proper values before proceeding to next step.

Press Enter key to skip optional parameters or use Default value.

Enter proper value for 'Country' [Default value : US] :

Enter proper value for 'Name' [Default value : CA] :

Enter proper value for 'Organization' [Default value : VMware] :

Enter proper value for 'OrgUnit' [Default value : VMware Engineering] :

Enter proper value for 'State' [Default value : California] :

Enter proper value for 'Locality' [Default value : Palo Alto] :
```

6. Similar to the previous inputs, provide the details and type in Y to complete for the remaining certificates, as shown here:

```
Please configure MACHINE_SSL_CERT.cfg with proper values before proceeding to ne
xt:
Press Enter key to skip optional parameters or use Default value.

Enter proper value for 'Country' [Default value : US] :

Enter proper value for 'Name' [Default value : CA] :

Enter proper value for 'Organization' [Default value : VMware] :

Enter proper value for 'OrgUnit' [Default value : VMware Engineering] :

Enter proper value for 'State' [Default value : California] :

Enter proper value for 'Locality' [Default value : Palo Alto] :

Enter proper value for 'IPAddress' [optional] :

Enter proper value for 'Email' [Default value : email@acme.com] :

Enter proper value for 'Hostname' [Enter valid Fully Qualified Domain Name(FQDN)
, For Example : example.domain.com] : vc1.vcloud.local

You are going to regenerate Root Certificate and all other certificates using VMCA
Continue operation : Option[Y/N] ? : 
```

7. Once the certificates are updated, the services are stopped and started, flagging completion.

# Generating certificate signing requests with the vSphere Certificate Manager

In certain organizations, for security or compliance reasons, a third-party or external certificate authority may be required. In such cases, the vSphere Certificate Manager can enable you to create the appropriate **Certificate Signing Requests (CSRs)**. This can then be sent to the certificate authority to obtain the appropriate signed certificates. In the following recipe, we shall walk through the creation of CSRs.

## Getting ready

All the steps in this recipe would be carried out from either an embedded deployment or on a **Platform Services Controller (PSC)**. Ensure that you have the appropriate access credentials to the respective systems. In the following recipe, we will perform the steps from the vCenter Server Appliance with Embedded PSC.

## How to do it...

1. Log in to the vCSA. Key in the command `shell` at prompt to access the shell.
2. The vSphere Certificate Manager utility can be invoked by the `/usr/lib/vmware-vmca/bin/certificate-manager` command.
3. Choose option `1. Replace Machine SSL certificate with Custom Certificate`:

```
root@vc1 [ ~ ]# /usr/lib/vmware-vmca/bin/certificate-manager

            |
            |    *** Welcome to the vSphere 6.0 Certificate Manager   ***
            |
            |                 -- Select Operation --
            |
            |    1. Replace Machine SSL certificate with Custom Certificate
```

4. Provide the credentials and choose the first option to create the CSR:

```
Please provide valid SSO and VC priviledged user credential to perform certificate operations.
Enter username [Administrator@vsphere.local]:
Enter password:
     1. Generate Certificate Signing Request(s) and Key(s) for Machine SSL certificate

     2. Import custom certificate(s) and key(s) to replace existing Machine SSL certificate
```

5. Provide the output directory to store the CSRs, similar to the following screenshot:

```
Please provide a directory location to write the CSR(s) and PrivateKey(s) to:
Output directory path: /root/ssl_repos
```

6. Provide the certificate-specific details and validate that the CSR is created:

```
Enter proper value for 'Country' [Default value : US] :

Enter proper value for 'Name' [Default value : CA] :

Enter proper value for 'Organization' [Default value : VMware] :

Enter proper value for 'OrgUnit' [Default value : VMware Engineering] :

Enter proper value for 'State' [Default value : California] :

Enter proper value for 'Locality' [Default value : Palo Alto] :

Enter proper value for 'IPAddress' [optional] : 192.168.1.10

Enter proper value for 'Email' [Default value : email@acme.com] :

Enter proper value for 'Hostname' [Enter valid Fully Qualified Domain Name(FQDN), For Example : example.d
2017-11-12T06:53:06.767Z    Running command: ['/usr/lib/vmware-vmca/bin/certool', '--genkey', '--privkey',
key', '/tmp/pubkey.pub']
2017-11-12T06:53:07.367Z    Done running command
2017-11-12T06:53:07.368Z    Running command: ['/usr/lib/vmware-vmca/bin/certool', '--gencsr', '--privkey',
key', '/tmp/pubkey.pub', '--config', '/var/tmp/vmware/certool.cfg', '--csrfile', '/root/ssl_repos/vmca_is
2017-11-12T06:53:07.574Z    Done running command

CSR generated at: /root/ssl_repos/vmca_issued_csr.csr
     1. Continue to importing Custom certificate(s) and key(s) for Machine SSL certificate
```

7. Choose second option to exit the certificate manager.

# How it works...

A CSR is an application sent to a certificate authority to obtain a digital certificate. It is quite possible that to maintain certain compliance standards the default certificates may need to replaced by external certificates. The first step in enabling this process is generating a CSR. The certificate manager utility derives a CSR based on user input of the attributes of the entity for which a certificate is requested for.

# Replacing all certificates with custom certificate

As previously discussed, if for specific reasons an external CA needs to be used in the environment, we would need to obtain the appropriate certificate and replace it across the components in the vSphere environment. In the following recipe, we replace the machine SSL certificate with the one obtained from the CA.

# Getting ready

A prerequisite for replacing the certificate is to ensure that you have created the CSRs and sent it to the CA to obtain the signed certificates. You would require the following:

- A valid machine SSL custom certificate (`*.crt` file)
- A valid machine SSL custom key (`*.key` file)
- A valid signing certificate for the custom machine certificate

# How to do it...

1. Log in to the vCSA. Key in the command `shell` when prompted to access the shell.
2. The vSphere Certificate Manager utility can be invoked by the `/usr/lib/vmware-vmca/bin/certificate-manager` command.

3. Choose option 1. `Replace Machine SSL Certificates with Custom Certificate`. Choose option 2 and provide the file location of the files obtained from the CA and continue, as shown in the following console window:

```
Option [1 or 2]: 2

Please provide valid custom certificate for Machine SSL.
File : //root/ssl_repos/newcerts/MACHINE_SSL_CERT.crt

Please provide valid custom key for Machine SSL.
File : /root/ssl_repos/newcerts/machine_cert.key

Please provide the signing certificate of the Machine SSL certificate
File : /root/ssl_repos/newcerts/signed.crt

You are going to replace Machine SSL cert using custom cert
Continue operation : Option[Y/N] ? : █
```

# Reverting the last performed operation by republishing old certificates

In the event that there are issues with certificates populated in the most recent certificate-related operation, you can revert to the previous state. A backup of the certificates is stored in BACKUP_Store and can be invoked as required. It is also important to note that this can only take one step back, that is, undo the last operation.

## How to do it...

1. Log in to the vCSA. Key in the command `shell` when prompted to access the shell.
2. The vSphere Certificate Manager utility can be invoked by the `/usr/lib/vmware-vmca/bin/certificate-manager` command.

3. Choose option `7. Revert last performed operation by re-publishing old certificates`:

```
Option[1 to 8]: 7

Please provide valid SSO and VC priviledged user credential to perform certificate operations.
Enter username [Administrator@vsphere.local]:
Enter password:

You are going to revert all certs with certs backed up in last operation.
Continue operation : Option[Y/N] ? : Y
```

4. Confirm by typing in `Y`.

# How it works...

Certificates are sensitive in nature and could cause multiple issues if replaced incorrectly. This is due to the strict compliance needed and the procedure that heavily depends on user input. There is every possibility that certificates have incorrect entries or errors requiring the user to be able to rollback. For this reason, an operation is invoked to modify the certificates and a copy of the current certificate state is stored in a backup repository. This enables the user to be able to undo the last operation by invoking the utility and restoring it to the previous state. Caution needs to be exercised as only the last operation can be undone and not the historical changes.

# Resetting all certificates

The certificate manager utility also allows a reset all certificates option that would replace all existing current vCenter certificates with the those signed by VMCA. This can be used, typically, as a corrective measure for issues or errors faced while performing certificate replacement.

 This will cause all the custom certificates that are currently in VECS to be overwritten.

# How to do it...

1. Log in to the vCSA. Key in the command `shell` when prompted to access the shell.
2. The vSphere Certificate Manager utility can be invoked by the `/usr/lib/vmware-vmca/bin/certificate-manager` **command**.
3. Choose option `8. Reset All Certificates`:

```
Option[1 to 8]: 8
Do you wish to generate all certificates using configuration file : Option[Y/N] ? : Y

Please provide valid SSO and VC priviledged user credential to perform certificate operations.
Enter username [Administrator@vsphere.local]:
Enter password:

You are going to reset by regenerating Root Certificate and replace all certificates using VMCA
root.cfg file exists, Do you wish to reconfigure : Option[Y/N] ? : Y
```

4. Confirm by typing in `Y`.

# How it works

The process is similar to the previous recipe of reverting to a previous state; however, we may need to go back a few steps. While this can be achieved through virtual machine snapshots, we risk losing other environmental data by going back to specific snapshots. Hence, there was a specific use case to be able to only undo all certificate-related changes. The certificate manager utility provides the `Reset all Certificates` option for this use case. In essence, all existing certificates are replaced by VMCA-signed certificates, similar to the way the components were originally deployed.

# 16
# Using vSphere Management Assistant

In this chapter, we will cover the following recipes:

- Deploying the vMA appliance
- Preparing VMware vMA for first use
- Configuring VMware vMA to join an existing domain
- Adding vCenter to vMA with AD authentication
- Adding vCenter to vMA with fastpass (fpauth) authentication
- Adding an ESXi host to vMA
- Reconfiguring an added target server
- Running CLI commands on target servers

## Introduction

**vSphere Management Assistant (vMA)** is a Linux appliance that enables remote management of your vSphere environment via its command-line interface. The tool does not offer a graphical user interface. It was originally developed to replace the service console to run scripts or agents that are programmed to interact with the vSphere hosts. It comes packaged with vSphere CLI and the Perl SDK. vSphere CLI shouldn't be confused with vSphere PowerCLI. While vSphere CLI is a bundle of Linux commands that can interact with the vSphere hosts, the latter is a Windows PowerShell plugin and executes PowerShell cmdlets.

It's also important to note that 6.5 is the last release of vSphere Management Assistant, since it's being deprecated. In this chapter, we will learn how to deploy and configure the appliance for use with vSphere environments.

# Deploying the vMA appliance

vMA appliance deployment comprises of the following steps:

1. Download the appliance from the portal. Extract the files.
2. Deploy via the vSphere Web Client onto an ESXi host.

# Getting ready

The vMA appliance will be deployed as an appliance on an ESXi server. It is a single virtual machine appliance. The ZIP bundle containing the OVF and the related files can be downloaded from the My VMware portal at `https://code.vmware.com/tool/vma/6.5`. Once the files are downloaded, extract the files.

# How to do it...

The following procedure will help you deploy the vMA appliance using the vSphere Web Client interface:

1. At the vSphere Web Client interface's inventory **Home**, navigate to **Hosts and Clusters**. Right-click on the ESXi cluster and then click on **Deploy OVF Template...**.
2. In the **Deploy OVF Template** wizard, select the **Local file** option and then click on the **Browse...** button.
3. Select all the files from the extracted location and then click on **Next** to validate the file and continue with the wizard, as shown here:

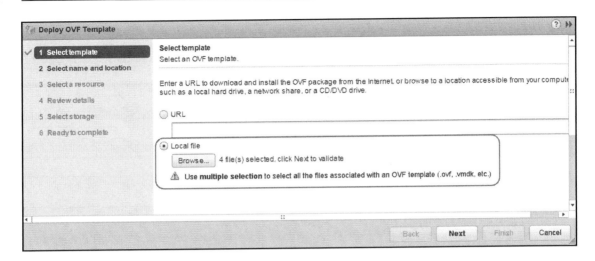

4. Provide a unique name for the appliance. Choose a host or cluster to host the appliance and review the details, as shown here:

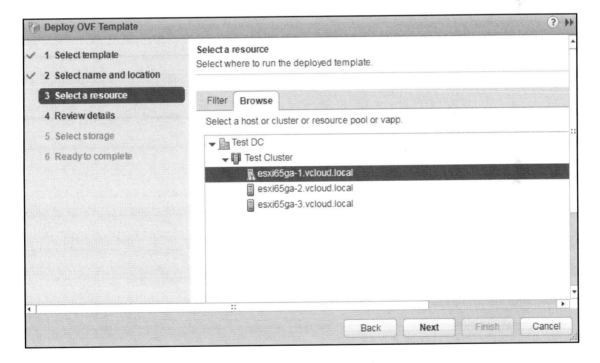

5. Choose a datastore to store the appliance. Choose an appropriate network (to connect with the hosts and vCenter).

6. Review the inputs provided for accuracy, as shown here, and click on **Finish**:

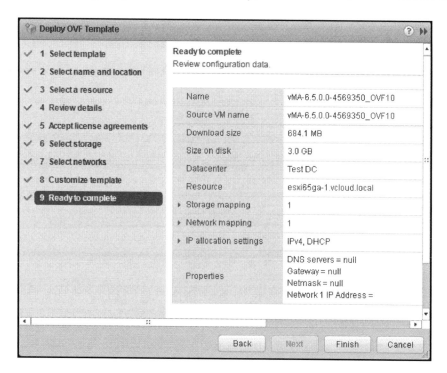

# Preparing VMware vMA for first use

After vMA is deployed, it will need to go through a few initial configuration steps before you can begin using it. The configuration is done at the appliance's guest operating system level:

The vMA appliance runs **SUSE Linux Enterprise Server (SLES)** 11 SP3 as the guest operating system.

1. Power on the vMA VM and wait for the VM to boot up and display the network configuration main menu, as shown in the following screenshot:

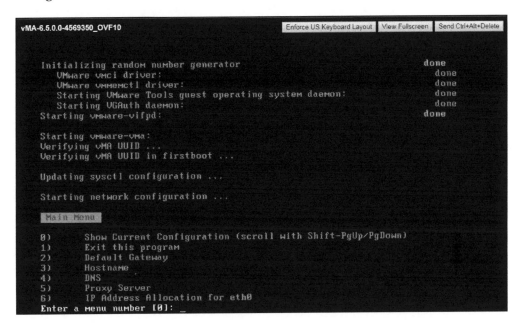

2. Enter 0 to check the current configuration and note that no information is populated yet and the appliance needs to be configured, as shown here:

3. Enter 6 to select `IP Address Allocation for eth0` and supply the static configuration or choose DHCP:

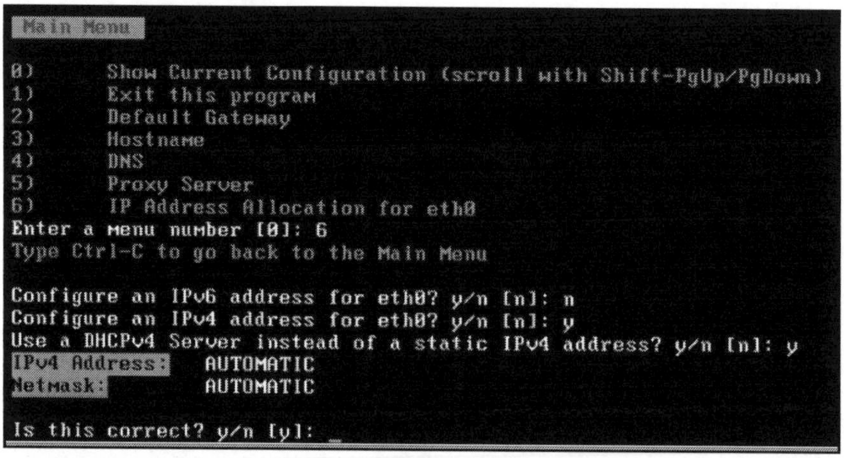

```
Main Menu

0)      Show Current Configuration (scroll with Shift-PgUp/PgDown)
1)      Exit this program
2)      Default Gateway
3)      Hostname
4)      DNS
5)      Proxy Server
6)      IP Address Allocation for eth0
Enter a menu number [0]: 6
Type Ctrl-C to go back to the Main Menu

Configure an IPv6 address for eth0? y/n [n]: n
Configure an IPv4 address for eth0? y/n [n]: y
Use a DHCPv4 Server instead of a static IPv4 address? y/n [n]: y
IPv4 Address:     AUTOMATIC
Netmask:          AUTOMATIC

Is this correct? y/n [y]:
```

4. Enter Y to confirm the configuration; this would apply the network configuration to the `eth0` interface.

5. Enter 0 to validate and confirm successful configuration, as shown here:

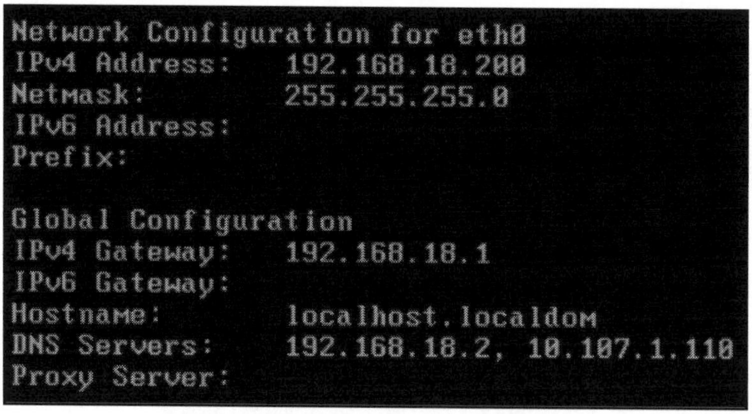

```
Network Configuration for eth0
IPv4 Address:    192.168.18.200
Netmask:         255.255.255.0
IPv6 Address:
Prefix:

Global Configuration
IPv4 Gateway:    192.168.18.1
IPv6 Gateway:
Hostname:        localhost.localdom
DNS Servers:     192.168.18.2, 10.107.1.110
Proxy Server:
```

6. Enter 1 to choose to exit the network configuration.

7. Set the password for the `vi-admin` user by keying in the default password `vmware` to something user-specific:

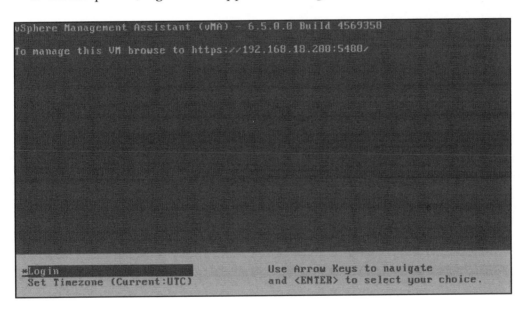

```
Starting password configuration ...
The root account is disabled in this vMA virtual machine, which means no one can
 log in as root. The administrator account for vMA is called "vi-admin". In orde
r to log in to vMA, you need to log in as this user. This user has been pre-crea
ted in the vMA, and its password needs to be set now. Please enter a secure pass
word for the account now.

Please provide a password for the vi-admin user. If you are prompted for an old
password for this user, enter vmware.
Old Password: _
```

8. On completion, log in to the appliance through a browser with the IP details:

```
vSphere Management Assistant (vMA) - 6.5.0.0 Build 4569350

To manage this VM browse to https://192.168.18.200:5480/



*Login                                        Use Arrow Keys to navigate
 Set Timezone (Current:UTC)                   and <ENTER> to select your choice.
```

# How it works...

Once the appliance has been configured for first use, you can perform various operations from the console of the appliance and its management home page. The vMA appliance can connect over the network to the vCenter and ESXi hosts through port 5480 and can run various commands/operations to either retrieve information or make modifications.

# Configuring VMware vMA to join an existing domain

VMware vMA can be configured to join an Active Directory domain and subsequently use an AD user to log in to the appliance and run the remote commands against the targets. This allows for scalable access control and delegation to a wider user base in comparison to local user management.

## How to do it...

The following procedure will guide you through the steps required to configure vMA to join an existing Active Directory domain:

1. Log in to the vMA console or SSH to it as the `vi-admin` user. Issue the following command to add the vMA appliance to the domain:

   ```
   Syntax: sudo domainjoin-cli join <domain-name> <domain-admin-user>
   Example: sudo domainjoin-cli join vcloud.local administrator
   ```

   ```
   vi-admin@localhost:~> sudo domainjoin-cli join vcloud.local administrator
   Joining to AD Domain:   vcloud.local
   With Computer DNS Name: localhost.localdom

   administrator@VCLOUD.LOCAL's password:
   Warning: System restart required
   Your system has been configured to authenticate to Active Directory for the
   first time.  It is recommended that you restart your system to ensure that all
   applications recognize the new settings.

   SUCCESS
   ```

2. You can further confirm that the task is successful by querying the status by executing the `sudo domainjoin-cli query` command and observe if the output reflects the appropriate domain, as shown here:

   ```
   vi-admin@localhost:~> sudo domainjoin-cli query
   vi-admin's password:
   Name = localhost
   Domain = VCLOUD.LOCAL
   Distinguished Name = CN=LOCALHOST,CN=Computers,DC=vcloud,DC=local
   ```

# Adding vCenter to vMA with AD authentication

You can add vCenter servers to vMA with AD authentication. This is considered to be more secure than the default fastpass authentication, which maintains a local cache of the credentials.

## How to do it...

The following procedure explains how to add the vCenter server to the vMA by using AD authentication:

1. Log in to the vMA console or SSH as `vi-admin`. Now, issue the following command:

   ```
   vifp addserver <vCenter> --authpolicy adauth --username
   <domain>\\<domain admin>
   or
   vifp addserver <vCenter> --authpolicy adauth --username
   <domainuser>@<domain>
   Examples:
   vifp addserver vc1.vcloud.local --authpolicy adauth --username
   administrator@vcloud.local
   ```

2. Issue the `vifp listservers` to verify that the server has been added, as demonstrated in the following screenshot:

   ```
   vi-admin@localhost:~> vifp listservers
   vc1.vcloud.local          vCenter 6.5.0    4602587
   ```

We can observe from the screenshot that the vCenter has been added and the version details have been displayed.

## How it works...

vMA authenticates and adds the vCenter to its fold of servers maintained. Once this is done, all commands can be executed against the hosts managed by vCenter without providing the host credentials. In other words, vCenter becomes a proxy for the hosts and provides a seamless platform to remote CLI management.

# Adding vCenter to vMA with fastpass (fpauth) authentication

You can add vCenter servers to vMA using the standard fastpass authentication. This method provides a mechanism to cache the target server credentials on the vMA machine, so that you don't have to authenticate every time you execute a command against the target server.

## Getting ready

The domain user or its AD group should be assigned at least a read-only role at the target vCenter server.

## How to do it...

The following procedure will take you through the steps required to add a vCenter to vMA by using the fastpass authentication:

1. Log in to the vMA console or SSH as the `vi-admin` user. Now, issue the following command:

   **`vifp addserver <vCenter hostname/ip address> --authpolicy fpauth`**
   Example:
   **`vifp addserver vc1.vcloud.local --authpolicy fpauth`**

2. Issue the `vifp listservers` command to verify that the server has been added, as shown in the following console screenshot:

```
vi-admin@localhost:~> vifp addserver vc1.vcloud.local --authpolicy fpauth
Enter username for vc1.vcloud.local: administrator@vsphere.local
administrator@vsphere.local@vc1.vcloud.local's password:
This will store username and password in credential store which is a security ri
sk. Do you want to continue?(yes/no): yes
vi-admin@localhost:~> vifp listservers -l
vc1.vcloud.local          vCenter  fpauth  6.5.0   4602587
```

# How it works...

Unlike AD authentication, the fastpass mechanism stores the username and password information in the local credential store. As observed in the preceding screenshot, it is indeed a security risk. The information is stored in `/home/vi-admin/vmware/credstore/vmacredentials.xml`.

# Adding an ESXi host to vMA

Instead of adding a vCenter server to vMA, it is possible to add just the individual ESXi hosts. This is particularly useful if a single vCenter is used to manage multiple data centers and you do not want to expose all the ESXi hosts managed by the vCenter to the vMA appliance.

# How to do it...

The following procedure will take you through the steps required to add a vCenter to vMA by using the fastpass authentication:

1. Log in to the vMA console or SSH as the `vi-admin` user. Now, issue the following command:

   ```
   vifp addserver <ESXi hostname/ip address> --authpolicy fpauth
   Example:
   vifp addserver esxi65vc1.vcloud.local --authpolicy fpauth
   ```

2. Issue the `vifp listservers -l` command to verify that the server has been added, as shown in the following console screenshot:

```
vi-admin@localhost:~> vifp addserver esxi65ga-2.vcloud.local --authpolicy fpauth
root@esxi65ga-2.vcloud.local's password:
vi-admin@localhost:~> vifp listservers -l
vc1.vcloud.local          vCenter fpauth  6.5.0   4602587
esxi65ga-1.vcloud.local ESXi    fpauth  6.5.0   4564106
esxi65ga-2.vcloud.local ESXi    fpauth  6.5.0   4564106
vi-admin@localhost:~>
```

## How it works...

Adding host to vMA works with a similar syntax as the vCenter; however, instead of prompting for a username to authenticate with, it defaults to the root user for authentication and then creates the `vi-admin` user on the target server for subsequent authentication attempts.

# Changing the authentication policy

If the fastpass authentication does not comply with the security requirements, you can change the authentication mode to AD-based authentication. In this recipe, we shall walk through the steps to re-configure the authentication policy from one to another.

## How to do it...

The following procedure will help you change the authentication policy of a target that has already been added to vMA:

1. Issue the following command:

   ```
   vifp reconfigure <servername> --authpolicy adauth
   Example:
   vifp reconfigure esxi65ga-1.vcloud.local --authpolicy adauth
   ```

2. Note that the host `esxi65ga-1.vcloud.local` authentication mode now depicts a `adauth` from `fpauth`, as shown in the following screenshot:

```
vi-admin@localhost:~> vifp reconfigure esxi65ga-1.vcloud.local --authpolicy adauth
Enter username for esxi65ga-1.vcloud.local: vi-user
vi-admin@localhost:~> vifp listservers -l
vc1.vcloud.local          vCenter   fpauth   6.5.0   4602587
esxi65ga-1.vcloud.local ESXi      adauth   6.5.0   4564106
esxi65ga-2.vcloud.local ESXi      fpauth   6.5.0   4564106
vi-admin@localhost:~>
```

# Running CLI commands on target servers

In this recipe, we will learn how to issue commands on the added target vCenter Servers or ESXi hosts.

# How to do it...

The following procedures explain how to set a target server and issue direct commands to it. We will discuss all three methods.

## Method 1 – Issuing commands on the default target

Follow these steps to issue commands on the default target:

1. Set the intended server as the default target for all commands:

```
Syntax:
vifptarget -s <servername>
Example:
vifptarget -s esxi65ga-1.vcloud.local
```

2. Issue the CLI commands, as you would at an ESXi host's console, as depicted here:

```
esxcli system version get
```

```
vi-admin@localhost:~[esxi65ga-1.vcloud.local]> esxcli system version get
Enter username: root
Enter password:
   Product: VMware ESXi
   Version: 6.5.0
   Build: Releasebuild-4564106
   Update: 0
   Patch: 0
vi-admin@localhost:~[esxi65ga-1.vcloud.local]>
```

## Method 2 – Issuing commands by specifying a target server

The following are the steps required to issue commands by specifying a target server:

1. Issue the command specifying the server name:

```
Example:
esxcli --server esxi65ga-1.vcloud.local iscsi adapter list
```

2. Supply the username and password when prompted to obtain results, as shown in the following console output:

```
vi-admin@localhost:~> esxcli --server esxi65ga-1.vcloud.local iscsi adapter list
Enter username: root
Enter password:
Adapter    Driver      State     UID                                        Description
-------    ---------   ------    -----------------------------------------  ----------------------
vmhba65    iscsi_vmk   online    iqn.1998-01.com.vmware:esxi65ga-1          iSCSI Software Adapter
vi-admin@localhost:~>
```

# Method 3 – Issuing commands against a vCenter added as the target

Perform the following steps to issue commands against a vCenter added as the target:

1. Issue the command specifying the vCenter server and ESXi server:

   ```
   esxcli --server <VC_server> --vihost <esx_host> system version get
   Example:
   esxcli --server vc1.vcloud.local --vihost esxi65ga-1.vcloud.local
   system version get
   ```

2. Supply the vCenter credentials to obtain the output, as depicted here:

```
vi-admin@localhost:~> esxcli --server vc1.vcloud.local --vihost esxi65ga-1.vcloud.local system version get
Enter username: administrator@vsphere.local
Enter password:
   Product: VMware ESXi
   Version: 6.5.0
   Build: Releasebuild-4564106
   Update: 0
   Patch: 0
vi-admin@localhost:~>
```

3. This method will only prompt you for the vCenter's username and password. It will not prompt you for the ESXi host's root password.

# 17
# Performance Monitoring in a vSphere Environment

In this chapter, we will cover the following recipes:

- Using esxtop to monitor performance
- Exporting and importing esxtop configurations
- Running esxtop in the batch mode
- Gathering VM I/O statistics using vscsiStats
- Using vCenter performance graphs

## Introduction

Any vSphere infrastructure, once deployed, needs to be monitored for performance during its life cycle. Continuous monitoring helps configure the infrastructure in a manner that maintains optimum performance to meet the business needs, which can bring cost savings. There are several methods and tools available, such as **vRealize Operations Manager (vROPS)**, which aids in performance monitoring. Unlike other monitoring tools, vROPS does what VMware calls predictive analysis and dynamic thresholding. It learns what is normal in an environment over time and provides recommendations, facilitates capacity planning, and allows policy-based automation. It can also monitor/manage environments. It is the tool that most infrastructures want to use to be efficient in IT operations.

This chapter primarily concentrates on native utilities embedded on the host and vCenter, such as esxtop, vscsiStats, and vCenter's performance charts. We shall introduce you to the tools that can be used in a vSphere environment to collect and review performance data.

# Using esxtop to monitor performance

The esxtop command line can be used to monitor the CPU, memory, storage, and network performance metrics. The default output of this tool can further be customized to display the information you need. The esxtop tool has two operating modes— the **interactive** (default) mode and batch mode. In the interactive mode, the screen output of the tool can be changed based on what or how much information you would like to view and in the batch mode you can collect and save the performance data onto a file.

# Getting ready

In order to run esxtop and view the output, you would need to connect to the ESXi host through an SSH client. Alternatively, you may also connect through a remote console; however, for better usability (copy, paste, logging, and so on), an SSH client is preferred.

# How to do it...

The following procedure will help you run esxtop and switch between different modes:

1. Connect to the console of the ESXi host through SSH or a remote console
2. Once you are at the CLI of the host, type `esxtop` and hit *Enter* to bring up the default interactive mode output

The following table will provide you with a basic list of keys to switch between the various statistics modes the tools can be in:

| Key | Statistics mode |
|-----|-----------------|
| c | CPU statistics |
| i | Interrupt vector information |
| m | Memory statistics |
| n | Network statistics |

| d | Disk/storage metrics |
|---|---|
| u | Storage device-specific metrics |
| v | VM-specific storage information |
| p | Power management configuration and utilization information |
| x | VSAN-specific metric information |

The previous table is a list is the primary metrics of each of the component, which can then further have categorizations. The list of interactive commands can be displayed by keying-in h , as depicted in the following screenshot:

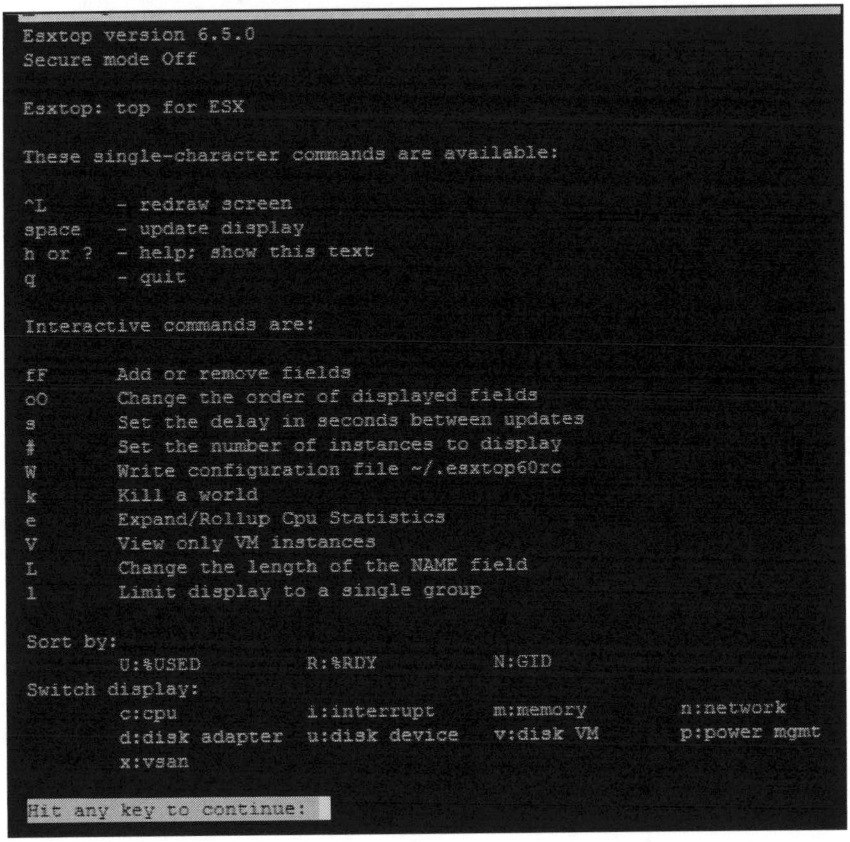

```
Esxtop version 6.5.0
Secure mode Off

Esxtop: top for ESX

These single-character commands are available:

^L      - redraw screen
space   - update display
h or ?  - help; show this text
q       - quit

Interactive commands are:

fF      Add or remove fields
oO      Change the order of displayed fields
s       Set the delay in seconds between updates
#       Set the number of instances to display
W       Write configuration file ~/.esxtop60rc
k       Kill a world
e       Expand/Rollup Cpu Statistics
V       View only VM instances
L       Change the length of the NAME field
l       Limit display to a single group

Sort by:
        U:%USED         R:%RDY          N:GID
Switch display:
        c:cpu           i:interrupt     m:memory        n:network
        d:disk adapter  u:disk device   v:disk VM       p:power mgmt
        x:vsan

Hit any key to continue:
```

Furthermore, for each component, there could be fields added or removed based on requirements. For instance, the CPU statistics view can be modified to included power stats. This will prove to be particularly helpful if the power management settings of the hardware may be affecting the performance of the workloads. In the following screenshot, we explicitly include the power stats to be displayed:

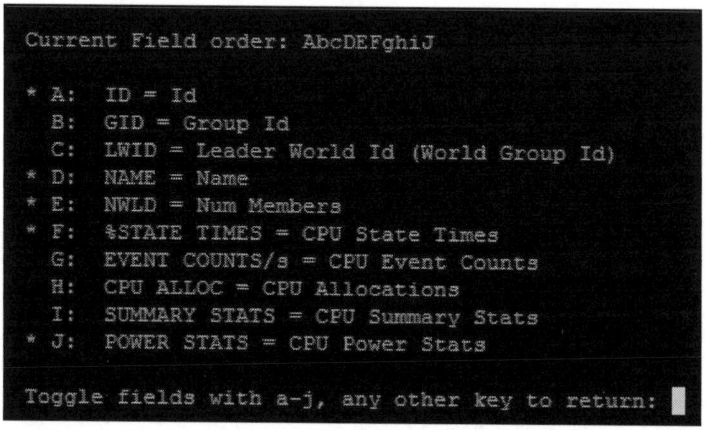

```
Current Field order: AbcDEFghiJ

* A:   ID = Id
  B:   GID = Group Id
  C:   LWID = Leader World Id (World Group Id)
* D:   NAME = Name
* E:   NWLD = Num Members
* F:   %STATE TIMES = CPU State Times
  G:   EVENT COUNTS/s = CPU Event Counts
  H:   CPU ALLOC = CPU Allocations
  I:   SUMMARY STATS = CPU Summary Stats
* J:   POWER STATS = CPU Power Stats

Toggle fields with a-j, any other key to return: █
```

# Exporting and importing esxtop configurations

All the output customization that is done during the interactive mode is lost the moment you exit the tool. You do have the option of exporting the output configuration to a file and re-importing the configuration to avoid spending time customizing the column output again.

## How to do it...

To export the esxtop configuration to a file, first launch esxtop, customize the output as required, hit the *W* key by shifting to uppercase, specify a directory path to save the configuration file, and then hit *Enter*, as demonstrated in the following screenshot:

In the previous example, we have created the `esxtopcfg` file. In subsequent attempts, you can initiate esxtop with the custom template with the following command:

```
Syntax:
# esxtop -c <filename>Example # esxtop -c /tmp/esxtopcfg
```

# How it works...

The default configuration file that is used by esxtop is `//.esxtop50rc`. To customize for different use cases, we modify the display of esxtop and store it in an alternate location.

# Running esxtop in the batch mode

As opposed to the interactive mode, for intermittent issues, you would most often want to target a specific time range and collect the statistics for a deeper introspection. Thus, you would invoke a batch mode or replay mode of data collection that can store snapshots of various metrics at every instance.

# Getting ready

We need access to the ESXi CLI via the console or SSH. You need to plan the duration to be captured and the number of performance snapshots needed. Based on the volume of data, ensure appropriate disk space is available to store the collected data.

# How to do it...

To run `esxtop` in batch mode, connect to the ESXi host's CLI and run the following command:

```
# esxtop -a -d <delay> -n <iterations> > exportfilename
Example:
# esxtop -a -d 10 -n 50 >perfstats.csv
```

| Switch | Effect |
|--------|--------|
| -a | This will gather all the esxtop statistics |
| -d | This inserts a delay (in seconds) between every performance snapshot |
| -n | This is used to specify the number of snapshot iterations that have to be collected |

# How it works...

Once exported, the comma-separated values can be viewed in Microsoft Excel, or can be imported into Windows Performance Monitor for analysis.

# Gathering VM I/O statistics using vscsiStats

The vscsiStats tools is used to gather the I/O statistics of a VM at a per-virtual-disk (vmdk) level. It can collect statistics such as the number of outstanding I/Os, size of the I/Os, and seek distance and latency.

# Getting ready

You will need access to the ESXi CLI via the console or SSH. Also, make note of the world IDs corresponding to the VMs that you would like to fetch the statistics for. The `esxcli vm process list` will list all the running VMs with their world IDs.

# How to do it...

To fetch the I/O statistics corresponding to a VM, you will need to find the `worldGroupID` corresponding to the VM. This is achieved by issuing the following command:

```
# vscsiStats -l
```

```
[root@esxi65ga-1:~] vscsiStats -l
Virtual Machine worldGroupID: 223557, Virtual Machine Display Name: vMA-6.5.0.0-4569350_OVF10, Virtual Machine Config File:
/vmfs/volumes/58466491-e35a329f-61f3-00505601a712/vMA-6.5.0.0-4569350_OVF10/vMA-6.5.0.0-4569350_OVF10.vmx, {
   Virtual SCSI Disk handleID: 8192 (scsi0:0)
}
```

Once the `worldGroupID` is obtained, we can execute the following command to fetch the statistics:

```
vscsiStats -s -w <worldGroupID of the virtual machine>
Example:
# vscsiStats -s -w 223557
```

The following screenshot depicts the output that is expected :

```
[root@esxi65ga-1:~] vscsiStats -s -w 223557
vscsiStats: Starting Vscsi stats collection for worldGroup 223557, handleID 8192 (scsi0:0)
Success.
```

The command will start a collection against every disk (vmdk or rdm) associated with the VM. The collection will continue to run for 30 minutes from the time it was started, unless you choose to stop it by using the `vscsiStats -x` command. Once the collection is complete or stopped, you can view the data gathered by the collection, based on the histogram type you need. The following are the histogram types that are available:

| Histogram type | Description |
|---|---|
| `all` | All statistics |
| `ioLength` | Size of the I/O |
| `seekDistance` | Logical blocks; the disk head must move before a read/write operation can be performed |
| `outstandingIOs` | Number of I/O operations queued |
| latency | I/O latency |
| Interarrival | Time gap between the VM disk commands (in microseconds) |

The following command syntax can be used:

```
Syntax:
# vscsiStats -w <worldGroupID> --printhistos <histogram type> -c <output
CSV>
Example:
# vscsiStats -w 223557 --printhistos outstandingIOs -c scsi.csv
```

# Using vCenter performance graphs

For the more convenient option to review performance data, vCenter captures performance data and depicts the output in forms of graphs. Although this may not provide the same level of flexibility and detail as esxtop, this serves the purpose for a high-level overview.

## Getting ready

You will need access to vCenter with a role that has the permission to view and modify performance charts.

## How to do it...

To be able to view the performance charts, have a look at the following steps:

1. Connect to the vCenter server and select an object/hierarchy you want to monitor performance for. Navigate to **Monitor** | **Performance** to bring up the performance **Overview** or **Advanced** view.

2. Performance charts can be pulled against a vCenter instance, a data center, a cluster, an ESXi host, or a VM. In the following screenshot, we look into the host CPU's past day performance:

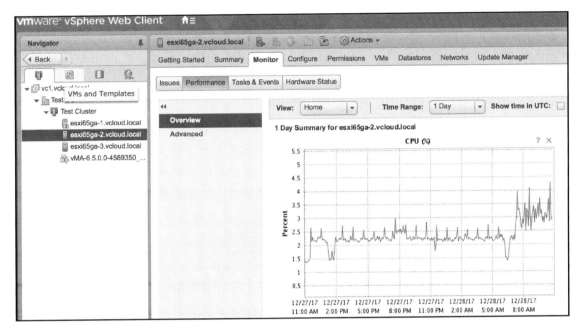

The Advanced view displays real-time data

3. By default, the real-time CPU data is displayed. You can switch between the different metrics available by using the dropdown at the top-right-hand corner of the chart.

4. You can change the chart options to customize the charts in terms of the metrics, timespan, chart type, and counters to be included. From the **Advanced** view, just click on the **Chart Options** hyperlink to bring up the options:

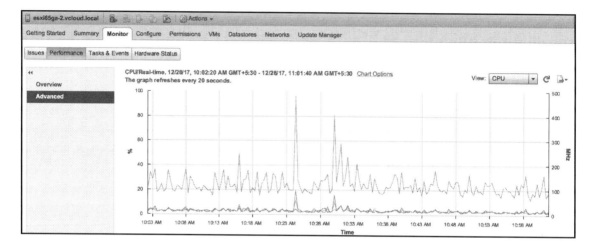

# How it works...

vCenter performance graphs collect data using collection intervals. vCenter uses four default intervals, namely a day, a week, a month, and a year. A collection interval defines the amount of time the performance data has to be stored in vCenter's database. Only the data for the collection intervals is saved in the database. In other words, the real-time performance data will not be saved. Every collection interval has a corresponding collection frequency. For example, the default collection interval frequencies are 5 minutes for a day, 30 minutes for a week, 2 hours for a month, and 1 day for a year.

vCenter performance charts support the following different chart types:

- Line charts
- Bar charts
- Pie charts
- Stacked charts

# Other Books You May Enjoy

If you enjoyed this book, you may be interested in these other books by Packt:

**Mastering VMware vSphere 6.5**
Andrea Mauro, Paolo Valsecchi, Karel Novak

ISBN: 978-1-78728-601-6

- Get a deep understanding of vSphere 6.5 functionalities
- Design and plan a virtualization environment based on vSphere 6.5
- Manage and administer a vSphere 6.5 environment and resources
- Get tips for the VCP6-DCV and VCIX6-DCV exams (along with use of the vSphere 6 documentation)
- Implement different migration techniques to move your workload across different environments
- Save your configuration, data, and workload from your virtual infrastructure.

## vSphere High Performance Cookbook - Second Edition

Kevin Elder, Christopher Kusek, Prasenjit Sarkar

ISBN: 978-1-78646-462-0

- Understand the VMM Scheduler, cache aware CPU Scheduler, NUMA Aware CPU Scheduler, and more during the CPU Performance Design phase
- Get to know the virtual memory reclamation technique, host ballooning monitoring, and swapping activity
- Choose the right platform while designing your vCenter Server, redundant vCenter design, and vCenter SSO and its deployment
- Know how to use various performance simulation tools
- Design VCSA Server Certificates to minimize security threats
- Use health check tools for storage and boost vSphere 6.5's performance with VAAI and VASA

# Leave a review - let other readers know what you think

Please share your thoughts on this book with others by leaving a review on the site that you bought it from. If you purchased the book from Amazon, please leave us an honest review on this book's Amazon page. This is vital so that other potential readers can see and use your unbiased opinion to make purchasing decisions, we can understand what our customers think about our products, and our authors can see your feedback on the title that they have worked with Packt to create. It will only take a few minutes of your time, but is valuable to other potential customers, our authors, and Packt. Thank you!

# Index